SHAKESPEARE AND TOLERANCE

Shakespeare's remarkable ability to detect and express important new currents and moods in his culture often led him to dramatise human interactions in terms of the presence or absence of tolerance. Differences of religion, gender, nationality, and what is now called 'race' are important in most of Shakespeare's plays, and varied ways of bridging these differences by means of sympathy and understanding are often depicted. The full development of a tolerant society is still incomplete, and this study demonstrates how the perceptions Shakespeare showed in relation to its earlier development are still instructive and valuable today. Many recent studies of Shakespeare's work have focused on reflections of the oppression or containment of minority, deviant, or non-dominant groups or outlooks. This book reverses that trend and examines Shakespeare's fascination with the desires that underlie tolerance, including in relation to religion, race, and sexuality, through close analysis of many Shakespearian plays, passages, and themes.

B. J. SOKOL is Emeritus Professor of English at Goldsmiths College, University of London. His many publications include *Art and Illusion in 'The Winter's Tale'* (1994) and, with Mary Sokol, *Shakespeare, Law and Marriage* (Cambridge, 2003).

SHAKESPEARE AND TOLERANCE

B. J. SOKOL

CAMBRIDGE
UNIVERSITY PRESS

CAMBRIDGE UNIVERSITY PRESS
Cambridge, New York, Melbourne, Madrid, Cape Town, Singapore, São Paulo, Delhi

Cambridge University Press
The Edinburgh Building, Cambridge CB2 8RU, UK

Published in the United States of America by Cambridge University Press, New York

www.cambridge.org
Information on this title: www.cambridge.org/9780521879125

First published 2008

Printed in the United Kingdom at the University Press, Cambridge

A catalogue record for this publication is available from the British Library

Library of Congress Cataloguing in Publication data
Sokol, B. J.
Shakespeare and tolerance / B. J. Sokol.
p.   cm.
Includes bibliographical references and index.
ISBN 978-0-521-87912-5 (hardback)
1. Shakespeare, William, 1564–1616–Knowledge–Sociology.   2. Shakespeare, William,
1564–1616–Political and social views.   3. Toleration in literature.   4. Social interaction
in literature.   5. Ethnic relations in literature.   6. Race relations in literature.
7. Religious tolerance in literature.   8. Interpersonal relations in literature.   I. Title.
PR3024.S66 2008
822.3′3–dc22
2008031151

ISBN 978-0-521-87912-5 hardback

For Mary Sokol, my collaborator, with love

Contents

Abbreviated titles

Unless otherwise noted all Shakespeare texts will be cited from the electronic version of the Oxford Shakespeare, edited by Wells and Taylor. This edition supplies the title abbreviations used in the notes, which follow:

1H4	*Henry IV, part 1*
2H4	*Henry IV, part 2*
1H6	*Henry VI, part 1*
ADO	*Much Ado About Nothing*
AIT	*All Is True (Henry VIII)*
ANT	*Antony and Cleopatra*
AWW	*All's Well That Ends Well*
AYL	*As You Like It*
COR	*Coriolanus*
CYL	*The First Part of the Contention (Henry VI, part 2)*
CYM	*Cymbeline*
ERR	*The Comedy of Errors*
H5	*Henry V*
HAM	*Hamlet*
JC	*Julius Caesar*
JN	*King John*
LC	*A Lover's Complaint*
LLL	*Love's Labor's Lost*
LRF	*The Tragedy of King Lear (Folio)*
LRQ	*The History of King Lear (Quarto)*
LUC	*The Rape of Lucrece*
MAC	*Macbeth*
MM	*Measure for Measure*
MND	*A Midsummer Night's Dream*
MV	*The Merchant of Venice*
OTH	*Othello*

PER	*Pericles, Prince of Tyre*
R2	*Richard II*
R3	*Richard III*
RDY	*Richard, Duke of York (Henry VI, part 3)*
ROM	*Romeo and Juliet*
SHR	*The Taming of the Shrew*
SON	*The Sonnets*
STM	*Sir Thomas More*
TGV	*The Two Gentlemen of Verona*
TIM	*Timon of Athens*
TIT	*Titus Andronicus*
TMP	*The Tempest*
TN	*Twelfth Night, or What You Will*
TNK	*Two Noble Kinsmen*
TRO	*Troilus and Cressida*
VEN	*Venus and Adonis*
WIV	*The Merry Wives of Windsor*
WT	*The Winter's Tale*

Introduction

A great deal has been written of late about early modern patriarchy, racism, bigotry, exploitation, hegemonic relations, oppression of 'outsiders', and 'containment' of human difference; it has often been claimed that these intolerant traits and practices are reflected from Shakespeare's culture into his work. A counterpoise seems in order in the form of an attempt to explore Shakespeare and tolerance.

Although there has been much research and debate about early modern tolerance, especially religious tolerance, little of this has been applied to Shakespeare studies, or literary studies generally. Indeed, I feel that a subject area of 'literature and tolerance studies' is needed, and hope my efforts may contribute somewhat towards that.

This Introduction discusses what 'tolerance' might mean in relation to a study of Shakespeare. It is a tricky question, although only a subdivision of the much-discussed issue of what tolerance means in general.

Some of the problems can be identified by posing a simple riddle: why is it that, in popular parlance, 'to be tolerant' and 'to tolerate some particular X' may seem in some sense diametrically opposed? For instance, to say that 'I tolerate gays' may be seen as offensive, because acceptance on such terms may seem derogatory and, in its condescension, not in accordance with 'being tolerant'. Allied with this paradox is the political/ethical question: should a programme to advance the social good of 'toleration' promote 'tolerant persons', or alternatively merely induce a public to 'tolerate X, Y or Z'?

I originally had hoped to dodge paradoxes and a need for fine distinctions by titling this work *Shakespeare's Tolerancy*, using a word called 'rare' by the *Oxford English Dictionary* (*OED*) yet seen in an English play of 1556. But I quickly realised that I had to use such formulations as 'to tolerate', 'to behave tolerantly', or 'to support toleration', and so had to share some of the problems of defining 'tolerance' faced also by historians, philosophers, political theorists, or framers of human-rights documents.

In addition, I have found that the topic of Shakespeare and tolerance forces me to use the word 'tolerance' in a way that does not square with its usual definition in most post-Enlightenment and modern philosophical discussions (although it may match up with much popular usage). The usual philosophical definition equates 'tolerance' with forbearance from hampering or harming persons or groups who are disliked because of their practices, beliefs, or even physical appearance (such as might be the case with 'racial intolerance'). It follows from this formulation that tolerance is pertinent only when some aspect of a person or group is felt to be morally or aesthetically unacceptable, or at least very offensive, and only when the party practising tolerance has sufficient power to oppress the party disliked (otherwise forbearance from oppression has no meaning). The requirement for dislike prior to tolerance is often expressed as being axiomatic, but sometimes a supporting argument is offered along the lines that it cannot be an instance of tolerance to accept or allow that which one likes, approves of, or agrees with.

Usages of 'tolerance' here, on the contrary, will orbit around a notion that 'tolerance' entails a person's willed or chosen extension of goodwill or sympathy towards a person, practice, behaviour, or belief that lies outside their usual experience – even towards someone or something shockingly or frighteningly strange.[1] My explorations will concern the forces driving the dramatised dynamics of such human interactions.

Because my focus will be on dramatised inter-personal relations, or on artistic representations of the inner aspects of situations that demand tolerance, another divergence will arise between the studies here and many of the numerous recent studies of early modern tolerance. These latter often concentrate on the emergence and underpinnings of modern 'regimes of tolerance', for example tolerationist legal or social arrangements. Many of these focus on collective mindsets or political forces, and question whether regimes of tolerance genuinely existed at all in the early modern or even the Enlightenment period. These revisionists typically argue that earlier 'liberal' scholars have perpetrated 'Whiggish' myths, and by misinterpreting the chronology, provenance, and original meanings of certain early developments have painted a false picture of an early modern and Enlightenment march towards toleration. Such revisionists, and those who counter them,[2] address a similar question: what processes produced our current political and conceptual commitments to tolerance? This, however, will not be the central question asked here. The main focus instead will be on Shakespearian dramatisations of successes or failures of tolerance.

Yet, of course, the present book cannot wish to be historically blind. It will always attempt to place Shakespeare's poetic explorations of the dynamics of tolerance within the contexts of his time and culture. Since the focus will be on tolerance as a choice expressed by dramatised agents, it will be especially important to question what sorts of choices were possible in the culture surrounding Shakespeare and his audiences. It will also be important to question what sorts of intolerance were possible within that historical culture, and what sorts (although possibly common in later times) may have been then unknown or impossible. With the help of recent scholarship I think I will be able to show that certain allegations made concerning some types of Elizabethan intolerance are anachronistic.

It may be useful, before beginning this, to discuss further why the definition of tolerance as merely non-harming cannot serve the purposes of this study. For one thing, within the concept that tolerance by definition must apply to that which is strongly disapproved of, there may be a paradoxical demand to tolerate persons or practices that are themselves intolerant or in other ways wicked. This paradox has been discussed at length.[3] It need not be further considered here, however, for Shakespeare never imputes any value to tolerating the intolerable – so an Iago, or an Angelo of _Measure for Measure_, does not attract our acquiescent acceptance.

Also, Shakespeare presents counter-possibilities to a notion that tolerance may arise or be called for only after dislike sets in, for he dramatises circumstances in which tolerance is required _before_ any dislike is established. These are circumstance in which confusion, anxiety, or uncertainty (rather than a settled and known dislike) arise in encounters with the seemingly outlandish or mysterious in humanity. Such encounters fascinated Shakespeare's time, when voyagers or explorers met unknown varieties of humanity with trepidation and surprise. The shock of such encounters was more strongly felt then, and more remarked on, than even quite soon afterwards. Then, also, Europeans did not automatically assume they possessed superiority over exotic others in sophistication, power, or even the ability to survive, for such overweening assumptions were not yet either justifiable or established prejudices.[4]

There is another level, as well, on which recent discussions of tolerance may run counter to an account of tolerance appropriate to Shakespeare studies. This may be encapsulated in the paradox that a simple like/dislike, attack/forbear model of tolerance makes possible a sharp division of attitudes from actions, thereby making room for an intolerant 'tolerance'. The important discussion of this paradox by philosophers and political theorists might be circumvented here by making the observation that for Shakespeare the mysteries of human motivations always matter. But because we live in a time dominated by questions of intra-ethnic and similar collisions, it is necessary, I think, to clarify the grounds of certain modern discourses so that these can be more clearly held to one side when they are inappropriate to discussions of early modern circumstances.

The action/attitude division concerning tolerance has recently been highlighted in an attempt by Andrew R. Murphy to desynonymise 'toleration' and 'tolerance'. In the preface to a political-theoretical book on seventeenth-century notions of toleration he writes:[5]

> Generally speaking, I shall avoid using the term 'tolerance' throughout this study. Elsewhere I have argued that we may avoid some long-standing conceptual confusions by using 'tolerance/intolerance' to refer to attitudes, and 'toleration/ antitoleration' to refer to institutional or behavioral phenomena. Without making that argument here, I shall merely suggest that *no* set of attitudes is necessarily related to tolerationist outcomes in politics.

The 'elsewhere' Murphy refers to is a 1997 article in which he reserved the term 'tolerance' for use only in the personal-attitudinal realm. That distinction has not taken hold in general, and in their traditional uses the *OED* defines both 'tolerance' and 'toleration' in terms of an 'action or practice', giving the verb 'to tolerate' and the adjective 'tolerant' meanings in both the attitudinal and actional spheres.

Terminology aside, it is very important to note Murphy's surprising assertion that '*no* set of attitudes is necessarily related to tolerationist outcomes in politics'. This has been echoed by many other writers. Many hold that a political 'regime of toleration' may be founded upon motives that include ones that are not tolerant at all – such as expedience, cynical indifference, relativism or amoralism, or prudential fears of consequences. Although some take exception to this,[6] others actually find reasons to prefer a 'regime of toleration' that is so founded. For instance, Bernard Williams has argued that since 'genuine' tolerance is equivalent to satisfying a Kantian demand for respecting others' autonomy as a good in itself, and since this kind of respect is unlikely to be widespread, it is 'as well' that the real-world 'practice of toleration' does not depend upon it.[7] Martin Walzer likewise describes a wide range of toleration-supporting, although not tolerant, positions, and holds that 'it is a feature of any successful regime of toleration that it does not depend on any particular form of this virtue'.[8]

According to such notions, any means of restraining violence against hated persons, communities, beliefs, or ideas is equivalent to toleration, and therefore toleration does not require individuals' inner tolerance or sympathy for others. That will not do for the purposes here, which are to examine tolerant impulses and behaviours represented in Shakespeare's plays. Here, in contrast, even restricted or symbolic violence may play a part in the dynamic development of tolerance. For Shakespeare's plays often represent robust expressions of friction arising from human differences, and such expressions sometimes in the end lead not only to peaceful coexistence, but also to an enlarged and more flexible sense of the humanity of others. The forms taken by eventually profitable human collisions or frictions, as depicted by Shakespeare, range from the wrangling of a Beatrice and Benedick (surely a more likely couple than Claudio and Hero) to the much more violent mistakings of Imogen and Posthumus, and include many instances of intra-communal jesting, friendly teasing, mock-insulting, and the mistaking of one identity for another (a Shakespearian favourite).

Another problem that arises for us with notions that tolerance consists of forbearance from harming is that tolerance is then only possible for those who are dominant or have a powerful upper hand. If accepted, this restriction would eliminate some of the most interesting Shakespearian explorations of tolerance, especially those involving *mutual* tolerance between the socially unequally empowered genders.[9] Bernard Williams has partially addressed the definitional one-sidedness that excludes a consideration of a symmetrical tolerance between unequals by making the distinction that toleration 'as a *political undertaking*...introduces the asymmetry [between groups] associated with the concept' but 'a tolerant attitude...can obtain just as much between groups who are not equal in power'.[10] However, Williams still apparently cleaves to the common notion that tolerance can arise only following disliking, for he claims that there must be a 'history or background of intolerance' to make 'room for the concept of toleration'.[11]

In summary, since Shakespeare can conceive of tolerance without prior disliking and of tolerance on both sides between unequals – and since he is prone to disfavour a vapid or indifferent response to human variances and to favour responses that are emotionally vivid – his reflections on tolerance do not match those commonly held by many current thinkers.[12] What we will meet in Shakespeare's portrayals of tolerance is the celebration of those who can transcend rancour arising from human differences, and the tragic disasters of those who are misguidedly or pathetically unable to do so.

Such assertions need to be tested against Shakespeare's plays and their contexts; this is to follow...

STRUCTURE, CONVENTIONS, AND THANKS

This book's six chapters pursue topics that often overlap. The first chapter's topic of humour and tolerance, for instance, will recur in every other chapter; two chapters are so closely linked that the last sentence of one becomes the first sentence of the next; the Afterword presents an example bridging the topics of every other chapter of the book. All this is not accidental.

My heavy reliance on others' researches is attested to by the bibliography. This contains as well a number of my own former single or joint efforts. Several of the latter are here amplified or revised; the topic of Shakespeare and tolerance has been on my mind for a long time.

A few points of convention or procedure should be mentioned. The term 'Elizabethan' will be used as a shorthand for the period of Shakespeare's lifetime except where this may cause confusion. Quotations from early works will not be modernised except where modern editions are used.[13] I have often used numerical evidence, some of which comes from measures applied to electronic texts. I am also very grateful for parish record data and analyses supplied for my use by the 'People in Place: Families, Households and Housing in Early Modern London' project of Birkbeck, University of London, the Centre for Metropolitan History at the Institute of Historical Research, and the University of Cambridge. I want especially to thank the co-directors of the project, Professor Richard Smith of Cambridge University, Dr Vanessa Harding of Birkbeck, and Dr Matthew Davies of the London University Institute of Historical Research. Professor Smith led me to the project and gave me illuminating initial and continuing advice, and the staff, especially Mark Merry, have been immensely helpful. My thanks also go to Leonora Gummer and David Moore-Gwyn at Sotheby's, London, for very kind assistance.

I have many others to thank for inspiration and help. These include my own students and those of Cynthia Lewis at Davidson College. I have also had the benefit of the astute comments of two readers for Cambridge University Press. Among the other scholars who have helped me in very generous ways several have patiently answered my questions or given me access to unpublished information. These include David Bevington, Hazel Forsyth, Alastair Fowler, Steven Johnson, Andrew Lewis, Charles Littleton, Steven May, Robert Miola, Steven Murdoch, Fred Rosen, Quentin Skinner, Richard M. Smith, Gary Watt, David Worthington, and Henry Woudhuysen. All errors and oversights, of course, are my own.

A NOTE ON THE COVER ILLUSTRATION

The cover reproduces the *Portrait of the Princess of Zanzibar with an African Attendant*, sold at Sotheby's on 14 June 2001 (lot 1). I am most grateful to the painting's owner, and to those thanked in the Introduction and to Sotheby's for arranging the permission for its use, and for supplying the image. This painting, by Walter Frier, is an eighteenth-century copy of a lost seventeenth-century original. See www.artnet.com/Artists/ LotDetailPage.aspx?lot_id=1C928D15FD04B3BD.

An inscription on the painting reads:

Sir John Henderson of Fordel, travelling in his youth through several parts of Asia and Africa from ye year 1618 to ye year 1628, was delivered into slavery by a Barbarian in Zanquebar on the coast of Africa. There a princess of that countrie falling in love with him, even to the renouncing of her religion and country, contrived the means of both their escape and getting aboard a ship trading up ye red sea landed at Alexandria where she died, whose picture John Henderson caused take with her black maid after their own country habit. From ye original picture at Oterston by W Frier, 1731.

(See 'In Zanzibar: Stone Town, Tanzania', by William Dalrymple, at www.travelintelligence.net/wsd/articles/art_52.html.) The romantic implications of this inscription and image overlap with many of the themes of this book: in particular, early modern attitudes to differences of nationality, religion, and 'race', gender relations, and slavery.

CHAPTER I

Shakespeare, jokes, humour, and tolerance

I. PROSPECTUS

Few topics [compared with humour] need as much prefatory apologism before receiving scholarly treatment.[1]

Humour, in its harder or softer forms, will be seen to play a significant role in relation to all of the kinds of tolerance in Shakespeare which the present study will consider. This is for reasons going beyond the self-evident fact that manifestations of tolerance in Shakespeare's plays are more likely to arise in genial comedy-like settings than in tragedy-like ones.

In fact harder or harsher rather than more genial forms of humour often accompany Shakespearian treatments of tolerance in both comedy and tragedy. Although festive and socially inclusive moods are often said to distinguish Shakespearian from classical or Jonsonian satiric comedy, some Shakespeare comedies contain judgmental types of humour situated far from the genial. In Chapter 4 on religion, for instance, we will meet in *All's Well that Ends Well* a long and complex series of linked jokes satirising issues arising in bitter and dangerous contemporary sectarian dissensions.

On the other hand, as we shall see in Chapter 5, a genial quip made by the Duke in *Othello* illustrates how Shakespeare gives space within a tragedy to tolerance-promoting jesting (a space, it will be argued, that is established only to be tragically stifled in that play).[2] The Duke's attempt at a conciliatory gesture using humour is mirrored in a number of Shakespearian and contemporary contexts that will be considered in Chapters 3 and 4; in these discord threatens to disrupt encounters between persons of diverse outlook or culture, and jokes are used to help rescue dialogue.

Such dialogue settings involving diverse persons might be bracketed with a range of other settings portrayed by Shakespeare in which convivial or at least peaceable assemblages make room for free-spirited interchanges between mismatched persons, allowing the give-and-take of easy 'conversation'.[3] Such give-and-take is well described when the contending suitors for Bianca in *The Taming of the Shrew* are invited to 'quaff carouses to our mistress' health, / And do as adversaries do in law – Strive mightily, but eat and drink as friends' (1.2.278–9).

To help with the appreciation of these and similar contexts in which humour or good humour abets tolerance, this first chapter will examine certain aspects of Shakespearian joking and humour in a more focused way than will be possible in the course of later discussions. It will begin by reviewing theories of humour, particularly 'denigration' theories and their alternatives, dating from before Shakespeare's time to beyond it. This will underpin a discussion of recently proposed theories (with possible Shakespearian application) to the effect that some seemingly denigratory humour which hinges on national or other stereotyping may conceal ploys intended to define and gain recognition for group identities. The present chapter will then attempt an analysis of Shakespeare's purposes in dramatising jokes that are failures, even dismal or repugnant failures; this will lead to discussions of joke patterns seen in the second *Henriad* and in *The Merchant of Venice*.

2. JOKES REQUIRE, AND REVEAL, SOCIAL PERSPECTIVES

Joking is not a simple matter. Across time or culture, and sometimes just across subcultures, jokes can be confusedly received or even mistakenly detected. Thus the transatlantic Professor Morris Zapp in David Lodge's comic novel *Changing Places* realises only belatedly that the populist presentional style of BBC Radio 1 is not at all a devastatingly clever spoof, as he first supposes, but is rather the thing itself. The point of this joke is that Zapp's fame is in hermeneutics. Or again, observing the wisdom in popular usages, it is worth considering the outraged phrase 'you must be joking!'; the exclamation suggests how the irony or indirection seen in jokes may produce ambiguity or uncertainty.

In fact, the present may not be an ideal moment for understanding jokes. According to the critic Warren St John, academic researchers agree that the folk tradition of trading and telling jokes has recently declined sharply, and moreover 'it's a matter of faith among professional comics that jokes … have been displaced by observational humor and one-liners'.[4] St John indicates that these changes have been attributed by various commentators to reductions of attention span, to an aversion to 'look-at-me' styles of social performance, to 'political correctness', or to a contraction of the range of agreed social standards against which humour might react.

Distance in time, and perhaps also a new puritanism, may create particular problems for the interpretation of Shakespeare's jokes. A valuable mode of access to them may be suggested by a remark made by the witty Rosaline of *Love's Labour's Lost*: 'A jest's prosperity lies in the ear / Of him that hears it, never in the tongue / Of him that makes it' (5.2.847–9). That is, historical work may aim to reconstruct what the ears of Shakespeare's time heard in his jests. Also, conversely, a literary analysis of dramatic contexts and patterns may reveal the likely register and thrust of an otherwise obscure Shakespearian joke, and these in turn may yield insight into the topical issues and the societal perspectives that formed the basis for its humour.

3. ANACHRONISMS AND DEFINITIONS

To give a reference point for the following I should mention that the *OED* does support non-anachronistic uses of the word 'toleration' in relation to Shakespeare: specifically religious 'toleration' (meaning 4.a.) dates from 1609, and more general 'toleration' (meaning 3) dates from 1610 or earlier.

A conscious use of anachronism may be valuable when we come to discuss currents of thought or feeling with which Shakespeare engaged but which in his time were still unnamed because inchoate or just nascent. On the other hand, history often produces divergences between partly kindred concepts,[5] and so uses of anachronistic terms may also may create confusions or encourage the framing of unbefitting questions. An example of an unbefitting question suggested by an anachronistic term might be: was Shakespeare a 'liberal'? The word 'liberal', meaning progressive, freedom-loving, or the like, was coined in the late eighteenth century; the concept may have arisen in the later seventeenth century, but in Shakespeare's time a 'liberal' position was not only nameless, but also, as a single ideological or conceptual package, inconceivable. Nevertheless, a connection that is very relevant to our discussion of Shakespeare is suggested by a distinction made by Sammy Basu between some proto-liberal proponents of toleration:[6]

What was absent from, and perhaps even antithetical to Locke but loomed large in certain other liberals (*avant la lettre*) – namely the Leveller Richard Overton (fl. 1640–60) and the Whig Anthony Ashley Cooper, Third Earl of Shaftsbury (1671–1713) – was the perception that humour was a mode of toleration vital to the viability of the then emergent liberal policy. For both, humour involved the perception of an incongruity that ruptures one's expectations, typically the sudden juxtaposition of the sacred and profane in revealing and meaningful ways. It thereby contributed to self-knowledge and political accommodation. In defending humour, both also warned that English liberal culture was carrying with it some redundantly heavy and humourless Puritan baggage.

If no full 'liberal' in the later sense, nonetheless Shakespeare represented 'heavy and humourless Puritan baggage' only in order to spoof it, and he did distinctly link humour and toleration.

Terminological anachronisms will be useful and hopefully not misleading in the following discussions of Shakespearian 'ethnic jokes'. According to the *OED*, in Shakespeare's time 'ethnic' was used only with reference to religions, and meant 'pertaining to nations not Christian or Jewish; Gentile, heathen, pagan'. For convenience I will be extending this term to its modern range (dated to after the mid-nineteenth century), so that 'ethnic' in 'ethnic joke' will refer to all sorts of groups differing from a majority, in nationality, 'race', language, or culture.

Like 'ethnic', the anachronistic word 'joke' is never used by Shakespeare himself. It was imported into standard English from the slang of the late seventeenth century. The closest equivalent word used by Shakespeare is 'jest', which is indeed used in nearly all of his plays and groups of poems.[7] But the denotation of 'jest' in Shakespeare's time was much broader than that of 'joke'; a jest could be a flippant inconsequential act, or a throwaway remark, or an elaborate prank, or even a confidence sting. Similarly, 'to jest' could be to taunt, chatter, banter, or be elaborately witty.

4. WHAT WAS FUNNY?

The lack of an exact correspondence between what a 'jest' was for Shakespeare's age and a 'joke' for ours connects with the famous riddle of what, in various cultures or times, makes certain verbal acts laughable. This question has been addressed repeatedly by physiologists, psychologists, social scientists, and nearly all of the big names in philosophy and literary criticism since antiquity. For philosophers, the question of human laughter has fed fundamental discussions: for instance, Aristotle, theorising on physiology, comments that humans are the only creatures that laugh.[8]

Many theories of verbal humour have been proposed, including ones attributing its laughter-evoking powers to surprise, incongruity, deflation, absurdity, release of repression, ambiguity, logical paradox, or a mixing of contradictory 'scripts'. But a clear majority among all those who have speculated on the question have settled on so-called 'derision theories' of humour, following Aristotle, who in turn followed hints in Plato.[9] In derision theories laughter is always caused by ridicule, and the targets of ridicule are always persons or human types that are ugly, absurd, inferior, or unworthy. A brilliant essay by Quentin Skinner outlines the evolution of the main theories of laughter up to and somewhat beyond the time when the mid-seventeenth-century philosopher Thomas Hobbes offered his own very famous version of derision theory.[10] Skinner shows that Hobbes returned to derision theory after a number of Renaissance thinkers had diverged from it by proposing, variously, that laughter may be kindly, civil, or even healthful because it corrects melancholia. Those included such important thinkers as Baldassare Castiglione and the physician Girolamo Fracastoro (the medical genius who first proposed a germ theory of infection).

Another important Renaissance view of humour (one of the few not discussed by Skinner) arises in Francis Bacon's 'On Discourse'. In all three published versions of this essay, starting from that of 1597, Bacon approved of a limited inclusion of jests in conversation in order to provide variety, as a sort of condiment or seasoning, but warned that one must be judicious in their use:[11]

> It is good to varie and mixe speech of the present occasion with argument, tales with reasons, asking of questions, with telling of opinions, and iest with earnest. But some thinges are priuileged from iest, namely Religion, matters of state, great persons, any mans present business of importance, and any case that deserueth pittie.

Since Bacon counselled avoiding jesting about politics, religion, power, weighty matters, or the pathetic, he may seem to have left few topics for what we call jokes aside from shaggy dogs, grapes, and light-bulbs.

In fact, Bacon had quite telling reasons for counselling against many kinds of jesting. These reasons connect with the fact that 'Of Discourse' was a guide to making profitable uses of sociability. So, just after recommending jesting, Bacon also recommended that conversationalists encourage others to talk about their own particular knowledge and skills:

> He that questioneth much, shall learn much, and content much, specially if hee applie his questions to the skill of the person of whome he asketh, for he shall giue them occasion to please themselues in speaking, and himselfe shall continually gather knowledge.

Bacon's belief that 'knowledge is power' applies here, but so does a view that flattery of experts may advance one's influence and power. Similar gains, on the other hand, might be hindered if one gave unnecessary offence. So Bacon inserted into the later versions of his essay – in between his recommendations of conversational jests and inquisitive flattery – a warning against impulsive or incautious jest-making:[12]

And generally, men ought to find the difference between saltiness and bitterness. Certainly, he that hath a satirical vein, as he maketh others afraid of his wit, so he had need to be afraid of others' memory.

Thus, for Bacon, restraints upon joking are necessary in order to advance the self-serving ends of making friends and avoiding enemies.[13]

   Others in Bacon's age perceived further reasons for avoiding jests that injure feelings. These are reasons of considerateness. For instance, Sir Philip Sidney's *Apologie for Poetrie* excluded from poetry's function of 'delightful teaching' any provoking of 'coarse amusement' by such comic turns as 'against lawe of hospitality, to jest at straungers, because they speake not English so well as wee doe'.[14] A widely used rhetorical manual by Thomas Wilson, in this and other ways closely following Cicero's *De Oratore*, generally condemned scurrilous jesting.[15] Wilson's position is similar to that suggested by Shakespeare's Beatrice in her castigation of Benedick's allegedly libellous wit (*Much Ado*, 2.1.127–32).

   Not a scurrilous, but even a deserved mockery, is condemned in Olivia's objection in *Twelfth Night* to the comic but cruel roasting of Malvolio: 'He hath been most notoriously abused' (5.1.375). Shakespeare's scoffers, right down to Sebastian and Antonio of *The Tempest*, are generally portrayed as untoward. Remarking on Shakespeare's 'sneerers', albeit from the standpoint of the Romantic age, Coleridge commented:[16]

Observe the fine humanity of Shakespeare in that his sneerers are all worthless villains. Too cunning to attach value to *self-praise*, and unable to obtain approval from those they are compelled to respect, they propitiate their own *self-love* by disparaging and lowering others.

   Kindness as a reason for avoiding cruel jokes was explicitly propounded by the French physician Laurent Joubert in his 1579 *Treatise on Laughter*. Joubert's treatise agreed with Bacon's warning against making jests that could irritate the powerful, but remarked also that it 'is of a great inhumanity to make fun of the miserable on whom we should take pity'.[17] Also, although Joubert held in accord with derision theories that

'The raw material of the laughable in speech is drawn from lampoons, gibes, derision, mockery, and remarks that are stinging, biting, equivocal, ambiguous, and which spring in any way from error', he added that 'All come from scorn and derision, which when serious and of consequence become harmful, but when light remain laughable.'[18] So, for Joubert, unkind derision that is not good-humoured or light is not funny, and should be avoided.

Thomas Hobbes, on the contrary, did not believe in the possibility of benign laughter. His convictions about human nature made him find nothing exceptional in cruel mockery causing pain through laughter. Yet Hobbes did not approve of laughter, which for him expressed the pleasure taken in the 'sudden glory' of a realisation of one's superiority, power, or dominance over another. Hobbes scornfully suggested that by laughing at those even more wretched than themselves persons of small ability 'keep themselves in their own favour … by observing the imperfections of other men'.[19] Their laughter is a badge of their unworthiness. But such baseness of motive was not for Hobbes the main reason why laughter should be suppressed; the reason was rather the safety of society. Since for Hobbes laughter is always denigrating, it always offends. It therefore always produces dissension. Allowing such dissension runs contrary to Hobbes's 'first and Fundamental Law of Nature; which is to seek Peace, and follow it'.[20]

Hobbes therefore presented a maximised sort of derision theory in which society's well-being, but no impulse of kindness, mandates limits on laughter. Quentin Skinner contrasts this Hobbesian position with several later views on laughter. The Augustan age in England typically found laughter lowering, and its writers advised the gentle to avoid it. Many Romantic literary critics, including Maurice Morgann, who extravagantly praised Falstaff,[21] thought laughter an expression of humane sympathy. Nearer our time, Freud and Nietzsche both found laughter revealing of hidden or denied drives, and both thought it possibly emancipating.

The most extensive twentieth-century study of laughter, that by Henri Bergson, reverts to a version of derision theory. Bergson holds that whenever something is laughable this is because it reveals some sort of automatism in a human being, something rigid or semi-mechanical. This elicits derision because humans should manifest the elasticity and responsiveness characteristic of vitality. So, Bergson holds, typical targets of laughter are narrow-mindedness, absent-mindedness, or self-obsession. He further argues that laughter is socially useful, but also inevitably unkind: 'in laughter we always find an unavowed intention to humiliate, and consequently to correct our neighbour'.[22] Bergson sums up:

Laughter is, above all, a corrective. Being intended to humiliate, it must make a painful impression on the person against whom it is directed. By laughter society avenges itself for the liberties taken with it. [Laughter] would fail in its object if it bore the stamp of sympathy or kindness. (197)

But is this so – must laughter always be bereft of 'the stamp of sympathy or kindness'? Or is the reverse possible: might laughter in some cases increase sympathy or reduce the likelihood of hatred or conflict?

Thousands of writers have addressed these and similar questions. Some have even constructed grids with theories of laughter on one axis and supposed listings of all types of humour on another, and considered how each theory matches up with each type of humour.[23] As serious as that is, I'd rather use the tactic counselled by Francis Bacon in 'Of Discourse', which consists of seeking the knowledge possessed by skilled practitioners of an art or craft.[24] Usefully, the screenwriter Max Eastman recorded the insights of some of Hollywood's great comics.[25] Groucho Marx told Eastman:

There are all kinds of humour. Some is derisive, some sympathetic, and some merely whimsical. That is just what makes comedy so much harder to create than serious drama; people laugh in many different ways, and they cry in only one. (370)

Surely Groucho is justified in claiming that comedy takes many shapes. Mae West's remarks ran similarly:

Ridicule is just one phase of humour and is not always the basis for a laugh, although it is a sure-fire short cut. In ridicule, too, all those who laugh are not necessarily amused. Sympathy may be aroused for the poor fellow who is the object of ridicule. (371)

Again, we will find use for Mae West's remarks on a possible counter-reaction of sympathy, and on the dangers of cheap laugh-seeking, when considering Shakespeare's dramatised joking.

5. SHAKESPEARE AND THE ETHNIC JOKE

Many Shakespeare plays contain comic remarks or interchanges which at least partly resemble what have more recently been labelled 'nationality' jokes ('Polish jokes', 'Scottish jokes', 'Irish jokes', etc.).[26] This was not unusual; A. J. Hoenselaars has shown that the English Renaissance stage very frequently displayed comic stereotyping of nationalities, both foreign and British.[27] But almost all of Shakespeare's critics have avoided addressing the issues raised by his nationality jokes, perhaps being shy of handling trivialities, or else fastidious of matters now judged shamefully incorrect.

A bold exception is Gary Taylor, who commends Shakespearian nationality jokes in terms of the pleasure they may give. Taylor develops his theory of a pleasurable reception being proper by drawing on personal experience; he reports himself having been in youth wholly unaware of the actual identity of the incredibly stupid 'Polacks' whom he often heard maligned in 'Polish jokes'. For him, as a child, 'Polacks' might as well have been creatures from outer space. Hearing them named signalled exactly and only: 'expect laughter soon'. Taylor suggests that today's Shakespeare audiences could benefit in terms of pleasure from adopting a similar outlook.[28]

I think that Taylor means that audiences may benefit from putting aside their aversions to the evils of bigotry, and replacing these with a sophisticated understanding that linguistic markers can serve wholly different purposes in varied contexts. Legitimate pleasure may be blocked unless it is realised that a narrative or textual convention need not necessarily reflect referents or realities external to itself.

It is true that humour researchers have shown that the groups named in typical stupidity-alleging 'nationality' jokes – be they Belgians, Kerrymen, Newfoundlanders, Sikhs, or others – vary only according to the origins of the joke-tellers, and are otherwise utterly interchangeable.[29] Because identical nationality jokes appear worldwide with differently named targets, it might be argued that such a joke's naming of a nationality is simply a marker for a genre of humour, a signal for an expectation of laughter (just as the mere naming of 'Radio Yerevan' cues smiling in Eastern Europe, as we shall see in Chapter 4).

But I wonder ... members of the nationalities used as 'markers' may justifiably be offended by the kinds of jokes that attribute colossal stupidity to them, even though an identical joke might be told elsewhere with a different target.

Moreover, in common with other theatrically staged nationality jokes of the era, those of Shakespeare did not typically allege a worldwide possibility: stupidity. Instead, they often assigned specific, although still prejudiced, differential characteristics to various national targets, as has been detailed by A. J. Hoenselaars.[30] Even so, specific stereotyping on its own is a dubious basis for brilliant humour. Perhaps, however, it might be a basis for depiction of a failed attempt at humour.

Such observations point towards a main focus of this chapter: Shakespeare's representations of poor or failed jokes. I will argue that these depictions need not be either inartistic or reprehensible; a dramatist may present unpalatable or embarrassing situations involving joking not for the sake of buying easy laughter, but rather to make salient points about individual or group relations, or about the social processes of joking itself. Thus it is worth giving serious attention to some ethnic jokes in Shakespeare which may not be at all successful as jokes, and may not be at all pleasant.

6. JOKE-MAKING, FAILURE, AND RISK

Many studies have insisted that humour is always entirely relative to context,[31] and it is certainly true that all jokes will not 'work' equally well with all audiences or in all settings.[32] Yet it is possible that certain aspects of the process of joking are similar in all periods and cultures.

I believe one such invariant characteristic of joking is that a true joke must be capable not only of succeeding but also of failing. The tyrant who elicits obedient hilarity through fear is therefore not truly joking. To a limited extent, then, jokes resemble scientific hypotheses, which, in order to be validated, must also be capable of being falsified or invalidated; jokes, like proper scientific theories, must risk failure and rejection because otherwise they cannot overcome these and 'work'.

A further, perhaps universal, aspect is that if the connection between a joke-audience and a joke-maker is in some way personal, the audience's awareness that joke-making must risk failure can strengthen eventual laughter. The process is as follows: their awareness that a friend's or acquaintance's joke may 'bomb', or fall flat, may induce in the joke-hearers a salutary anxiety or tension on account of their sympathetic dreading of – or perhaps their rivalrous wish for – an embarrassing failure. When a joke succeeds, the release of this tension may amplify the success of the 'punch-line'. The precariousness of jokes thus may supply the tension required for a pleasurable tension/release cycle, the release being laughter. Playwrights may, and Shakespeare did, imitate this pattern, placing both jokers and joke-hearers onstage.[33]

7. MORE HUMOUR THEORY, AND FALSTAFFIAN APPLICATIONS

Sammy Basu argues that joking need not be socially conservative, denying the inevitability of humour 'reinscrib[ing] the limit it temporarily transgresses'.[34] Thus he claims humour can advance 'dialogic ethics' and serve positively in 'political' dialogue (391–4). He offers three ways in which humour can act in this connection: as 'lubrication, friction and glue'. Jokes can be lubricants because they can promote 'goodwill', 'disarm', 'break … the ice'. They can be frictional because as 'fine grained social sandpaper' they can take the rough edges off what is hard to say or 'hard to swallow'. They can be glue because they are playfully sociable, and when shared can offer ways of 'reducing tensions … redrawing boundaries'.

The above summary conveys only a fraction of Basu's theories about humour serving an 'affirmative intersubjectivity', but is enough to make it clear that his theories bear implicitly on questions of tolerance. It is especially interesting in this connection that the three tolerance-promoting functions of humour – 'lubrication, friction and glue' – are incompatible, and yet there is no reason why any combination of them cannot be operative at once.

If joking can operate in several contradictory ways at the same time, each promoting tolerance, then perhaps the best place to look for Shakespearian materials illustrating such simultaneous functioning is in Shakespeare's most self-contradictory and complex comic figure, the Falstaff of the second *Henriad* (who is also, for most critics, Shakespeare's comic masterpiece).

But one might well ask: 'what 'a devil hast Falstaff to do with tolerance?'

It might seem a desperate answer to suggest that the tolerance of physical disability is in question, because Falstaff deploys humour to help others to accept his own vice- and age-produced deformities. However, it has been argued by David Ellis that among 'the many reasons for the appeal of Falstaff is that he has such a remarkable variety of ways for making others forget, overlook, or accept his physical disadvantages'. As detailed by Ellis, these ways are all comic, all allow Falstaff's entry into a youthful company above his social competence, and all induce others to laugh not at but '*with*' him.[35]

However, *pace* Ellis, Falstaff is presented not as a poor, fat, elderly man with increasingly many bodily diseases who seeks friendship, but rather, as Dr Johnson long ago described him, as an utterly charming and utterly incorrigible rogue.[36] To deal with Falstaff's famously unsettling mixture of charisma and wickedness in relation to tolerance and humour, it is useful to return to the before-mentioned topic of jokes failing or being vulnerable to failure. Falstaff's mixed resilient and precarious comic persona in the two *Henry IV* plays is labelled 'vitalist [… and] nihilist' by David Ellis, who relates it to an 'elegiac' mood felt by all who live long enough to see regime change.[37] I certainly agree with Ellis that Falstaff is not properly reducible to a supra-human force – a figure of misrule, carnival, the body, or anything else abstract or collective, irrepressible, and immortal (100). But I think that Falstaff's failures and failings, for Ellis suggesting 'the stereotype of the unhappy clown' (106), have rather a dimension that connects them with the vulnerability of all joking, and through that with issues concerning tolerance.

What has troubled many sensitive readers is that finally Hal will not tolerate Falstaff. To see why he cannot, it is necessary to note that Falstaff's comic performances present an incremental pattern. Falstaff is forced to find ever more contorted comic excuses for progressively more outrageous acts of greed, cowardice, dishonesty, or insubordination; thus he must increasingly hazard failure and embarrassment as he pushes his joke-excuses farther and farther into the realms of implausibility.[38] This correlates with a progressive decline in Falstaff's dramatic stature beside other characters, especially in *Henry IV, part 2*, as analysed in detail by Brian Vickers.[39]

Of course Falstaff is set up for some of his gaffes by cronies who delight in seeing him discomfited. Thus Hal is persuaded to participate in a very un-prince-like highway-robbery ploy, intended to double-cross Falstaff. This is simply because, as Poins puts it, 'The virtue of this jest will be the incomprehensible lies that this same fat rogue will tell us when we meet at supper' (*Henry IV, part 1* 1.2.183–5). And indeed here, as in all but a very few other cases,[40] Falstaff does pull off an excuse for his lying and cowardice by means of an audacious comic invention.

But, notoriously, Falstaff's skill fails utterly in his final encounter with Hal. Although worse and worse threats of 'open and apparent shame' for Falstaff (*Henry IV, part 1* 2.5.267–8) are the pattern of the *Henry IV* plays, the coronation scene contains the apogee of these when Falstaff appears at Hal's great event ill-companioned, road-stained, and ill-clad. Yet, abominably, Falstaff still calls out 'my sweet boy!' (*Henry IV, part 2* 5.5.43). The great let-down (for many) is that, in his infamous 'rejection' speech, Hal then prevents Falstaff from making his trademark comic excuses, commanding: 'Reply not to me with a fool born jest' (5.5.55).

In sober reality it must be admitted, however, that, by preventing the dismal failure of the joke trembling on Falstaff's lip, Hal's 'rejection' actually prevents Falstaff's crushing humiliation. For for no conceivable joke could succeed in overcoming Falstaff's grand violation of decorum. Moreover, Hal's reply to Falstaff nearly as much validates as rejects him. For Hal's lines beginning 'I know thee not, old man' in fact imitate a palpable Falstaffian style of stilted and canting platitudinousness:

> I know thee not, old man. Fall to thy prayers.
> How ill white hairs becomes a fool and jester!
> I have long dreamt of such a kind of man,
> So surfeit-swelled, so old, and so profane;
> But being awake, I do despise my dream.
> Make less thy body hence, and more thy grace.
> Leave gormandizing; know the grave doth gape
> For thee thrice wider than for other men. (5.5.47–54)

The tension developed at this juncture is nearly unbearable. We the audience, and Hal, and all present onstage, know that the wound-up watch of Falstaff's wit is about to strike. We know also that his joke must fail. Just as a grimace of anticipated embarrassment begins to spread however, quick-witted Hal wipes it away. He does in fact provide jokes, the usual ones about Falstaff's girth, age, and so on, and then tops them with a better one: he makes it part of the impecunious Falstaff's 'punishment' that he must suffer the receipt of a pension 'That lack of means enforce you not to evils' (5.5.67).

But this Falstaff-like, logic-puncturing joke has not assuaged critics who cannot forgive the new king for curbing the master joker. However, the structure of the play forces us to see that not Hal, but the logic of change itself, a 'turning o' th' tide' (*Henry V* 2.3.13), at last defeats Falstaff; time, which from the start Falstaff is said to ignore, does at the end catch up with him.

Finally, let me recap and identify a pattern. Until his final debacle Falstaff repeatedly succeeds in rescuing himself from deserved infamy by means of jokes that defeat logic and reality. For instance, he explains being overheard calumniating Hal in the tavern thus:

I dispraised him before the wicked, that the wicked might not fall in love with him; in which doing I have done the part of a careful friend and a true subject, and thy father is to give me thanks for it. No abuse, Hal; none, Ned, none; no, faith, boys, none. (*Henry IV, part 2* 2.4.322–8)

Aware of his own powers, Falstaff is also aware that he depends upon others to confer those powers on him; they do so on account of the pleasure they take from challenging him. Thus he comments on his doctor, who is catapulted into comedy even while delivering a bad prognosis:

Men of all sorts take a pride to gird at me. The brain of this foolish-compounded clay, man, is not able to invent anything that tends to laughter more than I invent, or is invented on me. I am not only witty in myself, but the cause that wit is in other men. (1.2.6–10)

Which is to say that Falstaff thrives within, and lives upon, a fellowship of mocking and retorts; he is rich in an economy of giving and taking non-harming insults. Shakespeare shows two tavern-drawers chronicling his fame:

The Prince once set a dish of apple-johns before him; and told him, there were five more Sir Johns; and, putting off his hat, said 'I will now take my leave of these six dry, round, old, withered knights.' It angered him to the heart. But he hath forgot that. (2.4.4–9)

Falstaff's 'girding', a participatory sport of mock insulting, has been called more recently 'joshing'. Joshing may promote tolerance by making comfortably familiar human differences or singularities that could otherwise cause alarm or disquiet. Self-joshing, as in Falstaff's bizarre acceptance that he is still young (his 'Young men must live' in *Henry IV, part 2* 2.2.88; also *Henry IV, part 2* 1.2.175, 3.2.320), may also lubricate or ease tensions.

But in Falstaff's stage trajectory any progression through joshing or self-joshing towards social bonding is shockingly fractured when his final impossible humour-sally fails miserably (although Hal charitably cushions that failure). Which brings us to the point of considering the dramatic functions that may be served by staging a range of failures of joking or humour.

8. DRAMA AND JOKE FAILURE

Some Elizabethan texts usefully distinguish between several varieties of failed jokes, and in particular between crude, ineffective, and malevolent ones.

Immediately following its dedication to both Oxford and Cambridge universities, Ben Jonson's 1606 *Volpone* contains a prologue boasting that it eschews the kinds of cheap comedy Jonson thinks would irritate such sophisticated audiences:

> Yet thus much I can give you as a token
> Of his play's worth: no eggs are broken,
> Nor quaking custards with fierce teeth affrighted,
> Wherewith your rout are so delighted;
> Nor hales he in a gull, old ends reciting,
> To stop gaps in his loose writing;
> With such a deal of monstrous and forced action,
> As might make Bedlam a faction;
> Nor made his play for jests, stolen from each table,
> But makes jests to fit his fable;
> And so presents quick comedy, refined
> As best critics have designed.

Jonson's 'best critics' decry comic uses of slapstick action, clichéd comic types, stale stage 'business', and the parachuting in of irrelevant jokes going the rounds of dinner tables.[41]

Woeful joke-making is also at issue when Shakespeare's Beatrice in *Much Ado About Nothing* complains bitterly that her adversary Benedick once said that she 'had my good wit out of the Hundred Merry Tales' (2.1.119–20). Here Beatrice refers to a 1526 printed collection of English jests,[42] first in a long line of sixteenth-century followers.[43] When, in about 1599, Shakespeare, via Beatrice, made a satiric swipe at this old collection he obviously expected his audiences to agree that it was hoary and outdated. For Beatrice, certainly, it is a book of stale and inferior wit, for she bristles at the accusation of having derived *her* 'good wit' from it, and retaliates by saying of Benedick:

Why, he is the Prince's jester, a very dull fool. Only his gift is in devising impossible slanders. None but libertines delight in him, and the commendation is not in his wit but in his villainy, for he both pleases men and angers them, and then they laugh at him, and beat him. (2.1.127–32)

This retort identifies a second category of bad jokes, far worse than those that are outdated or just flaccid: the category of scurrilously derogatory jokes. Such 'impossibly slanderous' jokes have impact simply as a result of their shock value. Beatrice claims that making them shows in Benedick a reprehensible dullness capable only of tickling the perverse palates of libertines.

Beatrice's discrimination between failures in jesting implies a distinction between two kinds of 'bad' jokes: feeble ones and repugnant ones. Feeble jokes are those deficient in wit or verve, while repugnant ones are obscene or revolting.

A distinction between feeble and repugnant ethnic jokes in particular has been examined by the philosopher Ted Cohen. Among other things Cohen shows that repugnant jokes may be at the same time not at all feeble, for he demonstrates some repugnant ethnic jokes that are quite witty.[44] It may therefore be argued that ethnic jokes especially have two independent dimensions of quality: they can be better or worse jokes in terms of slackness or wittiness; and, independently, they can be more or less acceptable or repugnant.

In such terms, *The Merchant of Venice* dramatises the telling of some fairly slack non-repugnant ethnic jokes, and some distinctly repugnant ethnic jokes which are, however, not wholly deficient in comic verve. It will next be argued that Shakespeare's inclusion of these jokes was not to please groundlings,[45] nor for purposes resembling Gary Taylor's hedonistic 'delight', but rather to serve significant artistic and thematic purposes.

9. ETHNIC JOKING IN *THE MERCHANT OF VENICE*

Near its start, *The Merchant of Venice* presents a string of comically weak but possibly ethically acceptable 'nationality' jokes. Then, deceptively soon afterwards, another ethnic joke appears that, while externally similar, is actually repugnant.

Portia's first ethnic jokes are the six 'nationality' jokes she makes in conversation with Nerissa mocking the national characteristics of six of her 'stranger', or foreign, suitors (1.2.38–97).[46] These closely follow Portia's admission of her world-weariness on account of her disempowerment with regard to her marriage choice (1.2.1–26); the ensuing jokes seem to me to convey an air of melancholy, perhaps even a desperate grasping for gaiety. The best among them is Portia's mock-serious, although perhaps not original,[47] command that to prevent her drunken German suitor from choosing her Nerissa should:

set a deep glass of Rhenish wine on the contrary casket; for if the devil be within and that temptation without, I know he will choose it. I will do anything, Nerissa, ere I will be married to a sponge (1.2.92–6).

Because of the way in which they are dramatically framed, Portia's first six nationality jokes are not wholly repugnant. Even though stereotyping lies behind a Neapolitan suitor who is horse-mad, one from the Palatinate (the Calvinist Rhineland) who is excessively dour, a French one who is extravagant in all his moods and actions, an English one who is monolingual and sartorially challenged, a Scottish one who is quarrelsome, and a German one who is constantly drunk,[48] nevertheless in each case Portia's wry descriptions are presented as if based on actual observations rather than on mere prejudice.

The reverse of that is true, however, in Portia's next suitor-bashing, slightly later in the same scene, in which she says of the Prince of Morocco: 'If he have the condition of a saint and the complexion of a devil, I had rather he should shrive me than wive me' (1.2.126–8). The crucial difference is that this time Portia has not actually observed the African prince, for the text shows he has not yet arrived (1.2.121–3). Indeed, no observation would have mattered, for Portia says that even if he has a saintly disposition his skin colour will trump his virtue, and she will not want to marry him. 'Complexion' meaning skin tone was a new usage in Shakespeare's age (*OED* 4.a); Portia puns on its older meaning (*OED* 3) as temperament or disposition (i.e. 'condition'). Portia's pun being perhaps fresh does not, however, negate the fact that it expresses outright prejudice, and that her gaiety, which expects a ready acceptance, is racist.

10. THE MOST REPUGNANT JOKE DEPICTED BY SHAKESPEARE

A further repugnantly racist quip is added to Portia's literally prejudiced prejudging of Morocco when she remarks just after he has failed the casket test:

> A gentle riddance. Draw the curtains, go.
> Let all of his complexion choose me so (2.7.78–9)

In fact, Portia's witty choice of the word 'gentle' in 'a gentle riddance' is multiply sinister. For one, it contains another pun. Although 'gentile' (spelled 'gentle') in Shakespeare's time usually meant a non-Jew or else a heathen or pagan (*OED* 1, 2), for Gratiano the eloping Jessica becomes 'a gentle, and no Jew' (2.6.51). Portia extends the same pun on gentile/gentle to Morocco, who is therefore aligned with un-gentle Shylock. In addition, Portia's unalloyed relief at her 'gentle riddance' of Morocco is heartless because she knows of his great loss on her account: just before she speaks he acknowledged in his 'farewell heat' speech (2.7.74–7) his undertaking never again to attempt to marry. Moreover, Portia's 'gentle riddance' distorts the standard locution 'a good [or fair] riddance' (see *OED*, 'riddance', 4). Here Portia reveals an attitude acceptable to Belmont at large: being 'gentle' in the sense of being well-bred (*OED* 2.a and 3.a) counts for more than any other value; good breeding prevails over any other 'good'.

But that is far from the most repugnant racialist quip heard in Shakespeare's Belmont; the prize for that must go to the clown Launcelot Gobbo. His outrageous joke is the moral nadir of the play, sinking below the baiting of Shylock, Portia's dismissal of Morocco, or Bassanio's denigration of an imagined 'Indian beauty' just as he wins Portia (3.2.98–9).

First, Gobbo teases his former ally and mistress, the New Christian Jessica, with:

this making of Christians will raise the price of hogs, – if we grow all to be pork-eaters, we shall not shortly have a rasher on the coals for money. (3.5.21–3)

Although he is a licensed clown, Gobbo's use of consumerist and dead animal imagery in connection with Christian conversion is jarring, as is his immediately preceding remark that Jessica was damned for being born Jewish (which violates Christian doctrine). Yet Jessica has always enjoyed Gobbo's being 'a merry devil' (2.3.2), and these are only lead-ins to the ugly joke that will follow.

The set-up for this joke begins when Jessica's husband Lorenzo enters and she reports to him that Launcelot:

tells me flatly there's no mercy for me in heaven because I am a Jew's daughter: and he says you are no good member of the commonwealth, for in converting Jews to Christians, you raise the price of pork. (3.5.29–33)

(Her words here 'no good member of the commonwealth' are ironic because *The Merchant of Venice* posits a commonwealth of Belmont where there is no scarcity of bacon, or anything else.) Lorenzo retorts with a counter-accusation against Gobbo, of fornication:

I shall answer that better to the commonwealth than you can the getting up of the Negro's belly. The Moor is with child by you, Lancelot! (3.5.32–7)

Here the 'commonwealth' is involved because it will have to deal with an unmarried mother, perhaps part of the Prince of Morocco's delegation; Lorenzo alludes to the much-discussed problem of Elizabethan parishes' reluctance to support illegitimate children and their mothers.[49] Gobbo replies:

It is much that the Moor should be more than reason: but if she be less than an honest woman, she is indeed more than I took her for. (3.5.37–9)

Lorenzo comments, 'How every fool can play upon the word!', referring no doubt to the quibbles in the multiple puns: 'more'/'Moor'; 'more' = greater vs. 'more' = pregnant; and 'take' = understand vs. 'take' = sexually use. But much more is going on in Gobbo's joke than simply his skill with what Lorenzo later calls disapprovingly the 'tricksy word'. Gobbo says that if the pregnant Moor is 'less than an honest woman' (and therefore a *dishonest* woman) she is 'indeed more' than he took her for. This amounts to a confession, or a boast, that Launcelot took her for less than a woman of any kind, for he 'took' her as an animal. With the greatest effrontery, he frankly jests that 'miscegenation' was for him just bestiality.

This repugnant joke aligns with a complex use in *The Merchant of Venice* of animal imagery, comprising almost eighty instances. Very often the images are of animals breeding. Correlative to these images was a legal position, described and theoretically applicable in Shakespeare's time, that made Jessica's and Lorenzo's sort of marriage – between a Christian and Jew – a very serious crime. Sir Edward Coke's *Institutes* associated such a marriage with sodomy and bestiality, and recorded an 'ancient law of England' demanding that 'the party so offending should be burnt alive'.[50] Indeed there had been a famous, if unusual, case of such a burning in Oxford in 1222.[51]

Such punishments might have been rare, but the equating of miscegenation with bestiality was still highly significant.[52] As we shall see in Chapter 6, such a take on miscegenation was by no means universal in Shakespeare's age. Yet, even beyond biblical injunctions, Shakespeare's age viewed the 'crying sin' of bestiality (about which Gobbo sexually boasts) with an anxiety fuelled by ideological terror. Actual indictments in Elizabethan England for bestiality were rare and convictions rarer,[53] yet the offence was violently condemned. According to the analysis of Keith Thomas this was because it violated an insecure yet crucial division of humans from animals.[54] So nudity, long hair, night work, nocturnal burglary, the play-acting of animal roles, and even swimming caused great anxiety.[55] For such reasons, wrote Thomas:[56]

Bestiality, accordingly, was the worst of sexual crimes because, as one Stuart moralist put it, 'it turns man into a very beast, makes a man a member of a brute creature.' The sin was the sin of confusion; it was immoral to mix the categories. Injunctions against 'buggery with beasts' were standard in seventeenth-century moral literature, though occasionally the topic was passed over, 'the fact being more filthy than to be spoken of.' Bestiality became a capital offence in 1543 and, with one brief interval [1553–62], remained so until 1861. Incest, by contrast, was not a secular crime at all until the twentieth century.

II. ON BENIGN SELF-MOCKING ETHNIC JOKES

It is with some relief that I now turn from Gobbo's atrocious 'joke' or filthy ethnic slur to consider instances of ethnic joking that are less distressing, and perhaps even salutary.

There is a curious fact, to be followed up at greater length in Chapter 3, that increasingly from about 1600 *English* playwrights displayed ethnic stereotyping in staged self-mockingly 'anti-*English* jokes'. Indeed, according to A. J. Hoenselaars, plays and dramatic characters satirizing the English in comparison with foreigners became a dominant theatrical mode throughout the Jacobean and Caroline periods.[57]

Precociously early for this trend, Portia in *The Merchant of Venice* derides her English suitor, the young baron Falconbridge, for lacking foreign languages and being deficient in dress sense (1.2.65–73). Slightly later in Shakespeare's career the witty Danish Gravedigger of *Hamlet* claims that the mad prince will go unnoticed in England, where 'the men are as mad as he' (5.1.150–1). Likewise, a jesting remark is passed by a French Lord in *All's Well* suggesting that Englishmen are less amorous than Frenchmen (2.3.94–6).

Another clue indicating a taste for self-mocking jokes in the Elizabethan period may appear if we again consider the pioneering joke-book *A Hundred Merry Tales*. Although it epitomised tedium for Shakespeare's Beatrice, according to a letter dated 9 March 1603 that very book was put to good use when it was read aloud to the ailing Queen Elizabeth:[58]

About 10 dayes since dyed the Countess of Nottingham. The Queene loved the Countess very much, and hath seemed to take her death very heavelye, remayning euer synce in a deepe melancholye, wth conceipte of her own death, and complayneth of many infirmyties, sodainlye to haue ouertaken her [including a] notable decay in judgement and memory, insomuch as she cannot attend to any discourses of governm[en]t and state, but delighteth to heere some of the 100 merry tales, and such like, and to such is very attentiue . . .

This report of the grieving and elderly Elizabeth's sudden 'notable decay in judgement and memory' may suggest that she was failing mentally. But if we consider the particular jokes in *A Hundred Merry Tales* we may be led to suspect something rather stranger in Elizabeth's 'delight' in hearing them.

Part of the background is as follows. The Welsh element in Elizabeth's Tudor ancestry may or may not have been significant in this,[59] but certainly Princess Elizabeth had been nursed and raised as a child by a Welsh-speaking governess, Blanche Parry. When Elizabeth was three Parry became the principal lady of her household; Parry was made a gentlewoman of the privy chamber when Elizabeth became queen, and was then effectively put in charge of the royal jewels and library. Parry became the queen's principal gentlewoman in 1565 and was said to wield considerable influence, some used in favour of Wales. When she died in 1590, aged over 80, Elizabeth commanded that Parry receive the burial rites of a baroness.[60]

In such circumstances, it is worth noting that a high proportion of the jokes in *A Hundred Merry Tales* are at the expense of either Welsh persons or clever, independent-minded women.[61] The queen and her old nurse were both spirited Welshwomen; how, then, could Elizabeth have enjoyed such jokes?

It is possible that Elizabeth may have responded to these jokes on the grounds – for which several humour theorists have argued – that the very 'minorities' targeted by some ethnic jokes may find them positive and tolerance-provoking on account of their 'sociability'.[62] Indeed, there are cases where the jokes have been promulgated by members of those very minorities themselves. A study by Christie Davies, for instance, reveals that Scottish writers produced a flood of joke-books in the nineteenth century with content alleging absurd degrees of Scottish parsimony or theological nit-picking. Davies concludes that mock stereotyping of national characteristics in self-depreciating jokes can actually help to establish and express a collective national identity.[63] Other humour researchers have offered the possibility that 'ethnic humor may perform a multiplicity of functions – some of which may actually increase ethnic group cohesiveness', or that as 'left-handed insults' ethnic jokes may really be 'compliments in disguise'.[64] Also suggestions have been made that self-denigrating ethnic jokes made by maligned groups may serve, in addition to 'salutary' purposes, defensive ones as well.[65]

My own personal recollection may help clarify such ideas. A joke circulated in the Jewish Brooklyn of my youth about a proud Jewish mother whose adored grown-up son gets into trouble whilst sea-bathing: she is seen running along the beach, crying: 'Help! My son-the-doctor is drowning.' In the milieu in which I first heard this joke, a mother of such a son would have ranked among the very fortunate, so this self-targeting ethnic joke was not, as some sociological commentators would have it, 'directed downwards in the class structure' in such a way that 'a middle class audience . . . laughs at the absent lower class of their own minority group'.[66] Something other than class antagonism was going on.

I also heard American Jews telling this same joke outside of their own communities, and this telling did not appear to me to expose masochistic Jewish self-loathing.[67] This was because the joke does not really assert that a Jewish mother is more concerned with the social or economic standing of her son than with his life. Calling out 'my-son-the-doctor' is not a symptom of her inhumanity or inordinate status-seeking, but rather a symptom of her habit; in her distracted state the mother simply does not notice the inappropriateness of her habitual boastful sobriquet. It is true that in this reading the frantic mother is acting mechanically, so Bergson's theory of laughter as a humiliating social corrective to mindlessness might apply. But I don't think so. For while this joke finds humorous the mother's aspirational pride, it does not disparage the basis of that pride. It implies, rather, that the single-minded dedication needed for advancement against difficult odds may create some silly distortions – but that this silliness is partly admirable, partly not-so-bad, and wholly human.

12. THE PROBLEM OF SHYLOCK

In the light of these considerations about self-mockery, let us now consider the problem of Shylock. As indicated above, I think that prejudice and bigotry are deliberately exposed by Shakespeare as pervasive in the play-worlds of *The Merchant of Venice*.[68] I nevertheless agree with those who believe that in swearing to pursue a bloody revenge Shylock becomes a very bad man, and a bad Jew also.[69]

It is true that Shylock is portrayed as sorely provoked, but Shakespeare only humanises him – does not excuse him – by showing this. Shakespeare constantly returns to the theme of treachery, and hardly any instance he presents is more bitter than when, as a result of his attempt to be 'friends' (1.3.136) with Antonio by attending a Christian social event, Shylock suffers the loss of his child, much wealth, and a memento of his wife. After that he seeks only revenge, and friendship is out of the question.[70]

My question is whether Shakespeare's presentation of Shylock's behaviour before his reaction to this bitter blow may hint at a lost, but once possible, comic outcome for him. The answer to this depends crucially on how Shakespeare framed Shylock's offer of an interest-free loan secured by what he calls a 'merry bond'. The word 'merry' appears often in *The Merchant of Venice*, and indeed merriness and its opposite melancholy are among the play's main themes. Some of the merriness of the play derives from Shylock's habitual joking; for instance, he puns: 'There be land rats and water rats, water thieves and land thieves – I mean pi-rats' (1.3.22–3). I would like to ask, radically, if at first Shylock could have been portrayed as intending only a joke by specifying a flesh bond, as he says, 'on a merry sport'?

Again, contextualising may help. The reputation of Venice as formerly a great international trading city supplied Elizabethan writers with an image of the sort of place that London was becoming;[71] by Shakespeare's time England was well advanced in the process of transforming feudal institutions into ones suited to a mercantile economy. Thus, despite continuing diatribes heard against the medieval sin of 'usury', charging interest on loans became legally possible in England in 1545.[72] In fact, the law effectively allowed the taking of interest of 10 per cent of the total of a loan (not per annum). So, under English law, Shylock could have legitimately asked Antonio for three hundred ducats as financing charges for his borrowing of three thousand ducats. But rather, Shylock offered Antonio a loan interest-free, only insisting that it be secured by a bond.

About the time when *The Merchant of Venice* was first seen new legal means of securing loans were being established; following the infamously complex Slade's Case of 1597–1602 other convenient contracts could replace the use of bonds, but conditional bonds such as Shylock's were in common use long after that time.[73] This was because a conditional bond with a penalty attached could ensure a lender repayment without recourse to expensive litigation. Such a bond was cancelled only if the loan was repaid on the due date; if not, the courts were obliged to enforce any penalty. In fact, the royal court of King's Bench held that a penalty should still be paid on a bond (for an already repaid loan) that was only *accidentally* not cancelled, and the principle behind this was supported in an important law treatise of the earlier sixteenth century.[74] The court in *Waberly* v *Cockerel* (1542) gave a Shylock-like reason for this: 'although the truth be that the plaintiff [lender] is paid his money, still it is better to suffer a mischief to one man than an inconvenience to many, which would subvert a law'.[75]

The typical penalty negotiated on a bond was twice the value of the debt, but Shylock demanded a pound of Antonio's flesh instead. Many flesh-bond stories, often but not always involving Jewish usurers, date back to the thirteenth century or earlier,[76] and a Jew demanding a pound of flesh features in an Italian Renaissance story which supplied many of the details for Shakespeare's play.[77] So Shakespeare had ample precedent for a tale of a very un-merry flesh bond, and might have followed them. On the other hand, he might have adapted them humorously. From Shakespeare's time until our own, new spins placed on old tales have provided a format for humour: witness how chivalric romances are metamorphosed into *Don Quixote*, or *Emma* into the film *Clueless*.

Alternatively again, Shakespeare may have been imitating a popular ballad, which was possibly written before *The Merchant of Venice*, in which the Jewish usurer Gernutus at first cunningly pretends that the flesh penalty that he all along intends to extract is only 'a merry jeast'.[78] Does *The Merchant of Venice* similarly imply that Shylock is setting out from the start to murder Antonio? Two pieces of evidence might be adduced to support this. One is Shylock's aside in Act One beginning 'How like a fawning publican he looks', during which he says he had long hoped to catch his old adversary Antonio off balance, or, as he puts it, 'upon the hip' (1.3.39–50). But just before this Shylock also says aside that he will never eat with Christians (1.3.33–5), yet later he does accept their invitation (2.5.11–15). So these asides indicate Shylock's habitual pique, but no clear intent to act. Similarly Jessica's testimony that her father had sworn that he would rather have Antonio's flesh than his money (3.2.282–6) proves only an obsessive animosity.

Stronger, if circumstantial, evidence leans the other way. We must not expect full consistency in a play or dramatic character, but it is surely basic to *The Merchant of Venice* that Shylock is a savvy businessman well able to judge the risks in ventures. Shylock emphasises that he holds Antonio to be 'a good man', and explains that he means a man good for the money he has borrowed (1.3.11–15). The audience are told repeatedly that Antonio's argosies will cover his borrowings from Shylock many times over, and that his ventures are widely dispersed. And there is no doubt that Shylock would know as much from 'news on the Rialto'. So Shylock would certainly anticipate Antonio's creditworthiness, not his bankruptcy.[79]

This would make it impossible for an astute Shylock to have planned all along to kill Antonio, for what successful financier operates on the vain hope of a remote chance? But then, if not by killing him, how else could Shylock envision getting even with his old enemy? Well, the rigid and melancholy Antonio is the only totally humourless character in *The Merchant of Venice*, so a satisfactory retaliation for wrongs done might lie in involving him in some kind of joke. Look, Shylock's joke could say, at how a Jewish moneylender demands a bond with a flesh penalty, but is forced to accept only the principal and no interest on his loan. Such a joke would mockingly exaggerate, and so undermine, the assumptions of Antonio's set – in the very mode described by several humour theorists. Tragically, any such aim fails when, after his disasters, and empowered by Antonio's bad fortune, Shylock abandons joking, and swerves instead towards vengeance.

13. CODA: DOES SHYLOCK MAKE ANTONIO INTO AN URBAN 'ARKANSAS TRAVELLER'?

That Shylock might have been originally planning a tolerance-promoting joke when demanding his 'merry bond', and was not feigning when he said to Antonio 'I would be friends with you' (1.3.136), is only a hypothesis. Jane Freeman explains that very little seems to be offered by way of reciprocation if this were the case.[80]

An alternative hypothesis is that much of Shylock's behaviour in the earlier part of the play serves a kind of humour that underdogs sometimes use to reassert their humanity while achieving some degree of revenge. Let us consider Shylock's clearly facetious quip, 'I cannot tell. I make it breed as fast', made in reply to Antonio's testy question 'is your gold and silver ewes and rams?' (1.3.94–5). Immediately after this, in the next line, Shylock attempts a further explanation beginning 'But note me, signor –.' Perhaps this was to be an explanation of the lengthy biblical analogies Shylock has just presented to Antonio: we will never know, because at this point Shylock is interrupted by Antonio, who interjects his own disdainful interpretation of Shylock's textual illustration.

In the following lines Shylock offers repeated mock self-deprecations in the style of 'I cannot tell . . . ' I will argue that, for those able to hear ironies, this mockery may allow despised Shylock to turn the tables on his despiser. Thus I will find a pattern in the whole interchange aligning it with a class of inverse ethnic jokes in which underdog figures show up their presumed 'superiors'.[81] Specifically, I will propose a match with the pattern of a sub-genre of inverted ethnic jokes known as 'Arkansas Traveller' jokes.

The traditional 'Arkansas Traveller' joke involves an American backwoods character who proves himself cleverer than his citified despiser. The prototype is a stage skit portraying a dialogue in rural Arkansas between a patrician city-type, a symbolic 'paleface', and a local frontiersman or squatter, a symbolic 'redskin'.[82] Throughout the skit the Traveller, lost and uneasy in the wilds, tries to get sense out of the countryman, but with little success. As the joke progresses the Traveller's haughty impatience causes him to become more and more overbearing. The countryman acts the part of a daft or slow-witted bumpkin, increasingly frustrating the exasperated Traveller. The countryman's naive simplicity is finally revealed to be a ploy enabling the exposure, in a punch line, of the Traveller's own slack wit and deficient capabilities.

A typical rendition runs:[83]

[The Arkansas Traveller, a city slicker, lost in the deep backwoods, is trying to get directions from a local hillbilly.]

A.T.   Which road do you take to Grassville?
H.B.   There ain't no use in takin' any; they got one there already.
A.T.   Does it make any difference which road I take?
H.B.   Not to me, it don't.
       [etc.]
A.T.   [his patience gone] You are not very smart, old man, are you?
H.B.   Nope. But then, I ain't the one that's lost . . .

Thus the hillbilly appears daft and limited until, in a sudden blaze of sense, he reveals the genuine incompetence of the Traveller.

At first in *The Merchant*, in accord with an Arkansas Traveller pattern, Shylock gestures his mock-stupidity in 'I cannot tell', in averring he 'had forgot' the term of the loan requested by Antonio, and then in feigning to remember it bumblingly: 'three months – you told me so' (1.3.66). Antonio, in dialogue with this mock-inept Shylock, fills the part of a palefaced would-be-patrician city-type at a loss in a wilderness beyond his civic walk. That wilderness is the territory of lenders and borrowers, where Antonio has never before strayed because of his would-be refined, absurd (for a merchant) fastidiousness, his fear of being dirtied by contact with capital markets, or, as he sees it, with usury.

Just like the uneasy Arkansas Traveller, the interloping Antonio cannot wait to get away. Like the locally knowledgeable hillbilly, only the savvy Shylock can help the interloper, and also like the hillbilly, Shylock is slow to do so. Like the Traveller, the finicky Antonio displays an increasingly irritable impatience with what is for him a base encounter. Like the hillbilly, Shylock thwarts the interloper's wish to move on by speaking lengthily and seemingly irrelevantly.

In Shylock's case, this lengthy speech takes the form of ruminations on biblical texts. Antonio's dismissive responses to these indicate that he believes Shylock to be merely a crude money-grubber. Again like the hillbilly, Shylock disingenuously plays up the assumed crudeness and stupidity. His 'I cannot tell' and 'I had forgot' are topped, brilliantly, by a mock-crude non-response to Antonio's insults, posed as if he had not understood them: 'Three thousand ducats. 'Tis a good round sum . . . ' (1.2.102).

Shylock playing a naive bumpkin serves to reinforce Antonio's prejudiced assumption that he is incapable of nuance or subtlety. Here, just like the Arkansas Traveller in the skit, Antonio is easily tricked because he is self-deluded. In fact Shylock finely judges his recitation of biblical stories: those to which he alludes all concern legalistic manoeuvres on the part of an underdog (the young Jacob) that lead to his God-ordained vindication. Shylock's allusions, then, might have revealed his real motives to Antonio had Antonio been capable of hearing them. Disastrously, Antonio shows himself incapable of appreciating the wit of his adversary.

CHAPTER 2

Shakespeare, gender, and tolerance

I. PROSPECTUS

Perhaps for good reason, relations between the sexes as portrayed by Shakespeare are not often discussed in terms of tolerance or intolerance. From the perspective of this book, in which tolerance is understood to require a possibility of making a choice against intolerance, the problem might be that in Elizabethan gender relations choice was not always a possibility. At the start of *The Merchant of Venice*, Portia, dominated by her late father's will, laments: 'O me, the word "choose"' (1.2.21–2). Some see early modern gender relations as the product of hierarchal or patri-archal ideologies determined by (or rationalising) oppressive and unjust social, economic, and legal arrangements beyond any individual's control. Much remains to be learned about such matters in connection with Shakespeare's time and culture.

From among such large questions a restricted but perhaps illuminating focus will be chosen for this chapter. This will be on Shakespeare's varied dramatic representations of men or women who react in ways specific to their dramatically posited situations to questions regarding gender and sexual relations. In some cases they manifest abnormal intolerance, and in others develop remarkable tolerance, relative to the possibilities available to them in Elizabethan culture.

Shakespeare, of course, had to frame his representations of gender interactions and attitudes within boundaries defined by his own society, although sometimes they were quite close to the edge of these boundaries, occasionally perhaps over the edge. Moreover, Shakespeare's transgressors of bounds are not always 'contained'. On the negative side, Othello is the only onstage wife-beater depicted by Shakespeare; wife-beating was dis-approved of in Elizabethan society,[1] and Othello proceeds to murder. On the positive side, no more must subversive humour always reinscribe the norms it challenges than must a witty and outspoken Shakespearian heroine, like Beatrice in *Much Ado*, settle into compliance like her long-suffering, silent, and 'wet' cousin Hero.

27

I refer to Shakespeare's dramatic representations of 'gender' inter-actions and attitudes in addition to his representations of 'sexual relations' because not only sexual behaviour and outlooks, but also how the sexes were represented or characterised by Elizabethan culture have a bearing on many of his dramatic constructions. In some very interesting Shakespearian places sexual distinctions and gender distinctions become partly decoupled; that is, human qualities nominally associated with one or the other gender are seen to be present in varying degrees in persons of either sex, and then manifest themselves in ways that are determinative for ques-tions of tolerance.

Only detailed studies of Shakespeare's intricate dramatic constructions can clarify such complexities. But it is possible to outline two main areas of relevant concern at the outset, because these are treated in a pair of classic studies of Renaissance ideas about women (other studies of men or manhood will be cited later).

One of these works is Ian Maclean's seminal investigation of the theological, physiological, political, legal, and philosophical bases for *The Renaissance Notion of Woman*. This study contrasts scholastic and Neo-platonic positions on the relative honour of the two sexes, which led to Renaissance debates in which Plato's philosophy was seen to champion women's equality with men, and Aristotle's philosophy their inequality.[2] Maclean then traces medical-scientific and social-philosophical advances of the sixteenth century that tended to reject inequality (43–6, 66–7). In addition to these sources of proto-philo-feminism, he also considers how philosophical systems of binaries gave rise to Renaissance concepts of gender distinctions (2–5, 27, 29–30, 37–8, 42–5, 53–4). In connection with this, Maclean discusses, among others, one concept that will be of par-ticular importance here: that specifically 'gendered' human characteristics can belong in varying degrees to members of either sex.[3]

Another classic study, Juliet Dusinberre's *Shakespeare and the Nature of Women*, concerns itself with one of the consequences of the male con-struction of gender, a long-standing tradition of anti-feminist diatribes and stereotypes. This often finds reflections in Shakespeare's plays, as when Hamlet prates 'frailty, thy name is woman', or in the fulminations against all women of Iago, Lear, Timon, Posthumus, and many others. Dusinberre shows that the often scurrilous, misogynistic literary trad-itions on which these outbursts were based – which found continuation in some contemporary braying satires, woman-despising sermons, and authoritarian conduct books – often attracted Elizabethan counter-attacks or ridicule.[4] Maclean also describes how in the wider European context a

'Renaissance intellectual joke' claiming that 'woman is not a human being' was repeatedly set up to 'reinforce the contrary position' and thereby satirise traditional authorities in theology, medicine, and law.[5]

These notions, of gender generated by pairs of opposing characteristics but these characteristics not necessarily unique to specific sexes, and of gender bigotry being subject to ridicule or even joking deconstruction, will serve the following analyses of Shakespearian representations of gender tolerance.

2. TOLERANCE (*SIC*) IN *THE TAMING OF THE SHREW*

The question of tolerance is central to *The Taming of the Shrew*, for the main plot of this play asks how (or if) an overbearing and even bullying man and a wilful and shrewish woman can learn to form a mutually respecting and socially effective partnership in marriage. The ideal of such a partnership, of what has been called a 'companionate marriage', was strongly influential in Shakespeare's age. In Chapter 4 we will further consider companionate marriage in relation to a Shakespearian treatment of its ideological and religious foundations; for here, suffice it to say that no one in the Padua of *The Shrew* believes that Katherina and Petruchio will ever make anything but a bloody battlefield of their marriage. But, as I think I can show, the play indicates that they are eventually able not only to work effectively together, but even to value one another so greatly that each becomes more like the other.

A key element of the following argument is a realisation, which I first presented some time ago,[6] that *The Shrew* follows closely certain ideas and language found in Books II and III of *The Faerie Queene*.[7] I did not then, but can now, comment on the impact of this on the dating of Shakespeare's play, but here confine this to a note.[8] What is crucial here is a carrying forward from the Spenserian connection to a demonstration of how the achievement of mutual tolerance in a companionate marriage is central to a play that some at least think is nearly unreadably malign and misogynistic in content.[9]

What Shakespeare borrowed from Spenser was a psychological formula dividing the passions into two opposed types, repeatedly called in FQ II and III the 'forward' and 'froward'. 'Froward' for Spenser designates the baulky, contrary, or perverse (motion away = froward motion), 'forward' the grasping, ambitious, or greedy (motion toward = forward motion). The origins of this opposition lie in scholastic thinking, which holds that a thwarting of the concupiscent passions or desires produces the strong passions of spite and anger.[10] William Nelson explicitly analyses Spenser's expression of the dichotomy of the 'forward' and 'froward' passions thus:[11]

the froward passion ranges in its manifestations from modesty and inactivity to grief, wrath, and suicide, . . . the forward passion takes such various forms as hunger for money, power, and glory; desire for ease, beauty, and sexual satisfaction.

Nelson then shows that many of the adventures in Spenser's Books II and III, of *Temperaunce* and *Chastitie*, allegorise such antithetical passions, for the characters in these Books are frequently misled by either too much or too little desire. Even more interestingly, Nelson detects a trend towards a single conclusion in all these adventures. This is that a pursuit of the Aristotelian mean between the forward and froward passions is not equivalent to, nor equal in merit to, true Christian temperance. Nelson points this out particularly with reference to the allegorical banquet in the house of Medina, who is called the 'golden Meane'. In FQ II.ii. Medina, actually sitting between them, can bring about only a temporary truce between her sisters Elissa (too little), described by Spenser as 'froward', and Perissa (too much), described as 'forward'.[12] Despite her courtesy Medina is still kin to her extreme sisters, and indeed excites their further mischief in II.ii.13.

Aristotelian moderation fails in Spenserian episode after episode. Sans Loy and Huddibras, suitors to Perissa and Elissa, are types of forwardness and frowardness too extreme to be bound by reasonableness, for the respective temperaments of these men are unmixed forward boldness and unmixed froward melancholy. The brothers Cymochles and Pyrochles, like the false-ideal ladies, Prays-desire and Shamefastnesse, are among many other pairs representing the destructive and misleading opposition of forward and froward. Mordant is propelled from the forwardness of lust to the froward extreme of suicide.

In the central episode of the Cave of Mammon, Guyon's froward abstinence is a dangerous and ignoble antidote to forward greed. Guyon resists all sustenance in greedy Mammon's cave with a froward fortitude perhaps too natural to him, and consequently is nearly dead after escaping the cave. The swoon he suffers is a symptom of his temperamental affinity with overly froward Shamefastnesse. He must learn that human survival requires not only sustenance but also all the objects of the forward passions; these objects must be elevated somehow above the dross of Mammon. Only Prince Arthur, 'flowre of grace and nobilesse', can save the helpless Guyon from Pyrochles and Cymochles, two brothers representing the forward and froward opposites. Arthur's entry portrays the need for a principle beyond these opposites in order to defeat despoliation by them; Guyon's eventual triumph does not result from the mixture in any proportions of forward and froward passions (as, for example, of lust with disdain). As Alastair Fowler points out, Guyon eventually 'resists concupiscence not by the institution of any opposite passion, but by his integration; by the spiritual "edification" of his nature'.[13] True temperance for Spenser is the transcendence of dualism, the marriage of matter and spirit. A synthesis, rather than a compromise, must be achieved.

This Spenserian framework, schematic in its allegorical statement, finds a direct application within the much more psychologically subtle and dynamic framework of Shakespeare's *The Shrew*. Because Shakespeare borrows Spenser's language of 'forward' and 'froward', his *paronomasia* in which 'a word is changed in signification by the changing of a letter or sillable',[14] simple word counting proves this. The word 'froward' appears eight times in FQ Books II and III but only two more times in all the remainder of FQ, and never again in the rest of Spenser's work. The same unusual word appears eight times in *The Taming of the Shrew* and only three more times in all the rest of Shakespeare's plays. The more common word 'forward' appears forty-one times in Books II and III of FQ, compared with forty times more in all the rest of Spenser's work. 'Forward' appears ten times in *The Taming of the Shrew*, considerably more often than in any other Shakespeare play.[15]

Moreover, in both FQ II–III and *The Shrew*, the terms 'froward' and 'forward' function as antitheses, and in both places they encapsulate very similar themes, as will be argued presently. But first it is necessary to mark some distinctions. For one, Shakespeare's Padua more closely resembles Elizabethan England than does Spenser's fairyland; I am referring in particular to female agency. Baptista Minola is an advanced Renaissance man who educates his daughters, but he still considers it necessary to arrange their marriages, and he sees their preparation for life in terms of that outcome alone. Spenser, by contrast, going well beyond the Italian Renaissance tradition of depicting a biblical or historical *virago* or strong woman,[16] produced an idealised female knight-errant, Britomart, the hero of FQ III, *The Booke of Chastitie*. She is described as an exemplar of the pre-eminent women knights who in 'antique times' bore 'most sway' in 'warres' and 'the girlond bore away, / Till enuious Men fearing their rules decay, / Gan coyne steight lawes to curb their liberty' (III.ii.1–6).

Shakespearian women certainly have lost 'their liberty' in that they do not pursue their lovers on horseback, as Britomart does, defeating evil males along the way. Rather, they are subjected, in many cases, to the

unjust 'curb' of coerced marriages. The plight of very young girls subject
to such coercion (as is Shakespeare's Juliet) led to Elizabethan scandals.[17]
But, despite the fact that in theory men and women made their own
choices of marriage partners, in practice higher-ranking Elizabethan
families made these choices for them, disregarding the canon law rule that
to be valid a marriage must be consensual. The free consent required by
law for the marriages of both men and women is overridden especially by
the many heavy-handed elders in Shakespeare's plays who attempt to
make unwilling girls marry against their wishes.[18]

Escaping from such oppression does not work well for Desdemona,
who defies the rule of her father only to put herself wholly into the power
of another man who then murders her (we will say more on gender
intolerance in *Othello* in Chapter 5). The conventional line, that a 'virtuous'
father knows what is best for his daughter, is enunciated by Nerissa in *The
Merchant of Venice* 1.2.27–34, and undone in the same speech when she
confirms that without any sensible care at all Portia's father has consigned
his daughter's future to an absurd 'lottery'. Egeus, the insistent father in
A Midsummer Night's Dream, is shown to have a wholly irrational
preference for one of his daughter's suitors over the other, and is ready to
kill her to enforce it; other Shakespearian fathers favour as suitors the
unpleasant Thurio and the hideous Cloten. Wise fathers do not seem to
be in great supply in Shakespeare (nor in the 'New Comedy' traditions he
sometimes imitates).

In *The Taming of the Shrew* Baptista Minola has a rational programme:
to get his shrewish daughter Katherina off his hands by marriage to
whomever will take her, and then to arrange the marriage of his younger
daughter Bianca to the maximum financial advantage. So in 2.1 the
apparently compliant Bianca is absurdly sold at auction without so much
as her presence, let alone her approval or consent. This must recall
Katherina's earlier question to the same marriage-brokering father: 'is it
your will / To make a stale of me amongst these mates?' (1.1.57–8). Her
'stale' could suggest something left standing and past its freshness, or a
decoy, a prostitute, a person used as means to an end, or even a ridiculed
cast-off lover; perhaps meant in multiple senses, it pungently expresses
Katherina's resistance to a familiar abuse of Shakespeare's time.

Katherina's language here and elsewhere is so striking that we may miss
how little of it there is. Before she makes her notorious public declaration
about female subordination in 5.2.141–84, Katherina is one of the most
taciturn of Shakespeare's heroines; electronic counting shows that
Katherina speaks 1,856 words in total (of which 364 are concentrated in

her notorious submission speech) to Petruchio's 4,815. Contrast this with Shakespeare's other comic heroines and heroes: Portia has 4,740 words to Bassanio's 2,611; Rosalind 5,949 to Orlando's 2,508; Viola 2,633 to Orsino's 1,690.[19]

This quantitative anomaly has a clear dramatic basis; in the earlier parts of the play Katherina's utterances are terse and anger-choked, and the reason for that is made apparent. She is intensely aware that the obedience expected of her contradicts the official doctrines that required free consent for a valid marriage formation; too high-spirited to abide by social pretexts or capitulate to hypocritical demands on her behaviour, she has long responded with an anger that has spoiled her marriage chances. Her sister Bianca, by contrast, makes no such gaffes, relying on backhanded means to get her own way. Bianca's double hypocrisy, her falsely pretended compliance with hypocritical practices, ignites Katherina's special anger. Jealousy plays a part too, for Bianca alone enjoys general esteem and multiple suitors. Katherina, who cannot bring herself to follow her sister's tactics, suffers a thwarting of her concupiscent passions; such thwarting, traditionally, produces spite and anger, or frowardness.

The adherence to that formula is quite clear, and indeed the word 'froward' is repeatedly associated with Katherina, who at the play's start has become famed in her city as 'stark mad or wonderful froward' (1.1.69). But later in the play the epithet 'froward' is also applied to other women, both by men (4.6.79, 5.2.124), and by Katherina herself (5.2.162, 174). 'Froward' is never applied to a man.

Katherina's infamous speech in which she acknowledges her own former frowardness, and blames the other wives for being 'froward, peevish, sullen, sour' (5.2.162), yields the play's concept: excessive frowardness is a mistaken bid for power, a flawed weapon of weakness. Its wounding baulkiness and negativity (lately it has been popularly labelled 'passive aggression') is self-hobbling, as seen both in the action of the play and in Katherina's conjunction in her speech of 'froward' with 'unable': 'Come, come, you froward and unable worms' (5.2.174).

Katherina, in her initial froward spite and wrath, gives way to violence (Folio stage directions TLN 877, 887 indicate that she is the only character who strikes a woman in the play). Tears are polysemous for Shakespeare; some of Katherina's are a delaying tactic. So, seeing that her hypocritical sister is her father's 'treasure' who alone 'must have a husband', she declares: 'Talk not to me. I will go sit and weep, / Till I can find occasion of revenge' (2.1.32–6). Infuriated by Bianca's quite different weeping as a bid for public sympathy, Katherina comments: 'A pretty peat! It is best / Put finger in the eye, an she knew why' (1.1.78–9). Here she alludes to a variant on the actor's trick with a concealed onion, which is divulged in the Induction 1.122–6. Seemingly, then, Katherina cannot abide pretence.

And yet pretence, illusion-making, or play-acting features repeatedly throughout the play.[20] In fact, it is a play in which almost nothing is as it first seems. It is particularly necessary to take this into account when considering the male 'forwardness' in the play which balances the female 'frowardness'. For instance, the play opens with the drunken, blustering[21] Christopher Sly threatening to 'pheeze' the 'Hostes', a female tavern-keeper whose glassware he has just 'burst' (TLN 2–10).[22] But neither this or any other beating of a woman by a man occurs in the play; Sly's threats are a tease, among others, misleading us into expecting that the play will resemble his own preferences in drama, 'a comonty, / A Christmas gambol or a tumbling-trick' (1.2.133–4): that is, a farce filled with knockabout, wooden-headed, slapstick male violence.

Almost all the rough-house in the play is described only, and occurs offstage. Tavern glasses are 'burst', Katherina's and Petruchio's saddles slip, with muddy consequences (4.1.50), and wedding ceremonies and celebrations are traduced. Onstage, Katherina deals out most of the play's violence, assaulting Bianca, Hortensio, Petruchio, and Grumio.[23] But we are at first misled into thinking Petruchio will be the play's fount of violence, for we initially encounter him in the midst of a crude 'knock me' joke (confusing the Elizabethan dative) leading to a slapstick assault on Grumio (TLN 584, 'He rings him by the eares'). There certainly is no textual warrant for staging Petruchio as a whip-wielding wife-tamer, although he *is* textually described as depriving his new wife, and himself at the same time,[24] of all physical comforts and conveniences. Thus he is a bully, and yet not a bully, in ways that need untangling.

Male 'forwardness' is certainly a feature of *The Shrew*, but is trickily presented. Several men in the play who initially seem not in the least swaggering, boastful, or appetitive turn out to be forward. The Lord of the Induction, who in his amateur scientific interest resembles a Renaissance 'virtuoso',[25] seems at first highly saturnine and aloof in producing theatre for an audience of one. Yet he is unmasked when he panders his own private sexual luxuries to Sly. The would-be ascetic philosopher Lucentio veers with comic rapidity into becoming a keen erotic pursuer of Bianca. Here the keyword appears; Lucentio marks his transformation by saying to his servant 'Go *forward*, this contents' (1.1.161, italics mine). Jealous of a rival's excessive keenness, two of Bianca's many suitors complain 'You grow too forward, sir' (3.1.1), and 'How fiery and forward our pedant is!' (3.1.46).

Petruchio's desires run the gamut of William Nelson's forms of forwardness, 'hunger for money, power, and glory; desire for ease, beauty, and sexual satisfaction'. Petruchio indeed describes himself as 'bold to show myself a forward guest' (2.1.51), and is seen by others as 'marvellous forward' (2.1.73). So we see that the 'forward' men in *The Shrew* inhabit its Induction and its 'New Comedy' Bianca sub-plot, as well as its 'taming' main plot. Although there are remarkably few plot links between those strands, contrasts and comparisons are suggested by overlaps of language and theme – especially concerning forwardness. The prime misleading gesture of the entire play is a suggestion that forward Petruchio will make the main plot cruder dramaturgically and more anti-woman than the Bianca wooing sub-plot. In fact, in terms of sophistication, Shakespeare toned down certain audacious Italian *commedia erudita* qualities of his source for the Bianca action, Ariosto and Gascoigne's play *The Supposes*,[26] leaving mainly a set of farcical 'New Comedy' conventions summed up in Grumio's remark: 'See, to beguile the old folks, how the young folks lay their heads together' (1.2.136–7). In terms of misogynistic stereotyping, Bianca and the Widow become baulky 'froward worms' after marriage, having been a 'young modest girl' (1.1.154) or epitomising 'Kindness in women' (4.2.41) before, so exceeding any anti-feminism in the main plot.

That main plot is built around misleadings. Immediately after Petruchio's entry as an absurd 'knocker' of Grumio fit for a taming farce, he presents himself in a highly contrasting verbal register, explaining that he has been blown into Padua by

> Such winds as scatters young men through the world
> To seek their fortunes farther than at home,
> Where small experience grows. But in a few,
> Seignor Hortensio, thus it stands with me:
> Antonio, my father, is deceased,
> And I have thrust myself into this maze,
> Happily to wive and thrive as best I may.
> Crowns in my purse I have, and goods at home,
> And so am come abroad to see the world. (1.2.49–57)

The firm and fresh tone here contrasts with that of all the language spoken by the first stilted and then puerilely smitten Lucentio, by Bianca's other besotted suitors, by hapless Baptista with his unmanageable daughters, and by the play's scheming servants. Petruchio speaks as a young man unencumbered by attachments and following only his own inclinations. He does not just react to difficulties, but rather actively seeks to test himself in a complex 'maze' (although, at this stage, Petruchio is unaware of the romantic intrigue afoot in Padua).

Aside from Katherina, Petruchio is unique in the play in not being taken in by the cunning Bianca. He says he pursues Katherina solely because she will bring him wealth (1.2.64–75). He is, however, no impoverished dowry-hunter like Bassanio of *The Merchant of Venice*; he declares himself, and later marriage settlement negotiations prove him to be, a rich and independent heir.[27] In addition to 'money', Petruchio clearly seeks the other forward goals listed by William Nelson: 'glory' (which he wins in trumps at the play's conclusion), and 'beauty, and sexual satisfaction'. For he finds in Katherina sexual charm, and tells her so:

> Kate like the hazel twig
> Is straight and slender, and as brown in hue
> As hazelnuts, and sweeter than the kernels. (2.1.248–50)

Katherina is evidently impressed by this. She is seen to be converted in some degree to 'forward' desire when she is upset by Petruchio's late arrival for the wedding (3.2.8–20), and even more so when she expresses her wish for forward pleasure and triumph at her wedding feast (3.3.77). However, these latter desires are thwarted; so Katherina says she will remain apart from her husband as long as she chooses (contrary to Elizabethan marriage law).[28]

Petruchio then enacts a virtually anthropological 'marriage by ritual abduction', pretending to steal his bride from her unwilling family, and thus expressing extreme young-male forwardness. Yet another crucial ingredient is mixed into this: although Petruchio seizes his woman by force, he at the same time pretends that her abduction is to protect and serve her, ranting, 'we are beset with thieves . . . / Fear not, sweet wench. They shall not touch thee, Kate. / I'll buckler thee against a million' (3.3.108–11). The pretence of service here is a key to how, in the rest of the play, a struggle between the 'froward' and 'forward' passions is able to resolve itself into a *mutual* triumph for both Petruchio and Katherina.

This is a pretence very different from the others seen in *The Shrew*. One sort is the false and sly self-presentation of the kind Widow and the demure-seeming Bianca, which evaporates as soon as the desired ends are attained. Another is seen in the Lord of the Induction's illusions, set up to amuse himself by beguiling the abducted Christopher Sly, and which again will not continue beyond the period of amusement. Yet another sort is seen in the disguising and pretences of Bianca's suitors and their helpers, who mainly befuddle themselves and dig deep pits to fall into by exchanging their identities.

By contrast, the play's most central illusion-making has a very different outcome. This is the illusion that Petruchio projects and sustains, starting from the moment when he 'rescues' Katherina from the wedding feast, to the effect that everything he does in relation to her is motivated by tender love and concern for her well-being. In the name of considerateness, framed so that 'all is done in reverent care of her' (4.1.190), he deprives her of food, sleep, personal adornments, and sexual comforts. Far from obtuse, Katherina recognises this tactic and reflects on it:

> But I, who never knew how to entreat,
> Nor never needed that I should entreat,
> Am starved for meat, giddy for lack of sleep,
> With oaths kept waking and with brawling fed,
> And that which spites me more than all these wants,
> He does it under name of perfect love. (4.3.7–12)

She understands the ploy: Petruchio holds that nothing is good enough for her, so she must have nothing. This forces her for the first time to entreat, and with this she realises that she has always been privileged, that her froward rejections of the goods of the world arose in the context of a pampered life. Now, like Christopher Sly, she must do without a soft bed and learn that comforts are not automatic.

Since, as Ann Thompson points out,[29] Petruchio deprives himself at the same time as he deprives Katherina, he becomes, or at least acts as if he has become, 'froward' in the rejection of comforts and pleasures. These include marital sex (4.1.159–93). A countervailing movement in Katherina is her discovery (through deprivation) of her own 'forward' appetites.

Following a new realisation of her own needs, Kate even discovers in herself compassion for the victims of Petruchio's frowardness. When Petruchio threatens to erupt she speaks in defence of a nervous servant who drops water (4.1.146); she heroically pushes a fallen horse off herself and bestrides deep mire to defend Grumio from being beaten 'because her horse stumbled' (as reported in 4.1.64–75); she attempts to defend the hapless Haberdasher's and Tailor's work spurned by froward Petruchio (4.3.69–70, 101–3). Perhaps this last is also a matter of keen acquisitiveness, again indicating a conversion from frowardness.

Thus, showing her desires, Katherina begins to become far less froward or surly than before, while Petruchio, refusing social contacts, goods, and comforts, becomes far less forward and peremptory than before. Petruchio begins so to resemble the former baulky Katherina that his servants remark 'he is more shrew than she' (4.1.76) and 'He kills her in her own humour' (4.1.166). That is, to 'tame' her, forward Petruchio borrows Katherina's former weapons of frowardness.

It is my belief that the effects of Petruchio's pretences, carried out in a plan to 'kill a wife with kindness' (4.1.194), are implied to be educative and transformative at least as much for himself as they are for her. For the play's end indicates that when Petruchio begins to restore to Kate her accustomed comforts, he cannot retract his kindly concern. That is, his illusion becomes real, his mask of a devoted husband grows to him.

To see if this is so, if Petruchio's forward concerns with the goods of the world become recentred on the well-being of Katherina, we must look to the play's final scenes. In these, the language of both Katherina and Petruchio alters radically.

The background is Petruchio becoming a baulky and surly killjoy – being aggressively froward – when he repeatedly threatens to spoil Kate's eagerly anticipated desire to visit Padua; by thwarting them, he whets Katherina's recently discovered strong desires. This leads to the pair's jesting, if that is what it is, on the journey to Padua at the end of Act 4. Prompted by Petruchio, Kate addresses the old man Vincentio, met on the way, as a 'Young budding virgin'. This causes Vincentio to address her as 'my merry mistress' (4.6.28–55). Either Vincentio is fooled and Kate has been thoroughly squashed and brainwashed, or his perception is correct and she is playing along with a joke. Just before meeting Vincentio, Kate had decided to agree to call the sun the moon in order to avoid Petruchio's threatened aborting of her wished-for visit home. Her words of submission then were:

> Forward, I pray, since we have come so far,
> And be it moon or sun or what you please,
> And if you please to call it a rush-candle
> Henceforth I vow it shall be so for me. (4.6.12–15)

Petruchio's response reprises Katherina's 'Forward, I pray', for he agrees to proceed, beginning 'Well, forward, forward' (4.6.25). It does appear that so long as matters are moving forward (and in a way that makes Kate happy) both are content, and perhaps even amused ('merry'), despite the froward perversity of demands for agreement with obviously absurd propositions.

This takes us to the final scene, where Katherina labels her former self, and the other wives, as they are now, 'froward worms'. In this scene containing her infamous speech Katherina speaks about twice as much as she does usually;[30] her language, which has formerly been curt and bitter, becomes highly fluent, while Petruchio stands mute and for the first time does not dominate the stage verbally.

Looking at its dramatic framing rather than content, we can see that in this speech Katherina at last comes forward to speak articulately, persuasively, abandoning the baulky weapons of her former frowardness. Her peroration beginning 'Come, come, you froward and unable worms' signals that she herself is no longer 'unable' through frowardness. Throughout this long speech, Petruchio (most uncharacteristically) holds his peace, yielding to Katherina centre stage, his forwardness converted to admiration and gratitude.

So her language and his silence combine to show that the two protagonists of *The Shrew* have moved towards one another, each becoming less tightly bound to respective male-forward or female-froward modes of being. The froward 'peevish, sullen, sour' aspects of Katherina's former outbursts of anger and scorn, and the madcap forward excesses of Petruchio's former defiant behaviour, are both moderated.

A simple formula that can be derived from this is that tolerance requires temperance. This, I think, is why Spenser divided his treatments of the froward/forward dichotomy between the books of *Temperaunce* (i.e. balance) and *Chastitie* (i.e. love) in FQ. It is also why Angelo in *Measure for Measure*, who is unbalanced in his own sexuality, cannot tolerate Juliet's and Claudio's.

But we have also seen that for Spenser the struggle between the extremes of froward Elissa and forward Perissa is not resolved by Medina (the mean), which is to say that a levelling or averaging of their differences will not resolve the tensions between them. What is required beyond the Aristotelian mean is the 'edification' of true temperance. What that might mean in *The Shrew* is a transcendence of forward/froward differences in a joint enterprise based on love and tolerance.[31]

There are plausible, if not requisite, theatrical readings in which Kate and Petruchio share in a humorous enactment with mutually satisfactory purposes when he bets on her obedience and she then plays the champion of female compliance. In such a reading the pair collude in Katherina's performance which exposes the other wives and wins Petruchio's wager. This would gratify Katherina's long-deferred desire to show up Bianca, her 'occasion of revenge', and also gain her general esteem. Petruchio would gain money and glory, classic forward goals.

Short of supposing a conspiracy afoot, a deliberate use of irony could still explain Katherina's rehearsal in her 'submission' speech of theories of female subordination so exaggerated that (as some have argued) many in Shakespeare's age would have found them ludicrous.[32] Thus Kate's mocking sense of humour could be seen here to operate in a more effective forward-type, rather than froward-type, mode; the target of her satire would be extreme patriarchal notions.

In Shakespeare's play a coming closer together of Katherina and Petruchio in terms of frowardness and forwardness allows each the better to appreciate the other. In his typical more idealising way, Spenser once analogously envisioned – in the extreme – a fusing of gendered representatives of the two modes, forward and froward,[33] making a single being of the two lovers Scudamor and Amoret.[34] This pair has been sorely afflicted by his forward male sexual cravings and her froward female sexual hesitancies; they are finally joined, indeed merged, when seen embracing in the penultimate stanza of Spenser's original version of Book III:[35]

> Had ye them seen, ye would have surely thought,
> That they had beene that faire *Hermaphrodite*,
> Which that rich *Romance* of white marble wrought,
> And in his costly Bath causd to be site:
> So seemed those two, as growne together quite.

Shakespeare also ends *The Shrew* with an embrace, less allegorical than Spenser's but nonetheless suggesting a reduction of gender friction and misunderstandings. This is signalled in the virtual stage direction of Petruchio's finally neither boisterous nor bullying, but appreciative and grateful, 'Why, there's a wench! Come on, and kiss me, Kate' (5.2.185).

3. GENDERING BINARIES: THE ELIZABETHAN FEMININE AND MASCULINE

Women are soft, mild, pitiful, and flexible –
Thou stern, obdurate, flinty, rough, remorseless. (*Henry VI, part 3* 1.4.142–3)

Her froward tactics do not bring Katherina Minola the autonomy or respect she craves, but they do attract a husband together with whom she is able contrive the means toward at least an increment of general esteem. In reality some Elizabethan women found additional ways to mitigate or partially overcome the effects of the legal and social structures that constrained or oppressed them, and some of these modes of pushing the boundaries were mirrored in Shakespeare's plays. Very briefly: Elizabethan wives taking an active, strong role within middling-class households[36] is reflected in *The Merry Wives of Windsor*; women in towns being entrepreneurial is reflected but exaggerated in the story of the successful self-employed artist Marina in *Pericles*;[37] women using the Church courts, local courts, or central conciliar courts to their advantage (although they were denied access to the common law courts after marriage) is mirrored in the stories of the litigant Isabella of *Measure for Measure* and of the 'lawyers' Portia and Nerissa of *The Merchant of Venice*.[38]

However, unrealistically, none of the aristocratic women portrayed by Shakespeare, like Portia in *The Merchant of Venice* or Olivia in *Twelfth Night*, are protected by the complex legal trusts by means of which the property of high-born Elizabethan women was typically preserved from the operation of the legal doctrine of 'coverture', by which a married woman's property became that of her husband.[39] On the contrary, Portia emphasises the absoluteness of the transfer of her property (3.2.149–74), and Olivia's amazed husband-to-be Sebastian marvels at it (4.3.1–4, 16–20).

But there is one other way in which some high-placed Shakespearian women do defend their own or their children's possessions: by going to war. Constance in *King John* attempts this with French aid, and Henry VI's (French-born) queen Margaret does so on her own behalf. Margaret is the target of the criticism in the gender-dichotomising epigraph quoted above, accused by the Duke of York of being 'stern, obdurate, flinty, rough, remorseless'. Since it was often seen as unseemly for women to pursue litigation,[40] how much more so would it have been for them to wage war, and show, as York says, unfeminine deficiencies of softness, mildness, and flexibility. York says this when he has been defeated militarily by Margaret and is about to be killed by her, but we are also invited by his dichotomies to remember that Margaret had not been able to tolerate her mild, pitiful, and (for her) excessively flexible husband Henry VI.

Shakespeare's depiction of Queen Margaret's bellicose temperament despising her husband's eirenic one, although similar to his depictions of Lady Macbeth and Goneril, is opposite to more typical gendered images in Elizabethan culture and writing. Next I will consider a more usual configuration and ask how far hyper-masculine bellicosity was seen by Shakespeare to correlate with men's intolerance of female-gendered human propensities, or of women in general.

Although he was dubious of ideologies that defined manhood in terms of militaristic 'honour' codes,[41] Shakespeare did address a topic that Elizabethans seriously debated and agonised over: how to accommodate the remaining vestiges, either dangerous or desirable, of the old codes of chivalry. Such concerns were entangled with a rising trend in the 1590s of interest in military valour and militaristic theory,[42] following which there were conflicting early Jacobean responses in favour of or against a chivalric revival.[43] It has sometimes been claimed that Shakespeare himself changed his earlier approval of a warrior code, becoming in his later writings an Erasmian pacifist.[44] Yet others argue that Shakespeare depicted pacifist outlooks in plays written throughout his earlier career,[45] or displayed dubiousness concerning chivalric honour in his earlier plays.[46]

However that may be, Shakespeare does show gender bigotry in a number of the men he represents as espousing militarism. For example, the impressionable and fatherless Bertram of *All's Well* takes lessons in maleness from the *miles gloriosus* Parolles, who 'knows himself a braggart' but pretends to be a 'gallant militarist' (4.3.335, 4.3.135). These include encouragements to Bertram to abandon his wife, seduce other women, and make martial reputation the sole serious focus of life (2.3.275–82, 3.5.16–28, 2.1.49–56).

Hamlet, another fatherless Shakespearian man, is deeply troubled about the connection between manhood and valour.[47] Especially in the second Quarto text (in the additional passage marked in the Oxford Shakespeare as A.J.), he expresses deep ambivalence about an 'honour' code based on quarrelsomeness and carelessness of consequences. Thus he marvels that Fortinbras would venture 'Two thousand souls and twenty thousand ducats' for a 'straw' (a valueless scrap of land which looms large only because its possession touches on reputation) and finds this way of thinking a diseased 'imposthume' (A.J.15–20). In his following soliloquy he inflates the death toll 'imminent' on account of Fortinbras' bellicosity to 'twenty thousand men', referring to Fortinbras ironically as 'a delicate and tender prince, / Whose spirit with divine ambition puffed...' (A.J.39–40). Yet he also uses Fortinbras' example 'gross as earth' to berate himself as over-scrupulous, with 'but one part wisdom / And ever three parts coward' (A.J.33–4).

Another of side of Hamlet's ambivalence about what is suited to manhood involves doubts over womanish emotionality. Although himself grieving her death, he ruthlessly parodies the claims to passionate grief of Ophelia's brother Laertes (5.1.270–81). Yet in an earlier context he has adversely compared his own coldness with the weeping of an emotionally labile actor shedding real tears for an imaginary Hecuba (2.2.552–82).

Hamlet's self-doubts about his emotionally responsive self contribute, I believe, to his misogyny (which will be taken up later). But just now I want to consider a few more Shakespearian men who denigrate what they feel is overly feminine in themselves. A handle on this becomes available if we consider the attitude in Shakespeare to men shedding tears. Dozens of Shakespeare's men find no problem with this,[48] but for others male weeping is seen as unacceptable, because unmanning. So there is a range of comments similar to Friar Laurence's rebuke to Romeo: 'Thy tears are womanish' (3.3.109).[49] Grieving Laertes longs to be rid of his shaming tears, saying misogynistically, 'When these are gone, / The woman will be out' (*Hamlet* 4.7.161–2). Lord Lafew in *All's Well* makes the comic excuse 'Mine eyes smell onions, I shall weep anon' (5.3.322); fatherless Coriolanus euphemises his weeping in the tough-sounding 'Mine eyes . . . sweat compassion' (5.3.197). The last example is not comic at all; Aufidius, maliciously recalling the occasion of Coriolanus' weeping, calls him 'thou boy of tears' (5.6.103) and thereby precipitates an excuse to assassinate him. Softened emotions in an unbalanced, fatherless, warlike young man like Coriolanus can be deadly.

Nonetheless, the majority of instances of masculine tears in Shakespeare are accepted as not unmanning, and indeed there was a powerful motif in Shakespeare's culture of what has been called 'lachrymose art', which celebrates weeping in connection with a melancholy view of the human condition.[50] Thus John Donne's persona in 'A nocturnall upon S. Lucies day' says 'Oft a flood / Have wee two wept', and the first five pieces (among others) in John Dowland's 1600 *Second Booke of Songs or Ayres* are all lachrymose, and include the enormously influential 'Lacrime' or 'Flow my tears', written to be sung by a man.[51] So there was a choice of outlooks in Shakespeare's culture, reflected in his plays, about whether it was unmanly to weep and show emotion. This breadth of choice has particular significance for the following reading of *Cymbeline*.

4. GENDERED TOLERANCE IN *CYMBELINE*

When he is forced to part from his clandestinely married wife Princess Imogen, Posthumus says: 'O lady, weep no more, lest I give cause / To be suspected of more tenderness / Than doth become a man' (*Cymbeline* 1.1.94–6). When we remember *Coriolanus* we might suspect this resistance to shedding tears to be an ominous hint at an exaggerated masculinity in the fatherless Posthumus, who also never knew his brothers (1.1.28–40). Other males in his vicinity who might have been models for him do not inspire confidence. In particular 'that harsh, churlish, noble, simple nothing, / That Cloten' (3.4.133–4), as Imogen calls him, revels in violence, even taking pride in doing physical harm to an opponent in a game of bowls (2.1.1–31).

Posthumus has been raised as the king's ward, and Cloten is the king's stepson; the main contention in the play is based on the fact that the wise Imogen loves Posthumus and detests Cloten. She has good reasons for both. In terms of a hyper-masculine bellicose disposition, Posthumus certainly fares better than Cloten, at first. Armed Cloten 'drew on' Posthumus, an unarmed exile, but he is fended off with such ease that Posthumus is not in the least perturbed. We are told, indeed, that Posthumus could have done, but does not do Cloten any harm, because he 'rather played than fought / And had no help of anger' (1.1.161–4). Thus Posthumus shows the courtly *sprezzatura* described by Baldassare Castiglione, combining his skill and valour with an ease of manner.[52] Following this 'action', leaving Posthumus unruffled, Cloten's aroma merits the advice that he should

shift a shirt. The violence of action hath made you reek as a sacrifice. Where air comes out, air comes in. There's none abroad so wholesome as that you vent. (1.2.1–4)

The sweaty, stinking, boastfully bellicose, swaggering Cloten utterly fails Castiglione's ideal, providing the nadir among the models of masculinity in *Cymbeline*.

However, another sort of courtliness than that seen in *The Book of the Courtier*, where men and women engage in easy and refined conversation, is seen in the Italy of *Cymbeline*. Immediately after leaving Imogen's sphere of influence Posthumus arrives in Rome and falls into a terribly erroneous mode of 'manliness'; among a swaggering all-male cohort, saturated with false values of chivalric 'courtesy', he boasts competitively of Imogen's chastity and wagers on it with Iachimo (1.4.33–166). Worse still, he provides Iachimo with an introduction to Imogen in order to test her. Such schemes for stress-testing chastity verge on accepting what has later come to be known as the foul-mouthed 'locker-room' stereotype of women's sexual inclinations;[53] Elizabethan theatrical representations of such schemes, as in *The Merry Wives of Windsor* or George Chapman's *The Widow's Tears*, show that husbands who set out to entrap their wives are despicable fools.

Posthumus is all too readily persuaded that Iachimo has prevailed with Imogen, and pays his bet with the ring she has given him. In defence of his 'honour', the exiled Posthumus then arranges by letter for Imogen's murder by proxy (3.1.1–17). The floodgates of misogyny are opened and Posthumus spews out declarations that women are the repository of all that is vicious: even in a man it is 'the woman's part' which makes him prone to 'lying...flattering...deceiving...Lust and rank thoughts... revenges...Ambitions, covetings, change of prides, disdain, / Nice longing, slanders, mutability, / All faults that man can name, nay, that hell knows' (2.5.22–7). Posthumus even laments that men must be born of women (2.5.1–2), 'soil[ing]', like Shakespeare's Troilus before him, 'our mothers' (*Troilus and Cressida* 5.2.136).

Models for misogyny surround Posthumus. In Italy, Iachimo and his falsely sophisticated friends find it easy to suppose all women corruptible: 'If you buy ladies' flesh at a million a dram, you cannot preserve it from tainting' (1.4.132–4). In England the king, on hearing about his wife's deathbed confession of treachery, finds it comforting to comment, 'O most delicate fiend! / Who is 't can read a woman?' (5.6.47–8), while Cloten becomes obsessed with the idea of raping Imogen in the most degrading manner he can imagine.

But within the culture Shakespeare inhabited such outlooks were countered by beliefs that women were born for salvation, had souls, and were not inhuman objects. In consequence, faced with physical evidence seeming to confirm that Imogen has been murdered Posthumus undergoes an amazing transformation. He now remembers 'noble' Imogen as Britain's 'mistress-piece' (5.1.10, 20) and bitterly regrets his action. Realising what he has done, Posthumus becomes fully reconciled with the memory of Imogen, not just forgiving her, but rather holding himself by far the more guilty party. In consequence, remaining fully convinced of her infidelity (on the basis of better evidence than is ever seen by Leontes or Othello), he wishes only to fight for Britain until he can 'die / For thee, O Imogen, even for whom my life / Is every breath a death' (2.1.25–7).

This is very surprising, but Anne Barton has brilliantly explained how the chastened Posthumus' revised estimation of Imogen's supposed infidelity as merely 'wrying but a little' (5.1.5), could indeed have been accepted by Elizabethans.[54] Barton's analysis of course upsets many assumptions about Elizabethan patriarchal attitudes.

I would comment further that Posthumus' tolerance of Imogen's small fault or 'wrying', as he comes to see it, shares nothing with the 'don't ask, don't tell' policies proposed by Shakespeare's other mistakenly convinced cuckolds, Leontes and Othello, who expound respectively on 'Alack, for lesser knowledge' (*The Winter's Tale* 2.1.40), and 'it harmed not me' (*Othello* 3.3.334). He never wishes, as they do, that his wife's infidelity might have occurred without his knowledge so that he would not have to suffer. By contrast, Posthumus wishes only that the gods had struck *him* down and 'saved / The noble Imogen to repent' (5.1.10). His tolerance of her infidelity has nothing self-serving in it.

Here we find implicit a distinction between a conception of 'tolerance' based on recognition of and respect for another, and one based on a grudging acceptance of that which is disliked, perhaps for selfish purposes. Although under some definitions Othello's or Leontes' wishful policies of disowning knowledge and compliance may be classified as 'tolerance', I would call them arguments of pseudo-tolerance based on cynicism and bitterness.

I will next argue that the deeper roots of the genuine tolerance seen in *Cymbeline* lie in the capacity of some in the play to combine within themselves both sides of the dichotomy of human potentialities that was definitive of gender divisions for Shakespeare's age. I will begin with Imogen's two long-lost brothers, two adolescent princes raised in a wilderness and unaware of their royalty. According to their guardian they are inclined by 'nature' to noble, manly, combative sports and hunting (3.3.79–98), yet are also exceptionally 'gentle' unless 'enchafed', by 'Nature' royally inclined to 'Civility' as well as to 'honour' and 'valour' (4.2.170–82). In them we see a combination of the warlike and the eirenic.

Moreover, the two princes show a tender side in the obsequies they say over the seemingly dead boy Fidele (really their sister Imogen, disguised and in a trance). The younger prince,[55] Arviragus, speaks beautifully at some length of the 'fairest flowers' with which he will 'sweeten' Fidele's grave (4.2.219–30), but then is interrupted by the elder, Guiderius, who objects to this overly poetic mourning:

> Prithee, have done,
> And do not play in wench-like words with that
> Which is so serious. (4.2.230–2)

His phrase 'wench-like words' here reveals a familiar, gendered, low opinion of the expression of emotion, yet Guiderius himself has just revealed his own grief: 'With female fairies will his tomb be haunted, / And worms will not come to thee' (4.2.218–19). Following this, the two brothers recite in chorus one of the most perfect of Shakespeare's lyrics, 'Fear no more the heat o' th' sun.' They do not *sing* this song, because, as one of them says, 'our voices / Have got the mannish crack' (4.2.236–7); in their self-conscious 'mannish'-ness they may be precursors of talking-bluesmen and rappers.

But theirs is only a comic and benign boyish hypermasculinity compared with the excesses seen in Cloten's reeking insolence. The play between various levels of masculinity and fears of 'wench-like' softness in *Cymbeline* is partly humorous, but becomes crucial when Princess Imogen presents within herself a kind of perfection in the balance of 'gendered' characteristics, and thereby teaches by example and helps bring many others to notable achievements of tolerance. Her image spreads an influence in a kind of chain-reaction (partly through Posthumus) to effect transformations throughout the play.

Imogen is humorous also when, unlike other cross-dressing Shakespearian women, ranging from the assured Portia to the terrified Viola, she comments on her adventures as a boy, 'I see a man's life is a tedious one.' She continues. 'Best draw my sword, and if mine enemy / But fear the sword like me he'll scarcely look on 't. / Such a foe, good heavens!' She is indeed courageous alone in the Welsh mountains, thanks to her 'resolution' (3.6.1–27), and a deeper courage emerges soon afterwards. When the death-imitating potion that she has accidentally taken wears off, she finds herself in the presence of a headless corpse which she mistakenly takes to be the body of her beloved Posthumus. This extreme event brings out within her what Elizabethans would have seen as a 'feminine' openness to emotion combined with a 'masculine' resoluteness. So, although deeply grieved, she still immediately takes the opportunity offered to serve (as the boy Fidele) the passing Roman general Lucius. But she insists first on giving funeral rites to the corpse she thinks is Posthumus. On hearing this, General Lucius remarks to his troops, marching to war:

> My friends,
> The boy hath taught us manly duties. Let us
> Find out the prettiest daisied plot we can,
> And make him with our pikes and partisans
> A grave. (4.2.397–401)

Thus, inspired by Fidele/Imogen, Roman legionnaires are taught that true manly duties require searching out the 'prettiest daisied plot' (reiterating Imogen's valiant brothers' talk of 'fairest flowers' and 'female fairies'). Imogen thus teaches that 'manly duty' requires sensibility.

On the other hand, there are many other examples of Imogen's courageous fortitude in the play aside from the obvious one, her resistance to all the 'assaults' (3.2.8) made on her to pressure her into accepting Cloten as her husband. For instance, once set on a dangerous mission to Wales to join Posthumus, she feels no apprehension and imagines no alternatives: 'I see before me, man. Nor here, nor here, / Nor what ensues, but have a fog in them / That I cannot look through / . . . Accessible is none but Milford way' (3.2.78–82). Determined to enter the enemy camp in disguise in order to gain knowledge of the erring Posthumus, she later says, believably, 'This attempt / I am soldier to, and will abide it with / A prince's courage' (3.4.183–5).

Imogen/Fidele is also morally courageous; when granted one free boon by Cymbeline, she does not, as generally expected, repay the Roman Lucius who has twice saved her from death, but rather says 'Your life, good master, / Must shuffle for itself' (5.6.104–5). Neither sentiment nor any (Ophelia-like) inclination to comply with expectations can deflect her from a focused quest to pursue what most concerns her, so she chooses as her boon that Iachimo be compelled to reveal 'of whom' he obtained the ring he wears, the ring that had been her love-gift to Posthumus (5.6.135–6).

Tough-minded but not cold-hearted, Imogen has by far the most passionate voice in the play. Ardour, sensitivity and strength are heard combined in her exclamations of grief (1.1.124–5), pride (1.1.140–4), anger (2.3.121–33), exultation (3.2.48–61), outrage (3.4.40–57), or joy (5.6.261–3); her utterances are remarkable for being always exceptionally salient but never wholly out of balance, sometimes mistaken but never frenzied or unhinged.[56] Also, although intrepid whenever needed, Imogen never seeks conflict for its own sake (even offering in 5.6.270 to condole with her father on her hated stepmother's death).

When faced with intimations that Posthumus has been unfaithful to her, Imogen, like Posthumus himself, does not incline to the pseudo-tolerance of disowned knowledge, but demands rather:

> Pray you,
> Since doubting things go ill often hurts more
> Than to be sure they do – for certainties
> Either are past remedies, or, timely knowing,
> The remedy then born – discover to me
> What both you spur and stop. (1.6.95–100)

Moreover, when Imogen is at first convinced that her lover has betrayed her, indeed that he has intended to murder her, she, like Posthumus, thinks of the perfidy of the opposite sex in general. She does not, like him, furiously disparage the adverse gender, but she does comment that in men:

> All good seeming,
> By thy revolt, O husband, shall be thought
> Put on for villainy; not born where 't grows,
> But worn a bait for ladies. (3.4.54–7)

But then (much more swiftly than he) she analyses such thinking as fallacious, acknowledging that 'True honest men' must still exist (3.4.58–64).

So, in all ways, what is excellently tolerant in Posthumus is a kind of shadow of the greater excellences of Imogen. Indeed, even after learning about his murderous plot, and showing the greatest imaginable non-masochistic tolerance (for Imogen is no patient Griselda), Imogen still thinks of her erring husband, lovingly, as: 'My dear lord, / Thou art one o' th' false ones' (3.6.14–15).

Finally in the play, inspired by the image of Imogen, Posthumus takes a great leap in the direction of tolerance and inspires all the other characters in turn to prodigies of new tolerance. But first Posthumus has to undergo a 'conversion to good'. This will be further explained later in this chapter, but is worth mentioning here because it supports the notion that a genuine tolerance of others requires a tolerance of the self.

That Posthumus *is* good, although suicidally inclined and not believing himself to be good, is seen on the battlefield, where Folio stage directions describe him sparing the life of Iachimo when he has him down, and helping to rescue the king who has banished him (TLN 2894–6, 2915–16). These are deeds both of martial prowess and of mercy and salvation, redefining what 'manly duties' can mean (thus recalling Imogen's lesson to Lucius' company). The image of Imogen is at the same time seen directly to affect Iachimo, who says upon being spared by Posthumus that his 'heaviness and guilt' concerning Imogen 'Take off my manhood' (5.2.1–9), and goes on to state that 'manhood…Knighthoods and honours' are cancelled by acts like his, so 'we scarce are men'.

Following this, however, Posthumus is still intolerant of himself, and seeks death by unnecessarily submitting himself to captivity and execution as an enemy of Britain. In prison he has a dream or vision in which he sees his two brothers and father and mother, all of whom he has never known. All plead on his behalf to Jupiter. The brothers, fallen war heroes, make the plea that on the battlefield Posthumus proved himself worthy of the heritage of the Leonati (5.5.164–74); the mother and father, however, decry Posthumus' sufferings as a result of his forced separation from Imogen and the 'taint[ing]' by Iachimo of 'his nobler heart and brain / With needless jealousy' (5.5.159–60). But finally and most importantly, Posthumus' dream plants a crucial idea when his mother pleads, 'Since, Jupiter, our son is good, / Take off his miseries' (5.5.179–80). For the notion that there is good in him specifically authorises Posthumus' conversion to good, and that allows his recovery.

Following the dream, Posthumus finds a written prophesy beginning: 'Whenas a lion's whelp shall, to himself unknown, without seeking find, and be embraced by a piece of tender air' (5.5.232–4). We do not require the help of the play's soothsayer to understand that Posthumus, surnamed Leonatus, is the 'lion's whelp' and that 'tender air' is Imogen in her role as woman. It is, however, interesting to hear the soothsayer adhere to a conjectural etymological derivation of the Latin *mulier* from *mollis aer*, meaning 'tender air', and also interpret *mulier* explicitly as 'wife' (5.6.444–6). Many in Shakespeare's world would have known that 'wife' is a secondary meaning, the first meaning being 'woman'.[57] So the play's young male lion will be embraced by tender 'woman', a figure oppositely gendered to himself.

In the play's super-complex recognition scene Posthumus is amazed when Iachimo, spurred by remorse, confesses to his villainy and affirms Imogen's chastity (5.6.139–209).[58] Posthumus' original 'covenant' with Iachimo was that if Imogen were proved unchaste he would not seek revenge, but if Imogen proved chaste, Posthumus would make Iachimo dearly 'answer' (1.4.154–61). But on learning the truth Posthumus does not do this, and rather calls only for a 'cord, or knife, or poison' to be applied to himself, as he still thinks he is guilty of Imogen's murder (5.6.210–27).

Imogen is next discovered alive; although she is disguised as Fidele, Cymbeline recognises her by her unmistakable voice, which he calls 'The tune of Imogen' (5.5.239). Then Imogen, as *mulier*, embraces Posthumus, expressing only mild rebukes.

So far the issue might seem to be more one of forgiveness than of tolerance, but the kinds of forgiveness seen in this play depend on great increments of tolerance. Thus Posthumus, having already concluded that infidelity is not the worst of sins, specifies Iachimo's fate: to 'Live, / And deal with others better' (5.6.420–1). Cymbeline then takes his cue from Posthumus, whom he now calls his 'son-in-law', and proclaims 'Pardon's the word to all' (5.6.423).

Former 'masculine' excesses of intransigence and belligerence in *Cymbeline* (such as in the condemnation of Cymbeline's captured Roman soldiers) are corrected not just because it is politic to do so. Both have the upper hand absolutely, yet Cymbeline and Posthumus extend pardon respectively to Belarius and Iachimo, who have done them genuine harm; I propose that this forgiveness is based on tolerance because I believe both realise the extent to which they themselves have instigated that harm.

Formerly, under the influence of his murderous second wife and her son Cloten, Cymbeline had been immune to his daughter's pain and only bellicose in his dealings with Rome. Still intransigent, Cymbeline intends to kill his Roman prisoners and punish Guiderius, who had vanquished

Cloten in self-defence. But then that dissolves, and following Posthumus' and Imogen's examples, the king forgives 'all'. Cymbeline now expresses a new, more creative identity by using gender-reversing imagery: upon regaining his three lost children he exclaims, 'O, what am I? / A mother to the birth of three? Ne'er mother / Rejoiced deliverance more' (5.6.369–71).

What Cymbeline next creates is a diplomacy to replace conflict, a new tolerance in British–Roman relations. Until this point the British king's language in the play has been uniformly dull, either prosaic or stilted. But at the play's very end Cymbeline's language gains remarkable sinews. Even though the winner of the day's battle, he at last forges a new British–Roman amity. In a vivid new register of speech,[59] he proclaims peace:

> Laud we the gods,
> And let our crooked smokes climb to their nostrils
> From our blest altars. Publish we this peace
> To all our subjects. Set we forward, let
> A Roman and a British ensign wave
> Friendly together. So through Lud's town march,
> And in the temple of great Jupiter
> Our peace we'll ratify, seal it with feasts. (5.6.477–84)

5. INTOLERANCE, REPENTANCE, REDEMPTION

Temperamental collisions of war-loving versus peace-loving dispositions, gendered as male versus female, were neither the beginning nor the end of Shakespeare's formulations of the problems of gender relations. Not only are Shakespearian women like Queen Margaret and Joan la Pucelle warriors, but many others, like Goneril, Lady Macbeth, Coriolanus' mother, and Cymbeline's unnamed Queen, encourage violence. The eirenic disposition may have been gendered, as York tells Margaret, but it is not firmly attached by Shakespeare to one sex.

Quite independently of discords between mildness and toughness, from near the beginning of his career Shakespeare had in mind a very different sort of gender difficulty. This is one in which the opposite sex, or sexuality itself, is a source of fear and aversion for reasons of deep-seated distrust or distaste. Here we come close to more usual notions of intolerance, for the genders are in such cases divided by a bigoted lack of respect or sympathy.

So, in such plays as *Love's Labour's Lost*, *Measure for Measure*, *Hamlet*, *Othello*, or *The Winter's Tale* we find characters who either despise or avoid contact with the opposite gender as if that gender were a 'racial', national, or cultural outsider group and subject to xenophobia. Sometimes such aversions are disguised as virtue, as they are by all three protagonists of *Measure for Measure*, who idealise their removal to intellectual ivory towers, rigorous halls of justice, or convents as motivated by higher ideals. But even then, such disguises wear thin in Shakespeare's representation, and show their undersides.[60]

The first premise of *Love's Labour's Lost* is the deliberate creation of an explicitly homosocial society. The King of Navarre banishes women from his court and orders all the men there to take vows to resist sensuality and contact with women in favour of supposedly higher philosophical aims. Promptly the king and his three leading courtiers fall in love with four visiting ladies of France. Witty Berowne, the courtier at first most dubious of the king's policy, falls for the dark-eyed and pale-skinned Rosaline, but only reluctantly. Berowne in soliloquy is not concerned about his oath-breaking, but rather expresses misogynistic objections to women in general:

> A woman, that is like a German clock,
> Still a-repairing, ever out of frame,
> And never going aright, being a watch,
> But being watched that it may still go right.
> Nay, to be perjured, which is worst of all,
> And among three to love the worst of all –
> A whitely wanton with a velvet brow,
> With two pitch-balls stuck in her face for eyes –
> Ay, and, by heaven, one that will do the deed
> Though Argus were her eunuch and her guard. (3.1.185–95)

Albeit with comic verve, this catalogue of gender-based hostilities expresses a tradition of loathing and fearing women's sexuality. However, lust trumps 'philosophy' and Berowne and his fellows attempt a comically maladroit, Petrarch-inspired, stilted and high-flown style of courtship. Eventually, having been put down by the witty ladies, Berowne attempts to apologise for his less than empathetic behaviour:

> O, never will I trust to speeches penned,
> Nor to the motion of a schoolboy's tongue,
> Nor never come in visor to my friend,
> Nor woo in rhyme, like a blind harper's song.
> Taffeta phrases, silken terms precise,
> Three-piled hyperboles, spruce affectation,
> Figures pedantical – these summer flies
> Have blown me full of maggot ostentation.

I do forswear them, and I here protest,
By this white glove – how white the hand, God knows! –
Henceforth my wooing mind shall be expressed
In russet yeas, and honest kersey noes.
And to begin, wench, so God help me, law!
My love to thee is sound, sans crack or flaw. (5.2.402–15)

Despite this attempt at a turnaround, which half-mockingly presumes that to speak 'broad' (using regional dialect) is to speak sincerely, the anthropologically wide gulf seen at the start of *Love's Labour's Lost* between the play's men and its women is not bridged. So the play ends without the concluding marriages expected in a comedy, or any assurances that these will ever take place.

I want particularly to consider one image in Berowne's unsuccessful repentance speech, as this initiates an interesting Shakespearian motif. It appears when Berowne attempts to make amends for his former dehumanising contempt of Rosaline's white body ('A whitely wanton', etc.) by praising her paleness in the beautiful monosyllabic line 'By this white glove – how white the hand, God knows!' (5.2.411).

The motif of a body part, particularly a hand, signifying a fear of, or revulsion from, sexuality arises again when in the 'closet scene' Hamlet conjures up his mother submitting to Claudius' loathsome 'paddling in your neck with his damned fingers' (167–9), and again when Iago says of Desdemona greeting Cassio 'Didst thou not see her paddle with the palm of his hand?', and insists that this is 'Lechery, by this hand; an index and obscure prologue to the history of lust and foul thoughts' (2.1.253–8).

This kind of imagery, which Berowne attempts to invert in praising Rosaline's white hand in order to make amends for his initial rejection of Cupid's 'almighty dreadful little might' (3.1.198), crops up again in a much deeper and darker way in *The Winter's Tale*. And indeed it is profoundly important to that play; but first let me contextualise it.[61]

Berowne had been waspishly dismissive of sexual desire in *Love's Labour's Lost*, calling it Cupid's 'plague', while much more seriously, early in *The Winter's Tale* Polixenes labels his own and his 'twin' Leontes' sexual desires as 'The doctrine of ill-doing' (1.2.72). Polixenes goes so far as to identify his and his friend Leontes' puberty, their 'weak spirits' being 'higher reared / With stronger blood', with the biblical Fall, even averring that without sexual awareness they could have avoided the inheritance of Original Sin: 'we should have answered heaven / Boldly, "Not guilty", the imposition cleared / Hereditary ours' (1.2.73–7).

It is a small step from loathing one's own desires to placing blame on the sexuality of others, and Polixenes promptly takes this step. Still using slick courtly diction, he alleges that the fall of the two blameless boys, whom he images as innocent and carefree 'twinned lambs', derived from 'Temptations' attributable to their future 'precious' wives (1.2.69–71, 78–82). These deeply offensive notions scandalise Hermione; yet in harmony with her nature, and in accord with an international diplomatic setting, she does not react as tartly to rank discourtesy as do the Ladies of France in *Love's Labour's Lost*. Instead Hermione replies, as if to exorcise anathema, 'Grace to boot!', and robustly continues 'Of this make no conclusion, lest you say / Your queen and I are devils' (1.2.82–4).

Thus in *The Winter's Tale* the content of Berowne's banter in *Love's Labour's Lost* 3.1.185–98 is unrolled theologically: sexuality causes men's fallen state and women are their 'Temptation' to sin. This sordid and heretical position is promptly if gently refuted by the wise Hermione in terms of her six-times-used word '*grace*', but despite this, Polixenes' notions of female sexuality as the source of evil take hold strongly in *The Winter's Tale*.

Such notions erupt with matchless intensity in the fantasy dictates of King Leontes' warped 'Affection', as he calls it (1.2.140), that is, his jealous paranoia. Leontes not only imagines his pregnant wife's sexuality as transgressive and adulterous,[62] but also that cuckoldry is universal in a luridly 'bawdy' world in which 'From east, west, north, and south, be it concluded, / No barricado for a belly. Know 't, / It will let in and out the enemy / With bag and baggage' (1.2.204–7). These fantasies lead to sarcasm, spite, revulsion, and a tyrannous contempt for truth.

All this raving seemingly follows from Leontes having observed his wife presenting her hand to his fellow king Polixenes in accord with courtly protocol. In his aside, Leontes sees that as a disgusting display of adulterous 'paddling palms and pinching fingers' (1.2.117), repeating the motif seen in *Hamlet* and *Othello*.

But even before drawing his delusional conclusions from that gesture, indeed just before, Leontes has already traduced an image of Hermione offering her 'white hand'; this was in connection with his own remembered courtship of her before she became his wife. Playfully asked to remember the courtship, he recalled how as a young woman Hermione had hesitated before agreeing to handfast with him in marriage, and sputtered ungratefully about 'when / Three crabbed months had soured themselves to death / Ere I could make thee open thy white hand / And clap thyself my love' (1.2.103–6). Note the ugliness of 'clap'.

The imagery of a loving pair holding one another's hands is half-redeemed in *The Winter's Tale* 4.4, during the sheep-sharing festival, when Polixenes remarks: 'How prettily the young swain seems to wash / The hand was fair before!' (364–5). But soon afterwards, thanks to the fact that his son intends to marry without parental consent rather than just take a concubine,[63] Polixenes sets out to despoil this idyll.

The image of a woman's offered hand is only fully redeemed in *The Winter's Tale* when Hermione as a statue miraculously transforms into Hermione redeemed from death. This transformation occurs just when the powerful voice of Paulina instructs Leontes: 'Nay, present your hand. / When she was young, you wooed her. Now, in age, / Is she become the suitor?' (5.3.107–9). Leontes obeys, re-enacting the long-ago handfasting which he had previously denigrated, and is amazed to discover: 'O, she's warm!' (109). The meaning of that discovery takes us, I think, to the heart of what tolerance means in Shakespeare's play.

Formerly, even when remembering his courtship of her, Hermione had seemed to Leontes a monstrous force and a non-person. His toxic fantasies and tyrannous behaviour lead to him throw away his family, and that in turn leads to his long, bitter remorse. On learning of his son's death, Leontes acknowledges 'I have too much believed mine own suspicion' and recognises 'My great profaneness 'gainst [the] oracle' (3.2.150, 153). He therefore commands that on the graves of his son and wife 'The causes of their death appear, unto / Our shame perpetual' (3.2.236–7). But shame is not enough to allow his recovery. Sixteen years later Leontes is famed as 'the penitent King' (4.2.6); only then does he fully confront the full horror of what he had done to his wife: 'She I killed? I did so' (5.1.17). So by the time of his statue encounter Leontes has achieved the first three of the four 'progressive steps' of Christian repentance,[64] 'conviction of sin, contrition, confession'. But these three steps are not sufficient for regeneration without the fourth and final step, a 'departure from evil' combined with the above-mentioned 'conversion to good'.[65] That conversion is seen in the statue scene of *The Winter's Tale*.

There, Hermione's once spitefully depreciated white hand ('open thy white hand / And clap thyself my love'), later defamed as lustful ('paddling palms and pinching fingers'), is transformed into a hand that is for Leontes a proof of the miracle of human life in another person, for it is perceived to be miraculously 'warm'.

Indeed, even before that warmth is confirmed in the flesh, it is realised in the spirit. This is thanks to Leontes' new ability to imagine Hermione as having been a fully autonomous living individual. Contemplating her image in his mind, awakened by viewing her memorial statue, Leontes casts his mind back to the time of his first wooing:

> O, thus she stood,
> Even with such life of majesty – warm life,
> As now it coldly stands – when first I wooed her.
> I am ashamed. Does not the stone rebuke me
> For being more stone than it? O royal piece!
> There's magic in thy majesty, which has
> My evils conjured to remembrance, and
> From thy admiring daughter took the spirits,
> Standing like stone with thee. (5.3.34–42)

These memories differ radically from Leontes' former bitter ones of 'three crabbed months' of frustration which had 'soured themselves to death'; now he imagines Hermione not as an object of his own frustrated desires, but rather in terms of her own 'majesty'.

Thus Leontes has overcome his former refusal to recognise another human person's reality, which led to rancour, ingratitude, petulance, and a disowning of psychic realities. Precisely these conditions have been theorised of late as underlying most tolerance-denying or tolerance-spoiling impulses.[66] Now Leontes sees the reality of another's 'life of majesty – warm life', and has no need to ask why Hermione once hesitated before becoming his loyal queen.[67] The statue stands in for a living person seen as possessing a unique, admirable, and indeed magical and majestic inner life, not as a focus for domination, idolatry, or denigration.

In this sense, for Leontes Hermione is alive in a way she has not been before. His misogynistic mania has been replaced by a new ability to imagine Hermione's separate identity; his strong sense of her now highly valued female otherness has at last overcome his dehumanising and hugely destructive gender intolerance.

CHAPTER 3

Shakespeare, tolerance, and nationality

the residence of continuance of one nation in one place is not of the
law of nature which beinge in itt selfe immutable would then admitt
no such transmigration of poeple and transplantation of nations as
in dayly experience we see.[1]

Of my nation? What ish my nation? Ish a villain and a bastard and a
knave and a rascal? What ish my nation? Who talks of my nation?[2]

I. PROSPECTUS

In Shakespeare's age political and cultural perceptions of what constituted
nationality tended to diverge: this circumstance will underlie the twofold
structure of this chapter.

On both sides of this divide, nationality in the Renaissance was often a
shifting or emerging concept, and certainly this was the case in Elizabethan
England. In terms of cultural mythologies, scholars and artists forged and/
or questioned British origin myths. In the realm of political constructions,
English lawmakers refashioned the limits of citizenship and alien status.

Moreover, mythic–historical and mythic–jurisprudential thinking joined
in novel, highly influential theories that an essential ancient Englishness was
the basis of the immutable English common law: scholars have argued that
these theories had a great deal of fictional content.[3] So in several ways English
nationality was both a prominent and yet an evidently constructed entity.

Because of the dual nature of the constructions of nationality in accord
with either legal specification or else with perceptions of cultural difference, this chapter will be divided into two portions, one of which could
be labelled 'Alien Statutes' and the other 'Exotic Foreigners'. These are
concerned respectively with the legal treatment in a home country of
sojourning or resident 'strangers', and with perceptions either at home or
abroad of 'foreign' groups as defined by differences of habits and speech.

The first section will explore disabilities imposed upon aliens by actual
or fictional law, and some tolerant counter-perspectives in which the

category 'stranger' was seen as largely arbitrary (hence the first epigraph above). The second section will consider the tolerance or prejudice implied by Shakespeare's dramatic portrayals of encounters between 'natives' and culturally 'foreign' others (hence the second epigraph above).

2. ELIZABETHAN ALIEN LAWS

Elizabethan perceptions of England's increasingly numerous resident 'strangers' were strongly impacted by economic relations, and by alien–native differences or affinities in history, culture, language, or religion. Legal definitions of nationality also crucially affected both 'strangers' and natives in Shakespeare's milieu, and may even have made a strong impression on Shakespeare's personal life.

Through the greater part of Shakespeare's literary career English nationality depended solely on birthplace, so that special Acts of Parliament were required to confer English nationality on persons born abroad. Even James VI of Scotland, prior to becoming James I of England in 1603, had problems about owning English land because of his non-English birth.[4] After 1609, however, as a result of the decision in the very important 'case of the *postnati*' (Calvin's Case, 7 Co. Rep. 1.), English nationality was acquired by allegiance to the English sovereign regardless of place of birth.[5] This case was instigated by James in order to determine if Robert Calvin, who was Scottish-born after James became king of England, was able to inherit land in England; the decision affirming that he could do so partially overcame the problem of James's inability to force through Parliament an Act of Union between Scotland and England. Calvin's Case had significance beyond Scotland as soon as it was decided, for in 1606–7 England had established its first long-lasting colony in North America, at Jamestown in Virginia, and the equating of allegiance to the English sovereign with citizenship had very significant impacts on colonial-born subjects from 1609 and onwards. These matters may well have had an impact on Shakespeare's treatment of colonies or empire in his late plays.[6]

There were three alternatives in terms of nationality status available to the non-native 'strangers' resident in Shakespeare's England. Many were allowed a special resident status as Protestant religious refugees, as will be discussed presently. Some applied for a status change that could be granted under the royal prerogative called 'denization'. Denizens had permanent rights of residence, but could not inherit or bequeath English land or hold office;[7] this status brought few advantages and was not often sought.[8] Finally, some among the many 'strangers' in England, albeit very few, could afford to be naturalised by means of very expensive Acts of Parliament.[9]

3. AN INFERRED 'ALIEN STATUTE': SHAKESPEARE'S MATCHMAKING

Known biographical facts, reanalysed, indicate that Shakespeare himself was positioned to appreciate some subsequently overlooked legal disabilities imposed on the 'strangers' of his London.

It is far from certain that the young Shakespeare served in the Roman Catholic household of the landowner Alexander Houghton of Lea Hall in Lancashire,[10] but it is certain that in his early middle years, centred on 1603, Shakespeare lived in the Calvinist artisan household of a member of London's Huguenot refugee community.[11] As is very well known, in 1612 Shakespeare provided testimony in a Court of Requests action showing that he had not only lodged during 1603–4 with the Huguenot family of Christopher Mountjoy at Silver Street in the City of London, but also had been on intimate terms with them; on the urging of the girl's mother, Shakespeare had acted as a go-between in the arrangement of a match between Mountjoy's sole heir, his daughter Mary, and his skilled former apprentice, Stephen Belott, also of Huguenot extraction.[12] Shakespeare's efforts succeeded and a marriage between the couple was solemnised on 19 November 1604 in the parish church of St Olave, Silver Street.[13] This story has often been commented upon, but some important aspects of it have been missed. These concern the impact on London's Huguenots of certain complex interactions between nationality law and marriage law in Elizabethan England.

By allowing residence to non-Anglican Protestant refugees, England, to a limited degree, joined some other parts of post-Reformation Europe in permitting a qualified religious pluralism. Factors such as scepticism, economic expedience, or the *politique* preference for social stability over orthodoxy led to the sanctioned coexistence of multiple confessions (including Catholics with various Protestant sects) in sixteenth-century France, the Netherlands, parts of Germany and Austria, Switzerland, and Poland.[14] It has also been argued that, in addition to reasons of state, the sincere desire of various confessions for religious freedom underwritten by mutual respect were factors in these developments in several places.[15]

England's first Stranger Church was established in the City of London in 1550 at Austin Friars. Inclined to 'reformed religion' himself, the boy-king

Edward VI donated this property and repaired it for the stranger congregation. In its first year this divided into a Dutch church at Austin
Friars and a French one at Threadneedle Street. The initial Walloon
congregation at Threadneedle Street enlarged considerably after French
Huguenot refugees arrived following the St Bartholomew's Day massacre
of 1572.

Concerning this influx Strype reports: 'The better Sort of the Queen's
Subjects were very kind unto these poor Protestants . . . But another Sort
(divers of the common People and Rabble, too many of them) behaved
themselves otherwise towards these afflicted Strangers, Men and Women,
who grudged at their coming hither, and would cal them by no other
Denomination than *French Dogs*.'[16] He adds that '*George Abbot*, D.D.,
afterwards Archbishop of *Canterbury*' preached against such language and
sentiments at Oxford, claiming that those:[17]

that were wise and godly, used those Aliens as Brethren; considering their
Distresses, with a lively Fellow-feeling: holding it an unspeakable Blessednes, that
this little Island of ours should not only be a Temple to serve God in, for
ourselves, but a Harbour for the Weatherbeaten, a Sanctuary to the Straunger,
wherein he might truly honour the Lord . . . And not forgetting, that other
Nations to their immortal Praise, were a Refuge to the *English* in their last bloody
Persecution in Q. *Mary's* Days.

William Lambard, in a 1576 topographical study of Kent, also defended
the French refugees, adding to Abbot's sort of reasons for tolerance a secular
one, the avoidance of provoking resentment. Lambard even attributed the
1066 Norman Conquest to 'the inveterate fiercenesse, and cancred crueltie
of this our *English* nation against foreignes and straungers'. That intolerance, said Lambard, led to a 'butcherly sacrifice' of some visiting Normans
by Englishmen who 'fearing (without cause) great harme, that these fewe
might bring unto them, did by ther barbarous immanite, give just cause to a
great armie to overrunne them'.[18] Then, recalling the recent surge of
Protestant immigration, Lambard continued:

It were worthy the consideration, to call to memorie, what great tragedies have
been stirred in this Realme, by this our naturall inhospitalitie and disdaine of
straungers, both in the time of king *John*, *Henrie* his sonne, King *Edward* the
seconde, *Henrie* the sixt, and in the daies of later memorie. But since that matter
is *parergon* . . . I will rather abruptly ende it, onely wishing, that whatsoever note
of infamie wee have heretofore contracted, among foreigne wryters by this our
ferocitie against Aliens, that now at the last (having the light of *Gods* Gospell
before our eyes, and the persecuted partes of his afflicted Church, as Guestes and

Straungers in our Countrie) wee so behave our selves towards them, as we may both utterly rubbe out the olde blemish, and from hencefoorth staye the heavie hand of the juste *Jupiter Hospitalis*, whiche, otherwise, must needes light upon such stubburne and uncharitable churlishnesse. (284–5)

Many, but not all, of England's Protestant 'Guestes and Straungers' were exiled under King Edward's successor, the Catholic Queen Mary.[19] Interestingly, despite Mary's proclamation of 17 February 1554 expelling all resident strangers without denizen status, 'the Privy Council received precious little help [in this regard] from the [London] city authorities';[20] this non-cooperation lends support to theories of a tolerant strain in English hospitality.[21] Mary's exiles were readmitted as allowed strangers by Queen Elizabeth, but she was far less keen on their churches' anti-prelatical constitutions and strongly 'Reformed' practices and doctrines than her half-brother Edward had been.[22]

In general, official attitudes to the Stranger Churches and the curious structures under which they operated (involving the Privy Council and latterly the Bishop of London) shifted from one reign to another in accordance with emerging ideologies, political or economic motivations, and the numbers in the refugee communities established in various parts of England.[23] On their part the Stranger Churches varied their 'Disciplines', or constitutions, over time, although the London Discipline of 1588 was widely adopted until 1644.[24]

Up to 200,000 Continental Protestant refugees may have fled to England between 1567 and 1590. The exact numbers of them settled in London in Shakespeare's time are difficult to determine,[25] but they certainly made a considerable presence.[26] Thus the workshops of their occupations, in particular their stoneworking workshops located near the Globe in Southwark, are alluded to familiarly in *King Lear* and *The Winter's Tale*.[27]

Although the term 'xenophobia' is sometimes used in discussions of Elizabethan relations with 'strangers',[28] as Nigel Goose points out this should refer to a 'deep antipathy'(*OED*), an ingrained intolerant attitude, that is not really equivalent to the sporadic or periodic outbursts of anti-alien sentiments seen in sixteenth-century London.[29] Nor need a motive of 'xenophobia' be attributed to those who sought economically to disadvantage England's 'strangers' in their landowning rights, taxation status, or through protectionist trading restrictions;[30] these derived from real or imagined economic fears,[31] not necessarily antipathies.

Goose also points to instances in Elizabethan practice, as well as stage fictions, of sympathy for and cooperation with alien strangers (111–17). He finds further indications of perhaps ambivalence, but not xenophobia, in a 'distinct lack of popular violence' in Tudor and early Stuart London against strangers 'after the serious disturbance of Evil May Day in 1517'.[32] On such bases Goose speculates that, following a 'last throw of the medieval dice' in 1517, and before political jingoism took hold, the period between 1550 and 1650 may have been an 'a veritable oasis of tolerance' in England toward strangers (129).

Yet Goose also mentions further upsurges of anti-alien agitation in London, all 'kept firmly in check' by the authorities, in 1550, 1563, 1567, 1586, 1593, and 1595 (119–20). As Charles Littleton has commented, it is pleasing and perhaps surprising to note that the economically and socially stressed London of the 1590s did not see more serious practical assaults on its industrious stranger communities.[33]

Official attitudes to these communities were divided. London's guilds sought restrictions on them in order to supplement or strengthen their own protectionist regulations,[34] yet Elizabethan Parliaments regularly rejected bills proposing these.[35] A 1589 parliamentary speech, probably by Henry Jackman, opposing one of a series of bills that intended to prohibit 'Strangers and Aliens' from retail trade in London,[36] takes positions well worth noting:[37]

I will not detayne you with mathematicall or philosophicall discourses to shew that the whole earth, beinge but a pointe in the center of the worlde will admitt no division of dominions, for *punctum* is *indivisible*, or that man (as Plato sayeth), is no earthlye but a heavenly creature . . . Neyther will I stand upon itt that the residence of continuance of one nation in one place is not of the law of nature, which beinge in itt selfe immutable would then admitt no such trans-migration of people and transplantation of nations as in dayly experience we see. But I will onely propose unto you two groundes of nature as more proper to this purpose: the one that we shoulde geve to others the same mesure that we would receave from them, which is the golden rule of justice.

Although religious principles and economic factors are then adduced as further reasons to defeat the bill, Jackman's starting-points are natural justice, the standing of the earth in the (post-Copernican) heavens, and the nature of man.

The language of this 1589 speech cites the 'Golden Rule' just as distinctly as Sir Henry Finch did on 21 March 1593 when he opposed another similar anti-stranger bill in Parliament.[38] So, although Finch's phrase 'let us do as we would be done unto' (507) is echoed by one of the May Day rioters in Shakespeare's portion of the collaborative playtext *Sir Thomas More* (156–7), this echoing is not unique. This undermines a suggestion made by P. Maas in 1953 that the similarity of the language used by Shakespeare's repentant rioter to Finch's language in Parliament supports a post-1593 dating of Shakespeare's contribution to *Sir Thomas More*.[39] Indeed, as we have seen, the Golden Rule was also invoked in George Abbot's 1572 Oxford sermon on the reception of the St Bartholomew's Day refugees.

Nevertheless, Giorgio Melchiori does accept Maas's argument, and holds that Shakespeare made his contribution to *Sir Thomas Moore* around 1593.[40] In further support of this dating Melchiori alleges that the context of Shakespeare's passage was the atmosphere surrounding the suppression in 1593 by the Privy Council of anti-stranger agitation in London. Here he may be standing on firmer ground, for the agitation of 1593 was more serious than any since 1517 because, as Goose puts it, of a 'congruence of expressions of resentment at various levels of the social hierarchy'.[41]

Some flavour of the nastiness coming from different subgroups in 1593 may be inferred from portions of an anti-alien libel published that year on behalf of 'The Artificers *Freemen* within the City and Suburbs in *London*', and of some verses placed on *the Wall of the Dutch Churchyard, on Thursday May the 5th* [1593], *between Eleven and Twelve at Night*.[42]

Doth not the World see, that you, beastly Brutes, the *Belgians*, or rather Drunken Drones, and faint-hearted *Flemings*; and you, fraudulent Father, *Frenchmen*, by your cowardly Flight from your own natural Countries, have abandoned the same into the Hands of your proud, cowardly Enemies, and have by a feigned Hypocrisy, and counterfeit Shew of Religion, placed your selves here in a most fertile Soil, under a most gracious and merciful Prince. Who hath been contented, to the great prejudice of her own natural Subjects, to suffer you to live here in better Case and more Freedom, than her own People. Be it known to all *Flemings* and *Frenchmen*, that it is best for them to depart out of the Realm of *England*, between this and the 9th *July* next. If not, then to take that which follows. For that there will be many a sore Stripe. Apprentices will rise, to the Number of 2336. And all the Apprentices and Journeymen will down with the *Flemings* and Strangers.

> You, Strangers, that inhabit in this Land,
> Note this same Writing, do it understand.
> Conceive it well, for Safe-guard of your Lives,
> Your Goods, your Children, and your dearest Wives.

Shakespeare, an 'upstart crow' according to Robert Greene's 1592 assessment, may have been a relatively recent arrival in London at the time of this agitation. Whenever he first arrived, in Elizabethan terms

Shakespeare then would have been seen as a 'foreigner', that is, a person from another part of England,[43] and as such likely to meet with many of the same resentments as did the 'strangers' under attack in 1593.[44] So personal experience may have inspired the empathy that is found in Shakespearian treatments of the abuse of strangers.

But common humanity alone, or humanity mixed with the same fears of disorder that led both City and national authorities to curtail the 1593 agitation, could have sufficed to ignite the vehement compassion heard in Shakespeare's *Sir Thomas More*'s deploring of the May Day riots of 1517:

> Imagine that you see the wretched strangers,
> Their babies at their backs, with their poor luggage
> Plodding to th' ports and coasts for transportation,
> And that you sit as kings in your desires,
> Authority quite silenced by your brawl
> And you in ruff of your opinions clothed:
> What had you got? I'll tell you. You had taught
> How insolence and strong hand should prevail,
> How order should be quelled – and by this pattern
> Not one of you should live an aged man,
> For other ruffians as their fancies wrought
> With selfsame hand, self reasons, and self right
> Would shark on you, and men like ravenous fishes
> Would feed on one another. (83–96)

>   You'll put down strangers,
> Kill them, cut their throats, possess their houses,
> And lead the majesty of law in lyam
> To slip him like a hound – alas, alas!
> Say now the King,
> As he is clement if th' offender mourn,
> Should so much come too short of your great trespass
> As but to banish you: whither would you go?
> What country, by the nature of your error,
> Should give you harbour? Go you to France or Flanders,
> To any German province, Spain or Portugal,
> Nay, anywhere that not adheres to England –
> Why, you must needs be strangers. Would you be pleased
> To find a nation of such barbarous temper
> That breaking out in hideous violence
> Would not afford you an abode on earth,
> Whet their detested knives against your throats,
> Spurn you like dogs, and like as if that God
> Owed not nor made not you, nor that the elements
> Were not all appropriate to your comforts

But chartered unto them, what would you think
To be thus used? This is the strangers' case,
And this your mountainish inhumanity. (133–56)

To this an apprentice replies 'Faith, a says true. Let's do as we may be done by.'

Yet a different incentive for the passion in these lines could be inferred if, as has been argued by many editors, Shakespeare did compose them around 1603.[45] For by then Shakespeare was lodging with the 'stranger' Christopher Mountjoy and his wife and daughter, and was intimately involved in their family life.

Having circled back to it, let us now look more closely at the Belott–Mountjoy marriage. In 1612 Shakespeare testified in a lawsuit brought by Stephen Belott. Belott complained about a missing marriage portion which, he claimed, had been promised to him before the marriage by his future father-in-law. Shakespeare and others could not recall significant details, so the equity Court of Requests found the claim inconclusive.[46] It ordered arbitration, and appointed as arbitrators the elders of the French Church in Threadneedle Street.[47]

These precise circumstances suggest certain paradoxes concerning the religious pluralism allowed to the English Calvinist Stranger Churches. By appointing the French Church's elders as arbitrators, the royal prerogative Court of Requests recognised the standing and authority of a Stranger Church. Yet, remember, Stephen Belott and Mary Mountjoy were married in an Anglican parish church, not in the French Church. Why was this so?

It is possible that they chose to be married as Anglicans in line with the religious conversions or semi-conversions made by some members of London's Protestant immigrant communities, an assimilation which is reflected in sixteenth-century wills and other documents.[48] Alternatively, Stephen Belott, like others, may have wished to avoid the much closer moral scrutiny to which the 'consistory' of the French Church subjected betrothing couples compared with the practice in Anglican churches.[49] Indeed the French Church records indicate that both Belott and his father-in-law Christopher Mountjoy were condemned as 'desbauchez',[50] and Mountjoy was actually excommunicated on 24 February 1614.[51]

However, telling statistics suggest that another explanation lies behind the choice of Anglican marriage rites by many of London's religious 'strangers' in Shakespeare's time. For the records of the French Church show that far fewer marriages were listed as taking place there, proportionally, than baptisms. A hint of this appears in some loose descriptions of London's Stranger Church records by John Southerden Burn. He mentions an 'earliest register...a thick folio in vellum, intituled "Du Dynche 13e Jor de Jenvyer, 1599"', which he says contains 'about 8800 baptisms and 800 marriages',[52] indicating an extraordinary ratio of eleven baptisms for each marriage. More reliable, indeed 'perfect', according to their editor,[53] are the preserved records of the French Church in London from 1600 to 1753. I have analysed these across the period 1600–16 and found a ratio of baptisms to marriages of 4.395:1.[54] This ratio is nearly constant year by year over that period.

To see if these Stranger Church data were anomalous I compared them with the same ratios for several other (Anglican) London churches. The figures for St Olave's, Silver Street (where Mary Mountjoy and Stephen Belott were married) yielded a ratio of baptisms to marriages of 1.843:1 in the period 1600–16. With the kind help the of the People in Place research project I found an overall ratio of 1.701:1 over 1600–1616 in a sample of five other London parishes, and similar statistics elsewhere.[55] Other data published for a completely different sample of ten London parishes over the period 1580–1650 show an average ratio of 2.52:1.[56] Thus the French Church ratio of baptisms to marriages, 4.395:1, appears to be about double the norm.

Such an anomaly could have been caused by a fertility rate following marriage among the French Church congregation that was double the average in London for the period. But if that were the case it likely would have been noted by those who commented on London's strangers taking up scant space and resources, and I have seen no such complaints. In the absence of that explanation, the statistics suggest that about half of those who attended London's French Stranger Church and later had their children baptised there chose to be married in Anglican churches, as did Mary Mountjoy and Stephen Belott.

It would have been prudent to do so, because in Shakespeare's time, although marriages could be formed validly elsewhere, some quite justified concerns attached to the legal status of marriages made outside of Anglican churches.[57] Such concerns were not paralleled in Shakespeare's time by similar legal doubts concerning baptisms.

4. EXPLAINING THE ANOMALY

In Shakespeare's time, marriage vows taken in Stranger Churches would have constituted fully valid *de praesenti* marriage contracts, for England retained the medieval laws making immediately valid and indissoluble marriages contracted by men and women who agreed to be married using words of present consent, such as 'I marry you.' There was no need for any particular religious or public ceremony, priestly blessing, endowment before the church door, or consent of parents.

Yet Elizabethan marriages made by consent alone, called clandestine marriages or marriages by spousals, fell foul of a peculiar legal anomaly. Although such *de praesenti* marriages were both valid in common law and accepted by the Church courts, they were also regarded as legally dubious because they did not conform to the requirements of the Elizabethan Act of Uniformity (1.Eliz.1 c.2), which continued in force until 1640. This Act made it an offence to marry other than by using all the rituals and rubrics prescribed in the 1559 Anglican Book of Common Prayer, although, critically, it did not invalidate such marriages.[58] The Calvinist Stranger Churches would not have used the 1559 Prayer Book solemnisation rituals and rubrics, for these, following a series of to-and-fro compromises through three revisions of the Prayer Book, went only part of the way towards the strongly Reformed religion the Stranger Churches upheld.

In fact, in Shakespeare's time and until well after, England lagged behind both Protestant and Catholic Europe in terms of marriage reform. Following the Council of Trent (1563) marriage in the presence of a priest was made mandatory for Catholics, but similar reforms in England had to wait until Lord Hardwick's Marriage Act of 1753. However, confusingly, the Tudor Acts of Uniformity did demand the use of the marriage ceremony set out in Cranmer's Prayer Book and its revisions. In all three revisions up to Shakespeare's day the Prayer Book's 'The Forme of Solemnisation of Matrimonie' specified the presence of an Anglican priest dressed not in a Genevan gown but in a surplice, and the taking of the Anglican, not Calvinist, form of Communion. Also, contrary to Reformed objections to 'idolatry', wedding rings or other tokens had to be exchanged.[59]

Moreover, *à propos* London's French Church, the Prayer Book liturgy was specified to be performed in English.[60] And, as noted, the Prayer Book marriage service included the taking of Communion, which London's allowed Calvinists did but rarely.[61] Thus doctrinally and liturgically the Prayer Book service would not have suited London's strongly Reformed Stranger Churches.

Note the religio-legal anomaly: a French Stranger Church was officially allowed its own congregation, was recognised by a royal law court as having moral authority over its community, could baptise infants and conduct religious services, but only the Established Church was capable of performing the legally demanded ritual of marriage solemnisation.

As will be seen in Chapter 4, in several places Shakespeare spoofed the Anglican solemnisation ceremonies and liturgy that both were and at the same time were not required for marrying, and which were very controversial. It is worth considering whether in doing this he reflected some sympathy for the difficult situation with regard to marrying of Huguenots and other allowed strangers in London, some of whom were his close acquaintances (scholars have suggested that several other refugee strangers besides the Belott-Mountjoys may have been well known to him).[62] If so, he was sympathising with a losing position, for from his time forwards Huguenots and other Protestant strangers came under increasing pressure to conform to Anglican marriage rules – so much so that in time Huguenot marriages were eliminated. First, from the 1630s Archbishop Laud and his followers challenged the Stranger Churches generally, suspicious that their Calvinist rites were like Puritan ones. In the Restoration period, in 1676, an attempt was made to punish the participants in a marriage made in the French Church of Canterbury, resulting in a defence that the Consistory Court was 'not "thoroughly versed in the graunts made to the Walloones" by Charles II and his predecessors'.[63] Still later the Marriage Tax and Marriage Registration Acts of 1694 and 1696 made Huguenot marriages doubly expensive, and slowed them to a trickle.[64] The long-standing marriage difficulties of Calvinists and Nonconformists finally became insuperable thanks to the long-awaited reforms in the 1753 Marriage Act; these required an Anglican solemnisation for any marriage except those of Quakers, Jews, or members of the royal family. All marriages made in Nonconformist churches remained dubious until the Marriage Act of 1836.[65]

So in Shakespeare's time a path had begun that led to the full intolerance of Protestant strangers' marriages, a subtle yet deep-rooted form of discrimination. As we have indicated, living as he did intimately with some of them, Shakespeare had personal reasons to take note of that.

5. A CRUEL ALIEN STATUTE: SHAKESPEARE'S TALE OF THREE CITIES

We have seen that the Act of Uniformity effectively disadvantaged Elizabethan alien strangers, including some personally known to Shakespeare. Next we will examine some fictional instances in Shakespeare's plays of more explicit and harsher discriminatory statutes aimed at alien strangers. The abrupt manner in which these are mooted by Shakespeare may make them seem merely plot devices, but I will argue that they have an oblique impact that might indicate an intent rather to display the cruel evils of nationality intolerance.

The first and the clearest example of these Shakespearian alien statutes appears in *The Comedy of Errors*. In this play multiple confusions caused by the mistaken identities of two sets of twins lead to many 'errors' of perception or judgement regarding a range of matters, including sexual jealousy, witchcraft practices, and financial probity. But, I will argue, neither sexual nor spiritual nor economic foundations are nearly so destabilised by the play's plot machinery as is national identity.

A pair of anti-alien statutes are prominently posited at the very start of *The Comedy of Errors*: an undisclosed 'rancorous outrage' leading to a feud has resulted in a mutual trade embargo and reciprocal 'rigorous statutes' being established in two cities. These statutes impose the death penalty on anyone apprehended in either city who had been born in the other, unless that party pays a substantial ransom (1.1.5–22). These laws of Syracuse and Ephesus are repeatedly referred to throughout the play; mutual distrust between the populations seems also to have arisen, as indicated by the 'those people' and 'they say' kind of remarks made by the Syracusian Antipholus about the city of Ephesus:

> They say this town is full of cozenage,
> As nimble jugglers that deceive the eye,
> Dark-working sorcerers that change the mind,
> Soul-killing witches that deform the body,
> Disguised cheaters, prating mountebanks,
> And many suchlike libertines of sin. (1.2.97–102)

International rivalry and xenophobic prejudices would not have appeared outrageously unfamiliar to an Elizabethan audience, and sharp enmity between former trading partners, such as England and Spain, was not unknown to them. But there are also more outlandish aspects to the Ephesus–Syracuse axis posited by Shakespeare. Antipholus of Syracuse not only fears the sorcerers that he has heard inhabit Ephesus. On arriving there he describes a hallucinatory sense of being in a city where neither language nor culture is unfamiliar, and yet he is wholly unknown; even before the first errors about identity arise in the play, he says that he will wander into Ephesus town and 'go lose myself' (1.2.30). And then, recalling being bereft of his family, he describes his emotions in soliloquy:

> I to the world am like a drop of water
> That in the ocean seeks another drop,
> Who, falling there to find his fellow forth,

> Unseen, inquisitive, confounds himself.
> So I, to find a mother and a brother,
> In quest of them, unhappy, lose myself. (1.2.35–40)

Antipholus' sense of his loss of identity, expressed in his repetition of the phrase 'lose myself', anticipates many others' painful sense of their identities dissolving following the play's multiple ensuing confusions.[66]

So, on one hand, the Ephesus of *The Comedy of Errors* is a place where identities are decentred, the world defamiliarised. But on other fronts this Ephesus is in many ways contrived to resemble familiar aspects of Elizabethan England. It will be useful to spell out some of these. Ephesus, like London, is distinctly a mercantile city. Therefore, although the play sets all its action in Ephesus (it observes the unity of time as well), it also constantly alludes to commerce, travel, and differing nationalities and places. Merchant voyages are planned, handshake contracts made, credit-worthiness assessed, and actions for debt pursued, just as they would have been in Shakespeare's London.

The wide international scope of Ephesus' trade is signalled by frequent mentions of varied coinages. A Syracusian ransom is described as being in 'guilders' (1.1.8) and an Ephesian merchant requires 'guilders' for a voyage to Persia (4.1.3–4). These two references are unique in Shakespeare, and it may be noted guilders were a coinage originating in parts of northern Europe from which the majority of London's resident Protestant 'strangers' originated. The Ephesian ransom sum required for Egeon is, however 'a thousand marks' (1.1.21), and there are repeated confusions throughout the play over a different, misdirected thousand marks (1.2.81–4, 2.1.59–64, 3.1.8); Elizabethan legal documents often specified 'marks' as a money of account (a mark equalled 13s 4d). Later a chain, purse, and ring are valued in 'ducats' (4.1.28–30, 4.1.105, 4.3.83, 4.4.13, 4.4.135, 5.1.387, 5.1.392); other moneys are named as in 'angels' (4.3.40), and there is a pun on 'a thousand pound a year' (4.1.21). All such currencies would have been known in London's bustling world of commerce.

Travel is frequently mentioned in the play, as when Egeon recounts his five years of 'Roaming' every 'place that harbours men' in search of his lost child (1.1.132–6). Interestingly, although he passed from 'farthest Greece, / . . . clean through the bounds of Asia', he only encounters harm when, homeward bound, he risks coming to Ephesus. Here something unfamiliar to Elizabethans is premised: very easy overseas travel was not a commonplace experience, and Elizabethan travel narratives (such as Sandys's or Coryate's, which will be discussed later) were couched as revelations of the unfamiliar.

Nevertheless there was a model for Shakespeare's England of frequent travel to Europe: many among England's allowed Protestant 'strangers' found refuge so close to their original north European homes that they more resembled the immigrants of our own jet aviation age than those of a former steamship era. That is, many of them shuttled back and forth between the Continent and England on business or personal missions.[67] So geographical mobility as seen in *The Comedy of Errors* may well have been associated by Elizabethans with their own well-known aliens.

Yet one geocultural aspect of *The Comedy of Errors* would have struck original Shakespearian audiences as entirely different from western European models. That is that the play's imaginary Ephesus, Syracuse, and Epidamnum implicitly belong to a universal classical (perhaps Hellenistic) eastern Mediterranean. By 'universal' I mean that these city-states are posited to possess a culture and dialect so much in common that a citizen of any one of them can be entirely confused with a look-alike citizen of another.

It seems to me crucially important that *The Comedy of Errors* is so contrived that national differences in it are recognisable only legally or politically, not by language, accent, gesture, dress, and so forth. Indeed, the connection of national differences with places is so far from 'immutable' (see the first epigraph above) as to make such a connection seem entirely inessential, and national differences only arbitrary products of laws or decrees.

To reiterate: cruel as the fictional alien laws of the play are, they cannot obliterate the fact that the play's world does not posit enough linguistic or cultural difference between nationalities to make look-alike citizens of different nations distinguishable even to their wives or long-standing servants. The mistaken identification of separately raised twins in the play provides more than comic confusion; it also shows up the hollowness of legalistic nationality distinctions.

These points are sharpened by means of certain structural ironies. Egeon's long establishing speech (1.1.31–136) tells us that both of the Antipholuses and both of the Dromios were born in Epidamnum; in Elizabethan terms, all four are native citizens of there and nowhere else. Yet the very next scene begins abruptly with Antipholus of Syracuse being advised upon his arrival in Ephesus:

> Therefore give out you are of Epidamnum,
> Lest that your goods too soon be confiscate.
> This very day a Syracusian merchant
> Is apprehended for arrival here,

And, not being able to buy out his life,
According to the statute of the town
Dies ere the weary sun set in the west. (1.2.1–7)

Antipholus would tell no lie in saying that, for we have just learned that
he was born in Epidamnum; yet he is identified in the Folio as 'of
Syracuse' and has passed his entire conscious life there. This emphasises
how nationality is framed as an arbitrary designation.

Egeon, the merchant mentioned to Antipholus as running foul of the
anti-alien law, does not deny his Syracusian nationality; the play begins
with his arrest encountered *in medias res* and his expression of being
resigned to dying. Although his pitiful situation may seem only a minor
strand in the mesh of a comedy of farcical confusions, yet his story starts
and finishes the play, and its melancholy pervades it. The passivity of
Egeon in the face of losing his life solely because of a legally assigned
identity contrasts sharply with the anger and outrage of many other characters who are thrust by plot convolutions into difficulties that challenge
their self-perceived identities.

That is, Egeon, who accepts a non-essential categorisation of his
identity, despairs. Others who are mistaken about their national identities
(having been abducted as infants), or are so bewildered by accidents
caused by mistaken identity that their sense of self weakens, are angry and
rebellious. None of this is correctable until their 'real' identities are
revealed and a divided family is reunited. Then the Duke of Ephesus
finally reviews his former limited compassion, whereby he had allowed
Egeon only one day to raise his ransom, and grants a complete remission
of the fine (5.1.393). This great improvement in the terms of tolerance of
'strangers' accompanies a deconstruction of 'nationality'.

Most important in the story of Egeon is his utter blamelessness, and yet
hopelessness, in the face of the irrationality of his treatment by the anti-
alien law. Moreover, at the play's end it emerges that Ephesus's highly
valued Abbess (5.1.135–6) is in fact Egeon's wife and Syracuse-born. But
her native nationality is simply overlooked in terms of applying the alien
statute; the duke does not 'forgive' her the payment of a Syracusian's
ransom, and seemingly never thinks of requiring one. This image of
unthinking nationality tolerance illustrates that tolerance can consist of
simply not thinking intolerantly (tolerance embodied in a Shakespearian
silence will be considered in the Afterword).

This section is titled 'a tale of three cities' because the very existence of
Epidamnum as a place where no 'strangers' are threatened illustrates that
the city-states of Shakespeare's imaginary Hellenistic region are normally

peaceable and cosmopolitan in their relations. We could say that Epidamnum fits into the play's scheme of cities as a non-partisan mid-point
between Syracuse and Ephesus, a place where neither city has scores to
settle, but also a place of tolerant normality and sanity. Thus, having
learned of their birth there, the play's two pairs of once nationally dis-
severed twins exit, one pair to 'Embrace' (5.1.416), the other side by side
and 'hand-in-hand' (5.1.430).

6. FURTHER SHAKESPEARIAN ALIEN STATUTES: TALES OF THREE CITIES, AND ONE CITY

The handily produced sojourning Pedant of Mantua in *The Taming of the
Shrew* is threatened with a fate parallel with Egeon's, to die by law simply
because he is a Mantuan who has entered Paduan territory (4.2.82–3). He
is advised to pretend to be the rich merchant Vincentio of neutral Pisa;
although this is a ruse, he accepts the misinformation unquestioningly
(4.2.89–115). This twist serves plot purposes, but in imaging an easily
believable disunity and strife between Italian city-states it also illustrates
Shakespeare's interest in politically motivated intolerance of particular
nationalities. Again the proscribed Mantuan alien cannot be distinguished in Padua by any linguistic or cultural markers (although status
markers appear because the Pedant is said to resemble the merchant
he feigns only 'As much as an apple doth an oyster' (4.2.102)). So
Shakespeare twice tells stories involving three cities, one neutral and
another applying arbitrary anti-alien statutes to externally indistinguish-
able 'strangers' from the third.

In *The Merchant of Venice* Shylock falls foul of another anti-alien
statute, but there is no named or implied third place of safety for him.
Shylock's nationality is not likely to have been invisible,[68] and is certainly
not inaudible. His distinctive style of speaking will be discussed later in
this chapter, but it is notable that he himself speaks to Venetians of his
belonging to 'our sacred nation' (1.3.46), 'my nation' (3.1.52), or 'our
nation' (3.1.80).

In the course of the trial scene in *The Merchant of Venice* a Venetian
alien statute provides Portia with her means to defeat Shylock. This
particular 'vile alien statute', as one commentator has described it,[69] has
elicited negative comment ever since. Criticism of the legal proceedings in
the trial in *The Merchant of Venice* may be justified, but not for the reason
given by that commentator, which is that they violate a principle of
equality of all persons before the law.[70] For there was no Elizabethan

principle that such equality should be applied to women (as we have seen in Chapter 2), or to aliens (to whom it does not yet apply in most countries today). The law cited by Portia states:

> If it be proved against an alien
> That by direct or indirect attempts
> He seek the life of any citizen,
> The party 'gainst the which he doth contrive
> Shall seize one half his goods; the other half
> Comes to the privy coffer of the state,
> And the offender's life lies in the mercy
> Of the Duke only (4.1.346–53)

Such a criminal law punishing an intent is not, as such, unusual or objectionable. *Mens rea*, the mental disposition of the accused, was in Shakespeare's time, and is still, crucial in the legal definitions of theft and murder.[71] Solely plotting or intending – without performance – became criminal from 1352 onwards (plotting or imagining the death of the king, his wife, or eldest son entailed conviction for treason).[72]

The imaginary Venetian statute that criminalised attempts by aliens to kill natives was not incommensurate with such formulations. There was a problem or scandal, however, with the trial in *The Merchant of Venice*, which I think Elizabethans would have seen. This is that Portia applies her Venetian alien statute in the wrong sort of court.

Seeing a lawyer from Rome (which Portia pretends to be) advising on a commercial case brought in Venice by an alien against a merchant, and that court presided over by the leader of a trading city, would, I think, inevitably have suggested to Elizabethan audiences the tribunals – still being held throughout Europe – of the international Law Merchant. As I have explained elsewhere at greater length, these special tribunals were convened at markets, fairs, ports, cities, or boroughs (where they were typically presided over by mayors) to deal quickly and efficiently with mercantile disputes.[73]

The Law Merchant was imported into England over several centuries from various Continental trading centres,[74] a process simplified by one commentator, who asserts: 'At the close of the fifteenth and the beginning of the sixteenth centuries we had in England a Reception of the Italian mercantile law.'[75] Its aim was to facilitate trade, and consequently its courts administered a swift or summary style of justice based on internationally understood commercial principles. This helped build the confidence necessary to encourage international transactions (although sometimes these courts dealt with matters pertaining to natives only, as seen in the *pie poudre* court dramatised in Ben Jonson's 1614 play *Bartholomew Fair*). Interestingly, an actual merchant *pie poudre* court presided over by the mayor of Southampton vied with a travelling theatre company for the use of the town hall there in 1623.[76]

The echoes of Law Merchant for an Elizabethan audience in the trial scene of *The Merchant of Venice* would have been multiple: some may have recalled that such law was Italianate; summary judgment is offered somewhat informally in the presence of the leader of a city and other merchants; advice is taken from experts from other nations; at issue is a commercial instrument in the form of a bond. Moreover, Antonio and Shylock alike state that the court's justice must be seen to be even-handed, to protect the commercial reputation of Venice. So Antonio speaks of the 'justice of the state, / Since that the trade and profit of the city / Consisteth of all nations' (3.3.29–31), while Shylock says that if justice is partial: 'the danger [would] light / Upon your charter and your city's freedom' (4.1.37–8). In addition, in the *pie poudres*, and not in any other Elizabethan jurisdictions, commercial and criminal causes could be decided side by side.[77]

Despite all this, the imaging of a Law Merchant tribunal in *The Merchant of Venice* is peculiar. Law Merchant was based on a pragmatic need for good relations between traders, often of different nations and sometimes only transitorily present in the country where the tribunals were established. Its jurisdiction did not usually extend to sanguinary matters, and in Shakespeare's England its jurisdiction over even commercial matters may have been shrinking.[78] I still believe, as I did before, that a Law Merchant tribunal is alluded to in *The Merchant of Venice*,[79] but now I want additionally to stress that the aims of such courts were to promote friendly solutions to differences, often by requiring compromise. This is to say, those courts promoted practical tolerance; in fact it has been argued recently that the international Law Merchant played a highly significant role as a model in the 'grand saga' of the emergence of religious tolerance in early modern Europe.[80] The mission of Law Merchant, to promote international exchange and cooperation, would have seemed shockingly traduced as the trial of Antonio veered off into the realms of revenge and nightmare. Law Merchant, essentially tolerant in its aim to promote agreement and constructive interchange, was perversely imaged by Shakespeare in *The Merchant of Venice* to point up the horrors of intolerance in both Jews and Christians.

7. STAGES, STEREOTYPING, AND EXOTIC 'FOREIGNERS'

This brings us to the second division of this chapter, where we will consider perceptions of 'national' differences in habits, language, or culture, rather than nationality as defined by law. Previously we have had to use the Elizabethan term 'stranger' in places where the more convenient modern word would have been 'foreigner', because for Elizabethans 'foreigner' could refer to a person from a different region of one's own country as well as to one from abroad. But now, because only cultural differences are the focus, these terms can (and will) be used interchangeably. Henceforth, a 'foreigner' (for a Londoner) can be someone from provincial England, Wales, Cornwall, Scotland, Ireland, or from further afield, so long as they appear or sound exotic.

English theatrical portrayals of exotic foreign appearances or speech, or of exotic English characteristics as viewed by foreigners, have been extensively studied, especially by A. J. Hoenselaars. He claims that between 1558 and 1642 there were distinct shifts in the modes of such portrayals of foreignness.[81] Early Elizabethan plays tended to portray foreigners as outlandish and as perfidious, vicious, or economically threatening. Later Elizabethan plays tended to stereotype the behaviour of various types of foreigners in specific ways, often to emphasise contrasting English virtues.[82] From the later 1590s through the early 1600s foreigners were treated more sympathetically, or found acceptance in the worlds of comedies.[83] Finally, in numerous Jacobean and Caroline plays notable vices or follies were exposed in English characters who were often contrasted with virtuous foreigners,[84] and sometimes plays exhibited reverse stereotyping, with English figures taking on supposedly foreign vices.[85]

Some Shakespearian examples seem to match such patterns. For example, in *The Merchant of Venice* (c. 1596) the Prince of Arragon exhibits what Elizabethans called 'Spanish haughture',[86] but in *Henry VIII* (c. 1613) Henry's Spanish-born Queen Katherine is, as Hoenselaars puts it, 'redeem[ed] . . . restore[d] . . . rehabilitate[d]' when she appears both humble and kind.[87] Indeed there may be reverse stereotyping when the stereotypical 'pride and cruelty' of Spaniards is attributed, justly according to Hoenselaars, by Spanish Katherine to the English Cardinal Wolsey.[88]

As we have seen in Chapter 1, supposedly typical English characteristics are also mocked in *The Merchant of Venice*, *Hamlet* (c. 1600), and *All's Well* (c. 1604). Yet Hoenselaars's notion that from about 1600 English writers so often negatively depicted English 'self-images', and positively depicted foreign 'heteroimages', that this created 'a national identity crisis in the world of the theatre',[89] may be exaggerated. For, as has been discussed in Chapter 1, 'joshing' about or even negatively self-imaging eccentric foreign characteristics may be a bid to promote tolerance and cohesion, rather than derogatory in intent.

Moreover, some English writers deplored derogatory representations of foreigners. As mentioned earlier, Sir Philip Sidney objected to the mocking of foreign-sounding English speech, holding it: 'against lawe of hospitality, to jest at straungers, because they speake not English so well as wee doe'.[90] Hoenselaars identifies many similar objections going back to 1572, some of which imply that negative stereoptyping of foreigners is usually based on projection.[91]

8. SHAKESPEARE AND STEREOTYPING

In Shakespeare's early *Henry VI* plays, Queen Margaret and Joan la Pucelle fulfil the roles of ambitious, devious, and promiscuous French-women in accord with stereotypes. Joan's own stereoptyping of her countrymen, 'Done like a Frenchman – turn and turn again' (*Henry VI, part 1* 3.7.85) is not a humorous or benignly self-defining quip.

But a comparison of Shakespeare's two Venetian plays shows a turning away from stereotyping foreigners and towards mocking English self-stereotyping. So in *The Merchant of Venice* Portia's stereotypical drunken German suitor is seen as a hopeless sot and 'sponge' (1.2.83–96),[92] but in *Othello* Iago claims that it is 'in England' where 'they are most potent in potting. Your Dane, your German, and your swag-bellied Hollander – drink, ho! – are nothing to your English' (2.3.70–3). Drunkenness as a national trait is also treated, much more complexly, in *Hamlet*, a play usually dated mid-way between the two Venetian plays.

Although *Hamlet* is set largely in Denmark, it is saturated with an 'international theme';[93] particularly important for us here are the concerns it voices regarding adverse national reputations. An instance appears in the Gravedigger's quip that in England Hamlet's madness would not be 'seen', because in England 'the men are as mad as he' (5.1.150–1).[94] But Hamlet's madness is an ambiguous matter; his self-styled 'weakness and melancholy' may not have been assessed by all in Shakespeare's audiences as of the deluding sort that Hamlet himself fears (2.2.600–5).[95] His melancholy could have been seen rather as of the sort connected since Aristotle with studiousness and deep intelligence.[96] Indeed, some may have associated Hamlet's mental gifts and 'prophetic soul' (1.5.41) with well-known theories deriving from Ficino connecting melancholy with 'genius, even prescience'.[97] So Shakespeare may have wittily refashioned a theatrical negatively self-imaging ethnic joke into one of those 'left-handed insults' that are 'compliments in disguise'.[98]

That possible doubleness, however, pales in comparison with the complexities arising when Hamlet comments bitterly about a widespread stereotyping of Danes as dipsomaniacs. Despising Claudius as always, Hamlet explains to Horatio that the raucous noises offstage accompany the king's traditional public nocturnal display of drunkenness, but has to admit that it has been a longstanding custom for the Danish king to 'Keep...wassail', probably also stumbling about dancing, as he 'drains his draughts of Rhennish down' (1.4.8–13).[99] Hamlet comments next that:

> to my mind, though I am native here
> And to the manner born, it is a custom
> More honoured in the breach than the observance (1.4.16–18)

In the second Quarto text only, this is followed by Hamlet's reflections:

> This heavy-headed revel east and west
> Makes us traduced and taxed of other nations.
> They clepe us drunkards, and with swinish phrase
> Soil our addition; and indeed it takes
> From our achievements, though performed at height,
> The pith and marrow of our attribute.
> So, oft it chances in particular men
> That, for some vicious mole of nature in them –
> As in their birth, wherein they are not guilty,
> Since nature cannot choose his origin,
> By the o'ergrowth of some complexion,
> Oft breaking down the pales and forts of reason,
> Or by some habit that too much o'erleavens
> The form of plausive manners – that these men,
> Carrying, I say, the stamp of one defect,
> Being nature's livery or fortune's star,
> His virtues else be they as pure as grace,
> As infinite as man may undergo,
> Shall in the general censure take corruption
> From that particular fault. The dram of evil
> Doth all the noble substance over-daub
> To his own scandal. (A.B. 1–22)

In 1818 Coleridge said that the above passage has 'the excellenc[y]' of 'finely revealing [Hamlet's] predominant...ratiocinative meditativeness';[100]

it does give a remarkable account of the nature and origins of national stereotyping, and so for our purposes is well worth reconsidering.[101] First it might be noted that Hamlet's word 'custom', although frequently used by Shakespeare, appears most often in *Hamlet*.[102] In Shakespeare 'custom' refers to an individual's habits either good (e.g. healthful, as in *Hamlet* 2.2.299) or bad (e.g. 'damned' as in *Hamlet* 3.4.36), or else to long-established cultural modes or practices.[103] In Hamlet's complaint, the Danish king's drinking 'custom' is seemingly of the second sort, linked to cultural traditions and alleged national traits. However, some have proposed that Hamlet's bitter feelings about the false impression made by a 'mole of nature' are deeply rooted in his concerns about a personal 'defect', not a national one.[104]

My view is that in musing on an ill 'custom' alongside a despised 'mole of nature' Hamlet deliberately conflates two kinds of censure: that of disliked national traits, and that of discreditable personal defects. Thus the simile beginning 'So, oft it chances in particular men' offers not just an analogy between a personal plight and a national one, but also reveals that the slights directed at Danish nationality are felt by Hamlet as equivalent to personal grievances; an individual may be reductively stereotyped through the overestimation of a small fault into no more than an embodiment of that fault, exactly as a nation might also be.

Then the 'ratiocinative' Hamlet plunges into deeper cogitation, further exploring his analogy and speculating about the question of which among individual, hereditary, or societal causes are most significant in producing adverse human traits. He proposes three different causes for his imaginary person's 'mole of nature'. These are: 'their birth', 'the o'ergrowth of some complexion', or 'some habit that too much o'erleavens / The form of plausive manners'. I will attempt to unravel these three alternative causes.

The first, 'their birth', is placed in apposition with 'his origin', and so it expresses what we now call genetic causes. Given the ignorance in Shakespeare's time of genetic mutations, 'birth . . . origin' would have been seen as determined by breeding alone.[105] The second alternative cause, the 'o'ergrowth of some complexion', encapsulates a humoral understanding of human differences; in Shakespeare's time a dominant 'geohumoral' theory (to be discussed in Chapter 6) connected individual or national constitutions with environmental causes, and so assigned typical propensities to particular climates or regions. Hamlet's third alternative cause, 'some habit that too much o'erleavens / The form of plausive manners' must be construed in terms of plausive meaning praiseworthy (*OED* 'plausive', 2a.), and 'o'erleavens' meaning overdone or puff[ed] up (*OED* 'overleaven[ed]'). But are habits that cause formerly good manners to become disastrously over-blown subject to individual choice and agency, or must such control be collective? Hamlet's remarks on unworthy 'customs' may indicate an unsettled response to this question. Young Hamlet is not a Danish drunkard, but does this sort of choice make him into an alienated, deracinated, or overly cosmopolitan figure? It is not evident that the 'breach' rather than 'observance' of the wassail custom is an option available to any Danish king, no more to Hamlet's father than to his uncle.

Thus I think that Hamlet is unsure whether his 'mole of nature' is a correctable blemish, a disposable imperative, or an imperative so firmly cemented to persons or cultures as to leave little scope for change. But even if alteration is impossible, Hamlet's main complaint remains that perceptions of particular nations or individuals, unduly overwhelmed by real but minor distastes, are no better than rank prejudices. So Hamlet's analysis calls for tolerance of perceived blemishes (whether in groups or persons), where a balanced view would shrink these to insignificance in comparison with evident virtues.

9. SHAKESPEARE AND FOREIGN SPEECH

The main marker of foreignness for Shakespeare is language use, although this is a complicated matter. Not so complicated, however, that it does not disrupt claims to the effect that Shakespearian foreignness was really not foreign at all. One critic claims, for instance, that for Shakespeare 'a foreign setting had little essential significance, reflecting little of national characteristics', and that Shakespeare's 'Jaques is no Frenchman; Gobbo (despite the name) no Italian...Shakespeare's foreigner holds only a suggestion of the alien; the essence is English.' He adds, 'Beneath an infinite variety of surface appearances, the enduring sameness of humanity remained.'[106] Also considering human universals, G. K. Hunter identified mixed applications in Shakespeare's plays of both a new observational geography and an older 'myth-bound' or religiously inspired one. According to Hunter, Shakespeare used this older geography, which saw the world from the perspective of a fast-receding common European culture, to obtain 'a freedom to concentrate on essential moral problems'.[107]

Certainly Shakespeare's portrayals of Othello, Shylock, Caliban, and others show his interest in humanity-in-common, even in the presence of extraordinary differences of culture or origin. Nonetheless, this does not mean that Shakespeare always aspired, as another commentator has it, to reach 'a plane where ethnicity is outdistanced by universality'.[108] Indeed, at the other extreme from universalising, Shakespeare sometimes employed foreign or exotic nations as proxies to particularise attention to specific aspects of England and the English;[109] we may see more Elizabethan issues reflected in Shakespeare's Vienna, Rousillion, or Illyria than even in the Windsor of *The Merry Wives*.[110]

Nationality issues are often alleged to have been the focus of Shakespearian topical allegories. Thus arguments have been advanced claiming that the succession problems in *Hamlet* and *King John*, or the national identity of Posthumus in *Cymbeline*, reflected on the standing of James I or of Scots in general in Britain.[111] Gonzalo's 'plantation' discourse in *The Tempest* has often been connected with Elizabethan Ireland.[112] Such allegations join many others in a range of studies of how Elizabethan literature may have mirrored newly emerging concepts of English, British, or Anglo-Irish identity.[113] So there is a universalising Shakespeare for some critics, and a topical nationality-issue allegorising Shakespeare for others.

On another less rarefied plane, sometimes Shakespeare dramatised foreigners as really foreign, marked as such by their culture and especially by linguistic differences, in order to explore challenging interpersonal encounters. However, some perplexing, or sometimes amusing, complications arise in Shakespeare's (inevitably gestural) presentations of 'foreign' dialects or languages. In *Love's Labour's Lost*, for instance, French spoken in and around the court of Navarre is staged as English, although an English of which the lucidity is threatened by unrestrained courtly euphuism or poeticism. The fact that the dialogue of the play is implicitly translated *from* French is utterly spoofed when Berowne is abashed by his slip of the tongue, and accepts rebuke, for his pretentiousness in using the word 'sans' for 'without'. Rosaline's 'Sans "sans", I pray you' (5.2.416) alludes to the fact that using 'sans' was an English poeticism. In fact, 'sans' is used by Shakespeare himself for metrical purposes in elevated poetic passages in nine plays, although only once in prose, by the pedantic Holofernes of *Love's Labour's Lost*.[114]

Shakespeare's fine meta-theatrical quip regarding French-speaking Berowne's apology for his use of 'sans' likely spoofs the anti-foreign-word-import 'inkhorn' debate of his time.[115] But it also points towards certain problematics that arise from the convention that most foreign speech was rendered as English on the Elizabethan stage. For instance, in the play worlds of *All's Well* English stands in for both French and Italian as used in a Tuscan war. Yet the gulling of the *miles gloriosus* Parolles involves vamping up an incomprehensible foreign gibberish, a jargon that is misidentified as of 'the Moscows regiment' by the self-styled 'manifold linguist' Parolles (4.1.70, 4.3.241). It is called by one of its users 'linsey-woolsey' (4.1.11), which links it imagistically with the play's 'The web of our life is of a mingled yarn, good and ill together' (4.3.74–5). So we have in the same play Italian or French, languages familiar to Elizabethans, rendered as plain English, but an (imaginary) more exotic language rendered as babble.

This context helps point towards the first of two salient facts I need to raise about the English language of Shakespeare's time: that English was not then a language widely known or used internationally. Parolles, captured by the 'Muscovites', requests 'If there be here German or Dane, Low Dutch, Italian, or French, let him speak to me' (4.1.72–3); signally, 'English' is not on his list. Also, among Portia's derisive comments on her 'stranger' suitors in *The Merchant of Venice* is that 'Falconbridge, the young baron of England' is incomprehensible: 'You know I say nothing to him, for he understands not me, nor I him. He hath neither Latin, French, nor Italian... He is a proper man's picture, but alas, who can converse with a dumb show?' (1.2.63–70). Even prosperous resident aliens of England such as Doctor Caius, the French physician in *Merry Wives*, are unable to avoid 'abusing... the King's English' (1.4.5), and Hoenselaars finds it a notable virtue in Spanish-born Queen Katherine in *Henry VIII* that in contrast with other stage Spaniards, and in contrast with 'great ambassadors' to England from Europe who 'speak no English' (1.4.56–66), she has learned English and insists on using it in international discourse rather than Latin (3.1.41–9).[116] Thus educated persons from abroad, including the razor-sharp Portia, lack knowledge of Shakespeare's tongue, and a foreign-born but long-resident English queen is praised for learning it.

A scant international knowledge of English explains the comic business of the French Princess Katherine in *Henry V*, who requires an English lesson (and gets one filled with bawdy bilingual puns). The implications of her 'Il faut que j'apprenne a parler' (3.4.4–5) have been confused by the important linguist N. F. Blake, among others. *Pace* Blake, the French king and queen of *Henry V* are not portrayed as speaking 'excellent English and [living] in a court where others also spoke standard English';[117] Blake overlooks the stage convention that allowed Shakespeare to represent this king's and queen's excellent French by using excellent English.[118] Hence he is mistaken in finding it contradictory that their daughter Princess Katherine 'speaks only a broken English'.[119] She needs English lessons, and struggles in the courtship scene, because she and her environment are not English-speaking. Thus her language deficiency does not lack 'verisimilitude', as claimed by Blake and some others,[120] although it may still, as Blake suggests, correlate with Katherine's 'defenselessness, her youth and her charm'.

Blake is also on good grounds in finding that Katherine's 'broken English' conveys some 'humour...but no touch of vulgarity'.[121] In general, linguistic chauvinism is not a typical feature of Shakespeare's plays; perhaps because of the contemporary far from dominant position of English worldwide, Shakespeare's portrayals of foreign or otherwise 'broken' language usages tended to take on a humorous, but not a denigratory, tone. This, of course, has a significant bearing on Shakespeare's dramatisations of tolerance versus intolerance of 'strangers' or foreigners.

10. SHAKESPEARE, LANGUAGE, AND NEW ARRIVALS

Shakespeare's broadest exotic-language users are newly arrived comic 'foreign' figures such as Doctor Caius or Don Armado. These are represented quite differently from Shakespeare's long-resident foreigners like Shylock, Othello, and Caliban, or his regional Britons.

Oddly languaged Caius and Armado are presented as amusing, but are not coarsely (as Sidney put it) belittled. Although noting Caius' 'broken English', Hoenselaars still points to the doctor's doughty courage in the face of the proposed duel in *Merry Wives*, his 'overdog' ability to turn tables on the xenophobic Host who had gulled him, and, perhaps most importantly, the 'significant' fact that Caius obtains the support of Anne Page's mother in his wooing of her.[122] Although Caius is not successful in his courtship, thanks to this parental support he is not so humiliated by the failure as is the typical stage foreigner who, as Hoenselaars writes elsewhere, becomes 'the butt of scorn' and 'excels in failure' in his 'amorous pursuits of highly desirable English maidens'.[123]

It may seem more unlikely that we will find any tolerance in the depiction of the absurdly verbose Don Armado of *Love's Labour's Lost*. Anti-Spanish feeling ran high in England from the mid-sixteenth century and increased in the later Elizabethan period, so that Spaniards were often ridiculed on English stages.[124] Yet, despite that, some sympathy and tolerance are evident in Shakespeare's portrayal of Armado.

Armado is described as the 'Spaniard.../ that makes sport / To the Prince and his bookmates' (4.1.97–9), that is, as some kind of figure of fun. But, although he is a sort of jester to the pretentious courtiers of Navarre, Armado's stilted bearing and absurd diction only exaggerate their absurdities. Moreover, in certain ways Armado's humanity and manhood are seen eventually to exceed those of the courtiers.

I would like to propose in this connection a small extension to a Jacobean grammarian's sixfold division of British dialects into: 'the general, the Northern, the Southern, the Eastern, the Western, and the Poetic'.[125] To these I would add another dialect variant, the courtly. Excessively courtly language is repeatedly effectively disapproved of by Shakespeare because in his plays at worst it covers up falsity, and at best it communicates shallowly or risibly. Some of its users, such as Osric, who is mocked in Hamlet's parody of overblown court speech (in the second Quarto text only, A.N.7–14), are foppish time-servers.[126] Others, like Oswald in *King Lear*, deploy courtesy or discourtesy as a political weapon. A courtly-insincere style of diction proves to be very dangerous indeed in several late Shakespearian contexts: courtly-insincere language covers up corruption in Antiochus' court in *Pericles*; the brittle courtly cadences of an Italian, Frenchman, Dutchman, Spaniard, and Posthumus in *Cymbeline* 1.4 advance the boasting that leads swiftly to dangerous contention; in *The Winter's Tale* 1.2 hyper-polite, brittle, and elaborate courtly language does not restrain, and may in fact advance, a break with reality and rupture of amity having long-lasting disastrous consequences.[127]

In Shakespeare's early play *Love's Labour's Lost*, however, courtly fashions and fads mirrored in affected speech patterns are subjected mainly to gentle mockery. Most mocked is the pompous Spaniard Don Armado. Yet, despite his high-flown rhetoric, Armado is, uniquely in the play, a victorious lover; so he is not just verbose and ineffective, as was the case with typical Elizabethan stage-Spaniards such as Arragon in *The Merchant of Venice*.

However Armado's erotic success is with a promiscuous country wench; to what degree this heterogamy mocks the 'refined traveller of Spain' (1.1.161) is open to question. Formerly I connected Armado's wooing mainly with an Elizabethan aversion to lustful misalliances, but I would revise that emphasis now.[128] Some unequal Shakespearian marriages (as of Olivia and Sebastian in *Twelfth Night*, 'dowerless' Cordelia and France in *King Lear*, or Florizel and Perdita in *The Winter's Tale*) are brave, romantic, and not ill-fated; Armado frames his wooing likewise, somewhat ridiculously comparing himself with King Cophetua (1.2.104–11 and 4.1.64–79). The ribald image of Armado proposing in high-flown written language to his pregnant (by another) and illiterate Jaquenetta might seem to render him contemptible, but we might remember that in Chapter 2 we encountered Anne Barton's remarkable disruption of the usual assumption of an unmitigated Elizabethan horror of cuckoldry.[129] Moreover, Armado's commitment 'To hold the plough for [Jaquenetta's] sweet love three year' (5.2.870) might not at all imply degradation. The despicable courtiers of *The Tempest* will not sully their hands with manual work, and they abuse the labouring sailors during the shipwreck,[130] while virtuous Prince Pericles in similar circumstances 'cried "Good seamen" to the mariners, / Galling his kingly hands with haling ropes' (S.15.104–5). Shakespeare's foreigner Don Armado may therefore be rendered, amusingly but tolerantly, as braver, more industrious, and more successful than his native-born mockers.

II. 'WHAT ISH MY NATION?': SHYLOCK'S DIALECTS

The second salient point about the Elizabethan English language alluded to above is that the English of Shakespeare's time was not standardised, but was rather rapidly acquiring new vocabulary and structures, and was deeply fissured by what we now call 'dialects'.[131]

Before turning to Shakespeare and British dialects, an important analogous case may be considered. Language was a marker in Shakespeare's time of perceptions of nationality even where political nations did not yet exist, or else had been conquered and merged (e.g. Wales or Cornwall). So, for instance, there was no Italy or Germany, but there were Italians and Germans.[132] In an interesting possible parallel, although there was no territory in view, Jewish Shylock of *The Merchant of Venice* speaks repeatedly of 'our sacred nation' (1.3.46), 'my nation' (3.1.52), 'our nation' (3.1.80), and adds that Venice's prosperity depends on fair dealing with 'all nations' (3.3.32), including his own. The sense in which Shylock belongs to a Jewish nation apart from other Venetians,[133] and yet is still a Venetian, is shown by peculiarities of his diction. This, rendered by Shakespeare from Italian into English, has been said by some to approximate to a dialect or even foreign-inflected variant.[134]

As has been discussed in Chapter 1 in connection with Shylock's mock-naive 'Arkansas Traveller' stance and other styles of humour, he often speaks in peculiar registers. His terse locutions, frequent repetitions, odd hesitations, self-answered questions, and other verbal peculiarities have been alleged by some to indicate 'language at a reduced and primitive level', 'plainness', or 'literalism'.[135] But I agree rather with Jane Freeman that Shylock's odd diction and cadences brilliantly and inventively serve a range of rhetorical ploys.[136] Simultaneously with serving such artifices, I believe, Shylock's quirky diction provides audiences with a window on his internal hesitancies and self-checking process of ratiocination. Thus I also agree with Freeman that in various places Shylock's uses of rhetorical figures make 'his thought process audible', show him giving 'conscious attention to his own words', 'reveal his awareness of his own reasoning process', present 'an analytical mind at work', or express 'the intensity of his focus'.[137]

To this I would add that an audience can not only hear Shylock thinking, but can see that he is repeatedly not properly heard as a thinking being by others onstage. So I have argued that Shylock warns Antonio about a threatened revenge when he retells the story of Jacob and Laban, but he is not understood.[138] His offers of friendship are also promptly misapprehended, leaving it open to serious question whether they might not be sincere.[139] Ironies concerning Shylock's misheard and derided dialect highlight his isolation and exclusion, and add to a sense of a dire lack of tolerance in his Venice.

12. 'WHAT ISH MY NATION?': BRITISH DIALECTS

The fact that the English language did not have a standard dialect in Shakespeare's time leads to the question: did Shakespeare's many portrayals of distinctive regional dialects entail ridicule, indifference, or sympathy?

Many have commented on British dialects represented by Shakespeare. Jonathan Hope, for one, makes the extreme claim that 'one of the most striking things about Shakespeare's treatment of language is the lack of comment on, or representation of dialect'. After naming a few exceptions to this, Hope offers that in Shakespeare's England: 'everyone had [a regional dialect], so why comment on it? . . . If everyone had a dialect, then variation is the element speakers swim in, not commented upon because there is no non-dialectal position from which to find dialectal variation strange.'[140] This of course goes directly against my claim, commenting on Shylock's distinctive diction, that Shakespeare used dialect speech patterns to indicate that certain of his characters were isolated from their surrounding cultures.[141] Which is right then, dialects as dramatically indicative, or dialects as invisible?

The majority of commentators have found the dialects indicative in various ways, but not necessarily of social approbation or status. Thus, while commenting on Shakespeare in relation to the contemporary Italian *commedia dell'arte* which employed humorous dialectal voices, Allardyce Nicoll insisted that dialect use did not impact on status:[142]

During the period of the Renaissance national and local dialects had not been ironed out into the flat uniformity which in many countries is our present ideal; and it would be as absurd to find in the different speech forms in these countries a division by class as it would be to argue that Sir Walter Raleigh's broad Devonshire at the court of Queen Elizabeth marked him out as a parvenu, or that King James I's strong Scots accent was a sign of his lack of culture.

However, more recently, in a time when prime emphasis is often placed on early modern oppression or 'containment' of alien voices or cultures,[143] some commentators have insisted that King James and Walter Raleigh, for example, were mocked and denigrated on account of their regional dialects.[144] Of course political enmity or jealousy (as of James's favoured Scottish courtiers) did prompt adverse comments on dialect users, but that does not prove that regional speech was disrespected *per se*.

The above contradictory views show that there are open questions about how users of foreign dialects were regarded in Shakespeare's culture. One possible indication of attitudes may lie in an observation by Brian Vickers that 'No foreigner in Shakespeare speaks verse.'[145] However, this may not apply to dialect users whose speech is rendered into clear English in accordance with above-mentioned stage conventions. For instance, King Duncan and Macbeth, and their courtiers, speak English verse nearly untouched by Scotticisms.[146] Yet it has also been claimed that 'Shakespeare would have known from reading Holinshed' that these 'had all been Gaelic speakers'.[147]

In fact, British dialects are never fully rendered by Shakespeare. The voice of Captain Jamy in *Henry V*, which 'is considered as the first representative of Scots speech in English literature',[148] provides only a gestural (if recognisable) sketch of Scots, and technically actually mirrors a generalised Northern dialect.[149] Likewise, although Mortimer's wife speaks and sings charmingly in actual Welsh in *Henry IV, part 1* 3.1 (to Hotspur's displeasure), the dialects used elsewhere by Shakespeare to portray Welsh characters speaking 'broken' English are not fully founded on Welsh, nor are they consistent. Thus N. F Blake finds that in portraying Evans in *The Merry Wives* 'Shakespeare is prepared to exploit the low comedy of a Welsh voice as much as he can', but to the Welsh-inflected speech of Fluellen in *Henry V* he gives only a 'flavour of Welsh'.[150]

Giving Fluellen 'the flavour of a regional variety' of English,[151] rather than satirically portraying his dialect, would have served Shakespeare's purposes if, as Blake puts it, his aim in *Henry V* was to 'show Henry's glory in that his appeal could unite such a seemingly disparate army'.[152]

The uniting of that army in *Henry V* is not always smooth sailing. The varied nationalities within King Hal's army – Welsh, Irish, Scottish, and English – are seen to be reluctantly welded into a 'band of brothers' partially through the agency of 'joshing' ethnic jokes which display, but also show the comic side of, British ethnic diversity.[153] One of those jokes involves the disguised King Henry pretending to be a kinsman of the Welsh Captain Fluellen and so receiving a challenge to Fluellen from the boastful English Pistol (4.1.52–64); the outcome in 5.1 is that Pistol is thrashed by Fluellen and forced to eat a leek, and is admonished by the English Captain Gower to show respect for the Welsh nation he has despised and its 'ancient tradition'.[154] The dishonoured Pistol resolves to become a bawd. But the play ends with national conflicts resolved, and even French and English differences are reconciled through the celebration of a marriage comically contracted by means of stumbling but well-intentioned endeavours to traverse linguistic and cultural divides.

Prior to that end, of particular interest here is the dissension in the famous 'four captains' scene, found only in the Folio version of *Henry V* (not the 1600 Quarto). Here the English Captain Gower, Welsh Captain Fluellen, Scottish Captain Jamy, and Irish Captain MacMorris meet on the battlefield in the hurry and stress of war, but Fluellen still wants to discuss classical military precedents and theories. To a degree, the Welsh-dialect-speaking Fluellen may be modelled in this regard on the Bolognese-dialect-speaking, pedantic, and long-winded 'Dottore' stock character of the *commedia dell'arte*.[155] But Fluellen deserves far more respect as a skilled soldier and patriot than the Dottore does as an intellectual;[156] as the king himself says, 'Though it appear a little out of fashion, / There is much care and valour in this Welshman' (4.1.83–4).[157] And in fact, through his malaprop verbosity and extravagant 'figures and comparisons', Fluellen may even serve as the play's channel for conveying the uncomfortable import of 'Harry of Monmouth's' betrayal of a friend (Falstaff), which half-parallels that of the classical 'Alexander the Pig' (4.7.11–49).[158]

In the lead-up to the fracas in the 'four captains' scene, then, not wholly ridiculous Fluellen extravagantly praises Scottish Captain Jamy for knowing and adhering to Roman military theory and decorum (3.3.21–37), and conversely dispraises Irish Captain MacMorris (3.3.15–18). MacMorris replies that he is more committed to actions than to words (3.3.49–57). Then the unfortunately prolix Fluellen sets out to expound for MacMorris's benefit his view of persons 'of your nation', whereupon MacMorris explodes, as if anticipating a national ethnic slur: 'Of my nation? What ish my nation? Ish a villain and a bastard and a knave and a rascal? What ish my nation? Who talks of my nation?' (3.3.66–8).

Tempers fray quickly, and soon MacMorris offers 'I will cut off your head' (3.3.76). Captain Gower then intervenes with, 'Gentlemen both, you will mistake each other' and Captain Jamy backs him up with the immediate comment 'Ah, that's a foul fault' (3.3.77–8). Various explanations have been offered of this interchange and MacMorris's outburst.[159] Also Gower's and Jamy's following remarks have been interpreted variously.[160]

In addition to other readings, one with a sharply comic import needs to be considered. In this, the threats of violence that come before are intentionally and entirely ignored by Gower, and this is done in a very humorously 'deadpan' manner. So, in Gower's remark 'Gentlemen... you will mistake', the word 'will' predicts a 'possible' future while deliberately eliding the palpable present and immediate past. This hypothetical concern of Gower's about what *might* happen is highly comic, coming as it does on the heels of what *has* just happened. By pretending to a selective deafness or stupidity, and thereby in a sense by cancelling what has just happened and replacing it with an alternative reality, Gower offers the antagonists a face-saving alternative to acting on their just-made threats. Jamy's daft mock-sagacious comment that to 'mistake each other' is a 'foul fault' neatly matches, and even overtops, Gower's gesture; it appears to be hyper-unaware of the just-heard angry threats of decapitation. So Jamy's comic understatement backs up as well as unmasks Gower's, while both open up a way to 'save face' and bypass impending conflict.

Humorous peace-making among the captains thus serves not only an obvious need to continue as a unified army in battle, but is also an attempt to extricate from angry dissension the tolerant impetuses in a dialogue seeking mutual understanding.

CHAPTER 4

Shakespeare, tolerance, and religion

I. A REPRISE

I have just claimed that in *Henry V* 3.3 Captains Jamy and Gower intervene humorously in an attempt to 'extricate from angry dissension the tolerant impetuses in a dialogue seeking mutual understanding'. I will next argue that their action and its humorous mode find an exact analogue in a very remarkable, but not wholly unprecedented, work by Shakespeare's contemporary Jean Bodin.[1] Only there the parallel action is intended to stop dissension over religious rather than national differences.

2. JEAN BODIN'S DIALOGUE BETWEEN SEVEN RELIGIOUS OUTLOOKS

Although unsigned, the *Colloquium of the Seven about Secrets of the Sublime* was almost certainly written by Bodin (and no other), late in his life, probably between 1588 and 1593.[2] Originally circulated in Latin and French manuscripts, it became a famous and eagerly sought 'underground' text, but remained unprinted until long after Shakespeare's lifetime.[3] Bodin's *Colloquium* is important for our purposes because it shows that western European culture in Shakespeare's age was capable of imagining wholly open-minded intra-religious dialogue; in addition, as just mentioned, it dramatises the protection of that dialogue in a manner eerily similar to that witnessed in *Henry V*.

The *Colloquium of the Seven* consists of a series of dramatised conversations between a Roman Catholic, a Muslim, a Calvinist, a Lutheran, a Natural Philosopher, a Sceptic, and a Jew. In consequence of this wide diversity of participants, Bodin's work cannot be understood in terms of merely *politique* concessions to religious pluralism.[4] Five of the seven faith outlooks represented in it had no impact on the civic stability of Bodin's France.

Bodin's seven participants meet at the elegant house of the Roman Catholic Coronaeus, a host who provides a cultured, pleasant, and convivial

90

setting.[5] There they candidly compare their views on religion; yet at at the book's end they agree that public discussions of that sort would not be safe, and afterwards they 'held no other conversation about religions'.[6]

Coronaeus provides privacy, allowing for the expression of differences of inner belief, and actively encourages vigorous and open, but courteous debate. Gary Remer has connected the *Colloquium* with increasing interest in the humanist rhetorical mode '*sermo*' or 'conversation'.[7] It is important to note, however, that the humanists' notion was that *sermo* should lead to the discovery of a single truth among contending options, but Bodin dramatises multiple viewpoints which do not, and cannot, ever converge. Thus no single truth, or single true faith, emerges from the *Colloquium*. However, it is claimed there that, thanks to a kind of 'chromaticism' (144–50), the multiplicity of ideas explored produces an 'enharmonic' 'harmony' (471).[8] In accord with this image, the participants' discussions are punctuated by songs sung and verses read, as well as by rare feasts provided by Coronaeus.[9]

Most often the discussions in the *Colloquium* produce concord. For instance, the Jewish participant Salomon says 'There is nothing which I bear more grievously than for piety implanted with the deepest roots, to be mocked; from this source civil disturbances and uprising spring which are too numerous to recount', and he illustrates this point with several examples of provocations leading to the persecution and expulsion of Jews. Octavius, the Muslim participant, adds to these an account of the persecution and forced conversion of the 'Moors of Granada, who were of the Arabic religion'. Then Fridericus the Lutheran and Curtius the Calvinist participants commend in turn two different late Roman emperors who supported religious toleration and pluralism; this is followed by a song about 'enharmonics' (471).

Yet sometimes Bodin's protagonists can disagree robustly, and some of their discussions even produce insults. Some particularly sharp acrimony appears in Book Four, when the Muslim Octavius is badgered, even derided, for his faith. The prelude to this is that Octavius, who was formerly a Christian, tells of his conversion to 'the Mohammedan faith' after he had been sold as a slave in Syria, following his capture by pirates 'on the shore of Sicily' (225). He reveals that, although he had been 'At last convinced by the arguments' (L. *Ad extremum rationibus victus acquievi*), his motives for conversion had been mixed. He admits that, after several years of proselytisation, and after reading a book by a Dominican who had converted to Islam, he also looked forward to regaining his freedom from slavery which he knew would follow his conversion. He even comments: 'Many are accustomed to embrace Mohammed and allow themselves to be circumcised in order to obtain freedom' (225). The Lutheran Fridericus immediately mocks such converts, whom he sees as apostates, by repeating a story from Pausanias:

Once I heard those who went into the cave of Trophonius were accustomed to leap about as if they were driven into madness by the demon. When their friends tried to call them back and had entered the cave, they joined the dancing. We see the same thing has happened to Octavius.

His aping of Octavius' word 'accustomed' (L. '*solent*'/'*solitos*') makes Fridericus' comparison particularly jeering in tone. To this gibe Octavius replies, with great dignity (227):

I pass over the insults by which the dignity of Mohammed is torn to bits by the disparagements of his adversaries. I stick to the substance, that is, the true and sincere worship of the one eternal God.

But soon afterwards, following a brief discussion of the need for ceremony in religion, the Calvinist Curtius again takes up the attack on Mohammed, alleging that he told deliberate lies 'to entice the untutored minds of the common people' (229). The Jewish participant, Salomon, adds his opinion that it is dangerous 'to offer men wicked pleasures in place of virtue and piety and to draw the unlearned by false promises beyond what is right' (230).

   Very interestingly, Octavius' reply to this incorporates views of religion and secular sovereignty that match Bodin's own, as expressed in texts written prior to the *Colloquium*. These writings of Bodin argue for a vision of state and Church that would promote the maintenance of good social order above all else.[10] So, Octavius begins 'I greatly admire the sentiment of Xenophon and Plato, namely, that it is justifiable and always has been justifiable for magistrates and physicians, as well as the nurses of infants, to lie to the people for the sake of the republic' (230). Salomon expresses disapproval of Octavius' 'lawgiver' Mohammed for using such tactics, but Octavius defends them as a means to a good end, the conversion to monotheistic beliefs of 'the peoples of Asia and Africa' (231).

   Next the discussion becomes quite heated again, this time concerning the acceptability of Arianism (which Octavius claims was the precursor to Islam). Just then, the text states, the host, Coronaeus, 'dismissed the gathering', halting the debate literally in mid-sentence. He announces the topic of an even more exciting discussion to follow, 'whether it is right for a good man to feel otherwise about religion than he confesses publicly', and hastily calls the participants away to dinner.

What is going on here is complicated not only in terms of ideas but also in terms of drama. It is evident that Coronaeus is acting as a peacemaker, and, aware that Octavius has been badgered, he promises a continued discussion after dinner 'so as not to seem to deny Octavius the right to speak' (232).

Immediately following this, at the start of Book V, Coronaeus takes steps to support Octavius in his beleaguered position. First Coronaeus commands the continued reading of a poetic tragedy written by Octavius, apparently a philosophical closet drama with an Islamic setting like those of England's Sir Fulke Greville (written 1595–1600). And the lines we hear from this play, including 'Let there be one all powerful commander for earth' (233), distinctly echo Bodin's own absolutist conceptions of sovereignty (as expressed in his 1576 *Six Books of the Republic*, which was translated into English by 1606).[11] Thus the Muslim's poetic art is set up to civilise and inform the other discussants at the Roman Catholic Coronaeus' house.

In fact Bodin's implied support for Octavius goes even further, for he gives him other views that also match with his own as expressed in 1576; that is, Octavius' derided remarks on the Islamic practice of freeing slaves who convert describes a practice that Bodin strongly approved in the *Six Books*. There Bodin claimed that the institution of slavery had been universal from classical times until about 1200–1300, and was alarmingly becoming 'againe approved, by the great agreement and consent of almost all nations' (34). He was relieved, however, that France was still resistant to slavery, as it had been for over four hundred years, and that even 'slaves of [foreign] strangers so soon as they set foot within Fraunce become franke & free' (41–2). In a more general way, Bodin questions 'Whether slaverie be naturall & profitable to a Commonweale, or contrarie unto nature and unprofitable?' (33); then, defying traditional views and Aristotle's authority, he sides with the 'the better' anti-slavery position of contemporary French lawgivers and concludes:[12]

Wherefore seeing it is proued by the examples of so many worlds of years, so many inconueniences of rebellions, seruile warres, conspiracies euersions and chaunges to have happened vnto Commonweals by slaues; so many murthers, cruelties, and detestable villanies to haue bene committed vpon the persons of slaues by their lords and masters: who can doubt to affirme it to be a thing most pernitious and daungerous to haue brought them into a Commonweale; or hauing cast them off, to receiue them againe?

Bodin's chief fear is that a revived use of slavery, with its inevitable cruelties and dangers, might return to infect and destroy France, as it had many former civilisations.[13]

Bodin also gives a historical account of the decline of slavery in most Christian countries by about 1250. This he attributes to an 'imitation' of 'the law of *Mohamet*, who set at liberty all them of his religion'.[14] Thanking Mohammedan ideas and practices for establishing a better moral standard, which was then imitated by Christians and Jews,[15] Bodin clearly stands out against those who would berate Islamic civilisation.

Implicitly, this would include the participants in the *Colloquium* who deride Octavius. However, in the *Colloquium*, Bodin's praise of Islam is presented obliquely. Equally oblique is the means that Coronaeus uses to steer robust exchanges in cross-cultural dialogue away from a rowdiness that is unfair to one participant. What Coronaeus does in the face of mounting dissent is to employ a ruse, announcing that dinner is served, in order to halt the discussion. That this is a ruse is apparent from the narrator's wry remark that at this point '[Coronaeus] realised the discussion about the most serious matters would have been drawn out too long' (232). This remark is similar to the mock-daft remarks made by Gower and Jamy in *Henry V* intending to defuse dissension there, for like theirs Coronaeus' intervention mock-ignores, and thereby helps to annul, a clash threatening to lead to destructive resentment.

Sadly for us, humorous conflict-deflecting tactics cannot always check the dissensions that threaten a developing tolerance. Identifying commonalities between Bodin's and Shakespeare's settings, in which such tactics are dramatised as successful, may indicate what is required for their effectiveness. Of course there are differences between Shakespeare's portrayal of an intra-ethnic encounter within an army during the hurry and stress of war, and Bodin's of a meeting of diverse believers in a cultured and leisured setting; for one, Shakespeare's captains would naturally be more irascible men than Bodin's urbane dialogists. Yet it may not be too much a Fluellenism to describe analogies that do pertain: Shakespeare's captains differ in nationality, Bodin's debaters differ in religion; the captains set out to compare differing views on military strategy, the debaters do the same about faith. Moreover, although in both Shakespeare's and Bodin's set-ups the protagonists may be drawn together in dialogue by some or all of simple curiosity, a desire to work together, and a perceived need for coexistence in a world shrunken by war, travel, migration, or trade, what is made explicit in both cases is an overarching motive that may be labelled epistemological desire. That is, the participants in both encounters set out to compare their own with others' views in order to increase their grasp of matters for which they have a strong desire for competence or knowledge, be these matters the best means to wage war, or to worship God.

Desire, together with the perceived possibility of some shared work towards fulfilling it, is what (in all cases in Shakespeare's plays) is seen to bridge national, cultural, gender, or ethnic divisions (or tragically to fail to bridge them). In Bodin's representation, religious differences do not fall into a separate category.

3. ARGUMENTS FOR RELIGIOUS LIBERTY IN SHAKESPEARE'S ENGLAND

As the last chapter has pointed out, after the Reformation various degrees of religious pluralism were allowed in several parts of Europe, for a variety of reasons. It has even been argued that King James argued for the toleration of Roman Catholicism in England, but that his 'respect for the inviolability of the human conscience was frustrated and he was not allowed to offer the toleration he wanted to the recusants because of the Pope's reaction; it did however help to anger and alienate the "Puritan" faction within the realm'.[16] James's pronouncements on this topic were complex or contradictory,[17] but certainly there were many other unambiguously conscientious calls in the post-Reformation era for the establishment of religious tolerance and the cessation of cruel religious persecution.[18]

Among the most famous of such early tolerationist demands were those expressed in Sebastian Castellio's dedication of his Bible translation to Edward VI of England (1551), and in his several published condemnations of the 1553 burning for heresy in Calvin's Geneva of the theologian Michael Servetus.[19]

Some recent scholars have argued that most pre-Enlightenment arguments for religious tolerance were either cynical, *politique*, or merely self-serving on the part of persecuted minorities. One, for example, holds that in England the Dutch Reformed stranger community, exiled under Mary, after their readmission by Elizabeth helped to persecute Anabaptists. This argument concludes, 'Those Protestants who considered tolerance and persuasion the only way forward, such as Haemstede and Acontius, remained an insignificant minority in the sixteenth century, often marginalised and victimised by their own co-religionists.'[20] Another holds that:

The occasional visionary thinker such as Dirck Coonhert should not disguise the fact that in the main, toleration in this period was only ever likely to be the party cry of the disappointed, the dispossessed, or the seriously confused . . . in the early modern period [toleration] was only ever a loser's creed; and one which, if the Calvinist church leaders of the Dutch Republic were anything to go by, could easily be abandoned when yesterday's persecuted minority became today's dominant elite.[21]

But sixteenth-century works like Castellio's, Bodin's, and many others[22] quite vividly give models for, or plead for, a non-self-serving tolerance, and these may have been widely impressive or inspiring.

Yet this does not in itself uphold a now often-disputed 'Whiggish' historical narrative in which 'liberal' principles of religious toleration steadily emerged and took root in the Europe of the sixteenth and seventeenth centuries. Lately opponents of such a historical narrative have scored some successes when re-examining particular cases in detail.[23] But, overall, the recent deluge of works on sixteenth-century pre- or proto-tolerance remains divided on such questions.[24]

Within the framework of such issues I will consider henceforth only pre-1616 English examples of calls for religious tolerance. The reasons are to avoid overloading the discussion, and to attend closely to the unique religious positioning of England in the post-Reformation world, which provided Shakespeare's immediate environment.

Comprehensive scholarly surveys of tolerationist writings show that early modern England did not produce many texts resembling those of eirenic humanists like Erasmus, radical theologians like Denck, Franck, Coornhert, or Castellio, or sceptical philosophers like Montaigne.[25] Notable among the relatively few pre-1616 English tolerationist writings is *Europae Speculum*. This treatise by Edwin Sandys was completed in Paris in April 1599, after three years of Continental travel. It at first circulated only in manuscript, but was later frequently republished and translated. Its first three editions, all titled *A Relation of the State of Religion . . . in the Severall States of these Westerne Parts of the World*, appeared in rapid succession in England between June and November of 1605,[26] just before the Gunpowder Plot.[27] They were ordered to be burnt by the Court of High Commission on 3 November 1605, possibly because Sandys had been very contentious in James I's first Parliament,[28] or possibly because his book, although often even tediously anti-papist,[29] also praises some Roman Catholics and Catholic practices.

Sandys's treatise evidently attempts to make balanced and objective assessments of Europe's contemporary religions. Yet some of its views clearly derive from ideology; thus it consistently condemns Islam and its followers, using terms like an 'impious abhomination' (Z3v) and the 'grand enemie the Turke' (S3v). But when Sandys describes the Protestants, Catholics, Greek Orthodox, and Jews he has observed, he conspicuously mixes sympathy and antipathy. For example, he approves of the 'Greeke Church, who beside their Great Lent, have three other Lents also in the yeare, though the other neither so long, nor yet so strict', and in the same paragraph notes parenthetically 'for even the Iewes and Turkes have their Lent, though different'. However, this ecumenical approval is embedded within an attack on the numerous private vices and social iniquities of 'Italian Romanistes', which are claimed to be held in check *only* during Lent (C1r).

Nonetheless, some offsetting praise is given to Roman Catholicism as well. Sometimes Catholic vices are simply compared with similar Protestant ones, as, for example, in a discussion of 'Martyrologie[s]' in which Sandys accuses both sides of partisan distortions of historical truth.[30] And sometimes particular aspects of Catholicism are said to be worthy of Protestant emulation, as, for instance, Catholic Italy's 'exceeding good provision of Hospitals and houses of pietie, for olde Persons enfeebled, for poore folkes maimed or diseased'.[31] Catholicism also has a political superiority over Protestantism, according to Sandys, in its 'vnitie... which proceeds from authoritie' (S3r).

Sandys condemns divisions between Lutheran and Calvinist factions not only because these advantage the Pope. They distress him also because they undercut his much-desired goal of a reconciliation of post-Reformation divisions within Christianity in what he calls a 'proiect of vnion' (S4r). Yet, on consideration, Sandys despairs of that goal, holding it to be nearly impossible (T2v). For he sees the Turkish empire as too enfeebled to force a unification for defence upon Western Christianity, Catholicism and Protestantism each too powerful for either to overcome the other, and both too stubborn to make accommodations (T1r–V3v). Thus Catholics will not give up their 'offensive ceremonies', while Protestants will not 'purge out that negative and contradictorie humour, of thinking they are then rightest when they are vnlikest the Papacy; & then neerest to God when furthest from Rome' (T1r–v).

Discussing his dreamed-of 'project', Sandys imagines a new Christian unity based on an ideal of religious tolerance in which 'it should be lawfull for each man to beleeve as hee found cause, not condemning others with such peremptorinesse as is the guise of some men of over-weening conceits' (T2r). Such men include those recalcitrant Protestants who are unable to 'finde [in Catholicism] some excellent order of government, some singular helpes for increase of godlinesse and devotion for the conquering of sinne, for the profiting of vertue: and contrariwise, in themselves... finde ther is no such absolute perfection in their doctrine and reformation, as some dreamers in the pleasing viewe of their owne actions doe fancie' (T1v).

If unity were achieved, writes Sandys, a religion might be founded 'whose rote is Truth, whose braunches are Charitie, whose fruites are good deedes, extending and ever offering themselves vnto all men, to the encouraging of friendes, and reclaiming of enemies'. Regarding 'his enemie' (he means Roman Catholicism, as all this appears in a context condemning the Inquisition), this religion would be satisfied 'onely to repress him, as maie disinable him thence forwardes from doing hurte vnto others' (Lɪv).

Sandys also hints at the specifics of that religion. He implies it should be led by the post-Reformation English Church, which uniquely in Europe shows the 'moderation and measure' required. For the English are 'the onely nation that walk the right way of iustifiable reformation, in comparison with other, who have runne headlong rather to a tumultuous innovations'. He continues that only in the English Reformation was seen 'a great part of their own Cleargie according and confirming themselves vnto it, no *Luther*, no *Calvine*, the square of their faith . . . The succession of Bishops, and vocation of Ministers continued . . . the more ancient vsages not cancelled.' With regard to the 'Church of Rome', English reformers, moreover, showed 'no humor of affecting contrarietie, but a charitable indevour rather of conformitie'; thus English Protestants 'concurring entirely with neither side, yet reverenced of both, are the fitter and abler to worke vnity between them' (V3v–V4r).

In the light of such ecumenical hopes and claims,[32] it is not surprising that Sandys showed a mixed response to the papacy. The body of Sandys's text is packed with familiar anti-Catholic accusations of forged miracles, sales of (or blackmail by) indulgences, a cruel Inquisition, subversive Jesuits, licentious friars, Roman censorship, and political skulduggery in the Catholic hierarchy. Yet Sandys is respectful of the current pope, Clement VIII, who, he says, 'carieth the name of a good Pope', being 'both good man, good Prince, and good Prelate' (O5v–P2r).

Wholly differing from Sandys's strategic vision of a reunified (Anglican) Christianity finding space even for a chastened papacy, Leonard Busher's little book of 1614, *Religions Peace or A reconciliation, between princes & Peoples, and Nations* is wholly idealistic in its plea for complete religious liberty.[33] This plea for total liberty of conscience was addressed, from the safety of Amsterdam, to James I and his Parliament. An exiled English Baptist, Busher undoubtedly hoped for an end to the the persecution of his sect. Yet very little specifically Baptist doctrine finds its way into his strongly Protestant, biblically oriented arguments.

Busher repeatedly urges two themes, the un-Christian cruelty of persecution, and the fact that the Roman Church is what *Revelation* calls 'a *mystery, great Babylon, the mother of whoredoms and abominations of the earth, &c.'* (46). Yet the first theme overrides the second, and the thrust of Busher's argument is that all religious expressions should be allowed, that 'Religions Peace' must trump all other goals. So, for instance, a repeated complaint against 'idol-bishops' (whom Busher blames for persecution), is put into second place when he writes 'I shall be content therewith, and so I wish all others; for we all ought to be content if we obtain liberty of conscience' (66).

Busher's plea is therefore not for a reconciliation or fusion of religions, like Sandys's, but for radical religious coexistence.[34] He sees this aim, indeed, as linked to other God-given ones:

For if the holy laws of God's word be practiced and executed after Christ's will, then shall neither king, prince, nor people be destroyed for difference in religion. Then treason and rebellion, as well as burning, banishing, hanging, or imprisoning, for difference in religion, will cease and be laid down. Then shall not men, women, and youth be hanged for theft. Then shall not the poor, lame, sick, and weak ones be stocked and whipped . . . neither the rich oppress the poor by usury and little wages. (69–70)

Then he associates freedom of conscience with many other biblically supported changes for England, including rights to divorce, manumission from servitude after six years, and also 'Then shall the Jews inhabit and dwell under his majesties dominion, to the great profit of his realms, and to their furtherance in faith' (71).

4. QUESTIONING SHAKESPEARE ON RELIGION

I will eventually try to locate a Shakespearian stance on contemporary religions in relation to the spectrum of positions on religious tolerance we have considered. This is a spectrum ranging from Sandys's political idea of a merger of European faiths in an English-led *via media*, through Busher's call for an unlimited 'liberty of conscience' despite his strong dislike of the prelatical, up to Bodin's image of a multiple-faith dialogue giving respect and dignity to every participant.

Clearly Busher's programme for total religious freedom was neither accepted nor acceptable in Shakespeare's time.[35] Even more unacceptable would have been Bodin's image of various Christians, Jews, Muslims, and even freethinkers participating as equals in dialogue, with each helping the others to strengthen, and not abandon, their separate beliefs. And even Sandys's John Stuart Mill-like proposal for the non-repression of a papist 'enemie', on the sole condition that he would not 'thence forwardes [do any] hurte vnto others', was far in advance of its time. Yet, although none of the proposals of Bodin, Sandys, or Busher was practical, yet they all presented visions of change. Forward-looking visions can sometimes suffuse literary productions even more than what is currently acceptable or practicable.

However, before I can proceed to ask where Shakespeare may have stood in relation to these three types of religious tolerance, I will have to confront a range of recent proposals that identify him as a religious sectarian and hence unlikely to be in favour of tolerance of any sort. These proposals take the form of biographical hypotheses which are then often linked to alleged specific but covert religious allusions in Shakespeare's work. Their claims, if accepted, would disrupt any alternative readings of Shakespeare's responses to religions, so we must pause to consider them.

Typically, the claim has been made that Shakespeare was, or nearly was, a secret Catholic. Thus his interests would have focused on religious tenacity and religious persecution, not tolerance. He would therefore, it is typically argued, have been extremely sensitive to the rigours and cruelties arising in post-Reformation religious conflict.

It cannot be denied that sectarian cruelties attracted much attention: we have discussed the scandal of Calvin's execution of Michael Servetus for heresy, the abhorrence shared by all of Bodin's dialogists for religious persecutions and expulsions, John Foxe and Edwin Sandys on martyrology, and Leonard Busher's impassioned plea for an end to 'burning, banishing, hanging, or imprisoning, for difference in religion'. No doubt, also, Shakespeare's plays indicate that he consistently despised cruelty. But a certain fact stands out despite this: for whatever reason, Shakespeare's few mentions of blood-soaked persecutions, such as punishment of heresy, are all either metaphorical or refer to historical anachronisms.[36] Thus Graham Greene was able to remark that although Shakespeare's 'huge world of comedy and despair' portrayed much of the Elizabethan scene, it wholly neglected the contemporary 'routine of the [religious] torture chamber'.[37]

Despite such an absence, starting from a premise of Shakespeare's Catholic family background Arthur Marotti has identified a range of possible allusions in various plays to the persecution of English Catholics.[38] One of these, a supposed subtext of *Titus Andronicus* in which the grotesque human suffering and sacrifices seen in that play's Rome stand in for post-Reformation Christian wars and martyrdoms, is supported in detail in a closely argued article by Nicholas Moschovakis. Moschovakis asks a type of question that could be applied equally to many similarly associative readings of Shakespearian sectarian concerns: does *Titus*, a play never touching on Christianity, necessarily evoke 'the pathos of the [Reformation] religious struggle'?[39]

The correct answer to such a model question may well be that, as Marotti has pointed out regarding another possible Shakespearian sectarian allusion, 'Shakespeare's audience probably did not perceive [such] material in a uniform way.'[40] That is, for some the four references to martyrdom in *Titus* might have suggested Reformation horrors, but for others the play's focus would have fallen squarely on the fascinating question of the downfall of ancient Rome.[41]

Similarly in other places where critics propose definite connections between strife in Shakespeare's plays and post-Reformation specifics, those connections may be associative by-blows of dramatisations of more universal themes. Both history and myth provide a surfeit of examples of shifts in values occasioning tragedies, such as in Euripides' *The Bacchae*, when a new cult comes to Thebes.

Even in *Hamlet*, which clearly does contain allusions to specific Renaissance sectarian doctrines and disputes, these may have been severely overplayed in some recent critical readings. For instance the play's image of Hamlet's father as an armed Ghost from purgatory may have alluded not so much to disputed Catholic doctrines as to a militaristic code that Hamlet feels is 'More honoured in the breach than the observance'.[42] For we learn that the former King Hamlet had killed the elder Fortinbras, indeed on the very day of Hamlet's birth (1.1.79–85, 5.1.140–5); despite his idealisation of his father, Hamlet, as an up-to-date humanistic scholar, might find such strong-armed approaches to diplomacy unpalatable. Such a 'secular' reading, moreover, could be translated niftily into a 'religious' one that reverses both of the more usual religious interpretations. In one of these Hamlet is a Puritan and in the other he finds reasons to regret the passing of Catholicism.[43] We could hypothesise Hamlet as neither, but at first as imaging pre-Reformation eirenic Christian humanism satirically mocking an old order, and then see him dragged disastrously into old-style chivalric single combat allegorizing the all-sundering conflicts of the Reformation and Counter-Reformation.

I have sketched several alternative readings of *Hamlet* in relation to the Reformation in order to suggest that no one of these commands assurance. All, it seems to me, undervalue the full universality of the meditation in *Hamlet* on the often outrageous human cost of great shifts of societal configurations or beliefs.

I am, of course, not suggesting by this that religion was unimportant to Shakespeare, nor joining those who would occlude this importance.[44] But I do suspect that circularity undermines many recently heard arguments alleging that Shakespeare's ambiguities or tenuousness about sectarian matters somehow indicate that these must have been centrally important for him personally and artistically. Such circularity most often begins with far from securely founded assertions about Shakespeare's personal or familial Catholic background, and then argues that Shakespeare's textual evasions of clear religious self-positioning evidence his secretive and fearful deep-rooted attachment to a persecuted faction.[45]

More subtly, using 'cultural poetics', Stephen Greenblatt gingerly rehearses the usual arguments suggesting Shakespeare's Catholicism, but does not 'need to believe that Shakespeare was himself a secret Catholic sympathizer'.[46] Without this certainty Greenblatt still proposes in *Hamlet* a nostalgia for England's Catholic past; Catholicism would have given Hamlet, or Shakespeare, a better chance to grieve over a father's recent death.[47] Such a speculative conflation of cultural memory with personal memory may serve to flesh out an imaginative reconstruction of Shakespeare's psycho-biography, but I wonder if fertile images of the loss of Catholicism are properly transferred to *Hamlet*? As suggested above, the bygone time suggested by the armed Ghost in *Hamlet* may be not a nostalgically viewed religious past, but rather an unregretted militaristic one. Or alternately, Greenblatt's 'pervasive pattern' of 'inconsistency' in the play (240), which indeed does mix Protestant with Catholic religious symbols, might imply a tolerantly syncretic or ecumenical religious outlook in *Hamlet*, rather than any fissive or nostalgic one.[48]

Moreover, even if Shakespeare when young did have a sensitive connection with zealously Catholic schoolmasters, neighbours, employers in Lancashire,[49] or parents,[50] much more certain facts show it very unlikely that he was later a secret papist, or traumatised by the plight of English Catholics. For if he had been, would he have chosen to live on familiar terms within a Huguenot Calvinist household? And yet, Shakespeare's portrayals of Malvolio, called a 'kind of puritan', or the 'precise' Angelo ('precisian' meaning Puritan), as well as the caricature of godly speech served up by Falstaff,[51] show it also impossible for Shakespeare to have been personally keen to see a more zealously Reformed religion. Shakespeare seems to have been committed to neither the pope nor Calvin; if asked to guess, I'd venture that he chose to live with the Mountjoys, and perhaps chose to associate with various Catholics, because he was deeply fascinated by all human outlooks including those foreign to his own propensities.

Some judicious close readers of Shakespeare's language and themes have detected Roman Catholic concerns and sensibilities in his work,[52] and others Protestant ones,[53] and I have no quarrel with either. But we might remark that Edwin Sandys, who as we have seen praised some Catholics and Catholic institutions, was the Protestant son of the combative and fiercely Reformed Archbishop of York of the same name.[54] Moreover, that Shakespeare's language resonates with Protestant texts may reflect mainly the fact that his culture at large was saturated by the language of the English Bible and of the liturgies and homilies of the Established Church.

In fact, several recent studies conclude that Shakespeare's plays were just like his England, culturally semi-Catholic and semi-Protestant.[55] For the majority of Elizabethans – those who were not engaged in recusant hunting, or professionally hampered by the demands of an Oath of Allegiance, or underground sectaries, or insurgents – religious tolerance is far from an impossible conception.

Pursuing subtle but debatable theological allusions in Shakespeare's plays may tell us less about such a situation than finding distinct engagements in Shakespeare texts with famously divisive contemporary religious issues, practical issues that had an impact on almost everyone's lives. Examples of such follow.

5. JOKES ABOUT RELIGION IN *ALL'S WELL THAT ENDS WELL*

Our discussion will next consider further connections of Shakespearian humour with religious differences, but this time not a genial humour, rather a rough and satiric one with dark undertones.

For convenience and for abbreviation's sake let me label crudely three factions in Elizabethan sectarian conflicts: moderate English Protestants, whom I'll call 'Anglicans', zealously Reforming English Protestants whom I'll call 'Puritans', and English Catholics. I will simply overlook here the many shades between and within these categories, such as recusant Catholics, church Catholics, parish Anglicans, proto-Presbyterians, proto-Laudians, and so on. This is because Shakespeare overlooks these, alluding only to the three rough categories named above in a run of jokes in *All's Well*. These jokes are not not entirely dissimilar to the modern sub-genre of jokes beginning 'A priest, a minister, and a rabbi . . .', that is, jokes hinging on tripartite religious divisions.

Since these jokes are both complex and topical, it is not surprising that the lines containing them are often simply cut in modern Shakespeare productions. It is surprising, however, that they have been overlooked by scholars with particular interests in Shakespeare's religious allusions, or especially those in *All's Well*.[56]

Quite a lot of detailed background has to be investigated before these jokes can be explained. To position them thematically within *All's Well* I must first mention the controversy over wardship in Shakespeare's time, and wardship's paradoxical interaction with Church laws requiring autonomous consent in the formation of marriages.

Through their rights to wardship Tudor monarchs or their assignees could direct the marriage choices of the children of some high-ranking families (determined by the type of tenure of land they possessed) who had become fatherless before they reached the age of majority. Very valuable wardship rights, including marriage, were sold to the highest bidders in the prerogative Court of Wards and Liveries, generating huge revenues. Just about when *All's Well* was written, a party in James I's first Parliament argued that this system was scandalous.[57]

The prudent Shakespeare moved his depiction of wardship in *All's Well* away from England, and made the widowed mother approve of rather than despair over the marriage imposed on her son. Nonetheless, the king's power to force young Count Bertram's marriage is treated as dubious.

A few years before he became Shakespeare's patron the young Earl of Southampton, a ward of Lord Burghley, was allegedly forced to pay a huge sum because he refused to agree to marry Burghley's granddaughter.[58] In law neither parents, guardians, nor monarchs could compel a marriage; indeed England still adhered to the medieval Church's ruling that required for valid marriage the consent of both parties. Yet it was still legal to compel a ward to pay a ruinous fine to avoid a forced marriage, because wardship was an economic commodity. The nature of a ward's marriage contradicted the ideal of 'companionate' marriage, and this ideal's promotion in a religious text will be seen to be the butt of the satiric joke we will be considering.

One aspect of English wardship law is exactly reflected in *All's Well*: Magna Carta guaranteed that a ward could refuse a forced marriage without paying fines if it led to his or her 'disparagement', meaning a marriage with someone either beneath them in rank, or diseased, defective, or insane. In Shakespeare's play the French king confers some kind of unnamed elevation of status upon the physician's daughter Helena, which, he implies, will suffice to forestall any such claim by Count Bertram (2.3.118–45). But this royal largesse (perhaps recalling James's sale of honours) only magnifies the problem of the imposition of an unwanted marriage choice upon a ward.

The problem of wardship was only an instance of a larger question that was causing legal and social perplexity in Shakespeare's time – namely how to regulate, for the social good, the nearly full autonomy in marriage formation theoretically allowed to men and women. The giving or withholding of economic marriage settlements by parents or others served this function to some degree,[59] but some sought tighter legal controls. These were brought in, following the English Reformation, only in the limited sense that certain prescribed actions and rituals ('posting banns', 'solemnisation') were required for marriage; however, as has been explained in Chapter 3, forming a marriage 'clandestinely', without the prescribed Anglican forms and rituals, although a spiritual offence, still resulted in a valid marriage.

Clandestine marriage or marriage by 'spousals' was an obsessive theme of the English stage, but, very unusually, *All's Well* 1.3 focuses on the opposite: the details of the requirements for making a 'solemnised', that is not-clandestine, marriage. By law, such a marriage had to be conducted following the rubrics and rituals specified in 'The Forme of Solemnization of Matrimonie' in the 1559 Book of Common Prayer.[60] Here is where the devil entered through the details.

The 1559 Prayer Book was the second of the revisions that followed Archbishop Cranmer's original version of 1549. These three versions reveal a kind of swaying in the Anglican settlement. The first, 1549, version was more Catholic-leaning than the very 'Reformed' second version of 1552. The revision of 1559, however, was slightly less Reformed, or Puritan, than that of 1552, and therefore failed to satisfy the desires of returning Marian exiles and others to advance the Reformation in England. Puritans especially objected to the 1559 marriage ceremony's requirement for ring-giving, which they held to be idolatrous, and to its inclusion of taking Communion; indeed any compulsory marriage ceremony, not being enjoined by the Bible (and empowering the Church hierarchy) offended some Puritans. Therefore, in defiance of the 1559 Act of Uniformity, some Puritan-leaning clergy covertly used alternative liturgies.

On the other hand, commissions to search out recusant Catholics investigated reports of unsolemnised clandestine marriages because many English Catholics, too, disliked the 1559 Prayer Book marriage ceremony. This was because of a Reformation bias in its liturgy, and on account of some of its doctrines on marriage. Catholics might have found especially untoward Cranmer's inclusion in the Prayer Book marriage service, retained in all versions, of a recitation by the priest of three purposes for marriage. These are first for procreation, second for avoiding fornication and sin, and lastly for 'mutuall society, helpe and coumfort'. That last notion, which has been associated by many historians with a new 'companionate' model of marriage,[61] was highly innovative, and certainly had not been seen before in 'any official liturgical marriage text'.[62] Cranmer cautiously placed it last among the three purposes of marriage, although the more radically Protestant theology professor, Martin Bucer, urged him to place it first.[63] Interestingly, this 'companionate' purpose is transposed to the first position in the official Elizabethan Homilie on Matrimony, an obligatory sermon.[64]

Now, at last, we may hear the first of the religious–ethnic jokes in *All's Well that Ends Well* 1.3. This arises when the clown Lavatch rehearses his three reasons to marry, spoofing the Prayer Book marriage ceremony.[65] The joke begins when Bertram's mother, the kindly Countess of Rousillion, rebukes Lavatch because of his reported sexual misbehaviour (1.3.8–12). In response to these accusations Lavatch deploys a mock-pious stance, while in fact effectively resembling the earlier court jester Touchstone, who had said frankly 'Come, sweet Audrey. / We must be married, or we must live in bawdry' (*As You Like It* 3.3.86–7). Excusing his desire to satisfy a sexual itch, the canting Lavatch thus begins with a sanctimonious-sounding plea to the Countess for financial support: 'I am poor,' he says, 'though many of the rich are damned. But if I may have your ladyship's good will to go to the world, Isbel the woman and I will do as we may' (*All's Well* 1.3.16–19). G. K. Hunter has interpreted the phrase 'go to the world' as one that 'must derive from the Catholic view of the essential carnality of marriage'.[66] If so, this would already point towards a confessional rift about the ideology of marriage.

Next, Lavatch launches into a parody version of the first Prayer Book reason for marrying, which is for 'the procreation of children to be brought up in the fear and nurture of the Lord'. Lavatch's perversion of this is: 'I think I shall never have the blessing of God till I have issue o' my body, for they say bairns are blessings'; note that he seeks a blessing for himself, and not the salvation of his child. The Countess then feeds Lavatch what he needs to develop his joke, asking him to 'Tell me thy reason why thou wilt marry.' Lavatch then parodies in turn, with cumulative satirical force, the remaining purposes for marriage given in the Elizabethan Prayer Book. The Prayer Book's second purpose, 'for a remedy against sin, and to avoid fornication', is translated by Lavatch into: 'I am driven on by the flesh, and he must needs go that the devil drives.' Thus, as well as traducing the Prayer Book, Lavatch also twists the meanings of traditional sayings or proverbs such as 'bairns are blessings' or 'the devil drives'.

Threefold cumulative structures are highly effective in comedy, and Lavatch applies this by topping his parodies of the Prayer Book's first two purposes for marriage in his version of the third, 'companionate' purpose. He starts with 'I have been, madam, a wicked creature, as you – and all flesh and blood – are, and indeed I do marry that I may repent.' Playing along, and noticing that each of his recitations makes use of some old saying or proverb, the Countess suggests that the allusion here is to 'Marry in haste, repent at leisure.' But Lavatch takes that proverb down an unexpected path. He links it with the stale Elizabethan jest that a certainty of cuckoldry comes with marrying, and then outrageously ties that to the Prayer Book's notion of companionate marriage for 'mutuall society, helpe and coumfort'. Such a marriage should provide a friend for life, and so Lavatch says to the Countess, 'I am out o' friends, madam, and I hope to have friends for my wife's sake.' She immediately picks up his drift, that these new 'friends' will be his wife's lovers, and he in response mock-justifies this by producing the syllogism: 'he that cherishes my flesh and blood loves my flesh and blood; he that loves my flesh and blood is my friend; ergo, he that kisses my wife is my friend.' Here Lavatch lampoons the third Prayer Book purpose for marriage, the specifically Protestant one,[67] and also the much older Pauline doctrine that man and wife become 'one flesh' (a phrase, by the way, which is included in the Prayer Book marriage service).[68]

This parodic joking is followed by two more jests in which Lavatch further alludes to contemporary religious divisions. First, he suggests that contending believers are not in essential matters different: 'young Chairbonne the puritan and old Poisson the papist, howsome'er their hearts are severed in religion, their heads are both one: they may jowl horns together like any deer i' th' herd.' His scurrilous theme is 'horning': the fish-eating old Catholic, who fasts on Fridays, and the meat-loving young Puritan who does not, are cuckolds alike. This leads on to Lavatch's exit lines, including: 'Though honesty be no puritan, yet it will do no hurt; it will wear the surplice of humility over the black gown of a big heart' (1.3.91–3), which jokingly allude to a contemporary sectarian 'vestiarian' controversy, also based on the Prayer Book, about which we will say more later.

What should we make of Lavatch's sardonic parody of a particularly controversial portion of the Prayer Book marriage service? The target of this derision is, I think, sectarian controversy itself, the hot divisiveness of the religious communities whose 'hearts', as he says, 'are severed in religion'. For in sequel to his parody Lavatch next derides both Catholics and Protestants, as he has just derided himself, for being destined to cuckoldry.

The tone in the parody supports this. Let's consider, for example, the mock-godliness in Lavatch's phrases such as 'have the blessing of God', 'the rich are damned', 'I have been . . . a wicked creature';[69] these partly resemble Falstaff's *faux* sanctimoniousness in the two *Henry IV* plays, but the implied motivation for their use is wholly different. Falstaff, when challenged to explain his egregious cowardice or dishonesty, often mimics a stern Puritanism outrageously at odds with his behaviour. For instance, he explains his habitual thieving with, ''tis my vocation . . . 'Tis no sin for a man to labour in his vocation' (*Henry IV, part 1* 1.2.104–5). This fools no one, yet deflects condemnation into admiration because of its vivacious audacity and ingenious slipperiness. By contrast, Lavatch's gestures of mock-godliness are not intended to delight roguishly; his humour is not genial but rather trenchantly satiric. Thus his gestures of self-denigration are opposites to Falstaff's deluded grandiosity and bidding for fame. Lavatch's scurrilous jests invite only infamy; the Countess calls him 'ever . . . a foul-mouthed and calumnious knave' (1.3.56–7).

Yet Lavatch's self-blazons of dishonour convey more than just cynical nihilist squalidity. On the contrary, in their extreme harshness they may be closer to Lear's Fool's value-laden paradoxes of folly than to Thersites' wild curses or Falstaff's base, if hilarious, evasions.[70]

6. SARDONIC LAUGHTER AT SECTARIANISM

A bitterly humorous inversion between wisdom and folly is a typical subversive response to circumstances that make systematic irrationality, no matter how stupid (for instance that of a domineering bureaucracy), unanswerable and uncontrollable.[71] In accord with this, in Eastern Europe before 1989, the mere mention of Armenian 'Radio Yerevan' evoked hilarity on account of a series of jokes that circulated in which a telephone-caller to this radio station, genuinely bewildered by double-think and lies, is answered by a gloomy 'expert' who typically begins with 'Yes, comrade, in principle, but . . .', and then presents a zany rendition of official advice.[72] A nice example, although lacking the 'but' clause, is:

CALLER   What shall we do in case of a nuclear war?
EXPERT   Cover yourself with a white bed-sheet and walk slowly towards the
         nearest cemetery.
CALLER   Why slowly?
EXPERT   So as not to cause any panic.

Logic gone topsy-turvy appears also in Lavatch's lines quoted above, 'Though honesty be no puritan, yet it will do no hurt; it will wear the surplice of humility over the black gown of a big heart' (1.3.91–3). These allude to the notorious 1559 Prayer Book rubric requiring the clerical use of 'such ornaments in the church as were in use by authority of Parliament in the second year of the reign of King Edward the sixth'.[73] This rubric was understood to require priestly surplices, which to some seemed papist clerical vestments, and thus 'caused anxiety and dismay among protestant subjects'.[74] In Lavatch's deliberately upside-down take on this, white surplices indicate 'humility', while the secretive black Genevan ministerial gowns that some Puritan clergy wore under their surplices conceal a prideful 'big heart'. Yet accusing Puritans of big-hearted (or black-hearted) pridefulness in their Nonconformity while equating the wearing of surplices with Christian humility is not simply an attack on Puritan pride, for shining vestments are *prima facie* more ostentatious than plain gowns. In the end only the paradox, transcending sectarian partisanship, stands out. Although not promoting tolerance directly, this scorns its absence.

Despite much recent speculation about his own religious partisanship, aside from in Lavatch's jests Shakespeare hardly ever explicitly names contemporary confessional communities. The few other exceptions are a couple of references to Puritans or precisians, as mentioned above, and the phrase 'spleeny Lutheran' used in *Henry VIII*. Nevertheless, Shakespeare often alluded to the controversial Prayer Book marriage ceremony. In *As You Like It* Jaques scorns the (seemingly Puritan) vicar Sir Oliver Martext, who holds it to be his 'calling' to conduct clandestine marriages omitting the Prayer Book requirements (3.3.96–7). Thus Jaques admonishes Touchstone: 'Get you to church, and have a good priest that can tell you what marriage is' (3.3.76–8). That would be to recite the Prayer Book's three purposes of marriage. On the other hand, the Prayer Book requirements are overlooked in the fact that none of the many lovers' rings mentioned by Shakespeare are exchanged during a marriage ceremony. In fact, all of the marriage solemnisations represented in Shakespeare plays are either interrupted, or else enacted offstage.[75] Examining that may bring us somewhat closer to understanding Shakespeare's views on the controversial Anglican rules.

The offstage marriage solemnisation ceremony reported in *The Taming of the Shrew* is a madcap affair. Petruchio is described bellowing out his consent to marry using a traditional Roman Catholic imprecation, 'God's wounds',[76] and then violently assaulting both priest and prayerbook:

> I'll tell you, Sir Lucentio: when the priest
> Should ask if Katherine should be his wife,
> 'Ay, by Gog's woun's,' quoth he, and swore so loud
> That all amazed the priest let fall the book,
> And as he stooped again to take it up
> This mad-brained bridegroom took him such a cuff
> That down fell priest, and book, and book, and priest.
> 'Now take them up,' quoth he, 'if any list'. (3.3.31–8)

Next, the stunned witness reports church wine sent flying about; this wild action alludes to highly controversial rubrics in the 1559 Prayer Book concerning the use of consecrated elements and the taking of Communion at weddings.

As has been argued in Chapter 2, the zany violence in *The Taming of the Shrew* is only misleadingly farcical, and rather has pointed significances (and, just as here, the violence is mainly reported and not seen in the play). The zaniness here is double edged. On the one hand, the rubric of Elizabethan Prayer Book directed that 'to take away the superstition, which any person hath or might have in the bread and wine' the Anglican Communion ceremony should use unconsecrated wine and ordinary white bread (not specially made wafers), and that 'if any of the bread or wine remain the curate shall have it to his own use'.[77] This is parodied in the offstage action in which Petruchio 'quaffed off the muscatel / And threw the sops all in the sexton's face, / Having no other reason / But that his beard grew thin and hungerly' (3.3.45–8); here he wildly exaggerates the Prayer Book's 'Reformed' denial of the real presence in the elements, and its rubric commanding the feeding of leftovers to the [hungry] clergy. On the other hand when Petruchio knocks down the book itself and the priest, he may seem to side with either Puritans, who found the Prayer Book ceremonially excessive (even in including Communion in a marriage ceremony), or Catholics (and not just Catholics), who found it deficient.[78]

Thus, Petruchio's wild actions and Lavatch's scurrilous jokes bear on the Prayer Book in similar ways: neither sides with specific sectarian demands, but both draw attention to sectarian divisiveness. My claim is that this is done precisely to protest against or mock that divisiveness. A somewhat similar craziness appears in the sonnet by John Donne beginning: 'Show me deare Christ, thy spouse, so bright and clear.'

Christ's spouse represents the true Church, and the poem expresses amazement that she has been disputably located in the three different homes of Protestant or Anglican, Calvinist, and Roman Catholic beliefs. Donne concludes:[79]

> Betray kind husband thy spouse to our sights,
> And let myne amorous soule court thy mild Dove,
> Who is most trew, and pleasing to thee, then
> When she'is embrac'd and open to most men.

Here promiscuous adultery is holy, and religious difference is irreligious. It is not surprising that this shocking poem remained unpublished until 1899.[80]

Bitter jests mocking religious polarisation would have been consistent with the view of Patrick Collinson that a silent majority in Shakespeare's England shunned the louder and more extreme sects of the age.[81] The responses of Shakespeare's audience to Lavatch's caustic jesting and deformed reasoning, or Petruchio's wild iconoclasm, may have reflected a deep perplexity, verging on despair, that doctrinal nuances could lead to murderous hatred.

7. CONCLUSION

There are two humorous passages in Edwin Sandys's *Relation* (curiously both of these have almost exact replicas in Thomas Coryate's famous 1611 *Crudities*).[82] In one, although Sandys finds some Jewish doctrine 'honourable and holy...drawing neere vnto the truth' (X3r), he misunderstands Italian Jews' rituals and liturgy (including keeping their 'bonets' on while praying) and so comments on their devotions: 'they are as reverend in their Synagogues, as Grammer boyes are at Schoole, when their master is absent' (X4r). In the other, Sandys points out with sympathy that the forced forfeiture of all their goods leaves 'nothing for a Iew converted but to be friared' (Y2v), that Jews 'preferre... Marriage before Virginity' (X3r), and this explains his earlier quip that in Italy 'as many Friars become Iewes, as Iewes become Friars' (X2r).

Shakespeare overlaps with Sandys in deploying humour when considering religious diversity, but there is no appearance that Shakespeare shares with him a vision of an Anglican-based reunification of universal Western Christendom. Also, although he shows a sense of humour very like Bodin's, Shakespeare's portrayal of the dire consequences of a dinner shared between Shylock and the Christians of Venice does not image, as does Bodin, any tolerant conviviality of differing religionists. Of the three discussed here, Busher's radical position on religious diversity seems to me closest to the position implied by Shakespeare's plays. For these exhibit bitter impatience with exclusive religious contentions or extremist demands, and thus imply that non-persecutory tolerance should trump all narrow sectarian aims.

CHAPTER 5

'Race', part one

The failure to allow for changes in the sense in which the word race has been used has important consequences, for those who misunderstand the past of their society are likely to misunderstand the present, because people judge the present in the light of what they believe the past to have been.[1]

1. PROSPECTUS

The following discussion of Shakespeare, tolerance, and what we now call 'race' will be divided between this chapter and the next. This one will concentrate on love and desire (including 'miscegenation'), while the next will be concerned with international topics like slavery and New World encounters. The present chapter will consider *Othello*, for example, as a play in which bigotry begets bigotry, that is, antipathy to a 'black' Moorish man leads to the evil stereotyping of a 'white' Venetian woman. The following chapter will analyse images of slavery in *Othello* and elsewhere, and will focus particularly on Prospero's two exotic servants in *The Tempest*.

2. 'RACE' IN SHAKESPEARE'S TIME

Throughout its (sadly continuing) life the spurious notion of there being a small handful of colour-coded, distinct human 'races' has always been both equivocal and historically unstable. This complicates current perplexities, and perhaps some confusion, over whether questions of 'race' are anachronistic in, or properly relevant to, discussions of Shakespeare's writing.[2] I am sorry to enter a dermatological prior to a dramaturgical nexus, yet some questioning of 'race' itself must preface a questioning of race in relation to Shakespeare.

Only one of the numerous distinct meanings of 'race' given in the *OED* need concern us: this is the one defined in 'race' 2, I.1.d: 'One of the great divisions of mankind, having certain physical peculiarities in common'. Any clarification offered by this definition does not outlast the

OED heading, which goes on to remark testily that 'even among anthropologists there is no generally accepted classification or terminology'. Perhaps the lexicographers' frustration arises because the 'great divisions' in question never had any reality except as constructs of bigoted ideologies. If so, when faced with the problems of defining 'race' for Shakespeare's age we will have to ask if that term had any meaning at all in common with its later uses.

To clarify discussion, henceforth (except in quotations) I will use the capitalised term 'Race' to refer to race in the sense of *OED* 2, I.1.d. Similarly (despite their being according to the *OED* equivalent terms) I will differentiate 'Racialist' from 'racist', reserving 'Racialist' to designate those who believe there are indeed a few human Races, and 'racist' to designate those showing antipathies toward persons or groups on account of skin colouring, hair textures, facial shapes, or other superficial somatic features.

In this sense, racists do not necessarily have to be Racialists;[3] indeed, without that fact this chapter might have to end here. For Racialist theories – for example, claims that humankind may be parcelled into two, three, or up to as many as eleven physically differing Races – were unknown in Shakespeare's time.[4] The earliest *OED* illustration of 'Race' used in the Racialist sense (2, I.2.d) is dated 1774. Moreover, despite a few very odd – seemingly desperate – scholarly attempts to find it,[5] the word 'race' bearing the sense 'Race' never appears in Shakespeare's language, or that of his contemporaries.[6] To highlight the total absence of 'race' in the sense of 'Race' from Shakespeare's own lexicon, we might note that by contrast his works do employ the word 'nation' – with meanings reasonably similar to modern ones – about forty times.

Moreover, further to confuse matters, even now there are many competing meanings for 'Race'.[7] When this uncertainty is overwritten by critics' strong feelings about current Race relations, literary studies sometimes show the effects of what communications engineers call 'crosstalk': that is, interference between diverse messages. For instance, some who see only socially constructed myths in Racialist conceptions still effectively essentialise Race by arguing that transcendence of Racial boundaries must inevitably produce 'alienation'. Various twentieth-century souls on ice have trod this path, and some Shakespeare critics, seemingly following in their footsteps, have described the 'noble Moor' met in *Othello* as from the start a cringing subaltern, or more subtly as a man destined by Racialism never to attain personal authenticity.[8]

On another level, many today view 'Race' as a vitally important political, economic, and sociological category despite its lack of any meaningful biological basis. These are often inclined to divide humanity into only two symbolic Races, the 'white' and 'black', thus making a well-deserved nonsense of any structural anthropological use of the concept Race. Although it has been convincingly argued that the words 'black' and 'white' were not yet used in Shakespeare's time as metaphoric signifiers for Race,[9] it will still sometimes be convenient here to adopt a language of Black and White, or Blacks and Whites (again I will use capitals to replace unsightly scare quotes).

Interestingly, Elizabethan usage of a term other than Race was partly analogous to a twofold division of humanity into White and Black. Of course, explorers and savants in Shakespeare's time and before had often remarked that diverse geographical places present a variety of human appearances, in terms of typical stature, hair colour or texture, skin tone, facial features, etc. By Shakespeare's time anthropological reports were available concerning such far-flung places as North Africa, sub-Saharan Africa, the Levant, south Asia, east Asia, and the Americas. Yet the peoples from all or any of those distant regions were on occasion each separately (and inconsistently) called 'Moors' by various Elizabethan writers.[10] In addition, the unstable category of 'Moors' could carry contradictory positive and negative valuations.[11] Although a 'Moor' could not possibly have referred then to what is meant today by those who speak politically and positively of 'people of colour', it is worth noting that a single if confused term was widely applied to non-European humanity in Shakespeare's England.

On the other hand, the unsteady definition of 'a Moor' for Shakespeare's contemporaries may tend to confirm that the boundaries of colour consciousness were not at all firmly erected in his time (and indeed 'Moor' often designated a national or religious category, rather than a Racial one). Moreover, human categories defined by pigmentation seem to have been at least semi-permeable in Shakespeare's own usage. Thus several of Shakespeare's dramatic or poetic characters are textually identified as 'black' or 'tawny', yet distinctly are not, in Racialist terms, Black. These include 'black' Thurio (in *Two Gentlemen of Verona* 5.2.10), 'Ethiope . . . tawny' Hermia (*A Midsummer Night's Dream* 3.2.258, 264), pale Rosaline said to be black in her eyes, face, and hair (*Love's Labour's Lost* 3.1.192 and 4.3.252–72), and, most intriguingly, Shakespeare's 'tawny', 'gypsy', or 'black' Cleopatra (*Antony and Cleopatra* 1.1.6, 1.1.10, 1.5.28 – see the Afterword). There was also, of course, the 'dark lady' of Shakespeare's sonnets. That these black, but not necessarily Black, Elizabethan literary figures were not unique is proved by the praise in Philip Sidney's famous sonnet sequence *Astrophil and Stella* of a black-eyed beloved.[12]

Perhaps the funniest contrarian literary treatment of female complexion seen Shakespeare's time, or any other, appears in *Love's Labour's Lost* in an interchange between the witty page Moth and Don Armado. Moth condemns the conventional beauty of red-and-white-faced ladies because the first of these colours can disguise ignoble 'blushing . . . faults', and the second ignoble 'fears', and so assures Armado that the 'complexion' of the biblical Samson's love was 'sea-water green' (1.2.80–101).

Because hot pursuit of connections between Race and gender can lead to endless complexities,[13] I will be minimalist in this chapter and not further comment on Shakespeare's merely darker than usual, green, or vari-coloured ladies, in terms of Race. But it might be noted that for Shakespeare and others of his time, female comeliness was able to transcend the colour-coded canonical norm of white-and-red perfection.

The least that we may conclude from all this is the unsurprising fact that differences of human skin pigmentation were not invisible to Shakespeare or his contemporaries. Just how significant they seemed to them is much more difficult to assess. For instance, Shakespeare's Hermia is rejected by Lysander on account of her dark complexion, and a few lines later she is insulted even more vigorously by Helena on account of her short or compact stature (she is called a 'puppet', to which she replies by calling the tall Helena a 'painted maypole' (*A Midsummer Night's Dream* 3.2.289–99)). References to the (short) stature of Moth in *Love's Labour's Lost* or Maria in *Twelfth Night*, as well as to the statures of Helena or Hermia, clearly serve varied purposes, including insulting, jocular, or affectionate ones. It thus appears that such physical peculiarities may have been amusing to, but did not seem of essential importance to, Shakespeare's milieu; for instance, without the interventions of Puck's philtre 'love in idleness' tall Helena and short Hermia seem to be equally attractive. Shakespeare makes light of 'height-ism' here, and so why might he not do the same of colour prejudice?

Yet, famously, several Black Shakespearian characters are heard to exclaim 'is black so base a hue?', to plead 'Mislike me not for my complexion', or to lament, love-lorn, 'Haply for I am black, . . . She's gone.'[14] These phrases show that Shakespeare portrayed within his Black characters distinct anticipations of an antipathy aroused by their skin tones. Moreover, in two casual remarks in plays of Shakespeare's middle period, both in contexts highly discreditable to their speakers, Pandarus uses 'a blackamore' as a metonym for an ugly woman in his mock-bitter comparison of Cressida with the slightly fairer-haired Helen (1.1.77), and, pointing to two portraits, Hamlet bitterly disparages his mother's love for

Claudius with the incredulous 'And batten on this moor?' (3.4.66). Such verbal uses suffice to establish that in Shakespeare's time racist attitudes were possibilities, if not Racialism and its theories of Race.

For lack of evidence, there is no way to break down the likely racist attitudes of Shakespeare's audiences along, so to speak, 'class' or status lines, although attempts have been made to do so.[15] Nor, despite attempts that have also been made,[16] are demonstrations of contemporary writings containing racist remarks useful for determining the likely 'average' attitudes of Shakespeare's audiences. For there are no data available concerning Shakespearian audiences' access to such materials, what, if any, alternative materials (especially word-of-mouth ones) might have influenced them, and what their responses to such materials might have been.[17]

There are, however, clear indications in Shakespeare's own work that an unquestioned racism could not have been the sole or even dominant attitude of his auditors. As remarked above, several of Shakespeare's Black characters manifest anxieties about possible racial intolerance, and some actually ask for tolerance. These figures necessarily speak with and to the conceptual possibilities of the time of their creation. This makes it clear that something like racial tolerance must have been an alternative to intolerance, and an alternative perceivable by Shakespeare's audiences.

And yet many recent commentators strongly emphasise a supposed monolithic racism pervading Shakespeare's actual and imagined worlds. In support of this, most quote certain Elizabethan texts; but it is worth noting that the variety of these texts has been small, and their uses very repetitive. In consequence, careful revisionist studies have recently re-examined or recontextualised the favourite texts or passages of those who have alleged a norm of Elizabethan racism.[18]

The texts in question include a few letters written by Queen Elizabeth in 1596 and 1601, which have frequently been cited as if they commanded the wholesale expulsion of Blacks from England, an ethnic cleansing.[19] In fact these letters ordered the deportation of a relatively small number (first ten, then eighty-nine) of 'blackmoores' or 'Negars and Blackamores', and for a specific purpose. Emily Bartels has reconsidered their motives in relation to Elizabethan suspicions of Spain (the Moors in question were former Spanish subjects). She has also shown that the deportations were intended to effect an exchange for the ransoming of an equal number of English prisoners held in Spanish captivity. Thus she judges that the whole affair was 'shaped, complicated and compromised by political and economic circumstances'.[20]

What has misled commentators is that Elizabeth's rhetoric did not match her intentions. One contradiction pointed out by Bartels is that although in 1601 Elizabeth stressed that many Blacks had 'crept into this realm' to the detriment of unemployed English persons, she actually sought to deport very few. There are also indications that Elizabeth's requests for masters to donate their Black servants fell on deaf ears. Bartels supposes economic reasons lay behind this reluctance (319), but possible resistance to surrendering members of the household (as English servants then were) to the hated Spaniards may have played some part as well in their masters' non-compliance.

Further observations might be added to Bartels's reanalysis. She suggests the possibility of a more racist tone to the second Elizabethan demands of 1601, as compared with those of 1596 (although she does not make the common error of interpreting Elizabeth's rhetoric as seriously demanding the expulsion of all Blacks). Against this, we might note first that in 1601 Elizabeth needed to compensate her Dutch intermediary for arranging the release of exactly eighty-nine captured Englishmen. In lieu of paying a cash ransom, Elizabeth seemed thriftily to have negotiated to supply the Spanish with exactly eighty-nine English-captured 'Negars or Blackamores'. This equality of numbers hardly speaks to any notion of the inequality of the Races. Indeed Elizabeth's chief pretext for the expulsion was that the 'Blackamores' had taken over Englishmen's jobs, not that they were inferior or incapable persons.

Another favourite passage that has been repeatedly cited in support of the proposition that Shakespeare's contemporaries were all Racialists appeared in a 1578 travel narrative by the sailor George Best. This expounds a theory that Africans are the descendants of Noah's accursed son Ham, or Cham, and that Africans are therefore, on account of Ham's sinful concupiscence, all destined to blackness and enslavement. For at least twenty years it has been repeatedly claimed that Best's notions represented a widespread characteristic Elizabethan belief,[21] although some classic studies did not agree.[22]

Yet the Bible-reading publics of Shakespeare's age would certainly have known that there is no scriptural authority for Ham's posterity being Black Africans, nor for Africans having to suffer the consequences of Noah's curse on Ham.[23] Indeed, recent scholarship has shown that the expression of a theory of Africans' derivation from the seed of Ham 'is rare' in other discussions of Africa contemporary with Best's,[24] and that, in general, any 'connection of Cham with Africa is contentious in the Renaissance'.[25] Even the very influential early work of Winthrop Jordan, which generally argues for Elizabethan racism, claims that 'When the story of Ham's curse did become relatively common in the seventeenth century it was utilised almost entirely as an explanation of colour rather than as justification for Negro slavery, and as such it was probably denied more often than affirmed.'[26] Also, a fascinating study by Benjamin Braude gives a surprising account of how claims of the Renaissance adherence to the connection of Ham with Africa and slavery were to a great extent a product of nineteenth- and twentieth-century scholarly Racialism.[27]

Another favourite text often selectively quoted to argue for widespread Elizabethan Racialism is John Porry's 1600 translation (with modifications and additions) of John Leo Africanus' 1550 *History and Description of Africa*. Yet the pioneer of the field of Shakespeare and Africa, Eldred Jones, holds that Porry's version of John Leo's study had a positive, or at least mixed positive and negative, impact on English estimations of Africa: Jones even suggests that modern Europeans give less credit to Africa's peoples and civilisations than Leo did.[28]

Such disagreements illustrate a diversity of opinion which a survey of Shakespeare criticism confirms. Among the hundreds of books and essays published between 1962 and 2007 identified as concerned with 'race' by the online *World Shakespeare Bibliography*, there is no consistency at all of either starting points or conclusions. Some kind of a path through this maze must be traced. An account of the hotly contested divisions between the many who hold that Shakespeare's age was racist, others who have objected that racism (no less Racialism) was not of great importance for Shakespeare,[29] and yet others who would qualify both those positions,[30] could be attempted, but might not be very instructive. A more helpful approach might be to consider how commentators on early modern England differ in their ideas about possible motivations for racism.

Two broad schools of thought are seen in a contrasting pair of classic theoretical works. The first is Margaret Hodgen's *Early Anthropology in the Sixteenth and Seventeenth Centuries*, which claims that because in England then 'no political or economic interest called for a theoretical imputation of debasement with respect to any group of dependent people', and because it was believed, in accord with Genesis, that all humans were created in a single act, 'neither skin color nor the natural anxiety caused by conflict with enemies such as the Muslims or the Tartars led to anything like what we now know as racial "tension".'[31] Thus, Hodgen held that Racialism in England must have arisen after Shakespeare, for there were in his time no political and economic interests to provoke it.

Contrastingly, another influential text, Winthrop D. Jordan's *White over Black*, asserts that English racist stereotyping and denigration of

African Blacks pre-dated by centuries their economic exploitation in the slave trade and on England's transatlantic plantations. Jordan found prejudicial English responses to Africans in several early texts, indeed the very texts usually cited by those who have followed him.[32] Jordan in addition proposed a theory of how such Racialism arose well before English New World colonialism. This is that inner explorations of the psyche prompted by the Reformation turned up images of what were seen as dark (often sexual) impulses in Europeans, while at the same time the accelerating evolution of a market-driven economy inspired widespread fears of insubordination, disorder, and rapaciousness; these negative images and fears of spiritual and other deformities were projected outwards by Englishmen, according to Jordan, mainly on to the newly encountered West African '*Negro* before he became preeminently the *slave*'.[33]

Whether or not Jordan's historical–psychological thesis is accepted in one form or another, it is still evident that a massive African slave trade, which served the English New World plantations first established in the later seventeenth century, was an impetus for Racialism. It is very important for our purposes not to pre-date such 'economic interests'. Such a historical error is very often seen, as for instance in the albeit lighthearted filmscript of *Shakespeare in Love*, where 'plantations' in Virginia are mentioned as contemporaneous with the first night of *Romeo and Juliet*; in fact, the very first English settlement in North America began at Jamestown a decade after the play's premiere.

The facts were that English slaving had taken only feeble first steps in the 1560s, and 'remained desultory and perfunctory in character until the establishment of British colonies in the Caribbean and the introduction of the sugar industry',[34] which was in the later seventeenth century. The earliest available evidence of English New World slaves derives from records of Africans delivered to Jamestown in 1619, although even these may have been indentured servants.[35] The fact that the first arrival of slaves at Jamestown post-dated Shakespeare's death in 1616, when placed in conjunction with the fact that the Jamestown colony had been labour-starved since its inception in 1605–6, speaks volumes to the proposition that England's was a slave-dependent economy during Shakespeare's lifetime.

Mistaken historical presumptions immersing Shakespeare's England in the Atlantic slave trade are often made implicitly, and are therefore hard to contest.[36] They are made usefully explicit in an article on *Othello* which describes 'inhospitality' towards Moroccan emissaries who visited London in 1600 as 'not surprising at a time when the English slave trade in

Africans [was] "a major economic foundation of English prosperity".[37] This error is useful because it is not cloaked in jargon, or wrapped in assumptions that non-assent must imply complicity with Racism/colonialism, and so may stand in for others that are more insulated from comment or correction.[38]

Let me clarify: I do not deny that racist or possibly even proto-Racialist sentiments may be detected in some of Shakespeare's contemporaries. But I do maintain that such sentiments were not the only ones possible or conceivable then. Indeed, many recent scholars have identified and analysed some unbiased, and even some sympathetic, Elizabethan accounts of Moors, Turks, East Indians, or Africans.[39] This joins contextual evidence in Shakespeare's work that points towards a possibility of choice for Elizabethans between tolerance and racialist bigotry.

Just such a choice is alleged as significant in the very critical essay cited above as containing the chronological error about the English slave trade. This essay also offers, intriguingly: 'The dramatic tension of *Othello* is set up between characters with racist attitudes and those in whom such an outlook is absent.'[40] Such a proposition will be carried further in the following discussions of *Othello*, which will propose that in a crucial instance a central character in this play is dramatised as replacing an attitude of tolerance with attitudes of intolerance.

Thus I will argue that Shakespeare not only represented a range of differing attitudes towards skin colour and the like, but also that he set out to portray dynamic progressions of tolerance or intolerance. To begin, let us consider certain inter-racial relations that could be headlined 'personal', although we will see that here, as often, no strict separation of the personal from the political is feasible.

3. 'MISCEGENATION' AND BLACK SEXUALITY

The word 'miscegenation' was a neologism of late 1863, invented to serve a political dirty trick or scam.[41] The context was the campaign for re-election of President Abraham Lincoln to a second term of office to begin in 1864. Referring to the ongoing Civil War, Lincoln's campaign slogan was the folksy, commonsensical 'Don't change horses in the middle of a stream.' A pair of Democratic Party activists, both New York City newspapermen, hoped to achieve precisely that result by provoking a Racialist backlash against the aims of the war. In a plot to derail Lincoln's campaign these two forged a pseudo-scientific tract titled *Miscegenation: The Theory of the Blending of the Races, Applied to the American White*

Man and Negro which urged inter-racial breeding both as biologically advantageous and as a way to improve America's racial composition. This they passed off as the work of abolitionists, and they circulated it widely in an attempt to shock or impress especially New York's recently arrived White immigrant workers (many of whom participated in anti-war agitation).[42] But the bulk of the Northern electorate was not impressed, and Lincoln was returned to office with a large majority.

Negative European opinions of inter-racial marriage had no doubt also arisen by the mid-nineteenth century, but perhaps not so much earlier than that as might be expected. Thus it is worth questioning Shakespearian critics' frequent comments to the effect that an Elizabethan would have felt 'the always potential pollutiveness of [Othello's] match with Desdemona (a potential which Iago merely serves to interpret and release)'.[43]

Evidence that in Shakespeare's age miscegenation was not necessarily viewed as 'unproper',[44] even less 'pollutive', arises on several fronts. For instance, Spanish laws of 1514, 1515, and 1556 specifically permitted intermarriage with New World 'Indians', and tacitly allowed intermarriage with Africans.[45] The British East India Company had a foothold in India by 1608, and it has been claimed that in its earlier years it strongly encouraged the marriage of both its upper and lower echelon officers with Indian wives, even paying special marriage subsidies.[46] Only after the late eighteenth century were disadvantages imposed on the numerous offspring of such mixed marriages;[47] it has been claimed that this 'new intolerance' first came to British India with a new Governor General, Lord Cornwallis, in 1786.[48] A suggested reason for this, not racist at all, was that Cornwallis, coming fresh from his defeat by Washington and his allies at Yorktown, 'was determined to make sure that a settled colonial class never emerged in India to undermine British rule as it had done, to his own humiliation, in America'.[49]

Certainly, turning back to Shakespeare's England, very little horror seems to have attached to John Rolfe, who, having married Pocahontas in Virginia in 1614, became a celebrity in London. Likewise, a painting of an olive-skinned princess with her black maid was proudly preserved by the family of (later Sir) John Henderson of Fordell, Fife, with an inscription telling how he had eloped with her when he was a slave in Zanzibar sometime between 1619 and 1628. The surviving 1713 copy of this picture appears on the cover of this book for readers to judge if any fear of pollutiveness is expressed.[50]

Nonetheless, many historically oriented readings of *Othello* assume that Iago's imagery of a monstrous or bestial marriage bed in the play represents a typical or even inevitable outlook of Shakespeare's time. Allied to this view is another common assumption: that Shakespeare's age saw Black sexuality as rampant, bestial, and transgressive.[51] Thus a sophisticated analysis claims that 'the "common sense" of the period' was sexually racist, and so would have accepted readily the 'images of monstrous coupling and animal imagery that kick start' *Othello*.[52]

Much more rarely has the historicity of such assessments been brought into question, although Ruth Morse has mocked those who assume Shakespeare attached sensuality particularly to Blackness by pointing to his ' "Roman" and yet sensuality-driven Antony'.[53] Although a 1998 essay by Kate Chedgzoy seemingly first accepts that: 'the relationship between Othello and Desdemona is informed throughout the play by the cultural attribution to black men, already well established by Shakespeare's time, of an excessive, animalistic, sexual appetite', it next gives reasons to doubt this, noting that: 'in so far as it puts the rhetoric of bestiality into the mouths of Othello's enemies, the play does not necessarily endorse these associations'.[54] In a similar vein, a 2003 discussion of *Othello* by Brian Niro points out that 'the inscription of beast and man is not solely reserved for overtly racialised characters', for it instances how animal images are applied by several speakers to the unmasked Iago.[55]

The proposition that Shakespeare's age assigned excessive and bestial sexuality to African Blacks, often assumed to be wholly true, though sometimes partly qualified (as above), may have to be entirely reversed. For Mary Floyd-Wilson has described an exact contemporary basis, solidly historically grounded, for an original audience of *Othello* to have found Iago's and Roderigo's allegations of Othello's bestial lust highly implausible. This is because, as Floyd-Wilson explains, there was a widespread belief in Shakespeare's time that a southern-born African would tend to have not an excessive, but rather a relatively *diminished* sexual drive.[56]

That flies in the face of the massed ranks of *Othello* commentary. But it also makes an entirely new kind of sense of the frank admission by Aaron the Moor in *Titus Andronicus* of his Saturnian reluctance to satisfy the erotic entreaties of his northern-born Gothic mistress Tamora (2.3.10–50), and of the insistence of the Prince of Morocco wooing Portia in *The Merchant of Venice* that his 'blood' is as red as that of 'the fairest creature northward born' (2.1.4–7). For, as Floyd-Wilson puts it, Portia's concern lest Morocco succeed as her suitor might in part be based on a fear that because of his African origin he 'lacks sexual heat' (43).

Such a fear would have rested on 'geohumoral' theories, as they are called by Floyd-Wilson, which were ancient in origin but, according to her, gaining 'new currency' in the sixteenth century (35). According to these theories natives of hot southern climates will have dry, cool, and melancholy temperaments, causing low libido and few jealous humours. Shakespeare's cognizance of these theories appears clearly, as Floyd-Wilson points out, in Desdemona's reply to Emilia's question 'Is [Othello] not jealous?' This is:

> Who, he? I think the sun where he was born
> Drew all such humours from him. (3.4.29–31)

This so precisely echoes geohumoral theories that Floyd-Wilson's reading cannot be denied.

But Floyd-Wilson also allows that alternative theories were available in Shakespeare's period.[57] She cites, for instance, Jean Bodin, who held that 'northerners are naturally chaste . . . southerners are lustful', yet she also shows that Bodin knew that his ideas were contrary to widely accepted geohumoral theories (36–8).

Therefore, although Shakespeare's audiences certainly could have encountered stereotypes of jealous, lustful, and sensuous Moors or Blacks,[58] it is unsafe to assume that their culture was wholly saturated with lurid notions of uncontrolled Black sexuality. Floyd-Wilson's great contribution, it seems to me, is to point out that counter-views, based on geohumoral theories, were widely available as well.

4. *OTHELLO*, LITERARY CRITICISM, AND MORALITY

Othello presents the most important case in point. Some have seen the portrayal in this play of an eloquent, civilised, sober, trustworthy, and in particular a sexually continent and not easily jealous Moor as an instance of Shakespearian moral exceptionalism.[59] Others have argued that this portrayal was driven by Shakespeare's aim to disrupt provocatively the reigning constructions or stereotypes of Blackness.[60] But sources cited by Floyd-Wilson show that Shakespeare need not have been provocative, or exceptional at all, in portraying Othello as thoughtful, civilised, and chaste.

In accordance with that possibility, Shakespeare depicts at the start of *Othello*, within one single fictional city, some figures highly respectful of Othello regardless of his colour, and others rabidly intolerant of him as a Moor. Therefore there seem to be choices to be made in that Venice. By contrast, a choice to be tolerant or not seems much less available in Shakespeare's earlier envisioned settings for *The Merchant of Venice*. As has been argued in Chapter 1, the xenophobic 'nationality jokes' heard in the Belmont of that play include some that are deliberately dramatised as bad jokes because repugnant ones (one even refers to an African woman as bestial). Moreover, the monocultural society of polite Belmont is dramatised as given to an often tacit or half-submerged, yet taken for granted, bigotry. Shakespeare mooting such differences between his two Venice-based plays seemingly illustrates that there are circumstances in which it is either more or less easy to choose to avoid intolerance and bigotry, or even to notice it.

Thus it seems that Shakespeare constructed in *Othello* a test situation in which a choice to be tolerant is relatively easily available, although not always availed of. Such a set-up is relevant to an intriguing discussion by the critic Nigel Alexander. In a discussion of literary-critical standards, even literary-critical morality, Alexander applied his steel-trap intellect to a famous 1693 essay by Thomas Rymer[61] that ridiculed the structure and substance of the 'bloody farce' *Othello*. In the course of this, Alexander considered Iago's disgusting slur, when referring to Desdemona's mis-cegenetic preference for a man not 'Of her own clime, complexion, and degree': 'Foh, one may smell in such a will most rank, / Foul dispro-portions, thoughts unnatural!' (3.3.235–8). Alexander's judgement was:[62]

In calling Desdemona 'unnatural' Iago expresses the crass, the vulgar view of her marriage. This is a point of view which carries death and destruction with it and is liable, at any period of history, to involve mankind in fatal and tragic action.

'At any period of history' is a big claim, and an exciting one. For present purposes, however, it will suffice to examine racist intolerance as tragic only in relation to Shakespeare's own time, and we may begin where Shakespeare did, with Aaron of *Titus Andronicus*.

5. SHAKESPEARE'S FIRST MOOR

I have been arguing that racist bigotry was not so endemic in Shakespeare's England as to be unquestionable, not so ingrained culturally as to have imposed an unchosen norm. Is this view challenged by Shakespeare's formulation of his first Moor, Aaron of *Titus Andronicus*, as a self-styled transcendent villain?

No minor figure, Aaron has the second-largest speaking part in the play (2,886 words and 279 lines, to Titus' 5,827 words and 466 lines).[63] On his first appearance he is presented in soliloquy glorying in the ele-vation to empress of his mistress Tamora (2.1.1–25). This soliloquy strikes a note very like that in the soliloquies of three White social-climbing Shakespearian power-seekers, the bastards Falconbridge and Edmund, and the self-made Richard III. And in addition to echoing their admissions of a love of power, Aaron also basks in the thought of Tamora's future adulteries with him, 'to wanton with this queen, / This goddess, this Semiramis, this nymph' (2.1.21–2). Thus preening, he lays claims to a strong sexual appetite as well as expectations of great power. But we should not take Aaron at his word but rather wait until we see him in action.

Aaron's first actions, seen immediately on the heels of this soliloquy, are to advise Tamora's egregious White sons that they should cease their contention over the love of the married Lavinia, and rather join together to rape her. They readily agree to this scheme, which Aaron counsels as a 'policy and stratagem' fitted to avoid the political risks of open attempts at seduction (2.1.105). Here, as mainly in the play, Aaron acts to promote violence, but is not violent himself.

The exceptions, where Aaron severs Titus' hand and murders Tamora's nurse, are acts of trickery and concealment respectively; these are relatively mild acts in a context in which the first thing seen is the hewing and burning of Tamora's living sons. So it comes as a surprise when near the play's end Aaron boasts of a past full of wild villainies personally enacted (5.1.124–44).

Indeed, throughout the play Aaron typically counsels sly and deceptive actions rather than direct ones. If we ignore his boasts and heed his actions we can see that Aaron is mainly an intellectual villain (just as geohumoralism would have a Moor be). His sarcastic asides, made while he teaches stratagems to Tamora's hideous sons, wittily show him to be far more intelligent than they are (2.1.37, 90). This is evident again when Aaron recognises the meaning of Latin poetic tags that the sons misread in 4.2.24–31.[64]

By and large Apron is not an attractive or amusingly evil character in the mould of Marlowe's Barabas, nor a merely grandiloquent one like George Peele's Muly Mohammet, England's first stage Moor.[65] Rather, in most of his appearances Aaron exudes his self-confessed 'cloudy melancholy' (2.3.33).[66] In this he is distinguished from most of Shakespeare's other dissembling mischief-makers, who are typically ebullient and charismatic.[67]

Yet, clearly, Aaron's melancholy is of the active and ingenious 'hot' sort, which was distinguished by Elizabethans from the paralytic and dulling 'cold' sort of melancholy mentioned above in relation to Hamlet.

It may be helpful to compare the active Aaron with the passive Egeon of *The Comedy of Errors* who, as we have seen in Chapter 3, spreads emanations of a despairing 'cold' sort of melancholy into his play. Egeon's sad resignation and readiness for a blameless death might seem as far as possible from Aaron's brilliant plotting and villainy. Yet melancholy Aaron and melancholy Egeon, both 'outsider' figures in their respective plays' settings, also share an extreme devotion to their offspring; indeed, both are self-sacrificing in this regard to the point of courting death.

That similarity might seem only accidental, because Egeon is presented as wholly passive, while on the surface of things Aaron would seem ferociously active. But is he? Here we may turn again to the researches of Mary Floyd-Wilson. As mentioned, she links Aaron's far lesser erotic keenness with the contrast between the Moor's southern and melancholy constitution and the Goth Queen's northern and active one. When deflecting Tamora's amorous advances in favour of pursuing 'Vengeance', as he puts it (2.3.38), Aaron nearly names these geohumoral differences exactly, using astrological terminology: 'Madam, though Venus govern your desires, / Saturn is dominator over mine' (2.3.30–1). Also, in accord with geohumoral theories, a Goth would be active and unreflective (Tamora's sons certainly are), while an African would be passive and thoughtful (as is Aaron).

So *Titus Andronicus* confronts Romans, Goths, and a Moor representing the three (middle, northern, and southern) geohumoral or proto-racial groups, all acting very badly. This is a pattern similar to that seen in Marlowe's *The Jew of Malta*, in which the three factions fighting for control of Malta are Jewish, Muslim, and Christian, and all are seen to be equally rapacious and amoral. But in Shakespeare's more subtly articulated play the diverse types portrayed are distinguished in accordance with geohumoral theories. Nonetheless, the play's supposedly temperate figures, its would-be balanced and civilised Romans, are as vicious and thoughtless as its Gothic northerners, and eventually are more cunning and vengeful than its African southerner.

On account of its expositions of an 'equal opportunities' prejudice, or wild anti-bigotry bigotry, we may read in *Titus Andronicus* a fierce repudiation of all intolerances based on received stereotypes; although this play demonstrates no tolerance on any side, it also mocks savagely any grounding for Racialist intolerance based on supposed superiorities.

What, then, is the status of the 'miscegenation' seen in the 'wilderness of tigers' of *Titus Andronicus*? It has been argued that a Black child's birth is only significant in the play as the proof of Aaron's violation of the patriarchal sexual possessiveness that is the greatest, and almost the only, transgression legally punished in the play's Rome; so Aaron's crime is adultery, and his 'blackness becomes important only after he is discovered to be evil'.[68]

It could be argued alternatively that the birth of this child is a redemptive exception to the hideousness generally seen in the play's Rome. After all, this birth is the only creative act seen in the play, contrasting with a seemingly endless sequence of lustful, possessive, murderous, or vengeful acts. In addition, there is a reading in which by choosing to spare Aaron's child (if this can be believed of the man who will half-bury and starve the father) the new emperor Lucius shows 'the Christian virtue of mercy, breaking the chain of eye-for-eye executions of sons'.[69] Moreover, the birth unquestionably occasions Aaron's self-sacrificing attempt to preserve his child, which ironically contrasts an 'amoral' Moor with a super-moral Roman, in that Titus willingly kills his son Mutius and daughter Lavinia (although Titus also attempts to ransom two other sons by sacrificing his hand).

Some have accepted Aaron's own boasting of active evil as the whole truth, and believe he 'figures as the consummate villain'.[70] Others have heard a heroic cry of racial defiance in Aaron's taunt to Tamora's White sons, who would destroy their Black half-brother: 'Ye whitelimed walls, ye alehouse painted signs, / Coal-black is better than another hue / In that it scorns to bear another hue' (4.2.97–9). My own opinion is that Shakespeare's sympathies in this play are not colour-coded, and so Lavinia's jeering concerning Aaron's Blackness (2.3.83), as well as that of Titus and Marcus in their black fly-killing dialogue (in the Folio only, 3.2.66–77), is intended to seem repulsive and grotesque. And so some critics' reading of Aaron's 'Is black so base a hue' as a sympathetic rallying cry may be justified.[71]

6. WHO IN VENICE OBJECTS TO OTHELLO'S MARRIAGE?

Shakespeare's main source for *Othello* was Cinthio's *novella* about a valiant Moor who marries and then murders a Venetian girl named 'Disdemona'.[72] Because that (unnamed) Moor proves an unreasonably jealous husband, Cinthio's Disdemona says she 'fear[s] greatly that I shall be a warning to young girls not to marry against their parents' wishes; and Italian ladies will learn by my example not to tie themselves to a man whom Nature, Heaven, and manner of life separate from us' (380). This remark is utterly out of keeping with the character Shakespeare gave to his

Desdemona, who never repents her marriage;[73] Thomas Rymer was only facetious when he wrote that *Othello* provides 'a caution to all Maidens of Quality how, without their Parents consent, they run away with Blackamoors'.[74]

There are many further contrasts between Shakespeare's and Cinthio's tales. For one (in accordance with geohumoral theories about southerners) Desdemona denies that her husband could be furiously jealous. But, conversely, Cinthio's Disdemona retorts to her husband's jealous anger with: 'you Moors are so hot by nature that any little thing moves you to anger and revenge'. Moreover, hearing this from his wife 'Still more enraged' Cinthio's 'Moor' (135). But in *Othello* Desdemona never makes racially stereotyping remarks. On the other hand, Iago says to Othello's face that Desdemona's miscegenetic marriage choice actually 'smells' perverse (3.3.234–8), and, bizarrely, Othello does not fly into a rage on hearing this (in this way being the opposite to Cinthio's unnamed Moor).

In another divergence, Shakespeare alters Cinthio's story in that *Othello* wholly reconstructs the protagonists' social situations. So Desdemona, unlike Disdemona, is made a patrician's daughter, and Shakespeare also elevates Othello, allowing him to claim royal lineage (1.2.22). These paired changes were not made by Shakespeare merely to avoid anticipating Ibsen's innovation of finding high tragedy in the domestic disasters of middling persons. They were necessary, rather, to underscore Shakespeare's conception of a high and beautiful love affair between a noble Moor and a very high-born Italian lady. That at least is my understanding of the impression given by the marriage portrayed in *Othello*. But to defend this I will have to answer the many who have argued that horror and disgust are the general reactions in the play to this pair's miscegenation; having attempted a general answer above in terms of societal norms, I will now turn to the text of the play.

It is very well worth asking just who in *Othello* objects to Othello's marriage. Certainly Iago objects vehemently, exposing from the start racist reasons, but also having other destructive motives which will be considered in Chapter 6. Roderigo too objects in racist terms, being Iago's dupe and demi-puppet. Roderigo is also a rejected suitor who seems to have become Desdemona's stalker: so Brabantio says, 'I have charged thee not to haunt about my doors / . . . My daughter is not for thee' (1.1.97–9). Brabantio constitutes the last of just three characters in the play who object to the marriage, but his motives are not, I will argue, basically racist.

We might note first that when Brabantio dismisses Roderigo under his window he calls him 'thee' in a disrespectful manner. The same disrespectful, familiar pronoun appears in the form 'thou' in Brabantio's interchange with Iago:[75]

BRABANTIO   Thou art a villain.
IAGO   You are a senator.

                                                                (1.1.120)

Here, I believe, Iago's quip about the high social standing of Brabantio reveals why Brabantio objects to the marriage.

Brabantio is wholly Shakespeare's invention (no father is seen in Cinthio); he is not only a senator of the Venetian oligarchy but a grandee so powerful as to have a 'voice... / As double as the Duke's' (1.2.13–14). In consequence, Brabantio's private grievances are allowed to interrupt time-critical war councils in 1.3.1–220.

As will be seen presently, Shakespeare very likely knew that the Venetian patrician class was a very small group. Its exclusive and prominent nature would help explain Brabantio's rage about his daughter making an unsuitable match, having rejected 'The wealthy curled darlings of our nation'. The scandal of this, Brabantio imagines, will produce a galling 'general mock' (1.2.68–70), causing his life to end with a bitter 'despised time' (1.1.163).

We learn as well that Brabantio has 'no other child' than Desdemona (1.3.195), and hear him use the rare term 'guardage' in his complaint she has 'Run from her guardage' (1.2.71). If 'guardage' is taken to imply guardianship, there may be an allusion here to the fact that in wardship a ward must be protected from 'disparagement' in his or her marriage. The three possibilities for disparagement listed by Coke are marriage to a lunatic, marriage to a person of inferior status (defects of blood), or marriage to a diseased or crippled person (defects of the body).[76] Desdemona's disparagement, which so pains Brabantio, could only be in accord with the second category. That is, Othello is seen by Brabantio as lacking a sufficiently high status to match with his daughter. In Shakespeare's age this objection would not have seemed foolish or pointless (as opposed to the merely arbitrary or wilful objection to Lysander posed by old Egeon in *A Midsummer Night's Dream*). So, although at first cast as the typical *senex* of a romantic comedy, crying brokenly 'Who would be a father!' (1.1.66), Brabantio deepens into performing a tragedy of his own, and unlike Egeon he dies of grief.[77]

Thus, I propose, Brabantio's tragedy is not primarily due to racism. Coke does not consider Race in his list of disparagements; in *The Tempest*, for instance, an Italian king marries his daughter to an African king.[78] To support this further, let me return to Brabantio's language. During an angry street confrontation, it is true, Brabantio does complain that Desdemona has run from his 'guardage' to Othello's 'sooty bosom' (1.2.171). But in the senate Brabantio says only that it is unbelievable that without witchcraft or drugging his young daughter would have fallen in love with Othello 'in spite of nature, / Of years, of country, credit, everything' (1.2.96–7). Thus he cites specifically Othello's advanced age, his nationality, his status, but not his colour.

In fact, previously Brabantio had been far from racist, and had rather 'cultivated' (as we say) Othello socially. Brabantio's apparent motive for this was to obtain knowledge from and about a man who had experienced a very different sort of life from his own (patricians were barred from military service in Venice, as we shall see). As Othello puts it:

> Her father loved me, oft invited me,
> Still questioned me the story of my life
> From year to year. (1.3.127–9)

In addition, Brabantio shows no responsiveness to Iago's slurs about bestial miscegenation, but only a patrician distaste for his indecency and indecorum. So, when Iago vents his venom under his window,

> Even now, now, very now, an old black ram
> Is tupping your white ewe. Arise, arise!
> Awake the snorting citizens with the bell,
> Or else the devil will make a grandsire of you.
> Arise, I say.

Brabantio replies only, 'What, have you lost your wits?' (1.1.88–92). Iago continues in his style, and so does Brabantio in his:

IAGO   ...you'll have your daughter covered with a Barbary horse, you'll have your nephews neigh to you, you'll have coursers for cousins and jennets for germans.

BRABANTIO   What profane wretch art thou?

IAGO   I am one, sir, that comes to tell you your daughter and the Moor are now making the beast with two backs.

BRABANTIO   Thou art a villain.

As noted above, Brabantio uses 'thou' here to indicate his contempt for the scandal-mongers. This is underscored imagistically when Brabantio's own imagery as it were denounces Iago's animal–sexual images (the same sorts of images we have seen endemic in *The Merchant of Venice*). Thus, less than twenty lines after Iago's farmyard image of a black ram 'tupping' a white ewe, Brabantio protests, 'My house is not a grange' (1.1.108), meaning not a farmstead fit for salacious talk of bestial copulation.

Because Brabantio repeatedly plays host to Othello, inviting him to enlarge on his life's 'pilgrimage', we may safely conclude that the stories told by Othello seem to Brabantio records of heroic virtue.[79] Desdemona responds so positively to Othello's history that she hints broadly that he might succeed if he were to woo her:

> She thanked me,
> And bade me, if I had a friend that loved her,
> I should but teach him how to tell my story,
> And that would woo her. (1.3.162–5)

Moreover, the Duke of Venice says he finds Desdemona's response not in the least perverse. To defuse a tense situation, he quips: 'I think [Othello's] tale would win my daughter, too' (1.3.170).[80]

Nevertheless, the Duke next advises Brabantio to 'Take up this mangled matter at the best' (1.3.172), and we must wonder what is mangled. The answer to that would have been apparent to Elizabethans; a long series of laws enacted up to and beyond Shakespeare's time provided civil or criminal penalties in cases of abduction, especially of an heir. Such laws are clearly alluded to in the Duke's promise to Brabantio to apply impartially 'the bloody book of law / . . . though our proper son / Stood in your action' (1.3.67–70). Yet in all these abduction or elopement laws free consent to a match on the part of a child who was not under age left her marriage intact. So no English law matched up with Iago's scare tactic when he warned Othello that, on Brabantio's urging, 'The law' had the power to 'divorce you' (1.2.14–17).[81] Once satisfied that Desdemona had given her full consent to her marriage, the Duke has no option but to confirm its legality, and to try to console Brabantio for his social loss.

This explains Brabantio's grievance.

Aside from him, Iago, and Roderigo, no one in Venice or Cyprus has a word to say against Desdemona's marriage. That is, no one until Othello, wholly out of character, displays public anger against Desdemona, and even strikes her. Witnessing this, the Venetian nobleman Lodovico, who although Brabantio's kinsman still regards Othello highly, remarks with shock: 'My lord, this would not be believed in Venice, / Though I should swear I saw 't. 'Tis very much' (4.1.242–3). Thus we may dispense with readings of 'Brabantio and his kin' being scandalised 'from the very first lines of the play' by Othello's 'miscegenous relationship with Desdemona'.[82]

7. VENICE'S FAME, OTHELLO'S INTEGRATION: THE 'NOBLE
MOOR' AND 'SUBTLE WHORE' OF VENICE

Before the crisis in *The Tragedy of Othello the Moor of Venice*, the often-heard sobriquet 'the Moor' for the famous general Othello is not used pejoratively except by Iago or Roderigo.[83] Rather, the term 'Moor' is regularly positively qualified, as in: 'valiant Moor', 'brave Moor', 'warlike Moor', 'the Moor my lord', 'Moor...a full soldier'. Three times in the play we hear of 'the noble Moor'.[84] So the Venetian society invented by Shakespeare is at first very far from disparaging the figure made by Othello. There is simply no textual warrant for such assessments as 'Othello endures a bevy of slurs and epithets, almost all of which serve to make him into a beast', and that 'a considerable proportion' of the play's Venetians describe the Moor in 'seemingly racist terms'.[85] Nor does 'the communal nature' of an assumed 'project' to stereotype and denigrate Othello show that Shakespeare was describing 'a distinctly racist community'.[86] Nor can I see any reason to connect Othello's Venice with the persecutory Iberian purity campaign that was ideologically suspicious of those held to have 'impure blood', the New Christians descended from Jews or Muslims forced to convert. Yet Michael Neill, among others, believes that that purity campaign was 'only an extreme symptom of a larger European difficulty that threatened to turn a phrase such as "Moor of Venice" into a hopeless oxymoron'.[87]

I am not alone in suggesting that, on the contrary, at the play's start we are presented with Othello well integrated into Venetian society, well accepted there, and comfortable with his dual identity as *both* Venetian and Moor. Matthew Dimmock, for instance, argues that Elizabethan England in practice, and also in its theatres, did not as a rule demonise or denigrate the civilisations of the south and east Mediterranean with which it willingly exchanged diplomats, and with which it hoped to trade. In accordance with this, Dimmock suggests that 'With Othello's entrance we are assured of his high status in Venice – a proposition familiar from the source material and made feasible by the proverbially "eastern" nature of the city state.'[88] Emily Bartels holds that Othello is 'so integrated into Venetian society that he can set the terms of both military and social action', and as the Moor 'of Venice' he has a 'dual rather than divided identity'.[89]

Like Dimmock, Bartels explains the possibility of Othello's integration by foregrounding commercial or imperialist reasons for eschewing racism,[90] effectively agreeing with Shylock's assessment that 'the trade and profit of the city / Consisteth of all nations' (*The Merchant of Venice* 3.3.30–1). But if we pursue historical contexts more specific to Venice than those examined by Dimmock and Bartels, then detailed support can be found for an image of a Venice tolerant of an exotic soldier not just for commercial advantage.

Such a context emerges from Hale and Mallet's incisive study of the military in Renaissance Venice, and especially the chapters on Venetian military manpower between 1509 and 1617.[91] These explain that one among 'many myths of Venice was that of a commercial governing class active at sea but passive, to the point of craven pacificity, on land'. Shakespeare and his audiences certainly could have known that 'myth', for Hale and Mallet show it to have been widely reported by, among others, Machiavelli, Contarini, Henry VIII of England, Bodin, Botero, and Lewkenor. They further comment that, 'like other aspects of the Myth [of Venice]', this one had 'a core of truth' (313).

The truth behind the myth, they suggest, was that Venice's very small numbers of ruling patricians abstained from leadership in war because all of them were needed at home for governing the city's land and sea empires. The Venetian law that no noble could command more than twenty-five soldiers was probably also intended to prevent the formation of armed factions and military take-overs. These arrangements produced a particular image of Venetian patrician culture: 'Dependence on foreign mercenaries was thus the carefully calculated price of [Venice's] political stability...the patrician was not militaristic...he was basically a statesman, a merchant and a patron of Church and learning.'[92]

Some details uncovered by Hale and Mallet concerning the dependence of Venice on hired foreign military commanders are particularly interesting in relation to *Othello*. For one, some of the soldiers hired by Venice earned its highest respect; in 1509 one family that had provided captain-generals for a century was even made, together with their descendants, honorary patricians (284). Also, Venice's military needs, as much as its trading needs, meant that it could not afford to be a xenophobic society. It hired *condottieri* not only from poorer parts of Italy, but also from Germany, Switzerland, Croatia, and farther afield, giving the Venetian forces a 'Noah's Ark quality' (315–17). Seemingly, even some Muslims were included: 'When captains, however scimitared and turbaned, arrived with the assurance that they and their men were Christians, or converts to Christianity, they were given the benefit of the doubt' (317).

Lewis Lewkenor's 1599 *The Commonwealth and Government of Venice* discussed and defended these military arrangements,[93] and impressive verbal and thematic echoes have been cited in support of Lewkenor's text being a background source for *Othello*.[94]

As David McPherson has explained, after its translation of Cardinal Contarini's 'highly influential' 1543 description of the Venetian state, Lewkenor's book contains a series of excerpts from five other Italian sources describing Venice.[95] Among the additional materials Lewkenor excerpts is a remark not directly mirrored in *Othello*, but nonetheless very interesting in relation to it. This remark suggests an additional reason, besides the fame of its (by Shakespeare's time declining) Eastern trade, why Venice may have been chosen by Shakespeare as a setting:

> above all other things this is most strange, that this [Venetian] aire by a special priveledge of nature doth agree with the complexions of all such strangers as resort thither, of what nation, or under what climate soever they bee born. (192)

Since prevailing geohumoral theories divided human groups by complexions derived from climate, this may suggest that Venice was by its privileged climate destined to provide a home for all kinds of 'stranger' inhabitants.

Lewkenor's book also describes another aspect of Venice's fame that is directly relevant to *Othello*. An excerpt, which Lewkenor says is taken from Girolamo Bardi,[96] describes a Venetian state officer empowered to oversee 'Mountebanks', 'Charlatanes', and 'publike women', that is, whores (182). This may first catch the attention of *Othello* scholars because Brabantio fears Desdemona has been 'corrupted / By spells and medicines bought of mountebanks' (1.3.60–1). But, more importantly, it also brings into focus the worldwide fame of Venice as a luxurious port city with an extensive sex industry.[97] This was so well known that even Lewkenor, who in general edits his materials to laud Venice, includes a matter-of-fact reference to a government official charged with overseeing prostitution.

Shakespeare and his audiences surely knew the bawdy reputation of Venice. That, however, also had a complication which can be seen mirrored in Ben Jonson's *Volpone* (written a year or two after *Othello*), and also in Thomas Nashe's pioneering picaresque 1594 novel *The Unfortunate Traveller*.[98]

Nashe's novel was dedicated to the Earl of Southampton in the same year in which Shakespeare dedicated a narrative poem to him. In it Nashe's narrator Jack Wilton and Jack's master, who is a fictionalised version of the Earl of Surrey, undergo wild adventures from the moment they arrive in Venice. Thanks to the machinations of one Petro de Campo Frego, a Venetian 'pandor' and 'practitioner in the pollicie of baudrie', and his accomplice Tabitha, a murderously inclined high-class Venetian 'curtizan', Jack and his master are soon framed as counterfeiters and imprisoned. They are delivered only thanks to the intervention of 'Petro Aretino' (52–63). The actual Pietro Aretino was in reality a famous sixteenth-century literary personality well known to Shakespeare and his contemporaries;[99] in Nashe's fiction, however, he is the Venetian 'searcher and chief Inquisitor to the colledge of curtizans',[100] and as such presents a sensationalised version of the Venetian official in charge of 'publike women' described by Lewkenor.

In much English Renaissance drama, not only Venetian 'public' women, but Venetian women in general, or even Italian women in general, were alleged to be either sexually 'frail' or cunningly lascivious.[101] Thus the audience of *Othello* would have had no trouble interpreting Iago's slurs that Desdemona is a 'super-subtle Venetian' (1.3.355), or that she may manifest Venice's bawdy 'country disposition' (3.3.205).

However, there was a complication. Ben Jonson's English Lady Would-be in *Volpone* tries to ape Venice's courtesans, but in *Volpone* a super-virtuous Venetian wife, Celia, despite being abused and pandered by her husband, resists all entreaties to adultery. And indeed, extreme female chastity also seems to have been a Venetian stereotype. Thus while in prison, Nashe's Jack Wilton meets the aptly named Diamante, the wife of an unjustly jealous Venetian magnifico who has abused her and called her a 'whore, strumpet, six penie hackster' (57). Despite this, Diamante remains 'immaculate honest' (58).[102] Diamante's initial extreme marital chastity and sexual innocence, like that of Shakespeare's Desdemona or Jonson's Celia, accords with the patriarchal implications of Venetian upper-echelon arranged marriage customs reported in Lewkenor:

> The marriages among the nobility, are for the most part alwaies treated of [i.e. arranged, negotiated] by a third person, the bride being never suffered so much as to behold her future husband, nor he her, till the marriage dower, and all things thereunto appertaining, bee fully agreede upon and concluded, which being done the next morning the Bridegrome goeth to the court of the pallace, & there the match being published, receiueth well wishing speeches and salutations form such of the nobility as doe enter into the pallace . . .

and so forth through many male-only ceremonies, until the married couple are first allowed to set eyes upon one another, albeit without speech and in a public setting (194–5).

So there were available to Shakespeare and his time images of Venice as a centre of whoredom and sexual licence, and at the same time a counter-image of upper-echelon Venetian women so sequestered from contact with men outside their households, and so controlled by the men within them,[103] that in their cloistered naivety they might not even be able to credit the possibility of sexual licence or adultery. Such a condition of radical innocence is reflected in Shakespeare's Desdemona (4.3.58–104). In fact, in terms of the fame of patrician Venetian families' extreme control over their daughters, Brabantio in *Othello* may even have been presented as unusually permissive in allowing Desdemona to have a say in rejecting (and presumably having sight of the curls of) 'The wealthy curled darlings of our nation' (1.2.69).

In *Othello*, then, we see the confrontation between several semi-realistic images related to fables of Venice. In one an assimilated 'Moor of Venice' gains great respect as a soldier, and in others an alleged 'whore of Venice' actually is not one. That confrontation, in my view, is the true setting for the play's tragedy.

8. OTHELLO: THE TRAGEDY

Referring to English-speaking culture at the time of its delivery – and of most of the century leading up to it – Helen Gardner's 1955 British Academy lecture commented on a 'distaste' for the heroic nobility which she found to be an essential attribute of the free-living Othello, and also of Desdemona after her achievement of freedom 'at a great cost'.[104] In her still-trenchant analysis, titled 'The Noble Moor', Gardner pointed out a great contrast between Hamlet, who is bound by history and family and convention, and Othello, who is free of all these and is therefore able with Desdemona to undertake 'a great venture of faith' (353–5). That venture is, of course, their mutual love. Gardner finds in that love prodigious beauty, and also truth; for her the real tragedy in *Othello* lies in the loss of an irreplaceable, individual, love between a noble and heroic man and woman.

It seems to me without doubt that *Othello* is both a painful tragedy and a love story, for it tells the story of a powerful love thwarted and destroyed. And this, it seems to me, ties directly to themes concerning tolerance in the play, for I will next argue that what destroys this love is precisely a failure of tolerance.

One way of describing the process whereby love is destroyed in *Othello* is to state that Iago's unreasoning hatred and suspiciousness become transferred to the once-noble Othello. Attempting to explain that, Anthony Barthelemy has suggested that Iago's own anxious sex obsessions are projected into Othello, and then connects Othello's denials of sexuality with his downfall:[105]

When Othello refuses Desdemona's final invitation to her bed [in 5.2.25], he rejects virtue and chooses evil...
   [in 1.3] Othello goes so far as to deny himself even the desire of 'proper satisfaction', a phrase that jars against Desdemona's request for the 'rites for why I love him'...Whereas Othello will later incorrectly choose abstinence...to defend his honor, here he chooses abstinence to defend his manhood.

This seems to me to go in a useful direction, but to go too far. For one thing it does not take into account the geohumoral theories discussed above whereby southern birth was supposed to have lessened sexual drive. In addition, I do not believe that 'abstinence' is a relevant issue in this play, despite the long history of hot debates among the learned as to whether Othello and Desdemona had consummated their marriage or not, and if so when, or if the general had time for this in his busy life.[106] Even though in *Othello* the final scene reveals the marriage bed more than fully occupied, the marital bedroom door is closed in this as in every Shakespeare play. (Yet it seems to me difficult to hear Othello speaking bitterly about 'her sweet body' (3.3.351) without supposing his knowledge of it).[107] Moreover, the newly married pair are evidently very much in love, despite whatever politeness, decorum, or ideology produces Othello's public gainsaying of 'the palate of my appetite'. So Desdemona, by her own courageous request,[108] is allowed to go to Cyprus with her husband. The play implies that it is then simply idyllic that Othello can enjoy his beloved military-camp life – his 'unhoused free condition' – and be together with his 'fair warrior' as well (1.2.26 and 2.1.183).
   What spoils this idyll no doubt has something to do with Barthelemy's and also Jordan's concepts, discussed above, of projections of perverse sexuality onto Blacks by Whites. Iago certainly harbours within himself toxic sexual fantasies (unfounded jealousy may be the least of these).[109] By projecting these outwards he inserts perverse images into Othello, and makes those images active. The images of Desdemona *in flagrante delicto* evoked by Iago, especially by his maddening question 'Would you.../ Behold her topped?' (3.3.400–1), so stick in Othello's imagination that a mesmerised 'Cassio did top her' (5.2.145) becomes his first explanation of the murder. And Iago's images so firmly take root in Othello's mind that they make him (wholly uncharacteristically) dishonourable. So, in his 'Pioneers and all...' speech (3.3.350–62) he wishes to be an ignorant if notorious cuckold (this is wholly unlike the remarkable sexual tolerance of Posthumus discussed in Chapter 2 above).

Yet I believe that something of Iago's that is even more destructive than evil sexual fantasies becomes planted in Othello; this is a scornful xenophobia, amounting to racism, and so extreme as to be perhaps even embryonic Racialism. I will explain that in a moment, but first want to point out that this concept extends the preceding argument that the Venetian world of *Othello* is by and large non-racist, to a proposition that the play itself may be best described as 'anti-racist'. That is, *Othello* neither overlooks 'racism' nor endorses it, but severely warns against it. It instructs us that foul racial insinuations like Iago's are likely, as Nigel Alexander put it, 'to involve mankind in fatal and tragic action'.

Now I will describe how Othello catches the virus of racism from Iago, and is then struck down by it.

Symptoms of racism, and maybe even Racialism, are seen in Iago from the play's start in his use of vile and pornographic imagery to place groups of human beings into categories that he holds to be despicable and subhuman.[110] Othello first shows severe symptoms of the same infection when he says to Desdemona, sarcastically, 'I cry you mercy then. / I took you for that cunning whore of Venice / That married with Othello' (4.2.92–4). He has already angrily labelled her 'whore' several times before, but only here does his Iago-inspired 'reasoning' emerge: Desdemona is a Venetian woman, the world knows what Venetians (especially females of that subhuman subspecies) are like, and so Desdemona must be a 'cunning whore'. Here, Iago-like, Othello sees in a person he should know well only the purported characteristics of a derogatory stereotype.

I believe that the same disease shows its symptoms in Othello's much-argued-over final speech (5.2.347–65). In the first half of this, Othello's language is not polluted by hate-talk, but rather is beautiful in its shaped cadences implying a self-aware self-command.[111] But nearer its end, Othello's final speech shows the ugly symptoms of his disease, an unheroic and indeed cowardly, Iago-like bigotry. I am amazed that critics who hear racial slurs throughout the play, even a 'bevy' or chorus of these from nearly every one in it, have not located them here.

We should remember that previously, even when describing the enemies who had enslaved him, Othello used merely the epithet 'the insolent foe'; those enemies were perhaps haughty or overbearing, but not despicable. Warfare, it seems, had been for Othello an honourable and glorious profession in spite of its cruelty, because his enemies had been men worth contending with. But in his final speech, when his life has ended and he knows it, Othello tells a tale of brutally quelling 'a malignant and a turbaned Turk', a subhuman creature whom he calls a 'circumcised dog' (5.2.361–5). And just before that Othello compares himself with an imagined 'base Indian', or else 'base Judean' tribesman (this intriguing textual crux is at 5.2.356, TLN 3658). In this simile he pictures the 'base' Indian/Judean as ignorant, despicable, wasteful, less than fully human. These almost casual descriptions of one person as a 'dog', and another as 'base', are Iago-like symptoms.

Let me make the pattern clear. Before Othello's final speech, all references in *Othello* to the Turkish adversary, except scurrilous Iago's in 2.1.117,[112] are respectful. Thus, throughout the council scene, Turkish leadership is seen as worryingly proficient: in strategy not 'unskilful' (1.3.28), and in foresight capable of 'a mighty preparation' (1.3.220).[113] Even the providential Turkish naval losses in the storm are described sympathetically by one Venetian as 'a grievous wrack and sufferance' (2.1.23). Most interestingly, Othello condemns Christian brawling and drunkenness with: 'Are we turned Turks, and to ourselves do that / Which heaven hath forbid the Ottomites?' (2.3.163–4). Literally he means, 'Please do not do the enemy's work for them by fighting among yourselves', and by 'heaven' he means that which destroyed the enemy fleet. But surely he alludes also to the Muslim prohibition of alcohol use, and in consequence to a, relatively speaking, greater Christian than Turkish barbarousness at work.

Thus the play shows at large tendencies contrary to denigrating Turks, against which Othello's concluding image of a villainous 'malignant and a turbaned Turk' stands out. This fellow is not one of those who enacts a skilful naval strategy with feints 'To keep us in false gaze', and who reserves a hidden 'after fleet' to perplex an astute Venetian Duke and his council (1.3.14–46). He is rather a crude, traducing, subhuman 'circumcised dog'.

Of course Othello projects upon his imaged turbaned 'dog' the hateful murderer that he himself has become. Still, in this projection, he appears as an Iago-like 'racial' bigot. By contrast, even after he has confessed to his dreadful act, no one, not even the distraught Emilia, shows Othello the degree of disrespect that he shows to the imagined adversary in his last speech, albeit an adversary whom he makes equivalent to himself.

Thus I am proposing a reading of *Othello* in which the desperately misled hero first turns into a racist despiser, perhaps even a Racialist one, of the heroic wife whom he reduces to the category 'Venetian women' (equating these with 'the cunning whore of Venice'). He later despises Turks, and Indians or Jews, as base and crude; and identifying with one of these, he kills himself.

I hope that such a reading will not seem shocking. To accept it one must accept that a Black man portrayed by Shakespeare may be capable of becoming a destructive bigot. To reject such a possibility, to my mind, is to lack the courage shown by Shakespeare in seeing that a heroic Black man may be, equally with a White one, capable of all human glories or failings. Likewise, for Shakespeare, a Jew like Shylock can be depicted as human enough to become an evil revenger: Shakespeare was not self-constrained to finding all Jews blameless.

What is seen in a more general sense is Shakespearian imaginary persons occupying relatively precarious political, material, or cultural positions – figures that may themselves be subject to discrimination – enjoined by implication to tolerance. A demand to practise tolerance and avoid bigotry is not restricted to those who are relatively more empowered than those they must tolerate. Shakespeare illustrates that if this is not observed, very harsh consequences may ensue.

CHAPTER 6

'Race', part two: Shakespeare and slavery

I. TYPES OF SLAVERY KNOWN TO ELIZABETHANS

In a particularly careful study of the tragedy of Atlantic plantation slavery,[1] Jonathan Schorsch dates the European emergence of notions corresponding with Racialism, finding that although most historians claim a later origin, some have dated this emergence to the second half of the seventeenth century (which is, of course, still well after Shakespeare's lifetime).[2] Starting from that point, Schorsch detects a process that he finds still continuing:

The hammering out of the precise meaning of the term *negro* or Black or *mulatto*, and the system of governing subjects assigned to each category, occurred over the course of two or three centuries – in fact have never ended.

If, as he says, such a process is still in progress, we are in the early twenty-first century living out the waning legacy of the massive, mainly eighteenth-century Atlantic slave trade (a fine example of a 'political or economic interest'), and so inhabit a highly racially sensitised culture. Was Shakespeare's culture similarly sensitised? To help answer that question we need to ask what views were taken in his England of slavery, and in particular what significances the word 'slave' had in Shakespeare's culture and in his plays.

Elizabethans were aware of three kinds of slavery: the enslavement of Africans or Native Americans employed by Spanish and Portuguese colonists in the New World; the enslavement of captives in war – in galleys or otherwise – who were not able to provide ransom payments; and the enslavement of those taken by corsair raiders on land or sea.

The relatively few Black servants kept as 'expensive, liveried status symbol[s]' by the fashionable in England *c.* 1600 experienced conditions entirely different from those imposed later on chattel slaves on English plantations abroad; they were likely rather to have been treated similarly to White English servants.[3] Even by 1700, John Baker finds within England 'no extensive use of slave labour, as in the colonies'.[4] Indeed, historians have noted that slavery was not legally possible within England itself after the Norman Conquest, which is generally true, although some slight qualifications of this point may be needed.[5]

Slavery of Native Americans and Africans in the Spanish New World became notorious throughout sixteenth-century Europe because of vivid accounts of its horrors written by, among others, the Spanish Dominican bishop Bartolome de las Casas and the Spanish Dominican jurist Francisco de Vitoria.[6] These writings and others alleged such severe atrocities that an image of Spanish cruelty in the New World emerged which was later called a 'Black Legend'.[7] Shakespeare must have encountered this famous scandal;[8] it even became fodder for such ubiquitous texts as the later editions of John Foxe's *Book of Martyrs* (which added it to an 'evil empire' characterisation of Catholic Spain).[9] Shakespeare also almost certainly read the stomach-churning account of Spanish New World cruelty and slavery in Montaigne's essay 'Of Coaches',[10] and quite possibly he read the 1579 *Histoire Nouvelle du Nouveau Monde*,[11] a French translation of the Italian Girolamo Benzoni's very popular travel book, which gives striking accounts of Spanish cruelties to Africans and Native Americans (some of which led to mass suicide). Moreover, several English publications promoting the Jamestown settlement in Virginia (including some accepted as sources for *The Tempest*) also censured Spanish New World cruelties and enslavement. The thrust of this propaganda was that England's settlements would behave much better than Spain's.[12]

At the same time the enslavement of 'White' Europeans, including many Britons, was a familiar fact of life for Elizabethans. It was frequently referred to in the theatre, especially by Heywood, Massinger, and Fletcher,[13] but less often by Shakespeare. Some of this slavery would have resonated for Elizabethan audiences with classical models of the capture and enslavement of enemy combatants in warfare, a practice likely to have been viewed as a more humane alternative to slaughter. Thus Othello is captured in war, and then sold and redeemed from slavery, and in *Henry V* the killing of French war prisoners requires special excuses (4.7.1–10).

A mixture of enmity and desire for gain motivated the raids for European slaves by Barbary pirates.[14] While traditionally using galleys in the shipping lanes and on the shores of the Mediterranean, by the early seventeenth century the corsair raiders increasingly used tall ships to sail into the Atlantic, and were 'taking captives as far north as Iceland' and from coastal villages of England and Ireland.[15] By sea the corsairs captured 'on average seventy to eighty Christian vessels a year between 1592 and 1609'.[16] The dangers of such capture were multiplied for Shakespeare's countrymen thanks to a burgeoning English trading involvement with the western Mediterranean.[17]

Christian captives taken by Muslim pirates on land or sea were sold in slave markets in North Africa, or sent onwards to the Levant. In accordance with an 'Eastern' pattern of slavery, these were valued either to raise ransoms or for their particular skills.[18] This pattern differed significantly from that of the African–Atlantic slavery which in later centuries increasingly provided raw labour to the New World.[19] However, many Europeans enslaved by Muslims were used harshly for labour; many were pressed into galley service, as were Islamic captives on Italian or Spanish galleys.[20]

Through the period 1580–1680 the average number of Christians enslaved in North Africa has been estimated as roughly 35,000, with many more held in the Levant or eastern Europe.[21] Nabil Matar points out that in Shakespeare's time Britons taken captive and sold as slaves were 'reported to have numbered five thousand in Algiers alone'.[22] Therefore, as Sujata Iyengar puts it, '"Slavery" to an early modern ear evokes white, rather than black, captivity.'[23]

Clearly, Elizabethan perceptions of slavery differed from those arising later in association with England's slave trade; it is necessary in fact to describe some rather unaccustomed Elizabethan aspects of the very term 'slave'.

2. SHAKESPEARIAN USES OF 'SLAVE'

The word 'slave' refers literally to a person owned by and controlled by another (in accordance with *OED* 'slave', I.1.a) only in a minority of its Shakespearian appearances. When it does so the slaves in question may be conventionally witty classical slaves, like the twin Dromios in *The Comedy of Errors*; these do not seem to be disgraced by their status. Or they may be military captives, as Othello once was. Othello describes this kind of slavery as an adventure, an attendant risk of war, and thrills Desdemona with his accounts:

> Of hair-breadth scapes i' th' imminent deadly breach,
> Of being taken by the insolent foe
> And sold to slavery, of my redemption thence. (1.3.135–7)

Here, as Camille Slights points out, Othello's accidental slavery is not seen as any kind of a disgrace to him.[24]

Moreover, for Shakespeare's age images of the 'Eastern' style of enslavement need not have involved degradation either. The above discussion suggests that the image of an early modern European abducted by pirates and then sold in an Eastern city would have seemed fairly realistic when portrayed fictionally by Jean Bodin in the story of Octavius in the *Colloquium* or by Shakespeare, who depicted Marina's capture and sale in *Pericles*. Neither of these characters is disgraced because they have been seized and sold. To gain freedom Octavius forsakes his original religion, but, as we have seen, he is a dignified proponent of his new one. Marina, sold into a brothel, is triumphantly autonomous and shines in her adversity. Not too realistically, she retains her virginity, earns a good living through art, redeems many libertine males, and wins a regal husband. It is clear that neither of these characters loses their self-respect when they lose their freedom; their form of slavery is like Othello's a mere accident of fate.

Modern expectations may be further confused, because other kinds of servitude coming short of chattel slavery were sometimes conflated with 'slavery' in Shakespeare's time. When condemning slavery, Jean Bodin did not differentiate between serfs and slaves; he saw them as equally presenting dangers to the state because of their social exclusion and consequent resentment.[25] The development of wage labour was more advanced in Shakespeare's England than in Bodin's contemporary France, and English serfdom had effectively ended with the liberalisation of vil-lein tenures,[26] so Shakespeare did not follow Bodin in this.[27] But he did sometimes broaden his meanings and have his characters use 'slave' to refer to an apparently 'free' servant or mere social inferior, as, for example, Costard in *Love's Labour's Lost* (1.2.146, 3.1.147, and 3.1.157), or Rome's or Antium's plebeians in *Coriolanus* (the former throughout, the latter in 4.5.175). In all these uses, except Coriolanus' derogatory ones, the term 'slave' is applied jovially to refer humorously to a mere underling or rascal (as in *OED* 'slave', I.1.c).

A more telling broadening of terms occurs in *The Tempest*, when on significant occasions both Caliban's and Ariel's servitude is referred to as slavery. This will be investigated in detail later, but for now let me mention that Andrew Gurr has identified Caliban in *The Tempest* with a lazy waged servant, and Ariel with an Elizabethan apprentice.[28] I cannot agree with the first assessment, because, although he grumbles, Caliban does not do so from a position of any autonomy at all. But I wholly agree that Ariel resembles a bound apprentice, and in fact have previously dis-cussed this resemblance together with some perhaps revealing numero-logical aspects of Ariel's renegotiated period of service.[29]

To add to that, I would like to mention that whenever Shakespeare describes a bound apprentice or servant seeking to shorten or terminate their indentures, the tone of his plays tends towards both the comic and the nervous. This may be because the roguishness of those fleeing service could be seen as droll, yet such freedom-seeking could also incite anxieties about 'masterless men' and destabilising indiscipline.[30] Thus dark images of disloyalty or insubordination colour both the story of Peter Thump vanquishing his drunken master in the lists in *Henry VI, part 2* 2.3.47–109,[31] and Jack Cade's sinister–comic remarks later in the play about his broken indentures: 'For I did but seal once to a thing, and I was never mine own man since' (4.2.83–4). Cade's remark is in support of his rebels' famous plan to 'kill all the lawyers'. Less threatening, but still packed with Jew-hatred, are the servant Gobbo's 'comic' internal debates in *The Merchant of Venice* 2.2.1–29 about breaking his contract to serve his master Shylock. Some kind of humour also colours Prince Hal's interchange with Francis, the apprentice tavern drawer who dreams of running from his 'indenture' (*Henry IV, part 1* 2.5.40–102). Least comic of all, because of the anger generated, is the scene in *The Tempest* in which Ariel begs to shorten his period of servitude, but perhaps this too ends comically with Ariel's incongruous promise 'I will ... do my spriting gently' (1.2.299). I am not sure how droll that might have sounded, but will return to the conflict presently.

Finally, by far most common in Shakespeare is the use of the term 'slave' as an insult, conveying disparagement or abuse (in accordance with *OED* 'slave', I.1.b, a 'term of contempt', labelled 'Now *arch*[*aic*]').[32] Its typical thrust is illustrated in Hamlet's self-condemning, 'O, what a rogue and peasant slave am I!' (2.2.552). Here Hamlet labels himself a 'slave' when he considers that, although a prince, he is yet crude in comparison with an imaginative, emotionally labile, compassionate actor, a mere player. Thus the epithet 'slave' identifies a person degraded in behaviour or sensibility.

Most, but not all, of Shakespeare's over two hundred uses of 'slave' berate someone as a churl, lout, wretch, rogue, reprobate, or knave. The exceptions include the few literal Shakespearian uses mentioned above, nine or ten figurative uses of 'slave of' or 'slave to' to indicate being morally dominated or fixated (corresponding with *OED* I.2.b, as in Hamlet's condensed 'passion's slave'),[33] and several uses where slavery indicates the services of a Petrarchan poetic lover.[34] But even in a play with a classical setting like *Antony and Cleopatra*, 'slave' can be a term of abuse, and not refer to actual slavery; so Cleopatra calls her 'hired' treasurer Seleucus (actually her con-federate in a double-cross!) a 'Slave, soulless villain, dog!' (5.2.151–3).

Also in *Othello* the word 'slave' is most often used as an angry insult, and then has no racial overtones. It is applied to Desdemona in 3.3.447,

Roderigo in 5.1.63, Iago in 4.2.136, 5.2.250 and 5.2.341 – and twice to
Othello after he kills Desdemona (first by himself in 5.2.283, and then by
Lodovico in 5.2.298). However, there are a few other uses of the term
'slave' in *Othello*. One is in Othello's story of being 'sold to slavery', discussed above, which does not attribute any baseness, nor indeed Blackness,
to him. Another is in Brabantio's complaint about his daughter's elopement
with Othello: 'if such actions may have passage free, / Bondslaves and
pagans shall our statesmen be' (1.2.99–100). Here Brabantio in 'bondslave'
exaggerates Othello's lower social rank compared with his own 'statesman'
one, complaining about his heir's 'disparagement' as discussed in the last
chapter;[35] 'bondslave' refers to Othello's non-patrician social position, not
his Racial status. Indeed, Bianca in *The Taming of the Shrew* 2.1.2 complains
that her sister intends 'To make a bondmaid and a slave of me', indicating
that she means to degrade her. Bianca (as her name says) is surely White,
although possibly a pagan.

   The one remaining exception in *Othello* to the rule that Shakespeare
characters mainly use the term 'slave' to abuse or condemn is very telling in
relation to tolerance. It will be the topic of the entire next section because it
throws light on Shakespeare's prime racist, Iago, who is the most intolerant
fictional person Shakespeare (and perhaps any author) has ever portrayed.

3. THE SELF-REPRESENTATION OF IAGO AS A SLAVE

We learn at the very start of *Othello* that Iago has been passed over for
promotion and feels himself trapped in a humiliatingly subordinate military
rank (1.1.7–32). This, however, seems inadequate to explain his later remark
that he is less well treated than 'all slaves'.

   Iago's claim arises in a context in which Othello insistently asks him to
'speak to me as to thy thinkings'. Iago angrily replies that he, like any
despicable slave, is entitled to a minimal portion of autonomy in the form
of the private possession of his inner thoughts:[36]

> Good my lord, pardon me.
> Though I am bound to every act of duty,
> I am not bound to that all slaves are free to.
> Utter my thoughts? (3.3.138–41)

In his sarcastic politeness, Iago here nearly identifies himself as a slave.

   An audience privy to Iago's scheming is aware of the irony that his
concealed 'thinkings' are no more than a simulated bait, a mummery,
concocted to arouse Othello's interest. Othello falls headlong into this

trap, and so it seems more than likely that Iago is pleased by his awareness that, far from being Othello's 'slave', he is fast becoming his psychological puppeteer.

Yet Iago's 'slaves' remark also seems to convey a sense of resentment that excites Iago himself. Why would he thus drive himself into a state of grievance? Certainly there is no sign that he does this to overcome any moral scruples. I propose that Iago persuades himself that he is a degraded subaltern, worse treated than pitiable downtrodden 'slaves', in order to pretend *to himself* that his machinations are the products of revenge, when in fact they are the products of emptiness, envy, and intolerance.

Iago is, of course, a blatant racist, and he also seemingly despises moral 'beauty'. That is, he hates Cassio because 'He hath a daily beauty in his life / That makes me ugly' (5.1.19–20). He similarly detests the 'Moor' and Desdemona because he realises they are respectively 'of a constant, loving, noble nature', and 'as fruitful / As the free [= generous] elements' (2.1.288, 2.3.332–3). But he finds for his own purposes other reasons to despise his victims, those whom he misleads and exploits. He labels Cassio a 'drunkard . . . drunk . . . fool' (2.3.55, 2.3.306, 2.3.344), Othello a 'credulous fool . . . unbookish' (4.1.43, 4.1.100), Roderigo a '[love-] sick fool' (2.3.47), and both Emilia and Desdemona 'foolish' (3.3.308, 4.1.172).

Thus Iago thinks his victims fools compared with himself. Yet he is no self-lover. Rather, I think, he derogates others because he finds himself, more than any other person, slavish, detestable, venial, weak, and – most of all – hollow. As much as he plants false convictions in others by means of distortions and innuendoes, he plants falsehoods in himself; for example that he must seek revenge because he has been cuckolded by Othello (1.3.379–80, 2.1.294–5) or by Cassio (2.1.306). His purpose in this, I maintain, is to deceive himself into believing that he has a real inner life. Similarly, while feigning to harbour thoughts kept from Othello, he simulates anger in order to persuade himself that inwardness is possible for him. But none of this inwardness is genuine.

Iago envies anyone capable of deep feeling, of genuine passion, and from this arises his need to control and then destroy them. This is his motive for attacking the play's lovers, but also in a simpler case for attacking Cassio. The latter can be more easily illustrated textually.

Iago is scathing when Cassio expresses his misery because his drunken misdeeds have cost him his 'reputation' (2.3.256–9), and scoffs dismissively 'Reputation is an idle and most false imposition' (2.3.262–3). But then, when Cassio shows he is less sorry for the loss of his own benefits than he is remorseful for his ill behaviour itself and its effect on 'so good a commander', the reductive Iago is reduced to silence and to a *non sequitur* (2.3.271–8). What checks Iago's cynicism is Cassio's expression of a capacity for strong feeling transcending the appetitive or selfish.

Grotesquely, Iago remembers Cassio's genuine feelings, and attempts to ape them, when he imitates Cassio's remarks about lost reputation in his own later pronouncement:

> Good name in man and woman, dear my lord,
> Is the immediate jewel of their souls.
> Who steals my purse steals trash; 'tis something, nothing;
> 'Twas mine, 'tis his, and has been slave to thousands.
> But he that filches from me my good name
> Robs me of that which not enriches him
> And makes me poor indeed. (3.3.160–6)

But, of course, Iago cannot clone Cassio's inward sorrow at having done wrong.

In this reading, Iago simulates his bitterness that, less than slave-like, he has no rights to his own private 'thinkings', in order to mask the fact that he has no inner thoughts, that nothing alive inhabits his inner landscape except his incessant scheming. What he finds truly shaming and intolerable is not that he has been cuckolded, or passed over for pro-motion, but that he must dissemble about having an interiority, even deceive himself by concocting false motives for vile plots. In consequence Iago invents an inscrutable persona for himself, becomes perfect in reducing self-tolerance as well as other-tolerance to the degree zero, and risks all to fill a vacuum with more emptiness. A despiser most of all of himself, Iago does after all tell the truth when he reveals his vision in which, less than a despised slave, he is bereft of any inward autonomy.

4. THE SLAVE IN *TITUS ANDRONICUS*

Three times the epithet 'slave' is very strangely linked to 'racial' qualities in *Titus Andronicus*. To frame these instances I will first briefly trace the more typical Shakespearian uses of the word 'slave' in the play.

Near the play's conclusion, when leading a Goth army into Rome, Lucius labels his captive Aaron the Moor a 'wall-eyed slave'. Lucius continues, calling the child Aaron has conceived with the adulterous Roman empress Tamora 'This growing image of thy fiendlike face' (5.1.44–5). It is possible that the linked derogatory physical descriptions here, 'wall-eyed' and 'fiendlike', are racist.[37] But even that would not assure us that Lucius' further term of abuse 'slave' (in 'wall-eyed slave') is also racist; of course, Roman slaves could be of any colour.

Yet Aaron's skin colour is often mentioned in the play, especially by himself. Thus, following his capture, in exchange for a promise from Lucius that his child will be spared, Aaron confesses to numerous horrendous crimes. When asked 'canst thou say all this and never blush?', Aaron replies, quipping about his colour, 'Ay, like a black dog, as the saying is' (5.1.121–2). Interestingly, none of the White Goth army present takes Aaron up on this, not even after he next boasts of a fantastic series of crimes prior to the play's action.

When Aaron is next seen, still in custody, Lucius calls him an 'inhuman dog, unhallowed slave!' (5.3.14). Here again, there is no necessary racial element in the insult 'slave'. For Aaron has boasted of despising all religions (5.1.70–85), so here 'unhallowed slave' may designate an atheistic villain, not a Black one especially.

The epithet 'slavish' is first heard in *Titus* in Aaron's initial soliloquy. In this he glories in his mistress Tamora's advancement to empress, and admonishes himself with: 'Away with slavish weeds and servile thoughts!' (2.1.18; the third Quarto and the Folio replace 'servile' with 'idle'). Here 'slavish' clearly means 'lowly' or 'degraded', modifying 'weeds' (is this metaphorical for his state of mind, or does Aaron actually smarten up his costume with 'pearl and gold' (2.1.19) from this point?).

That leaves the three very peculiar uses of 'slave' in *Titus* mentioned above; all are applied by Aaron to his newborn infant son in his arms:

> Look how the black slave smiles upon the father (4.2.119)

> Come on, you thick-lipped slave, I'll bear you hence,
> For it is you that puts us to our shifts.
> I'll make you feed on berries and on roots,
> And fat on curds and whey, and suck the goat,
> And cabin in a cave, and bring you up
> To be a warrior and command a camp. (4.2.174–9)

> Peace, tawny slave, half me and half thy dam!
> Did not thy hue bewray whose brat thou art,
> Had nature lent thee but thy mother's look,
> Villain, thou mightst have been an emperor.
> But where the bull and cow are both milk-white
> They never do beget a coal-black calf. (5.1.27–32)

In these contexts, 'slave' appears to be a term of affection, as do its modifiers 'black', 'tawny', and 'thick-lipped'. As we can see in the third passage above, Aaron only regrets his son not being White because this prevents him from being taken to be legitimate, and thus the heir to the empire. Aaron, who has called his child a 'Sweet blowze . . . a beauteous blossom, sure' (4.2.72), clearly does not despise its colour.

Thus here the son's Blackness is beautiful to the father. It provides a proof of crimes (adultery and treason), but is not taken to be a disgrace in itself. This illustrates a formula presented by Phyllis Braxton, who, writing about Aaron, claims that although evil was symbolically black for Shakespeare's culture, blackness was not evil.[38]

Aaron's own words support such a view. When resolving in soliloquy to become evil, he distinguishes his soul's chosen 'blackness' from his face's merely incidental colour: 'Let fools do good, and fair men call for grace: / Aaron will have his soul black like his face' (3.1.203–4). That is, despite being Black (in his face) he must deliberately *choose* to be evil; Eldred Jones long ago pointed out the importance of the expression of Aaron's moral autonomy in these lines.[39]

Moreover, in *Titus* the polyvalent term 'black' refers variously to the colour of mourning (stage directions 1.1.69), of alleged ugliness (3.2.66 and 4.2.66–7), of beauty (4.2.71–2), of pride (4.2.98–102), of shamelessness (5.1.122), of vengeance (5.2.50), and, as we have seen, of parental affection. Blackness in the play is not necessarily the Blackness of racism, although it may be. Racism, it seems, is an alternative and a choice, not a hegemonic mindset and an inevitability, even in the savage Rome of Shakespeare's *Titus Andronicus*.

5. 'SLAVES' IN *THE MERCHANT OF VENICE*

then must the Jew be merciful (*The Merchant of Venice*, 4.1.179)

the stranger that dwelleth with you shall be unto you as one born among you, and thou shalt love him as thyself; for ye were strangers in the land of Egypt: I am the LORD your God. (Leviticus 19:33–4)

Love ye therefore the stranger: for ye were strangers in the land of Egypt. (Deuteromony 10:19)

On the contrary, as we have seen in Chapter 1, racial or ethnic tolerance does seem an inaccessible alternative in both of the play-worlds of *The Merchant of Venice*, cosmopolitan Venice and monocultural Belmont. However, this play contains the unique explicit reference in all of Shakespeare's work to the actual operations of chattel slavery, and it is a disapproving one.

This reference comes when, in arguing for his legal right to mutilate Antonio in exchange for his money, Shylock makes a comparison with the uses Venetian Christians make of their 'purchased' slaves:[40]

> You have among you many a purchased slave
> Which, like your asses and your dogs and mules,
> You use in abject and in slavish parts
> Because you bought them. Shall I say to you
> 'Let them be free, marry them to your heirs.
> Why sweat they under burdens? Let their beds
> Be made as soft as yours, and let their palates
> Be seasoned with such viands.' You will answer
> 'The slaves are ours.' So do I answer you.
> The pound of flesh which I demand of him
> Is dearly bought. 'Tis mine, and I will have it. (4.1.89–99)

Thus, by claiming that he does no worse than his Christian detractors, Shylock retorts against the humanitarian objections they have raised to his taking a pound of Antonio's flesh.

Because of their biblical knowledge Shakespeare and his audiences would have recognised that Shylock surely would have known better and was being heavily ironic. For they would have known that multiple commandments in the Old Testament contradict the assumptions behind Shylock's remarks on slaves. For one, in opposition to Shylock's ironic 'Let them be free', meaning their masters would not free them, the Bible demands the manumission of Hebrew slaves every seventh year (males in Exodus 21:2; males and their children, to be treated kindly, in Leviticus 25:39–55; both sexes in Deuteronomy 15:12–18, here with a demand for generous parting gifts), and of all slaves (including non-Hebrews) in jubilee years (Leviticus 25:10). In opposition to Shylock's derisive 'marry them to your heirs', Exodus 21:9–11 provides explicit rules concerning a woman sold by her father to be betrothed to her master's heir. In opposition to Shylock's mocking 'let their palates / Be seasoned with such viands [as your own]', the Bible demands just this of the normally highly restricted priestly food: 'But if the priest buy any soul with his money, he shall eat of it, and he that is born in his house: they shall eat of his meat' (Leviticus 22:11). In general, the Hebrew Bible repeatedly demands fair, generous, and humane treatment for bound servants or slaves (Exodus 20:10, 21:20–1, 21:26–7, 23:12; Leviticus 25:6, 25:39–55; Deuteronomy 5:14; Job 31:13–15). The Bible's oft-repeated rationale for these injunctions is: 'thou shalt remember that thou wast a bondman in the land of Egypt, and the LORD thy God redeemed thee' (Deuteronomy 15:15).

In addition, in equating maiming Antonio with a permissible ill-treatment of animals Shylock defies Jewish laws mandating kindness to beasts (Exodus 23:5 and 12; Deuteronomy 22:4; Proverbs 12:10; Hosea 2:18 even speaks of a holy covenant with beasts). According to Keith Thomas, some early modern Christians may have been misled by biblical inter-pretations that overlooked or allegorised these Old Testament demands for the good treatment of animals,[41] but many ignored these glosses and regarded domestic animals 'in the way that Jews had before them, as essentially within the covenant'.[42]

Thus the disrespect with which Shylock refers to asses, dogs, and mules is also theologically suspect. It has been noted that *The Merchant of Venice* is packed with 'contemptuous or repellent' animal images;[43] of the roughly eighty vehemently negative references to animals in the play, thirty-three are made by Shylock. It may even appear that Shylock conflates Jewish dietary restrictions (which are pointed to, in the play, by Gobbo's 'bacon' jests) with an irrational revulsion against beasts ('Some men there are love not a gaping pig, / Some that are mad if they behold a cat!' (4.1.46–7)). This, a possible equating in *The Merchant of Venice* of the laws of Shylock's religion with irrational phobias, might be taken to indicate ignorant and intolerant leanings in the play itself, rather than in its characters, but I think not. For *The Merchant of Venice* repeatedly signals itself to be a play closely aware of details of scripture.[44] Certainly enough was known of the Old Testament by Shakespeare's audiences to recognise that the vengeful Shylock did not conform with either its letter or its spirit.

There is also a kind of sick joke that works on several levels in Shylock's 'slaves, . . . asses, dogs . . . and mules' argument. If heard carefully, this does not claim that Venetian chattel slaves may be wantonly mutilated or killed, but only that they are unfree, worked hard, and fed and housed coarsely. Shylock's argument by analogy that he may kill Antonio therefore presents a deliberate fallacy or solecism, which is also effectively a self-condemnation of his greater cruelty than that of the Christian slave-owners. There are also obscene dimensions to Shylock's bogus argument. In first equating slaves with animals (asses, dogs, and mules), and then in speaking of them 'married to your heirs', Shylock evokes the play's common images of beasts coupling, here with the stakes raised to human bestiality, in defiance of Exodus 22:19, and in harmony with other aspects of *The Merchant* discussed in the previous chapter.

Although they certainly knew the Bible, it is not nearly so certain that many in Shakespeare's milieu had access to rabbinical commentary or teachings. Yet it seems to me remarkable that Shylock's phrases about Venetian slaves virtually echo, in a reversed sense, the exact contents and language of a comment on Deuteronomy 15:12–15 in the Babylonian Talmud. The biblical context in Deuteronomy commands that the Jewish master give his male or female Jewish slave, who in accordance with the law must be granted freedom after seven years of service, generous parting gifts. Then the Bible considers the case where the slave does not wish to be freed 'because he loveth thee and thine house, because he is well with thee'. The Talmud commentary asserts that such 'being well' reflects the ethically correct method of treating slaves:[45]

Because he is 'well with thee': he must be with [i.e. equal to] thee in food and drink, that thou shouldst not eat white bread and he black bread, thou drink old wine and he new wine, thou sleep in a feather bed and he on straw. Hence it was said, 'Whoever buys a Hebrew slave is like buying a master for himself'.

This seems remarkably similar, in reverse, to Shylock's sarcastic 'Let their beds / Be made as soft as yours, and let their palates / Be seasoned with such viands.' However, since the Talmud was only first printed in Hebrew and Aramaic in Venice in 1520–3, it is hard to attribute the similarity to other than accident. Yet, if Shakespeare did somehow come to know of these injunctions, the passage on slaves would intensify his otherwise established portrayal of Shylock as a very bad Jew, sacrilegious and cruel.

Shakespeare is even less likely to have encountered the writings of his own near contemporary, the sixteenth-century Egyptian rabbinical authority, Radbaz, who had interesting views on slavery, race, and miscegenation. According to Jonathan Schorsch: 'Radbaz and later rabbis held that the [Black] Ethiopian Jews who were purchased as slaves had to be ransomed and freed, despite their deficient Jewish knowledge and practice, as they were descended from the tribe of Dan.' Radbaz also disallowed discrimination against Black Jews, commanding: 'permit this great congregation to marry into the congregation of Israel, to remove from them the hatred and strife [and] since they keep all the mitzvot as Jews, it is forbidden to call them slaves'.[46]

It is highly unlikely that Shakespeare could have known Radbaz's views on slavery. But he may have encountered the views of Jean Bodin or some of his French contemporaries.[47] As we have seen in Chapter 4, Bodin repeatedly discussed slavery;[48] in a 1576 work (published in English in 1606) Bodin explicitly compares Jewish rules regarding manumission of co-religionists to Muslim ones, and praises both if faithfully carried through.[49]

Whatever their source, Shylock's scornful references to Christian slave-owning practices present a heavily derogatory view of others, and of himself. His vision lacks all dignity and humanity, even if it is understood to be retaliatory on the part of a not-tolerated Jew of Venice. As such, it conforms with his earlier snarling remark: 'The villainy you [Christians] teach me I will execute, and it shall go hard but I will better the instruction' (3.1.66–8). There, at the climax of his often sentimentally read 'Hath not a Jew eyes? . . . ' speech, Shylock reviles the Venetian Christians by saying, in effect, 'I, a despicable Jew in your opinion, learn my evil from you, and will outgo you in it.' In so doing he consummately expresses both self-intolerance and other-intolerance. But we must remember that Shylock's outlook is not presented neutrally in *The Merchant of Venice*. The play's non-approval implies the existence of a counterbalancing frame of reference to that of both Shylock and the play's Christian bigots, an early modern frame of reference allowing a place for racial and ethnic tolerance.

6. 'SLAVES' IN *THE TEMPEST*: WHAT KIND OF SERVITUDE, 'WHAT SEAS, WHAT SHORES, WHAT ISLANDS'?

Profound and deliberate confusions of geography in *The Tempest* link with very complex applications of the term 'slave' to the two exotic inhabitants of Prospero's island, the native 'spirit' Ariel and the African-derived Caliban.

On one level, both of these figures are seen to be forced unwillingly, in the manner of Spanish New World slavery, into the service of a European settler. Certainly the model of their servitude is not that of a captive slave taken by Mediterranean pirates and subsequently sold for use, such as is evoked by the story of Marina's abduction in *Pericles*. And because the word 'slave' appears in *The Tempest* in harsh verbal attacks on the unwilling labourer Caliban, and also in a passage in which Prospero threatens Ariel with tortures, it could easily have reminded Shakespeare's audiences of the infamous legend of Spanish cruelty to New World slaves. Indeed, a 1610 Virginia Company promotional tract which Shakespeare probably consulted while composing *The Tempest* boasted that the English who intended to settle in Virginia would not enslave Native Americans, while the Spanish in their plantations had set out to 'preach the Gospell to a nation conquered, and to set their soules at liberty, when [they] have brought their bodies to slavery'.[50]

The imaging in *The Tempest* of an Atlantic style of slavery rather than a Mediterranean one confronts the frequently noted aspects of the play that tangle up Atlantic with Mediterranean motifs. A brief review of these is in order. Although it is clearly associated with Bermuda, there are also indications that Prospero's island lies within 'the Mediterranean float' (1.2.235), somewhere between Tunis and Naples. Yet this is an odd Mediterranean, for Claribel's 'Tunis' is twice said to be immensely remote from Alonso's Naples (2.1.115–17, 2.1.251–62).[51] There is also a contradiction between Ariel's claim that Sycorax was born in Algiers (1.2.262), and Caliban's statement that 'my dam's god', i.e. Sycorax's god, is the Patagonian deity Setebos (1.2.375).[52]

But the notorious sufferings of African or Native American chattel slaves reduced to commodified labour units and housed in the deadly barracks of Spanish mines, pearl fisheries, or plantations do not exactly match up with Ariel's or Caliban's servitude either. The orphaned Caliban had been raised within Prospero's household as an adopted child, but by the play's start has been exiled from Prospero's 'cell' to a nearby inferior 'sty' (1.2.344–50) and forced to provide involuntary labour. This labour could be understood as punitive, although it is also of economic value to Prospero (1.2.347–50, 1.2.312–15). Caliban's exclusion from Prospero's household causes him grief (1.2.334–8). Ariel, on the other hand, is summoned when needed from an ethereal sphere, and is never seen by Miranda, so he/she does not image a household servant. A better match for Ariel's servitude might have been seen in 1610 in the arrangements for bound employment under indentures of many of the new settlers at Jamestown, who served there for a period of years in exchange for their passage to Virginia.[53] Such English fixed-term indentured servitude was, of course, quite different from Spanish New World chattel slavery.[54]

7. THE TEMPEST, VIRGINIA, GEOGRAPHY, AND RACE

No doubt the composition of *The Tempest* had strong connections with English New World travel and settlement;[55] the play's shipwreck storyline derived directly from the amazing news that had just reached London in 1610 of the Gates and Summers party's reappearance following their apparent loss at sea a year earlier en route for Virginia.

Gates and Summers were the leaders of a flotilla of nine ships carrying about five hundred settlers to Jamestown in Virginia. Their flagship, the *Sea Venture*, was caught in a storm off Bermuda in May 1609. The other vessels sent news home of its apparent sinking, although it actually foundered on an island and all aboard survived. In an imperfect but close analogue in *The Tempest*, all aboard King Alonso's ship are miraculously saved on an island, although 'the rest o' th' fleet, / ... all have met again, / And are upon the Mediterranean float / Bound sadly home for Naples, / Supposing that they saw the King's ship wrecked / and his great person perish' (1.2.233–7).

Jamestown, the *Sea Venture*'s destination, was established by the London Virginia Company in 1606–7, and was a second attempt at English colonisation of the territory then called 'Virginia', following an earlier failure on Roanoke Island in 1585. It is the longest-held territory in the New World settled by the English.[56] One particular aspect of Jamestown, which I had not realised before in previous studies,[57] rests on a simple geographical fact: the latitude of Jamestown is within a degree of that of classical Athens (37°12′33″ N versus 37°58′47″ N, a difference of about 50 miles). Raleigh's settlement at Roanoke was a bit further south, at 35°52′55″ N (just below the Peloponnese); the Bermuda Islands, where Gates and Summers were shipwrecked (and which are named in *The Tempest*, 1.2.230), lie at about 32°18′ N, still within the Mediterranean ambit.[58]

By contrast, at 51°30′25″ N, London lies considerably northwards of Jamestown or Bermuda, and most of Britain lies further north still. The facts about Virginia's latitude relative to England's would have been extremely resonant in Shakespeare's age; latitude was after all the basis of the geohumoral theories which we have mentioned in Chapter 5, and which we now must investigate further.

Originating in Aristotle's *Politics*,[59] these theories emerged in Shakespeare's period with varying emphases; in one humankind was divided into three distinct categories according to latitude, with the ideal balance of 'spirit' (e.g. energy) and 'intelligence' at the centre (as it had been in Aristotle), in the other the similar differences as a result of climate were more continuously attributed according to latitude.[60] The theory emphasising a threefold division was expounded by Giovanni Botero, who placed the English among other northern peoples who are tall, strong, courageous, fertile, warlike, but inclined to heavy eating and drinking, and mechanical artificers rather than contemplative thinkers or any sort of intellectuals.[61] Botero even says of the 'Northern people' that 'their wittes consist in their hands'.[62] Jean Bodin also subscribed to a threefold division, but was more ready to allow for gradations within each zone, so that, for instance, 'although the English haue had great victories over the French, and conquered the country which lieth South to them, yet for these nine hundred yeres they could neuer expell the Scottish men out of the island'.[63]

The sharper threefold divisions of Botero are closer to a full-blown Racial theory than Bodin's version, yet Botero explains tolerantly that since each of the divisions of humankind 'haue their faults as well as their vertues', none should 'detract' from the excellences or 'taxe' the short-comings of the others.[64] Overall, both Bodin and Botero convey the same kind of distinctions, which are summarised by Bodin thus:[65]

The people therefore of the middle regions haue more force than they of the South, & lesse policie: and more wit than they of the North, & lesse force; and are more fit to commaunde and gouerne Commonweales, and more iust in their actions . . . euen as great armies and mightie powers have come out of the North; euen so the hidden knowledge of Philosophie, the Mathematiks, and other contemplatiue science, are come out of the South: and the politike sciences, lawes, and the studie thereof, the grace of well speaking and discoursing, haue their beginning in the middle regions, and all great empires haue bene there established.

Also, both Bodin and Botero view the English as Northern, and so forceful but deficient culturally and intellectually.

When theories such as these are compared by Mary Floyd-Wilson with later Racialism startling differences appear.[66] According to her, geohumoralism became 'the dominant mode of ethnic distinctions in the late sixteenth and early seventeenth centuries'.[67] This meant that 'the classification of people during this period still conformed to the ancient tripartite divisions of climatic regions – northern, southern and temperate zones . . . Ideally *moderate* complexions, in both appearance and temperament, belonged to those inhabitants of the middle, temperate region'; the Renaissance maintained beliefs in accordance with 'Classical geohumoral discourse' which:[68]

had depended on a Mediterranean-centered world, and relied on a logic of inversion to characterize the north and the south. As the barbaric outsiders of the *polis* or *oikumene*, white northerners and black southerners, or Scythians and Ethiopians, were paired together in intemperance but opposed in particular qualities.

That is to say, in accordance with such theories Black Africans were believed to be excessively intellectual but physically feeble, and the English, as northern Whites, were believed to be physically robust but dull-witted.[69] As a result Britons would tend to be valiant but uncivilised, or as one contemporary Englishman put it, 'blockish, uncivill, fierce and warlike'.[70]

The currency of such ideas makes it evident why many Britons apparently suffered from a kind of latitude envy, thinking the natives of middle or Mediterranean latitudes apt to produce intellectual and cultural achievements superior to their own. Many writers and dramatists contemporary with Shakespeare alluded to such notions,[71] and similar allusions continued throughout the seventeenth century, with at least eight in John Milton's writings.[72] The most famous of these appears in *Paradise Lost* when Milton expresses concern that his creative abilities may be unequal to writing his great epic. His theme, says Milton, excels those of all the ancients, and so he intends to rise to 'Things unattempted yet in prose or rhyme' (1:14–16). In his authorial introduction to Book Nine, Milton even belittles *The Iliad* and *The Aeneid*, and hopes to outdo them: 'unless an age too late, or cold / Climate, or Years damp my intended wing' (9:44–5). This passage, with its alliterative 'cold / Climate', and depressing verb 'damp', may indeed have been inspired by a passage on cold climates as a cause of 'dull' melancholy in Robert Burton's great psychological treatise.[73]

As far as I know, such geohumoral theories have not been tied to the geography of *The Tempest*, where a mixture of Mediterranean and Bermudan (and possibly Virginian) locales is at issue. Probably this is because these theories based on latitude classically were applied only to Old World longitudes. It seems that a notion of New World geohumoralism was excluded by Mary Floyd-Wilson when, introducing the tripartite north–south axis of European climate theory she prefaced the description with the proviso: 'Despite Europe's contact with the New World'.[74] I wonder if she need have done so (even though Aristotle and Strabo did not envision America, of course). For in fact there was comment in Shakespeare's time on the New World applicability of geohumoralism: both Bodin and Botero applied it to Magellan's reports on 'Giants *Patagones*', commenting that geohumoral influences on the far south of South America are just like those on the far north of the (European) northern hemisphere in producing men of huge stature and strength, but 'otherwise verie simple'.[75]

It is fascinating that an English translation of the same 'Histories of the Indies' that supplied Bodin with his information on these 'great and mightie' Patagonians supplied Shakespeare also with the name 'Sycorax', a deity named both by Magellan's 'giantes' and also by Caliban in *The Tempest*.[76] It has also been argued that Bodin's climate theory had an 'unmistakable' influence on Shakespeare's plays.[77] Moreover, again indicating a universal concept of climate theory, distinct fears were expressed in Shakespeare's England concerning the possible physiological unsuitability of English-born persons for residence at the southern latitudes of 'Virginia'.[78]

Taking all this together, I will now make a suggestion which will be tested in the remainder of this chapter. This is, that 'the still-vexed

Bermudas' and 'the Mediterranean float' of *The Tempest* (1.2.230, 1.2.235) are not only confounded or contrasted in the play, but also are imaged as in some ways equivalent. For in the geohumoral sense both are in the temperate middle zone, and therefore apt to produce peoples and cultures combining sound intellect with a vigorous disposition, and therefore able to sustain effective and successful societies.

If Shakespeare's world was mindful of the nearly equivalent latitudes of the Classical Mediterranean civilisations, of newly settled Jamestown, and of Gates's and Summers's Bermuda, some very odd reflections may arise. For Shakespeare's English countrymen, Northerners, were currently attempting to colonise Jamestown with ill success; we will next consider if their problems were seen to be a product of their own civility and civilisation compared with that of the Native Americans they encountered.

8. 'SLAVES' IN *THE TEMPEST*: GEOHUMORALISM AND ETHNOLOGY AT JAMESTOWN

we are taught to acknowledge every man, that beares the Impression of Gods stampe, to be not only our neighbour, but to be our brother, howe far distinguished and removed by Seas or lands soever from us.[79]

As mentioned, the shipwreck subplot of *The Tempest* distinctly mirrored the Gates and Summers party's famous Bermudan shipwreck and salvation; in fact, details of the play echo accounts of those events in contemporary written documents.[80] Shakespeare would have found in the same sources the details of the shocking sequel to the salvation story, and this too became prominent news in London.[81] After a year spent on their uninhabited Bermudan island, during which they built and provisioned two more ships, most of the passengers and crew of the *Sea Venture* succeeded in reaching Jamestown. They arrived there on 23 May 1610, after a very harsh Virginian winter had reduced the English settlement of over five hundred to a remnant of about sixty starving wretches, and this tragedy very nearly ended the colony. It was saved only by an opportune last-minute arrival of a new consignment of food and colonists from England. These matters were extensively described in a long eyewitness letter by William Strachey.[82] Shakespeare seems to have somehow read this private letter (dated 15 July 1610, unpublished until 1625), from which he adopted images and language for the storm scene in *The Tempest*.[83]

This letter, in common with other early published accounts,[84] emphasised the dreadful inefficiencies and rebellions that beset the failing Jamestown enterprise. Yet Strachey's and other texts did not attribute Jamestown's 1609–10 'starving times' solely to the idleness, insubordination, and civil ineffectiveness they described as endemic there. They also described as a main cause of the settlement's woes a well-organised Algonkian trade boycott, effectively warfare by sanctions, which had deprived it of food. Considerable chagrin attached in these texts to the spectacle of the Algonkian ability to live easily on the land, while the colony was unable to feed itself. Implicit also was a realisation that the Algonkians were united and well governed, while the English colonists were divisive and undisciplined.

In fact, according to rumours circulating in England, Jamestown had long been afflicted by its colonists' violence, rebellion, laziness, and disorder.[85] And even an *official* 1610 Virginia Council promotional tract confirmed that certain English renegades had 'created the *Indians* our implacable enemies by some violence they had offered', while detailing as 'an incredible example of [the settlers'] idleness' that 'some of them eat their fish raw, rather than they would go a stones cast to fetch wood and dress it'.[86] Such reports may have seemed confirmation of claims in a series of English-language pamphlets emanating from Catholic Europe that Jamestown's settlers were unfit, and were dragooned there unwillingly.[87]

By 1610 the circumstances at Jamestown were even worse than were claimed by Catholic propagandists. A manuscript by George Percy, who was the colony's president during the 'starving time', reveals renegading, mutinying, stealing food, drinking the blood of the wounded, disinterring and eating human corpses, murder and infanticide for purposes of cannibalism, hoarding at outposts while the main fort starved, and popular demands for a massacre of Algonkian women and children.[88] Such outrages make the settlers seem savages, not the Algonkians.

The representation in *The Tempest* of rebellion and rapacity on every social level on the part of Europeans stranded in a wilderness may well have been inspired by accounts of very recent events in Bermuda (where some rebels were hanged by Gates and Summers), and in Virginia. Moreover, at Jamestown, as in *The Tempest*, sojourning Europeans entirely depended upon the services of native inhabitants for material survival; Caliban is able to feed Prospero because, like the Algonkians, he is able to thrive in his environment. Also, Prospero and the Italian courtiers in *The Tempest* disdain physical work and workers; among other things,[89] this may be seen to mirror the situation in which an irate John Smith wrote to the Virginia Council in 1608 complaining 'Though there be fish in the Sea, foules in the ayre, and Beasts in the woods, their bounds are so large, they are so wilde, and we are so weake and ignorant, we cannot much trouble them', and so requested a different kind of colonist: 'When you send againe I intreat you rather send but thirty Carpenters, husbandmen, gardiners, fisher men, blacksmiths, masons, and diggers vp of tree roots, well provided; then a thousand of such as we haue.'[90]

Moreover a display in multiple parallel subplots of *The Tempest* of European greed for power sadly correlated with the tumultuous strife between contenders for the leadership of early Jamestown.[91] In the arts of government the northern-born English seem to have been very much bettered by the Virginians native to the temperate middle latitudes of Jamestown.

In addition, a number of Englishmen expressed admiration for the cultural achievements of the Virginians. Their mechanical skills as in making fishing weirs received particular praise (echoed in *The Tempest* 2.2.179).[92] So did their artistic abilities; for instance, the letter by Strachey about the *Sea Venture* (which Shakespeare somehow read) expressed admiration for the finesse involved in the manufacture of 'a delicate wrought fine kinde of Mat the Indians make, with which (as they can be trucked for or snatched up) our people do dresse their chambers ... which make their houses so much the more handsome'.[93] Even more interestingly, in another context Strachey reveals admiration for the *moral* culture, as opposed to the material culture, of the Virginian 'Indians'. This appears in a manuscript Strachey produced *c.* 1607–12 (quoted in the epigraph above) which notes that when playing their skilful version of football the Algonkians 'never strike vp one anothers heeles as we doe, not accompting that praise worthy to purchase a goale by such an advantage'.[94] One commentator notes that this passage portrays the Algonkians showing 'more sportsmanship than the British', and adds 'It may be remembered that Kent in *King Lear* expresses no high opinion of English football players.'[95]

In his famous 1588 *Report* on Virginia,[96] Thomas Harriot also analysed the Algonkians' material achievements alongside what he observed to be their moral excellences. As I have argued elsewhere, Harriot and his collaborator, the pictorial artist John White, strove to report the undistorted truth about the portions of Virginia they explored between 1585 and 1586.[97] Among the captions that Harriot wrote for engravings taken by Theodore de Bry from White's remarkable watercolour drawings of Algonkians,[98] two accompany images of abundant food being shared by Algonkian people, and read:[99]

they are verye sober in their eatinge, and drinkinge, and consequentlye verye longe liued because they do not oppress nature;

Yet they are moderate in their eatinge wher by they auoide sicknes. I would to god we would followe their example.

Harriot's text, which the images illustrated,[100] proved conclusively that the native inhabitants of North America had the means to be greedy or intemperate had they been so inclined.[101] Harriot therefore commented that he wished the English would follow the example of temperate moderation he observed in Virginia, which, he also wrote, is a place of 'holsome' climate in accordance with its middle latitude.[102]

Here again, then, an alignment arises between geohumoral theories of the temperance-inducing influence of middling latitudes and superiorities attributed to the Native Americans, who were at least in part models for Shakespeare's creation of the two natives of Prospero's island.

9. 'SLAVES' AND *THE TEMPEST*: FROM ABUSE TO RADICAL TOLERANCE

A simple objection might be made to the congruity alleged above of European cupidity and corruption reported from Bermuda and James-town with the Milanese plotting and murderous contention seen in the *The Tempest*, and of the contrasts of these with the Algonkian temperance, cohesion, and competence reported from Virginia. For the analogue in *The Tempest* with those Native Americans would be Ariel and Caliban. And isn't Caliban named after the New World's notorious cannibals,[103] and described as a 'salvage and deformed slave' in the First Folio's 'Names of the Actors'? And isn't Ariel first seen as a flighty and whining subordinate who, like Caliban, comes under the lash of Prospero's tongue?

The two final sections of this analysis of *The Tempest* will attempt to meet that objection, in the first by examining closely the confrontations in which Caliban and Ariel are abused, and in the second by showing that the images of these two are revised very positively as the play proceeds.

Prospero near the play's start uses nauseous epithets to describe or summon Caliban: 'A freckled whelp, hag-born'; 'Dull thing'; 'Thou earth, thou'; 'Thou poisonous slave, got by the devil himself'; 'Thou most lying slave'; 'Filth as thou art'; 'Hag-seed'; 'malice' (1.2.284; 1.2.286; 1.2.316; 1.2.321; 1.2.346; 1.2.348; 1.2.367; 1.2.369). Moreover, Ariel is first seen in *The Tempest* imaging a realistic sort of truculent Elizabethan household subordinate.[104]

Thus the Ariel we first see in *The Tempest* and the irascible Prospero of the play's start fall out badly over the remaining length of the term of service agreed between them:

ARIEL   Let me remember thee what thou hast promised
           Which is not yet performed me.
PROSPERO   How now? Moody?
           What is 't thou canst demand?
ARIEL   My liberty.
PROSPERO   Before the time be out? No more!
ARIEL   I prithee,
           Remember I have done thee worthy service,
           Told thee no lies, made thee no mistakings, served
           Without or grudge or grumblings. Thou did promise
           To bate me a full year.

                                                    (1.2.244–51)

As mentioned above, attempts to foreshorten agreed periods of service were typically represented by Shakespeare as both worrying and comic. But what follows from this interchange in *The Tempest* is actually very harsh. Prospero immediately accuses Ariel of having forgotten the torture from which he/she had been released by him, which Ariel denies. This denial, or its tone, draws from Prospero the shockingly abusive: 'Thou liest, malignant thing' (1.2.258). Prospero then goes on to remind Ariel of his/her sufferings at the hands of a former enslaver, the Algerian witch Sycorax, including the following significant words: 'Thou, my *slave*, / As thou *report'st* thyself, was then her *servant*' (1.2.271–2, emphasis mine). Here Prospero angrily contrasts 'slave' with 'servant', emphasising that Ariel, a self-*reported* 'slave' to Prospero seems to think he had only been a 'servant' to the cruel, torturing Sycorax. The sarcasm in Prospero's comparison reveals a mounting anger, and a sense of being betrayed. The betrayal was in Ariel's supposed ingratitude, for rather than enslaving him/her, says Prospero, he had released Ariel from an imprisoning torture lasting twelve years.

Prospero becomes so infuriated by his recollection of Ariel's allegation that he threatens to outdo the tyrant Sycorax, merely 'If thou more murmur'st' (1.2.295–6), and to subject Ariel to a reimposition, with an intensification, of Sycorax's tortures.[105] By contrast, the worst Prospero ever threatens the would-be rapist Caliban with are cramps and pinches. Pique overcomes proportionality, vengeance compassion, and hypersensitivity tolerance. Yet, at last in the play, Prospero comes to appreciate Ariel in his tender salutations at their parting (5.1.97–8 and 5.1.320–2), and to accept or 'acknowledge' Caliban as 'mine' (5.1.278–9).[106] That is, Prospero learns better: from whom he learns is truly remarkable.

10. 'SLAVES' IN *THE TEMPEST*: REMARKABLE SERVICE

Now I will attempt to strengthen the alignment, alleged above, of Ariel and Caliban with the images of the Virginian Algonkians reported on from Roanoke or Jamestown.

As previously noted, at the time of the writing of *The Tempest* the Virginia Algonkians were evidently very effective in the planning and execution of their trade warfare against Jamestown. In fact, when Gates and Summers arrived, the Fort was on the point of being burned down by the fleeing colonists so that they could not be forced to return. Of course, Ariel is an excellent planner and executor of plans; he is Prospero's agent in arranging for all the action in the play. Caliban, too, demonstrates skills of sound planning and of focusing on a plan. Thus, although he shows naivety amounting to folly when he offers his services to the European renegades Trinculo and Stephano, when it comes to plotting a usurpation, Caliban's strategy and focus far excel theirs. Caliban's planned rebellion is also far more intelligent in its aims than that of the upper-class Italians Antonio and Sebastian, whose assassinations and fratricide would gain them only the status of King of Naples (and king's aide), quite meaningless in the wilderness.

Also, eloquent material archaeological evidence recently excavated at Jamestown Fort reveals the practical services rendered to the early Jamestown community by the surrounding Algonkians. Some of these were household services, as indicated by fragments of Algonkian cooking implements excavated within James Fort.[107] More important still were the essential Algonkian services of food purveying to the settlement; material evidence again tells the story first of food voluntarily offered by the Algonkians, then of it purchased or extorted from them, and finally of it deliberately withdrawn by them.[108] This sequence so closely matches the evolution of Caliban's relations with Prospero's household as to suggest that Shakespeare must have had knowledge of Jamestown's economic woes.[109]

Ariel too offers much-needed food to sojourning Europeans in *The Tempest*, and he too then withholds it (3.3.19–82). So Ariel, as much as Caliban, displays parallels to Powhattan's very effective boycott of the English colony at Jamestown.

Moreover, the moral impact of Ariel and Caliban, like that of the Virginia Algonkians, severely disrupts European presumptions. Partly these are just presumptions of sufficiency; John Smith lamented the inability of the Jamestown settlers to take the 'fish . . . , foules . . . , and Beasts' that the Algonkians were able to purvey to them if they wished to. Likewise in *The Tempest* the native Ariel and Caliban are essential for Prospero and his household, and so Prospero says reluctantly of his 'slave' Caliban, 'We cannot miss him' (1.2.313).

But do the 'deformed' figure of Caliban and the ethereal one of Ariel have moral dimensions? I have mentioned that in his efficiency Caliban in effect rebukes the Italians by bettering them in practicality and purposefulness. Powhattan and his Algonkian confederation likewise showed far more resoluteness and effectiveness than did the endlessly contentious and ineffective leaders and colonists of early Jamestown. Thus both Powhattan and Caliban hold up a mirror to undisciplined Europeans to show them in a poor light.

There may even be a spiritual dimension to the figure made by Caliban. Many texts claimed that Jamestown's purposes included the conversion of the Algonkians to Christianity, holding them to be 'our bretheren: for the same God made them as well as vs, of as good matter as he made vs, gaue them as perfect and good soules and bodies as to vs, and the same Messiah & sauior is sent to them as to vs . . . they are our bretheren, wanting not title to Christ, but the knowledge of Christ'.[110] Thus Gates was instructed to 'with all propensenes and dilegence, endeavour the conversion of the natiues' when he became Jamestown's governor in 1610,[111] and a 1610 promotional pamphlet, taken to be a source for *The Tempest*, stated that conversion was the '*Principall*' motive for the settlement.[112] But if Caliban, tutored by Prospero, first learns to name the heavenly lights (1.2.336–8), he later condemns civil language as only a means to curse (1.2.365–6). He even comes to worshipping the drunkards' bottle of 'celestial liquor' or its bearers (2.2.114–15, 123–4, 141–2), and reverts to invoking the pagan god Setebos (5.1.264). Yet the European rogues of the play also swear upon their liquor bottle (2.2.118, 125–9) and attempt unchristian deeds. At the end of the play Caliban is distinguished from Stephano and Trinculo, and also their 'betters' Antonio and Sebastian, in that only he, not they, is able finally to resolve to 'seek for grace' (5.1.295).

The spiritual impact of the figure of Ariel is stronger still. Acting as a proxy for Prospero, he tests whether the Italians who had usurped Prospero are ready to repeat the deed, and finds that they are keen to usurp and murder King Alonso. On account of their unrepentance, Ariel offers the hungry Italians a banquet and then, as a Harpy, eloquently spoils it, and reminds them of their sins (3.3.68–82). This educative correction of the highest-placed of the sojourning Europeans is provided by an exotic island creature with strange manners and appearance.

Ariel's Harpy speech might be seen to be similar in its subversive moral thrust to the essay 'Of the Cannibals' in which Montaigne cites the exotic virtues of a newly encountered native Brazilian culture to mock any presumption of superiority in European mores. Of course, a passage from this very Montaigne essay (as translated by John Florio) is famously plagiarised by Gonzalo in *The Tempest* 2.1.149–62.[113] But in fact the Harpy speech is only a rehearsal for an additional educative function of Ariel that goes much further than any envisioned by Montaigne in that essay.

The moral instruction to the Europeans offered by Ariel as the Harpy is delivered on Prospero's behalf, but as the play unfolds we see Ariel as being capable of independently offering crucial moral instruction to Prospero himself. A fuller understanding of this surprising development is made possible thanks to a 1965 textual discovery by Eleanor Prosser.[114] Briefly, Prosser uncovered a second echo of Montaigne within *The Tempest*, besides the well-known quotation from 'Of the Cannibals', in Gonzalo's sentimental ruminations on an ideal plantation. This second echo is from Florio's translation of Montaigne's essay 'Of Cruelty',[115] which, as Prosser says, contrasts with 'Of the Cannibals' by praising not an extreme heroic stoicism, but rather a living virtue sensitive to mental pain and so capable of voluntary sacrifice. Ariel applies these ideas when he urges the angry Prospero to forgive his former enemies by allowing his 'affections' to become 'tender' (5.1.18–19). Prospero agrees to this, and in his noble speech beginning, 'Though with their high wrongs I am struck to the quick', he echoes, as Prosser discovered, the opening of 'Of Cruelty'.

So an exotic islander in *The Tempest* prompts a proud European princely magus to appreciate, as Montaigne put it in 'Of Cruelty', a 'vertue ... *more noble*' than merely benign 'goodnesse', or honourable vengeance, no matter how brave. Shakespeare therefore gives to his self-confessedly non-human native islander an extraordinary moral authority, one going far beyond the range of the admiration of mechanical skills or warlike qualities or barbaric arts often allowed to 'savages'.

This is an authority independent of rank, hierarchy, nation, climate, or 'race'. That this can be asserted, even by an outlandish servant, implies the presence of an unusual, even a radical, kind of tolerance by the end of *The Tempest* (although Ariel is not the only servant possessing a high moral standing in Shakespeare's plays).[116] And Prospero learning to tolerate those who (justifiably) show him to have been in the wrong shows one of the hardest-to-achieve kinds of tolerance of all those celebrated in Shakespeare's work.

From Shakespeare's perspective there was perhaps only one kind of tolerance even more difficult to achieve. That is tolerance following a perceived personal betrayal. A discussion of how tolerance of that sort features in two late Shakespeare plays, in one case also summing up all the other kinds of tolerance discussed above, will conclude this study.

CHAPTER 7

Afterword: tolerance as a species of love

LEAR	Be your tears wet? Yes, faith. I pray, weep not.
	If you have poison for me, I will drink it.
	I know you do not love me; for your sisters
	Have, as I do remember, done me wrong.
	You have some cause; they have not.
CORDELIA	No cause, no cause.

(King Lear (Folio) 4.6.64–8)

I will not be able to conclude in any real sense on a topic as vast and ramified as Shakespeare and tolerance. But a few larger questions can be addressed here near the end, and an illustration or two offered in support of some tentative answers.

These questions revolve around the topic 'is tolerance one thing or many things?' (To see it as one thing, by the way, is not the same as to allege that all forms of oppression – sexism, slavery, racism, xenophobia, religious persecution – must be mutually 'imbricated' or have a common origin.)

There has certainly been diversity in the details in the preceding chapters, perhaps suggesting a multiplicity of tolerances portrayed by Shakespeare. But there have also been overlaps between the various chapters, suggesting that a notion of tolerance might have some unity.

Indeed Chapter 4 mentioned a possibly universal or paradigmatic prerequisite for all of the varied sorts of tolerance depicted by Shakespeare. This would be the mutual possession of some desire coupled with a perceived possibility of some shared work towards fulfilling it. The kinds of this desire may vary; I have proposed in different places the possibilities of both epistemological desires, that is desires to know and to understand the unfamiliar, and of practical desires such as to become more effective in the worship of God or in the pursuits of war or of peace.

Let me reiterate a position expounded in Chapter 2, that gender-based divisiveness is a topic treated in many of Shakespeare's works, and is portrayed in some places as so extreme that men and women are as far divided from one another as are separate tribes or sects. Of course, the

169

main counter-force to the gender divisions and discords seen in such plays as *Love's Labour's Lost, Two Gentlemen of Verona,* or *Measure for Measure* is erotic desire, although epistemological or societal desires may play a role as well.

For Shakespeare, erotic desire, or love more generally, can overcome some very high barriers. Significant bars to mutual understanding are emphasised especially in the portrayal of the unlikely love affair at the core of *Antony and Cleopatra,* in which the two protagonists are mis-matched in their culture, temperament, gender, nationality, religion, and (in so far as this has meaning) 'race'. Thus their initial differences run the gamut of the themes of the present study. How Antony's and Cleoptra's love becomes a gateway to a remarkable tolerance will become the principal example in this Afterword.

Preliminary to that it is necessary to make a particular kind of dis-tinction. First we should note that much of the intolerance portrayed by Shakespeare lacks a rationally justified cause, and therefore is (in com-edies), or might have been (mainly in tragedies), overcome by means of a better will and understanding. But sometimes, as in the cases of Cymbeline and Belarius, or Posthumus and Iachimo, or Prospero and Alonso, or Cordelia and Lear, Shakespeare presents the theme of someone forgiving a person who has actually done them a great harm. Here is where the distinction I am after arises: the act of forgiving in such cases may or may not be inwardly equivalent to acquiring tolerance. *The Tempest* contrasted with *King Lear* can illustrate this difference.

I have argued at length previously that Prospero in *The Tempest* experi-ences monumental internal struggles on account of being 'struck to th' quick' (5.1.25) by (chiefly among others) a 'false brother' (1.2.92).[1] Antonio, that brother, never repents of his evils, and in consequence Prospero 'forgives' him only with a superadded condemnation: 'I do forgive thee, / Unnatural though thou art' (5.1.78–9). Then, Prospero's last words in the play to Antonio and his accomplice contain threats to expose their recent evil plots unless they behave (5.1.128–30), and again he forgives his brother with a superaddition:

> For you, most wicked sir, whom to call brother
> Would even infect my mouth, I do forgive
> Thy rankest fault, *all of them,* and require
> My dukedom of thee, which perforce I know
> Thou must restore. (5.1.132–6; emphasis mine)

Bitterness obviously persists in the strong reservation voiced in Prospero's phrase '*all of them*'; at the play's end Prospero's anguished questioning near its start, 'Mark his condition and th' event, then tell me / If this might be a brother' (1.2.117–18), remains unresolved. The absence of human comprehension, necessitated by Antonio's imperviousness, allows only Prospero's bare or necessitated forgiveness, not his tolerance. Nor should Antonio receive tolerance, for, as noted in the Introduction, Shakespeare never suggests that evil should be tolerated.

But, on the contrary, entirely no reservations or hints of bitterness appear in Cordelia's assuring her father 'No cause, no cause' in the passage quoted in the epigraph above. This stunning interchange, in which she pours grace on the repentant Lear, sublimely expresses absolute tolerance.

With such contrasts established, let us now consider *Antony and Cleopatra*. The character of Shakespeare's Antony is modelled on Aristotle's description of *megalopsychia*. With regard to forgiveness, that means being not 'mindful of wrongs; for it is not the part of a proud man to have a long memory, especially for wrongs, but rather to overlook them'.[2] Thus, bringing forward such a trait, Shakespeare went beyond his source in Plutarch and elaborated the story of the great generosity of Antony to the army-deserter Enobarbus after Enobarbus had betrayed him. The seemingly contrary meanness in Antony's resenting the independent achievements of his officers where these had benefited him, as described by Ventidius in *Antony and Cleopatra* 3.1.11–27 (and as only hinted at by Plutarch), in fact also accords with Aristotle's *megalopsychia*, for this makes men 'hear of [any service] they have received . . . with displeasure' (1124b 10–15: 993).

However, according to Enobarbus (echoing Plutarch), Antony all too readily acknowledges demeaning pleasures and trivial benefits conferred on him by his 'wrangling queen' Cleopatra. The austerity of Antony's *megalopsychia* is undermined by one of Shakespeare's greatest teasers and jokers.

But sometimes, when Cleopatra coquettishly or manipulatively misleads or betrays him, Antony becomes furiously angry and lets this be seen. This public anger is again no sign of *megalopsychia*; it seems that, in relations with Cleopatra, Antony's 'great-souled' pride, virtue, and restraint are consistently destroyed. At the play's worst moment, when Cleopatra has ruined him by fleeing the very sea battle that she had insisted upon, Antony supposes that she has betrayed him for Caesar's sake and calls her publicly, 'This foul Egyptian . . . triple-turned whore' (4.13.10–13).

But, of course, that is not the very worst moment of betrayal. Worse comes when Antony learns that, fearing his 'rage / Would not be purged', Cleopatra only falsely 'sent word she was dead' (4.15.121–2). This, a typical act of manipulative duplicity, is the other side of Cleopatra's penchant for delightful play-acting with which she had enchanted Antony. Then she sends a messenger to rescind the lie, but he arrives after Antony has mortally wounded himself in a bungled suicide attempt. He had intended to follow Cleopatra in a noble death ('I come, my Queen'); her self-serving fabrication has in effect murdered him.

To say this more moderately: because he does not fully understand her, Cleopatra has misled Antony, even after their long liaison (of fourteen years, according to Plutarch). There are some mitigating aspects of this. Cleopatra, for one, is a master dramatist and actor; she is even capable of duping the super-cunning Octavius Caesar out of his triumph. It is also to Antony's credit that he gives the Egyptian Cleopatra credit for a Roman-like resolution for suicide, and after his death his faith in her is justified. Yet, unmistakably, he misunderstands her, and we should ask what gaps, what causes, separate Antony from Cleopatra even at the point of their deaths.

One cause could be a difference of religion, which in their cases is linked to gender. As John Wilders points out, the Egyptians in Shakespeare's play repeatedly swear by or pray to the goddess Isis. Wilders adds that, according to source materials Shakespeare would have known, Cleopatra herself identified with and dressed up as Isis, and according to the same sources Isis was a goddess of mutability, multiplicity, fertility, love affairs, and of the 'female principle of nature'.[3] She thus represented principles in all ways contrary to a Roman ethic/religion that idealised manly hardness, consistency, self-denial, and continence.

Also prominent in the play are many mentions of Antony's and Cleopatra's difference in nationality (although nationality as a concept is problematised by the image of an expanding Roman empire in Shakespeare's most globe-hopping play). Does the play also imply concerns about a perceived difference of 'race', as many have alleged? Racial or colour awareness in the play is seemingly relative to points of view. Cleopatra is praised as a 'Rare Egyptian!' by one Roman commentator (2.2.225), and denigrated by another for her 'tawny front' and 'gipsy's lust' (1.1.6, 1.1.10). Antony, too, when furious with her, says Cleopatra 'Like a right gipsy hath at fast and loose / Beguiled me to the very heart of loss' (4.13.28–9).

To gauge the meaning of this we must ask what 'gipsy' or 'Egyptian' meant to an Elizabethan. Aspects of that meaning may be traced in a sequence of three Tudor statutes of 1530, 1554, and 1562 concerning (respectively) 'people' or 'persons' or 'vagabonds' (in all cases) 'calling themselves Egyptians'. The first of these statutes (22.H.8 c.10) expels them and seizes their goods with a restitution made of any stolen items. The second statute (1&2.Ph&M c.24) fines any importers or supporters of 'Egyptians', makes an Egyptian's continued residence a felony, but excludes from any 'hurt' or 'pain' 'persons commonly called *Egyptians* [who] shall leave that naughty, idle and ungodly life and company', and who will 'honestly exercise himself in some lawful work or occupation'. The last of the gipsy statutes (5.Eliz.1 c.20 – there were no more) extends the felony to those 'counterfeiting, transforming or disguising themselves by the apparel, speech or other behaviour, like unto such vagabonds, commonly called or calling themselves Egyptians'. It also allows native-born *Egyptians* to reside as citizens in *'England* or *Wales*' so long as they are 'in some honest service' or 'at home with their parents'. It is interesting to note the varied implications of these provisions, both practical and theoretical. Practically,[4] some, but actually few, 'Egyptians' were expelled or executed for felony. This was thanks, apparently, to lenient law enforcement, exceptions made on technicalities, or because native birth was proven. The worst persecution occurred in York in 1596 when one hundred and six were arrested and nine executed. As for theoretical implications, the second statute held that behaviour and not 'racial' identity defined the felony of being a gipsy. The third law made non-gipsies who behaved as gipsies subject to the same punishments as born gipsies; speech, apparel, and conduct – and not, for instance, skin colour or lineage – defined those accounted to be 'Egyptian' felons.

All this does not absolutely prove that Cleopatra was not seen as a Racial 'other', although Shakespeare was probably well aware that historically she was in fact the last of a Hellenistic Greek dynasty. But it does indicate a likelihood that Cleopatra's otherness seen in the play has far more to do with her gender, personal style, and conduct than with her descent or sunburned skin colour.

Now let us return to Antony bleeding to death, being ignominiously hauled up into Cleopatra's monument (4.16.43–61). He has time left to tell her not to 'Lament nor sorrow' at his death, and to advise her on whom around Caesar best to trust for her safety. This, his other-considering and brave death, restores Antony's status in terms of *megalopsychia*.

But more than that, what Antony does *not* say, nor show any inclination to say, shows him finally to be a full man in terms of tolerance. He indicates no impatience with, no tendency to rail about, having been induced to sacrifice his life by Cleopatra's dissimulation. He only wishes her to live on, her inimitable vitality intact, after his passing. It seems he has understood fully at last, and admires without reservation, the life-affirming principles by which she operates.

Then the play's Fifth Act shows that Antony's hard-won tolerance of Cleopatra and her Egyptian ethos wins her over in turn to his Roman values, or at least part-way there. It is impossible to paraphrase the intensity of the ending of *Antony and Cleopatra*, or to explain fully just how, amidst a welter of conflicting forces, Cleopatra becomes 'marble-constant' and dies a 'lass unparalleled'. But surely the apotheoses of the play's two heroes, and the heroism in both their good ends, has to do with a convergence between contrasting human types who at the end, by learning tolerance, each come to absorb from the other what is best in their differing human possibilities.

Notes

INTRODUCTION

1 Laursen, 1999a, 3, objecting to Walzer, 1997, 11, denies the label 'tolerance' to the open-mindedness central to kinds of tolerance mainly to be considered here. Yet Laursen and Nederman, 1998, 1, rejects pre-ordained limitations on definitions of tolerance or toleration.

2 See Chapter 4 for a brief account of several of these revisionists.

3 See the essays in Ricoeur, 1996.

4 Reasons for this included the palpably greater sophistication of some Eastern regions and the lack of the knowledge needed for mere survival in North America, where indigenous peoples were thriving; see R. Barbour, 2003, and Sokol, 2003.

5 Murphy, 2002, xiii.

6 So Williams, 1996a, 37, argues that neither indifference nor prudence can found 'an attitude of genuine tolerance' and MacCulloch, 1996a, 199–200, distinguishes from tolerance both 'concord by coercion' and 'concord by discussion'.

7 Williams, 1996b, 25.

8 Walzer, 1997, 52. Laursen, 1999a, 2–3, rejects Walzer's full range of tolerance-motives, holding that it is better to understand some of these as 'the other extreme [from persecution] rather than seeing them as brands of tolerance', yet agrees with Waltzer that a range of mixed motives, some ignoble, are vitally useful for a 'regime of tolerance'.

9 Even in ANT, where the restrictions of coverture and the like do not apply to the Queen of Egypt, she is politically a subordinate to Antony, who is her Emperor. Yet in WIV the women do seem to have the upper hand nearly throughout, as if coverture did not apply.

10 Williams, 1996a, 36.

11 Ibid.

12 In rejecting as insufficient 'a conception of toleration . . . implying a double negative' Galeotti, 2002, 226–8, comes closer than many modern treatments of tolerance to the ideas explored here, but even this, 227, considers toleration only where one party has a greater portion of asymmetrical power.

13 The availability of Early English Books Online (EEBO) and of Hinman's Folio facsimile, Shakespeare, 1968 has been invaluable. But, unless otherwise

noted, Shakespeare quotations will be from Wells and Taylor, 1989, with some character name spellings regularised. Play titles are abbreviated as in that edition.

1 SHAKESPEARE, JOKES, HUMOUR, AND TOLERANCE

1 Basu, 1999a, 378n.
2 Teague, 1994b, argues for an overall comedic pattern inflecting OTH.
3 On 'conversation' as a technical rhetorical term see Remer, 1996b, and see Chapter 4.
4 St John, 2005.
5 For example Hoenselaars, 1994, acknowledges an anachronism in uses of both 'cosmopolitanism' and 'insularity' in relation to Shakespeare. This makes a good case for Erasmus giving a conceptual equivalent to 'cosmopolitanism', but a much weaker case for transposing 'insularity' to Shakespeare's age as a concept applicable to WIV and H5 in which 'defensive regionalism' or 'aggressive expansionism' crowd out 'cosmopolitan views' (106). Chapter 3 will argue rather for a relatively open tolerant perspective on 'strangers' or 'foreigners' in both plays.
6 Basu, 1999b, 147–8.
7 The exceptions are the grim TIM, OTH, and LC.
8 Aristotle, 1941, 281: *De Partibus Animalium* III.10 [673]. But this is an attribute and not a definition like Plato's categorisation of humans as 'herds of featherless bipeds', *The Statesman* 266e, in Plato, 1966, 1031, translated as 'two footed herds' that are 'wingless'.
9 See Skinner, 2000, 4–6 and 8–11.
10 Skinner, 2002; also Skinner, 2004.
11 Bacon, 1862–74, 6:526, from the first, 1597, edition.
12 Ibid., 6:456, from the 1625 edition; in the the 1612 edition, ibid., 6:565, the warning consists only of the second sentence.
13 The Elizabethan stage may have been an even more dangerous venue for ill-judged joking than private conversations; it is likely, for instance, that an anti-Scots joke in *Eastward Hoe* led to the 1605 imprisonment of Ben Jonson and George Chapman, on which see Sokol and Sokol, 1996, 358–9 and notes. Restrictions on the Elizabethan stage are emphasised in Clare, 1999 and elsewhere, but Clegg, 1999, questions if the royal proclamations and treason statutes of the age greatly affected its writers. Bacon's point about the dangers of private discourse seems borne out in Ben Jonson's poem 'Inviting a Friend to Supper' (Jonson, 1975, 55–6), in which a host promises to allow in no government spy to report on his 'mirthful board'.
14 Sidney, 1961, 55–6, further discussed in the Chapter 3.
15 T. Wilson, 1553, lxxvii. Wilson's book was reissued in 1560, 1562, 1563, 1567, 1580, 1584, and 1585. See Howell, 1956, 98–110, on its popularity.
16 Foakes, 1989, 187.
17 Joubert, 1980, 25. This aspect of Joubert's treatise is not discussed by Skinner.

18 Ibid., 24.
19 Hobbes repeated his ideas on laughter in several places, untangled in Martinich, 1995, 176.
20 See Skinner, 2002, 172.
21 Morgann, 1972, 143–215.
22 Bergson, 1911, 136.
23 Monro, 1951.
24 This Baconian tactic is identified as belonging to a 'maker's knowledge tradition' in Pérez-Ramos, 1988.
25 In Eastman, 1937, which is severely critical of derision theories.
26 Nilsen, 1993, 223–4, provides a bibliography of studies of modern nationality jokes.
27 See Hoenselaars, 1991, 1996, and especially 1992.
28 See Taylor, 1985, 112–61.
29 Nilsen, 1993, 219–20, tabulates the tellers and targets.
30 Hoenselaars, 1991, lists the characteristics thus assigned to various nationalities; Hoenselaars, 1992, discusses how interchangeable or specific these were.
31 E.g. Krishna-Menon, 1931.
32 Radically, LeFave and Mannell, 1976, 117, suggests that 'ethnic jokes' may not really exist except in certain contexts, by showing that derogatory stereotyping jokes may not seem to be jokes at all to an insulted outgroup, while stereotyping that is unfunny in itself may be perceived to be a joke by a bigoted ingroup.
33 I am grateful to an anonymous reader for pointing out a very direct example of this in TN 1.5.64–8 where Feste's shocking public remarks on Olivia's brother's soul are redeemed by means of a witty punchline.
34 Basu, 1999a, 392.
35 Ellis, 2005, 96–8.
36 Johnson's comment is quoted in full and masterfully analysed in Vickers, 1968, 89–90. See also J. D. Wilson, 1953, 1–14.
37 Ellis, 2005, 104–6. Does this confuse Falstaff with Shallow?
38 This incremental pattern comprises in 1H4 robbery with restitution, corrupt use of the King's press leading to most soldiers being 'peppered', sack in a pistol case, playing possum, Hotspur's corpse stabbed; in 2H4 it comprises contempt of court, debts and marriage promises denied, the calumny of a Prince, an attempt to ruin the realm.
39 Vickers, 1968, 118–41.
40 I cannot agree with Ellis, 2005, 104, that Falstaff's run-ins with Prince John and with the Chief Justice are 'Glasgow Empire' comic flops, because in each Falstaff's adversaries are lured into the trap of 'girding' him (2H4 1.2.141–2, 4.2.55). But Falstaff's punning sack-in-pistol-case excuses do 'bomb', and simply infuriate Hal (1H4 5.3.53–5).
41 Teague, 1994a, 20, suggests Jonson despised laughter, but on the contrary his self-deprecating poetic jokes could have had no other purpose than to cause hilarity. See, for instance Jonson, 1975, 55–6, 145, 129–39: in 'Inviting a Friend

to Supper' the speaker promises to spring no new verses on the guests at his 'mirthful board'; 'My Picture Left in Scotland' describes 'My mountain belly, and my rocky face'; the 'Celebration of Charis' presents an erotic tragicomedy of age and ugliness.

42 This very rare book is reproduced in Hazlitt, 1887, which discusses its authorship, v–x.

43 See Maslen, 2003, and Woodbridge, 2003. Holt, 2004, describes the traditions of the classical Philogelos and the humanist Poggio Bracciolini (1380–1495), and points out, 187, that Caxton included a 'sampling of Poggio's jokes' in his 1484 translation of Aesop.

44 See T. Cohen, 2001, 69–86, for (shocking) examples.

45 See the theory of dual Shakespeare audiences in Girard, 1991a, 249.

46 Oddly, these six are called 'four strangers' in 1.2.120.

47 Botero, 1611, 8, reports that: 'The Spanish women terme the Germans, *molles pisces*, that is, spongie fishes, for their continual drinking.'

48 See Hoenselaars, 1992, on standard stereotypes of foreigners, 1991, 1996, on Shakespeare's caution with these.

49 See Sokol and Sokol, 2003, 157, 224n.

50 The 'Destestable and abominable' sin of sodomy is discussed in Coke, 1644, 58–9; the biblical category 'Calamanita peccata' is noted, and Fleta's punishment, which was burial alive. Ibid., 89, describes an English common law punishing Jewish/Christian intermarriage with burning; here 'Sodomitae' are mentioned 'Contrahentes cum Judaeis', and the same law of Fleta (lib. I, ca. 35) as was cited in relation to sodomy is also noted 'Contrahentes'. A contemporary hand in the British Library copy 508.g.5(2.) annotates alongside, 'But if converted he shall not be burnt.' Pollock and Maitland, 1898, 2:549, considers an alternative view that burial alive was more appropriate than burning for Christians married to Jews.

51 Pollock and Maitland, 1898, 2:584, describes how Stephen Langton 'degraded and handed over to lay power a deacon who had turned Jew for the love of a Jewess. The apostate was delivered to the sheriff of Oxfordshire, who forthwith burnt him [. . . This] prompt action seems to have surprised his contemporaries, but was approved by Bracton.' These proceedings became famous for legal and political reasons discussed in Maitland, 1911.

52 Bestiality is equated with Moorish–European miscegenation also when envious Iago describes newly married Othello and Desdemona as beasts coupling (1.1.88–9 and 117–19). Indeed Caroline Spurgeon reveals that 'contemptuous or repellent' animal imagery dominates *Othello* (Spurgeon, 1935, 335). And at last Othello compares himself to a 'base Indian' (or in the First Folio text a 'base Judean', TLN 3658 – citations using TLN references will be from the Folio facsimile Shakespeare, 1968). He then stabs himself self-imaged as a 'circumcised dog' (5.2.364).

53 See Boehrer, 1994, 123–50.

54 See Thomas, 1983, 38–9, 92–142.

55 Ibid., 38–9. Coke's *Institutes* held that night was the time 'wherein Beasts runne about seeking their prey' (Coke, 1644, 63).

56 Thomas, 1983, 39.
57 Hoenselaars, 1992, 217–18, 229.
58 Furness, 1899, 72, quoting S.P. Venetian, 9 March 1603.
59 The ideological importance of Tudor Welshness is outlined in Yates, 1947, 48–9.
60 See the Oxford DNB article by Peter R. Roberts; a Parry biography by Ruth E. Richardson will appear too late for this study.
61 See Hazlitt, 1887, x, on the Welsh aspect of the *Merry Tales*. Welsh stories appear in folios: v recto; twice on ix verso; xiii verso; xvii recto and verso; xxi verso; xxiv verso. In fact, Powers, 1994, argues, based on defamation actions, that Welshness was the favourite topic for nationality jokes in the period.
62 Schultz, 1989, T. Cohen, 2001, 69–86, and LeFave and Mannell, 1976.
63 C. Davies, 2002. This adds that that many 'Jewish jokes' told by Jews work similarly.
64 LeFave and Mannell, 1976, 119, 118.
65 Boskin and Dorinson, 1985.
66 C. P. Wilson, 1979, 220. See also Zillmann, 1983, 92, which claims that in 'disparagement humor' mirth is proportional to 'the negativeness of the affective disposition toward the disparaged party and to the positiveness of the affective disposition toward the disparaging party'. The seven studies of ethnic humour in Chapman and Foot, 1977, 237 86 reach similar conclusions, but a well-taken point in the summing up, Mintz, 1977, 287, is that the jokes offered in the experiments were not very funny.
67 See Boskin and Dorinson, 1985, 87. Riley, 2000, 164, suggests that those who assert that Jewish self-hatred inspires the phenomenon of Jews making 'Jewish jokes' show 'a wooden response, in the face of language's highly effective powers to query the very identification that it will perpetuate only if its own latent irony is neutered'.
68 For further details see Sokol, 1992, 1995a, 1998.
69 Yaffe, 1997, especially 164–5, holds Shakespeare 'indicat[ed] . . . Shylock might have avoided his legal catastrophe by simply sticking to the moral teachings of his own religion', including biblical injunctions to mercy. Noble, 1935, 168, points out that the Old Testament apocryphal Ecclesiasticus 8.2–5 contains the exact doctrine of Portia's 'We do pray for mercy, / And that same prayer doth teach us all to render / The deeds of mercy' (4.1.197–9), and argues, 3, 23, 36, and 43, that the Apocrypha were much better known to Shakespeare's age than to ours, and that Ecclesiasticus and Job were Shakespeare's favourite biblical books. Moreover, Jews are enjoined by the *Kol Nidre* prayer *not* to cleave to angrily formed vows, as Shylock repeatedly says he will do in: 3.3.5; 4.1.225–6 three times; 4.1.237; and 3.2.282–6 by report.
70 Nevo, 1980, 130–1, offers a persuasive reading in which Shylock changes his intentions after these events.
71 See W. Cohen, 1982; Hoenselaars, 1993; Levin, 1993; Mullini, 1993.
72 See Holdsworth, 1903, 8:110–11 on 37.H.8 c.9, which, although nominally punitive, effectively allowed the taking of interest at 10 per cent. Shylock's commercial acumen would not have offended an Elizabethan audience.

Shakespeare himself bought income-generating tithes and purchased London properties as investments – activities which were perfectly acceptable in his milieu.

73 See Sokol and Sokol, 2004 under ON THE CASE regarding Slade's Case, and also under DEBT, and BOND.

74 St German, 1975, 77–9.

75 For more detail see Sokol and Sokol, 2004, 36–8.

76 See Shakespeare, 1977, xxviii–xxix and 156–74.

77 Reprinted in Shakespeare, 1977, 140–53.

78 Reprinted ibid., 153–6.

79 Despite this Gleckman, 2001, 87, proposes the possibility that although 'risk averse', still 'Shylock may in fact be so extraordinarily cunning and patient that he can predict from the earliest words Bassanio speaks to him . . . almost the entire future course of the play'. Such an ability would give Shylock demonic powers contrary to Shakespeare's representation of him as flawed but human.

80 Freeman, 2002, 171, puts it: 'Shylock extends an offer of friendship. We cannot know if it is a heartfelt offer, for it is immediately rejected by the smugly self-righteous Christians.'

81 For example, there is the joke about an Irish building worker, presumed to be ignorant, who is asked to describe the difference between a 'joist' and a 'girder', and replies that the first wrote *Ulysses* and the second wrote *Faust*.

82 The 'Arkansas Traveller' is actually both a famous nineteenth-century comic skit and a bluegrass folktune. In performance these two were often combined, sometimes with the Arkansas hillbilly playing the tune on a fiddle, and the Traveller playing it on a banjo.

83 This abbreviates an example from Bluestein, 1981, 11. The internet supplies numerous longer versions, some including music.

2 SHAKESPEARE, GENDER, AND TOLERANCE

1 See Sokol and Sokol, 2003, 129–38.

2 I. Maclean, 1980, 16–26, 54, 60.

3 Thus ibid., 62, refers to the idea expressed by Torquato Tasso in 1582 that the virtues required for both sexes are the same, but that some of these are more dominant or important for one sex than for the other.

4 See Dusinberre, 1975, 175–98, on Elizabethan anti-woman traditions, and 176–81 on counter-attacks. Fletcher, 2002 explains how some male-authored Renaissance texts nominally in defence of women may have been framed as polemical exercises, or intended ironically, while others were genuine.

5 I. Maclean, 1980, 85–6.

6 Sokol, 1985.

7 All quotations will be from from Spenser, 1961, cited hereafter as FQ.

8 A lengthy discussion in Morris, 1981, 50–65, suggests dating SHR to 1589. But reflections to be described here of FQ II–III in SHR indicate that either SHR

was written after FQ I–III was published in 1590, or that Shakespeare had pre-publication access. Arguing for an 'early-start chronology' dating of H6 1–3, Honigmann, 1982, 74–5, suggests Shakespeare read and assimilated FQ II–III before its publication in 1590. The six commendatory verse writers in the 1590 FQ volume did have such access; moreover Fraunce, 1588, E3r, quotes a stanza from FQ II (II.iv.35). H. Maclean, 1968, 399–400, indicates that in a letter dated 2 April 1580 Spenser told Gabriel Harvey that the composition of FQ had begun, and that by 1582 Spenser reportedly said he was 'well entered into' this work. So there was certainly some coterie pre-circulation of parts of FQ; the question is whether a ms. of FQ II–III might have pre-circulated outside of coterie circles. Black, 2001, reviews echoes of FQ in Marlowe's 1587 *Tamberlaine part 1*, reveals further echoes in *part 2*, and describes a recently discovered unpublished commendatory poem to FQ dating itself 1588 – all these suggesting that it did. Steven May at the CELM seminar in London on 10 May 2007 showed seven more echoes in *Tamberlaine part 1* and further discussed the 1588 poem; he argued for a wide pre-publication circulation of FQ I–III and other courtly poems. Therefore it seems possible for SHR to have been written before 1590, although of course dating it 1591–2, as in Thompson, 1984, 1–3, or later, is not ruled out. My own view is that the sophisticated SHR is not a very early play.

9 This frequently met visceral position has been expounded with detailed underpinnings in Downs-Gamble, 1993, and Maguire, 1995.

10 As Alastair Fowler kindly explained to me privately. Fowler, 1960, 146, pursues this distinction in FQ Book II, although not referring to Spenser's 'forward' and 'froward', in terms of 'two modes of corruption, ireful and appetitive, strong and weak – a dichotomy which runs throughout [Spenser's second] book'.

11 W. Nelson, 1963, 178–203.

12 Elissa is introduced in the very stanza, FQ II.iv.35, which Fraunce, 1588, E3r, quoted pre-publication. See note 8 above.

13 Fowler, 1960, 185.

14 The figure is thus described in Fraunce, 1588, D5 recto and verso. Expressing inverse notions by inverting two letters may reveal an aspect of Spenser's wit derived from Plato's *Cratylus* and the 'reality' of language; see Craig, 1969.

15 See Osgood, 1915; Bartlett, 1965; and Shakespeare, 1995b. HAM Q2 correctly gives 'forward' where folio HAM TLN 470 (1.3.9) misprints 'froward'.

16 This led to notable paintings by Botticelli and many others, and to a group-biography of illustrious women, Boccaccio, 1964.

17 See Young, 1988, and Sokol and Sokol, 2003, 30–64, especially 37–9.

18 For an excellent overview of English Renaissance dramatic representations of enforced marriages see Atkinson, 1986.

19 These word counts were performed on Wells and Taylor, 1989 using my own WCSPEAK program.

20 Excellent studies of illusion-making in SHR include Seronsy, 1963, Righter, 1967, 94–6, and Daniell, 1984.

21 The humour in Sly's threatening resembles Ralph Kramden's in the television classic *The Honeymooners*, such as: 'I'll give you the world of tomorrow, Alice – you're goin' to the moon!'

22 Morris, 1981, 133n., points out that Sly's word 'pheeze' in Shakespeare's text provides one of the few points of verbal overlap between Shakespeare's *The Taming of the Shrew* and the similarly plotted anonymous *The Taming of a Shrew* (which uses 'fese'). We may note in addition that the tavern worker threatened at the start of *A Shrew* is male, 'a Tapster, beating out of his doores *Slie Droonken*' (Anon., 1594, A2r; Holderness and Loughrey, 1992, 103). This renders *A Shrew* more violent and less thematically subtle.

23 See SHR stage directions, TLN 877, 887, 1007, 1096, and 2010. Male servants are assaulted by Petruchio and Vincentio TLN 1776 and 2434.

24 Thompson, 1984, 117n. and 118n., notes to 4.1.148 and 4.1.170–8, explains it is 'clear that Petruchio will himself suffer the deprivations he imposes on Katherina'. The updated Thompson, 2003, 28, 125n., and 126n., echoes this.

25 On English virtuosi and their scientific pastimes see Houghton, 1942.

26 *Supposes*, staged privately at Gray's Inn in 1566, in Gascoigne, 1907, 1.187–243, reveals that Bianca's prototype and her lover have been enjoying one another sexually for five years without marriage; yet they are unpunished and unblamed, as they are in Ariosto's original. Shakespeare's adaptation of this for a plot in SHR resembles Anthony Munday's of Pasqualigo's *Il Fedele* in his *The Two Italian Gentlemen* (*c.* 1584); the latter is called in Melchiori, 1994, 86, a 'cleansing for an English audience [of] the loose morality of Italian "commedia erudita"'.

27 See Sokol and Sokol, 2003, 179–83, on how extraordinary Petruchio's settlement is.

28 Although Stone, 1979, 661–2, claims 'about a third' of 'older peers' and their wives lived apart between 1595 and 1620, absconding wives could find themselves forced by the Church courts to return to their husbands (but if maltreatment was proved there they could obtain orders for a legal separation, possibly with alimony). See Sokol and Sokol, 2003, 142–3 and 144–8.

29 Thompson, 2003, 28, and 125n. and 126n.

30 She appears in nine scenes, and in this one speaks 23 per cent of her total word count.

31 See Nevo, 1980, 35–52, which finds in the play a love-match, and the actors and editors cited in Sokol, 1985, 316n. Daniell, 1984, 25, proposes that the 'Good Marriage of Katherine and Petruchio' involves them growing 'to share an ability to use theatrical situations to express new and broadening perspectives in a world as unlimited as art itself'. This is close to what I have claimed, although without the Spenserian framework.

32 Kahn, 1975, bases its argument on the palpability of such an exaggeration in SHR. A similar exaggeration is evident in the above-mentioned repetitions of a Renaissance humanist 'intellectual joke' in which pretending to argue that 'woman is not a human being' was used to 'reinforce the contrary position' (on these jokes see I. Maclean, 1980, 85–6).

33 Spenser did not often associate the genders with forward and froward passions: he presents pairs of men like Cymochles and Pyrochles, or of women like Elissa and Perissa, representing the froward and forward. But Shakespeare did; in SHR frowardness usually implies female insubordination, much as it does in TGV 3.1.68–9, when Silvia is described by her angry father as 'peevish, sullen, froward, / Proud, disobedient, stubborn, lacking duty'.

34 This vision no doubt alludes to Aristophenes' myth of erotic fusion in *Symposium* 189e–193b, Plato, 1966, 542–5.

35 This ending, printed in 1590, in Spenser, 1961, 517, was changed (and the Scudamor–Amoret strand re-opened for further development) in the 1596 quarto which included Books I–VI. The later version is printed ibid., 516.

36 On the Elizabethan ideology see T. Smith, 1583, 13, on the couple: 'ech obeyeth and commaundeth other, and they two togeather rule the house', although ibid., 101–5, repeats the patriarchal rules of coverture and inheritance; see also Stretton, 2002, 44.

37 Nevertheless skilled Marina turns over her income in accordance with the Eastern model of slavery (see Chapter 6), and finally she marries the not wholly plausible Lysimachus. In London, entrepreneurial widows in artisan trades were not uncommon, and typically remarried. The model of Emilia Bassano, poet, musician, chancery litigant, and feminist, might have been known to Shakespeare.

38 See Sokol and Sokol, 2003, 7–8, 118–29, and 137–8, on the legal restrictions on married women as a result of the doctrine of coverture, and Shakespeare's reflections of these. On Elizabethan women's legal position see Anon., 1632 (written about 1600), and Prest, 1991; on women litigants see Cioni, 1982, 1985; Stretton, 1994, 1998, 1999, 2002.

39 Typically these trusts were set up by families. See Sokol and Sokol, 2003, 58, 7–8, 122–5.

40 See Stretton, 1999, 196–7, which cites Juan Luis Vives, and Todd, 1999, 69–70.

41 See R. H. Wells, 2000b, and B. R. Smith, 2000. Very interestingly, Biberman, 2004, treats the construction of two kinds of masculinity and Elizabethan anti-Semitism as interconnected.

42 Studies relating these interests to the Elizabethan theatre include Breight, 1996; De Somogyi, 1998; Taunton, 2001.

43 For instance, R. H. Wells, 2000a, finds in COR an implicit opposition to the chivalric cult growing around the Prince of Wales.

44 See Marx, 1992, and R. H. Wells, 2000b.

45 See R. S. White, 1999, on 1H6, CYL, RDY, TIT, ERR, HAM, AYL, and ADO.

46 See Melchiori, 1994, 61–3, 128–31, and passim. This makes the interesting point that the origin of the Garter Order, which epitomised Elizabethan honour, connected sexual conquest with military power.

47 Yet most discussions of Shakespeare on manliness centre on MAC; see Brooks, 1963 (originally 1949), Ramsey, 1973; Harding, 1969; and Zimmermann, 2006.

48 See: TGV 2.4.130; RDY 2.5.70–2, 5.2.37; TIT 2.3.289, 2.4.55, 3.1 throughout, 3.2.48–51, 5.3.89, 100, 151, 174; ROM 5.3.15; 2H4 3.1.62, 4.3 throughout; ADO

1.1.24–8, 5.1.285, 5.3.16–17; TN 5.1.238–9; OTH 5,2,357–60; LRF 3.6.19–20; PER S.18.25–6; CYM 5.6.268–9, 353; WT 3.2.237–9, 5.2.141–3; TMP 5.1.15–17; AIT 4.2.24–30, 5.1.153–8, 5.2.206–8.

49 These include AYL 3.4.2–3; LRF 1.4.277–9; MAC 4.3.232; COR 3.2.110–17; TIM 5.2.40–3.

50 Rooley, 1983, 14.

51 Donne, 1960, 40. On the influence of 'Flow my Tears' see Rooley, 1983, 17–20. The tune was so famous that a collection of instrumental consort variants, *Lachrimae*, was published by Dowland in 1604. On Dowland's melancholy, as either artistic, philosophical, or career-related, see Rooley, 1983, passim, R. H. Wells, 1985, and Poulton, 1983, respectively.

52 Castiglione, 1975, 46–9.

53 This view of women is expounded upon by Shakespeare's foul-mouthed Iachimo, Pandarus, and Parolles.

54 Barton, 1994, 3–30. This examines Elizabethan cultural and legal norms concerning marriage and shows how, without having sexually consummated his spousals, Posthumus could have recognised the intimate details of Imogen's body described by Iachimo.

55 Arviragus seemingly says he is sixteen years old in CYM 4.2.200, but 1.1.63 and 5.6.338 both say he was abducted twenty years hence. I think sixteen is right, because the princes have just-breaking voices, and the sundered families in Shakespeare's other Romances are reunited after twelve to sixteen years.

56 Imogen never sinks beneath hysteria, although many Shakespearian men do. In CYM Pisanio too never collapses although he is consistently misinterpreted, even by Imogen. A servant who remains loyal when disobedient, truthful when lying, Pisanio resembles Belario of Beaumont and Fletcher's *Philaster* (which I believe influenced CYM rather than vice versa).

57 See I. Maclean, 1980, 72, on etymological questions such as of a possible derivation of *mulier* from *mollica*, and if *mulier* must refer to a married woman.

58 The plot may be overwhelmed here by its own complexity, for in Posthumus' dream his father already said this was so (5.5.157–62).

59 *Pace* R. S. White, 1999, 143, which claims that pacifist voices in Shakespeare are 'muted'.

60 Sokol, 1991 describes how three successive scenes of MM are structured around rhetorical figures of repetition by means of which Vincentio, Isabella, and Angelo are each shown in parallel ways to be fiercely intolerant of their own and others' sexuality. Each idealises their intolerance by self-praising their own asceticism, and identifying themselves with 'good' cultural institutions (philosophy, religion, law).

61 The following continues parts of the argument in Sokol, 1994a, adding the realisation that leonine madness is overcome by gender tolerance.

62 Sokol, 1994a, 31–54, argues that here Shakespeare depicted a specific non-anachronistic psychopathology, the couvade syndrome.

63 See ibid., 85–141, on this concubinage.

64 The four 'progressive steps' are described, with biblical sources cited, in Milton, 1825, 348–9 (*Christian Doctrine* Book 1 Chapter 19).

65 The consequence of a lack of that fourth step is well illustrated in the conclusion of MM. Sokol, 1991, argues that in addition to the above-mentioned patterning showing the three main protagonists all at the outset sex-adverse, further rhetorical patterning indicates that at the end two of these protagonists' foibles are confessed. But it remains questionable whether either the Duke or Angelo is converted to good; their marriages at the play's end, especially that of the death-desiring Angelo, seem devoid of much potential for joy or renewal.

66 See Hinshelwood, 2007, 1–3, on the personality disorder underlying intolerance, and especially racism.

67 She might have hesitated because of Leontes' peremptory, leonine, disposition, which remains still visible when he overrides Paulina, insisting that 'no foot shall stir' (5.3.98).

3 SHAKESPEARE, TOLERANCE, AND NATIONALITY

1 Ms. of 1589 speech printed in Hartley, 1981, 2:481 – on context and author see below.

2 H5 3.3.66–8.

3 See Sharpe and Brooks, 1976; Thorne, 1985a, b, c; Berman, 1994; Raffield, 2005; and for an approach to these matters in connection with Elizabethan literature, Lockey, 2006.

4 See Lane, 1995, 469–70.

5 See Dummett and Nicol, 1990.

6 See Sokol and Sokol, 1996, 369–74, on Calvin's Case in relation to TMP, and Floyd-Wilson, 2002, for speculations connecting Posthumus of CYM with the *postnati*.

7 See Lane, 1995, 468–9, on how this prohibition came about.

8 According to Luu, 2005b, 60–2, only 7 per cent of the 'strangers' in the City of London were denizens in 1593. Ibid., 62–3, describes the difficulty for strangers of obtaining Freedom of the City.

9 Ibid., 63.

10 See Chapter 4 on this seventy-year-old theory and its recent proponents.

11 Schoenbaum, 1986, 264, and Schoenbaum, 1981, 39, show that Christopher Mountjoy was censured by the French Church, so his family were not 'absent' from that congregation as is claimed 'apparent' in Nicholl, 2007, 101. The Mountjoys were likely in England for religious reasons, as were the majority of Elizabethan Huguenots, although Scouloudi, 1987, 43–4, holds that by 1573 'about one third' of London's strangers may have come to England 'for economic reasons'.

12 The Shakespeare–Belott–Mountjoy story is retold with interesting topographical details in Schoenbaum, 1986, 260–4. Schoenbaum, 1981, 20–9, contains facsimiles of documents, and an imaginative reconstruction of the events in Nicholl, 2007 provides transcripts, 279–307.

13 The Register of St Olave, Silver Street, spells Belott as 'Plott'; A. H. Nelson, 2000, kept at the London Guildhall library, analyses the register.

14 Lecler, 1960, 2:486–91 gives an overview, and for details see: 1:268–9 on Maximillian's and 1:285–6 on Rudolph II's empire; 1:398–9 on the 1573 Warsaw Confederation; 1:402–6 on Stephen Bathory's extremely liberal regime in Poland (1576–86); 2:5–184 on France; 2:191–315 on Holland.

15 See Christen, 2004; a need for a better understanding of daily contacts and interpersonal relations in such multi-faith communities is stressed ibid., 433, and in B. J. Kaplan, 2004, 501.

16 Strype, 1725, 2:169. 2:1688–70 further describes their reception.

17 Ibid., 2:169–70, which adds this was published in 1600.

18 Lambard, 1576, 284.

19 Indeed Goose, 2005a, 15, indicates that as many as 40–50 per cent of London's aliens may have remained there during Mary's reign.

20 Ibid.

21 R. Wilson, 2005, argues such a theory, placing it in opposition to an exaggeration of the position in Fiedler, 1974.

22 See Grell, 1996b, on the re-admission of the Reformed communities.

23 The twelve chapters of Goose and Luu, 2005, present excellent studies of these developments.

24 The sole copy of this 1588 Discipline, which survived in Norwich, is discussed in Schickler, 1892, 1:340–56; see also Briggs, 1978, 103–4, and Pettegree, 1986.

25 Pettegree, 1990, 297, states that over 50,000 settled 'mostly in London' between 1540 and 1600, but Grell, 1996a, 1–33, finds the question of numbers present at any time complex because of the return of some exiles to the Continent, and the double exile of some to England. Ibid., 4, suggests a total immigration of 100,000 (revising others' estimates of 200,000) between 1567 and 1590, and, 5, suggests a rough estimate of 10,000 refugees in London in 1590. The official 'Returns' of strangers in London of 1562, 1566, 1568, 1573, 1583, and 1593 listed far fewer, but as Scouloudi, 1987, 43–4, and Goose, 2005a, 15–19, point out these were deficient.

26 See Hunter, 1964, 45–6; Zito, 1991, 47–9; and on the Welsh in London Emrys Jones, 1981.

27 LRF 2.2.57–9; on WT see Sokol, 1989, 56–65, 206–7.

28 For instance in Nicholl, 2007.

29 Goose, 2005b, 111–12.

30 See Luu, 2005b, 58–68, on the complex history of such restrictions.

31 Goose, 2005b, 111, 121.

32 Ibid., 111. Yet ibid., 118–19, acknowledges the deterrent effects of the punishments of the 1517 rioters – which was drawing and quartering for treason. On how these rioters were found treasonous see Bellamy, 1979, 18–19.

33 Littleton, 1995, 147. Luu, 2005a, 196–9, details particular stresses in the 1590s.

34 On these local regulations and how they were often circumvented see J. P. Ward, 2005. On how their increased enforcement contributed to an early

seventeenth-century decline in the stranger communities see Luu, 2005a, especially 196–9.

35 Repeated failed moves against London's strangers are detailed in Strype, 1725: 3:543 (1588), 4:167–8 (1593), 4:212–15 (1594), 4:352 (1599), 4:353 (1601). Assurances from King James (1603) made to the Dutch Church in London are printed ibid., 4:386–7. Scouloudi, 1987, 46–51, treats the opposition to the disadvantaging of London's strangers and the effects of informers, Denization, and Naturalisation.

36 In addition to those in the last note, Hartley, 1981, 2:95, records a 'byll ageynst sellinge bye retele bye strangiers' rejected on second reading on 9 March 1585, and, 2:399, records another 'bill redd for prohibicion of strangiers born [to] use retayle' on 7 March 1587.

37 Transcribed in Hartley, 1981, 2:480–3, here 481, from BL Landsdown 55, fol. 188–9. This is discussed ibid., 2:409–10, and said to be probably composed by Jackman but 'We cannot know if it was delivered.' The 1589 bill is also discussed in Strype, 1725, 3:543, which comments also on another 1588 bill (defeated at second reading) intending to impose extra taxes or 'Stranger's *Customs*' on 'their Children'. Jackman's speech is transcribed also ibid., 3 Appendix: 242–4.

38 Debates on a 'Bill against Aliens selling by way of retail any Foreign Commodities' on 21 and 23 March 1593 are reported in D'Ewes, 1973, 505–7 and 508–9. Also see Hartley, 1981, 3:134–9, 142–4, 145–6, 147–8, 176. Finch's *Oxford DNB* biography by Wilfred Prest shows that he had personal sympathies with Reformed religion.

39 Maas, 1953.

40 Melchiori, 1994, 24–8, which further claims that Shakespeare revised Anthony Munday's original which approved the 1517 riots. See Hoenselaars, 1992, 50–3, and ibid., 43–50, which compares STM with other stage depictions of anti-stranger agitation.

41 Goose, 2005b, 120.

42 Strype, 1725, 4:167 and 4:168. Shapiro, 1992, 185, prints a newly found ms. continuation of the verses.

43 I am told this early modern meaning of 'foreigner' encompassing English non-locals (*OED* 2) was still current in Norfolk in the 1960s; on its Elizabethan use see Gwynn, 1985, 3, and Luu, 2005b, 60.

44 Goose, 2005b, 123–4, discusses the similarity of Elizabethan treatment of English-born (regional) 'foreigners' and overseas-born 'strangers'.

45 Wells and Taylor, 1989, dates STM 1603–4; the arguments of others who concur are surveyed in G. Blakemore Evans's introduction to STM in Shakespeare, 1997.

46 On the Court of Requests see J. H. Baker, 1990, 138–9 and Stretton, 1998.

47 Schoenbaum, 1986, 264.

48 Widespread, at least partial, religious assimilation in the course of one generation is illustrated by means of a survey of wills in Pettegree, 1990. Assimilation is also investigated in Littleton, 1995, and Goose, 2005a, 3–9. Grell, 1996a, 5, suggests that especially in the 1560s many of London's

Protestant refugees stayed 'outside the confines of the foreign [stranger] churches'. Littleton, 2003, 97, suggests that by King James's time many of second-generation Protestant refugee stock became lukewarm about their religious backgrounds, so that 'dual membership in [the English and French] churches was common, perhaps even the norm'. Referring to 1593, Pettegree, 1986, 303, points out that 'The Returns of Aliens indicate that some 25 percent of strangers regularly attended the English parish churches.' Yet, as mentioned above, those returns were incomplete.

49 Littleton, 1995, 154, claims 'Many couples thwarted by the [strict rules of the French Church] consistory married in the English Church instead. Marriage in the English Church was apparently quicker and easier than in the French Church.' Pettegree, 1986, 186, offers a similar view.

50 Schoenbaum, 1986, 264.

51 Schoenbaum, 1981, 39.

52 Burn, 1846, 31. What this volume might have been is not identified in R. Smith, 1972.

53 Moens, 1896, 1:iii.

54 The data are in ibid., 1:1–209.

55 The five sample parishes are St Pancreas Soper Lane, St Mary le Bowe, St Mary Colechurch, St Martin Ironmonger Lane, and All Hallows Honey Lane. The ratio rose gradually to reach 2.323 by 1660. Between 1600 and 1630 in these five parishes and in Clarkenwell parish the ratios all approximated to 2.0. These data were very kindly supplied to me and permission was given to use them by the 'People in Place' project acknowledged in the Introduction.

56 Finlay, 1981, 59 (Table 3.3), lists these ten parishes and their data. A graph, ibid., 61 (Figure 3.5), shows that this ratio was fairly constant. The concluding graph in the classic Wrigley and Schofield, 1981, after 779, indicates a national average for this ratio of approximately 3 across the interval 1580–1650. These last data are not wholly comparable with the others, however, because Wrigley's analyses are of the population of England and not London, and also adjust their figures generally upwards by means of sophisticated approximating tactics.

57 Difficult legal-historical and literary-historical questions about such marriages are addressed in Sokol and Sokol, 2002, 93–116, and were more extensively addressed by them at the Shakespeare and Law conference at Warwick University on 9 July 2007.

58 Neither did the first Act of Uniformity in 1549, or its 1552 successor, invalidate them.

59 However, the marriage gifts of gold or silver named in the first 1549 Prayer Book had disappeared by the time of the third version of 1559. Shakespeare implicitly responded to debates over such 'idolatry': see Sokol and Sokol, 2003, 82–92, and Chapter 4 below.

60 A French-language Prayer Book was published by 1551 for use only in the Channel Islands and Jersey, and revisions followed; the complicated history of these and other translated versions of the Prayer Book is described in Muss-Arnolt, 1914. Latin or Greek translations of the Prayer Book were

allowed for study in the universities, and use of a Latin version was allowed in Gaelic-speaking parts of Ireland. According to Spicer, 2005, 101, the Sandcroft Stranger Church was unusual to the point of uniqueness in adopting for its use (in the 1630s) 'a French translation of the liturgy and rites of the Church of England'.

61 Ibid., 97.

62 Schoenbaum, 1986, 174–5, suggests that Richard Field, who printed VEN in 1593, was probably known to Shakespeare since their mutual Stratford childhoods. In 1588 Field married Jaqueline, the widow of his deceased apprentice-master the Huguenot printer Thomas Vautrollier, and took over Vautrollier's Blackfriars printshop. Ibid., 260, suggests Shakespeare may have met the Mountjoys through Jaqueline Field ,who knew Mme Mountjoy from the French church. Ibid., 169–70, speculates in addition about Shakespeare's possible acquaintance with the London-resident Italians Paolo Luchese, John Florio, and Emilia Bassano. Honigmann, 1985a, adds to a list of Shakespeare's possible 'stranger' associates: Peter Street, a possibly Huguenot property developer or 'carpenter' who built the 1599 Globe; Geerart Janssen, who carved Shakespeare's Stratford effigy and that of Shakespeare's friend John Combe (d. 1614); whichever of the two Martin Droeshouts engraved the First Folio likeness, which Honigmann argues is based on a life drawing made *c.* 1610; an as-yet untraced Dorothy Soer.

63 Gwynn, 1995, 215.

64 6&7.Wm.3 c.6, and 6&7.Wm.3 c.35. See Gwynn, 1985, 162, 180.

65 See Moens, 1896, i:iii.

66 Also in ERR Adriana claims she has merged her identity with her husband's using the same simile as Antipholus. Her 'A drop of water in the breaking gulf' (2.2.129) expresses the inextricable mixing which in her opinion is the consequence of a married pair sharing one 'self' (2.2.122–49); this conveys confusion between the legal doctrine of coverture and the Christian doctrine of 'one flesh' (see Chapter 2), but also perhaps a dire reflection on her marriage.

67 See Littleton, 2005, 178–83. Many Protestant refugees who immigrated to England re-emigrated 'home', and some, following changing circumstance re-immigrated to England a second time: see Luu, 2005a, 192–4 and 206–7. In consequence of multiple immigration the consistories of the London Stranger Churches often needed to investigate immigrants before allowing membership, especially to those suspected of having apostasised, as is described in Littleton, 2005, 179, 186.

68 In MV 4.1.171, does a pretence at judicial impartiality, or a similarity in appearance, cause Portia to ask, when entering the trial scene, 'Which is the merchant here, and which the Jew?'

69 Kornstein, 1994, 79–81.

70 Ibid. See also Kornstein, 1993, and Schotz, 1991; the latter goes so far as to suggest that Portia 'makes up' the law of Venice to suit her needs, and that it never existed.

71 The complexities involved are outlined in Sokol and Sokol, 2004, under 'MURDER', 'ROBBERY', and 'FELON'.
72 The Treason Act 25.Edw.3 st.5 c.2 was followed by numerous others, especially under the Tudors. See Bellamy, 1979. The Act of 1352 also made it 'petty treason' for a servant to kill a master, a wife a husband, or a monk his superior, but there performance and not just intent was required.
73 See Sokol, 1992, and Holdsworth, 1903, 1:536–8.
74 See Holdsworth, 1903, 1:526–73, 5:60–154, 8:99–300.
75 Plucknett, 1956, 663.
76 Gross, 1908, xviii.
77 This combination was known in English Law Merchant courts although it was rare in Continental ones according to ibid., xxiv. See also Holdsworth, 1903, 1:536. A criminal jurisdiction of the sort described by Holdsworth is portrayed explicitly in *Bartholomew Fair* when Adam Overdo soliloquises 'Many are the yearly enormities of this Fair, in whose court of Pie-powders I have the honour during the three days sometimes to sit as judge' (Jonson, 1979, 43: 2.1.42–4).
78 See Holdsworth, 1903, 1:539–40 and 1:568–73, and J. H. Baker, 1986: Sokol, 1992, 61–2, discusses a supposed decline or absorption of Law Merchant up to 1700.
79 Sokol and Sokol, 1999, attempts to put to rest an old notion that the equity court of Chancery was suggested.
80 Oberman, 1996, 29–30, which places the 'protection of law' for heretics, and 'law merchant' as practised by the citizens of Amsterdam and by Jewish exiles on a level with the intellectual work of Erasmus, Reuchlin, Castellio, and Locke.
81 See Hoenselaars, 1992, passim and 237–44.
82 See ibid., 19–20; Brennan, 1994; and Hoenselaars, 1998. For a comprehensive account of Shakespeare's responses to varied localities and their peoples see Sugden, 1925.
83 Hoenselaars, 1992, 53. Ibid., 20–1, proposes social and political causes for this change. Moreover, ibid., 53, holds STM was the last (and most outspoken) play portraying London's 'alien problem'.
84 Ibid., 217–18, 229.
85 Thus ibid., 98–9, 115, 201, and 242 describes Englishmen staged as outdrinking proverbially bibulous Flemings or Dutchmen, and English merchants more rapacious than Italian ones, 103–4. In another stereotype reversal, an Italian merchant is portrayed as much more unscrupulous than a Jewish one, ibid., 174–5, 254n., and 278–9n.
86 This phrase is quoted by *OED* from Fulke Greville's *Life of Sidney*, which was published in 1652 but written 1610–12.
87 Hoenselaars, 1992, 20, 27, 109.
88 Ibid., 133–4.
89 The phrase is repeated in ibid., 243; Hoenselaars, 1991, 167–70; and Hoenselaars, 1998, 97–100.
90 Sidney, 1961, 55–6; see Hoenselaars, 1992, 70–1, and Hoenselaars, 1991, 163–4.

91 Hoenselaars, 1991, 159–62 and Hoenselaars, 1992, 21–4, mention Thomas Wilson (1572), George Gascoigne (1576), Philip Stubbes (1583), Thomas Wright (1601/1604), Francis Bacon (1605), Barnaby Rich (1606), John Barclay (1614), Fynes Moryson (1617), and Richard Young (1638).
92 See Hoenselaars, 1991, 165–7, on theatrical stereotypes of North European dipsomania.
93 See Petronella, 1984.
94 Stage representations of Englishmen as 'mad' are discussed in Hoenselaars, 1992, 80, 164–7, 234–5, 242, 277.
95 Babb, 1944, 106–10 agrees, finding Hamlet's melancholy a destructive, black and cold humoral affliction.
96 See ibid., 58–67.
97 Trevor, 2004, 6, thus describes the 'estimable sadness' of 'genial' melancholy in the 'Ficinian tradition'. See Klibansky, Panofsky, and Saxl, 1964, especially 217–77, on this tradition. Yet Trevor, 2004, 63–86, also holds that Galenic medical theory was diluting Ficinian theory by Shakespeare's time, so that 'the positive influences' of melancholy 'are not easily separable from its negative associations . . . and the possible onset of dementia' (65–6). But Babb, 1951, 58–67, finds the theory of melancholy contributing to genius still 'the popular concept . . . in sixteenth- and seventeenth-century Europe' and the one 'most significant to the student of literature'. R. H. Wells, 1985, connects melancholy with Elizabethan ideas of genius in relation to John Dowland's music.
98 LeFave and Mannell, 1976, 119, 118.
99 The notion of Claudius' wild dancing arises from readings of 'the swagg'ring upspring reels' in HAM 1.4.9–10 as a wild dance. These originated in Steevens's 1778 comment that the 'vp-spring' was a German dance, on which see Jenkins, 1982, 208n., and the commentary to TLN 613 in Kliman, 1996.
100 Foakes, 1989, 83.
101 Interpretations in Hoenselaars, 1991, 158, Hoenselaars, 1992, 80–1, and Hoenselaars, 1996, 19–21, respond favourably to the argument in Andrews, 1983, linking Hamlet's notion of a 'mole of nature' with ideas found in Thomas Wright's *The Passions of the Minde in Generall* (which Andrews argued was in ms. by 1598, and so could have been seen by Shakespeare before he wrote HAM). However, these ideas are not unique; in Shakespeare, 1987, 357n., G. R. Hibbard finds similar ones in Thomas Nashe's 1592 *Pierce Penilesse*.
102 Bartlett, 1965, lists 'custom' nine times in HAM ('monster custom' in the second Quarto text only), followed by six times in COR, and no more than three times in any other play. Shakespeare, 1995b, produces slightly different counts but the same pattern.
103 Exceptions are 'custom' in the sense of business or patronage given to a shop, place of entertainment or commercial outlet (as in OED 'custom', 5), as seen in SHR 4.3.99, MM 1.2.82, and (metaphorically) WT 5.2.98.
104 Trevor, 2004, 78–9, argues the 'one defect' Hamlet speaks of must be his own melancholy. This, I feel, would reductively diminish Hamlet's breadth of mind as reflected in his speech.

105 Alternative beliefs based on deterministic theories of 'judicial' astrological influences at birth were in sharp decline by Shakespeare's time; see Sokol, 2003, 49–50, 102, 151–3. Aside from those there were also theories of defects inherited because of 'maternal impression', or as a result of forbidden sexual practices (intercourse during menstruation); on the first see Reeve, 1989 and Japtok and Schleiner, 1999, and on the decline of belief in the second see I. Maclean, 1980, 29 and 39, and Whatley, 1619, 21–4.

106 Lievsay, 1985, 239–40.

107 Hunter, 1964, 52, also in the conclusion of the enlarged essay Hunter, 1978a.

108 Levin, 1993, 29, thus comments on Shakespeare adaptations by Verdi, but clearly has in mind the originals as well, for ibid., 20, comments 'although Shakespeare could easily spin off such caricatures [as of Portia's foreign suitors in MV], his fundamental concern was with human beings.'

109 However, Locatelli, 1993, rightly points out tensions in Shakespeare's identifications of foreign places with English ones, so that an Italian city could be at once a stand-in for London or Stratford and also a place to be condemned for its foreign propensities.

110 For instance, English Puritan demands for harsh moral legislation (on which see Kent, 1973) are mirrored in TN and MM, and scandalous English wardship practices in AWW.

111 See Hadfield, 2004, regarding HAM; Lane, 1995, regarding JN; and Floyd-Wilson, 2002, regarding CYM.

112 Yet Shakespeare alludes explicitly to Elizabethan Irish conflicts only once, in a passage only in the Folio of H5. The Chorus there compares the victorious return of Henry V from France with Essex's anticipated victorious return from Ireland:

> Were now the General of our gracious Empress –
> As in good time he may – from Ireland coming,
> Bringing rebellion broached on his sword,
> How many would the peaceful city quit
> To welcome him! Much more, and much more cause,
> Did they this Harry. (5.0.30–5)

It is notable that Henry's French victory is said to provide 'much more cause' for celebration than Essex's hoped-for one.

113 See Edwards, 1974, 66–94, 103–30, which reviews earlier work in this field and advances it, and Hadfield, 1994, which traces parallel topics in non-Shakespearian literature. CYM has been interpreted in terms of English foundational myths in Marcus, 1988, in terms of civility and 'Britishness' in Floyd-Wilson, 2002, and in terms of 'Britishness' versus 'English particularism' in Feerick, 2003.

114 LLL 5.1.81. 'Sans' is also used in the mock stichomythia in LLL 4.4.69–79, in Jaques's peroration 'Sans teeth, sans eyes, sans taste, sans everything' (AYL 2.7.166), and to describe Duke Prospero's former self-deluding 'confidence sans bound' (TMP 1.2.97).

115 See Blank, 1996, 40–52, which discusses language use in LLL but misses this.
116 Hoenselaars, 1996, 23–4, holds that Spanish-born Queen Katherine's 'self-conscious command of English' shows her truthfulness, and also reveals a link between her and Princess Elizabeth.
117 Blake, 1981, 87.
118 However, some other French aristocrats' speeches are peppered with flourishes of French and/or contain heavy Gallicisms in H5 3.5.5, 3.5.11, 3.5.15, 3.7.14, 4.2.3–6, 4.5.2, and 4.5.6, and of course French must be actually heard in the scene showing Pistol's incomprehension of the French Soldier in H5 4.4.
119 Blake, 1981, 87.
120 Hoenselaars, 1996, 25, quoting Lance Wilcox, also accepts a theory that in contrast to Katherine there is an 'easy mastery of [English] by the rest of the French aristocracy'.
121 Blake, 1981, 87.
122 Hoenselaars, 1992, 58–60, 238.
123 Hoenselaars, 1991, 162, repeated in Hoenselaars, 1998, 89.
124 See Hoenselaars, 1992, 17, and passim, and Brennan, 1994, 46–9. Antipathy to Spain is argued to have been very significant to *The Spanish Tragedy* in Mulryne, 1996. A background to LLL in anti-Spanish sentiment is outlined in Londré, 1995, 9–10, but Brennan, 1994, 59–62, disagrees, claiming that religious and other factors produced both positive and negative responses to the Spanish in English literature.
125 Quoted in Blank, 1996, 3, from Alexander Gill's *Logomia Anglica* of 1619. Other Renaissance discussions of dialect are surveyed in Blank, 1996, 7–32.
126 P. Berry, 2004, claims Hamlet's 'alienation from courtly style or decorum in language' throughout the play.
127 See Chapter 2 on CYM 1.4; on the 'frigid euphemism' in WT 1.2 see Sokol, 1994a, 24–6 and 173.
128 My rethinking of Sokol and Sokol, 2003, 65, accords with a comment in Londré, 1995, 10, that, given Elizabethan prejudices, it is surprising Spanish Armado 'should be such a complex character in whom there is no imputation of villainy and very little of cowardice'. However Armado's erotic success is not treated there.
129 Barton, 1994.
130 See the discussions of 'work' in Sokol, 2003, 125–6, 138–9, 164, 170–80.
131 Blank, 1996 treats both the great rate of Elizabethan neologism, and the development of concepts of dialect.
132 Theatrical representations of Germans and Italians are extensively analysed in Hoenselaars, 1992.
133 Shapiro, 1992, 167–80, discusses how Elizabethans viewed the notion of a Jewish nation.
134 Biswas, 1996, 6–9, places the bizarre English 'pronunciation' and peculiar 'speech habits' of Shakespeare's French, Welsh, and Spanish characters in parallel with those of Shylock, the Prince of Morocco, and Othello.

135 Rosen, 1997, 69, 71, 76.
136 Freeman, 2002, 153–72, holds that even Portia must learn from Shylock's formidable rhetorical abilities.
137 Freeman, 2002, 155, 156, 158.
138 Sokol, 1998.
139 See ibid., 162–4, and Freeman, 2002, 171.
140 Hope, 2004, 6–7. Ibid. does however allow that if not region, then status and education were noted judgmentally when revealed by 'use of words and decorum of construction'.
141 Likewise Othello's voice may indicate his 'alienation', on which see E. Berry, 1990, and Biswas, 1996. Othello standing apart from his surrounding culture for reasons other than colour is discussed also in Hunter, 1978b.
142 Nicoll, 1963, 46, which offers alternately that dialect in *commedia* served 'the purpose of enriching the total design and for that of offering characteristic qualities to the members of the company', and then mentioned a 'play inspired by the commedia dell'arte, Vergilio Verucci's *Li diversi linguaggi* (1609), wherein all attention is concentrated upon the forms of speech used by the characters – Claudio's French, Pantalone's Venetian, Zanni's Bergamask, the Pedant's Sicilian, the Captain's Neapolitan, and Franceschina's Matriccian'.
143 My own doubts about the most famous essay about containment of alien voices appear in Sokol, 1994b, and are further contextualised in Sokol, 2003, 48–96.
144 Highley, 2004, 54–5 cites Blank, 1996, 80, in support of a claim that Raleigh was 'ridiculed for his pronounced Devonshire accent'. But I can see no support for this claim there. However Blank, 1996, Chapter Five, does argue there was an attempt made to 'Anglicize the British Isles'.
145 Vickers, 1985, 390.
146 See Maley and Murphy, 2004, 6–7, on the rarity of Scotticisms in MAC.
147 Highley, 2004, 58. This essay argues that MAC mirrors James's own attempts to extirpate the Scottish languages.
148 Kniezsa, 1991, 1.
149 See ibid. and Blake, 1981, 85–6. Blank, 1996, 160, also alludes to this. It is denied in Maley and Murphy, 2004, 15.
150 Blake, 1981, 90.
151 Ibid., 84–5, states that Fluellen's usages 'increase the flavour of a regional variety, though some are genuinely Welsh'.
152 Ibid., 86.
153 Powers, 1994, 109, strongly agrees. Ibid., 110, reviews the frequency of Scottish jokes on the stage of Shakespeare's time, and claims, 120, that 'much of the *Henriad* can be seen as an elaborate Welsh joke'.
154 According to Pugliatti, 1996, 145–7, the traditions in conflict are not the Welsh wearing of a leek on St David's Day, but literary ones, for this argues that Fluellen represents a 'new comedy' which is submissive to authority and which triumphs in H5 over an 'old comedy' represented by Pistol which is 'non-conformist, subversive'.

155 On the Dottore see Nicoll, 1963, 56–7.

156 Respect for Fluellen implied by the play is strongly argued in Harries, 1991, 162–74.

157 Fluellen is highly effective in dealing with Pistol and his cronies in 3.2, gives sound advice to English Captain Gower in 4.1.66–82, is brave and loyal in the 'Williams' episode in 4.8, and eventually unmasks Pistol's cowardice.

158 Contrary to Pugliatti, 1996, 145–7, this would make Fluellen non-subservient; as Blank, 1996, 138–9, puts it, it would give him a voice that makes 'the King . . . subject to Fluellen, rather than the other way around'.

159 One possibility, elaborated upon in Edwards, 1974, 75–7, is that as an Anglo-Irish citizen MacMorris is 'indignant that a Welshman . . . should think of Ireland as a separate nation from the great (British) nation which the Welshman apparently thought he belonged to'. However, ibid., 75, also draws attention to a more usual perception of MacMorris angrily anticipating a bigoted account of his 'nation'. Blank, 1996, 137, summarises (in order to contradict) the influential views of New Historicists and Cultural Materialists to the effect that the dialects of the speakers in this interchange deny them not only dignity, but also political or cultural autonomy or authenticity.

160 T. W. Craik, in his notes to Shakespeare, 1995c, 214–15, holds, for instance, that Gower's '*you will*' means 'you are determined'.

4 SHAKESPEARE, TOLERANCE, AND RELIGION

1 Bodin, 1984, written *c.* 1590, discusses sixteenth-century and earlier analogues (xlvii–lxii), including works by Pico, Erasmus, Montaigne, Guillaume Postel, and, in a note to xlvii, the ancient Jewish *Book of the Khazars*. Popkin, 1998, discusses Bodin's Jewish orientation.

2 The earlier date is argued in a note to Bodin, 1975, xxxvii–xxxviii. Malcolm, 2006, 97–100, reviews some reasons to support this but prefers the dating 1590–3. Malcolm, 2006 argues for Bodin's authorship despite contrary arguments in Wootton, 2002.

3 See Bodin, 1984, lxvii–lxix, on the early mss.; on the early circulation see Popkin, 1988. On keenness to possess mss. see Bredvold, 1924, which claims Milton possessed a copy, as does Bodin, 1984, lxix. The first complete printed edition was a Latin text edited by Ludovicus Noack, Schwerin, 1857, available as an e-text, Bodin, 1970.

4 Earlier Bodin himself had supported *politique* notions, but Remer, 1996a argues that in the *Colloquium* he changed his former position on religion. Other French philosophers decried *politique* pluralism; Zagorin, 2003, 91, describes it as 'a practical concession and political expedient' and points out that La Boetie denounced it and Montaigne only accepted it 'as the alternative to civil strife'. In fact the *politique* solution was unstable; see Benedict, 1996.

5 See Kuntz, 1998c.

6 Bodin, 1975, 471. All citations in English are from this translation; the Latin text sometimes cited is Bodin, 1970.

7 Remer, 1996b, 3–37, discusses '*decorum*' of '*sermo*', and 211–27 Bodin's *Colloquium*.

8 This harmony achieved within diversity is discussed in Kuntz, 1998b, and in Remer, 1996a, which replies to critics of the *Colloquium*.

9 See Kuntz, 1998a, c, d.

10 See Bodin, 1606, a translation of 1576.

11 See Bodin, 1606, 34.

12 Ibid., 44.

13 Ibid., 38–9, 45. See Heller, 1994, on Bodin on slavery.

14 Bodin, 1606, 40.

15 Nevertheless ibid., 43–5, details the 'deceit' of many Christians, Muslims, and also Jews who defy their own ordinances against enslaving converts.

16 LaRocca, 1984, 35–6, which holds that James's desire for toleration lasted beyond the first few years of his rule in England. The more often expressed notion that this lasted only until about 1606 is seen in Lecler, 1960, 2:407–8. That it had appeared in some form seems apparent from the objections seen in Busher, 1846, 46, a 1614 text which will be discussed below.

17 See LaRocca, 1984, passim.

18 See Laursen and Masroori, 1999, an annotated bibliography of such writings and secondary works on them. W. K. Jordan, 1932, Lecler, 1960, and Zagorin, 2003, consider many of these writings in detail.

19 See Laursen and Masroori, 1999, 233, for a bibliography. Especially Zagorin, 2003, sees Castellio as initiating the Western ideas of tolerance.

20 Grell, 1996, 181.

21 Pettegree, 1996, 198.

22 See W. K. Jordan, 1932, mainly on Protestants, and Lecler, 1960, mainly on Catholics.

23 Thus MacCulloch, 1996a, finds Cranmer's tolerance conceptually and practically meagre. As mentioned above, Grell, 1996, finds London's returned Protestant strangers ready to persecute as they had been persecuted, and Pettegree, 1996, detects a lack of tolerance in Holland on the part of those who had formerly been persecuted. Limitations of Dutch tolerance of Anabaptistism are also considered in Zijlstra, 2002.

24 All the essays in Grell and Scribner, 1996 are dubious about European early modern tolerance, while the essays in Laursen and Nederman, 1996, Laursen and Nederman, 1998, Laursen, 1999, and Nederman, 2000, find toleration not a unique development of the Enlightenment West, but rather widely manifested in other cultures, times, and places. Murphy, 2002, holds that the politics of religious toleration in several seventeenth-century settings was not necessarily based on 'liberal' principles, and that anti-tolerationists could have a well-principled concern for good social order. Yet B. J. Kaplan, 2004, identifies tolerance-in-practice in multi-faith early modern Holland, despite intolerant pronouncements. Coffey, 2000, argues for a sophisticated return to the idea of an English progress to an idealistic religious tolerance (especially after 1640), and Zagorin, 2003, finds a similar progress beginning in Europe with Castellio.

25 Laursen and Masroori, 1999, lists 130 tolerationist authors between 1500 and 1700, with only a small minority English and most of those post-1616. The comprehensive W. K. Jordan, 1932, in considering England, finds, aside from Sandys and Busher: 1:303–65, Acontius, a follower of Castellio; 1:366–7, the jurist Gentilis; the Baptists Thomas Helwys (2:274–84) and John Murton (2.298–314); and, 2.351, the 'moderate' Thomas Palmer.

26 See Rabb, 1963 on the editions.

27 Ibid., 325–8, and the Oxford DNB article on Sandys by Theodore K. Rabb, contradict contemporary claims that Sandys's book was first published without his consent.

28 See Rabb, 1963, 328–9.

29 From the start of Sandys, 1605, through to H1r (the sections numbered 1–27 out of 58), Sandys castigates the idolatry, corruption, hypocrisy, cruelty, and despotism of the 'Church of Rome' and especially 'Italian Romanistes'; similar remarks recur throughout the rest of the book. Citations are from this edition, STC 21716.

30 Ibid., I4r–K2r, sections 31–2. But immediately after this, section 33 begins by accusing the Catholic Church of having a 'pollicie' of propaganda or 'false newes', and Sandys subsequently describes the truth-destroying Spanish Inquisition as 'the greatest slaverie, that ever the world hath tasted' (L3r).

31 Ibid., C1v. Even this is hedged with a following comment that the great social inequalities of Italy, based on exploitation, require such charitable helps.

32 These were very probably inspired by the aims of Fra Paolo Sarpi, whom Sandys knew in Venice. See Rabb, 1963, 334–6, on Sarpi's 1608 annotations to Sandys's text, later published in Italian, French, and Dutch.

33 I have consulted Busher, 1614, but will cite from Busher, 1846, which transcribes a 1646 second edition.

34 Coffey, 2000, argues that Busher's argument was unique before the English Civil War.

35 Some, however, may have shared Busher's hopes for the conversion of Jews to the true apostolic faith (Jews re-admitted 'to the furtherance of their faith' Busher, 1846, 71); following this, Busher also expresses a hope that religious liberty will evoke a spirituality antipathetic to 'false [Christian] ministers', meaning Catholic ones (71–2).

36 See Sokol and Sokol, 2004, under HERESY; heresy was no longer officially a crime in Shakespeare's England. Witchcraft also was not treated as heresy under Elizabethan statutes, and this has a bearing on MAC discussed in Sokol, 1995.

37 Quoted in Marotti, 2003, 225–6. Milward, 1973, 69, agrees: 'there are no certain references in Shakespeare's plays to the sufferings of English Catholics'.

38 Marotti, 2003, 219, 226.

39 Moschovakis, 2002, 460.

40 Marotti, 2003, 224.

41 As proposed in Liebler, 1994, and West, 1982; both are commented on in Chapter 5.

42 Bridging these views, Foakes, 2005, associates the Ghost in HAM, the unique Elizabethan stage ghost seen in outdated armour, with the anachronistic theology of the Catholic past.

43 As in Hassel, 2003, and in Greenblatt, 2001, respectively.

44 These are critiqued in Moschovakis, 2002, and in McAlindon, 2001.

45 R. Wilson, 2004, finds Shakespeare secretively but intensely aware of the dangers and sufferings of English Catholics; its dense argument is undercut by much historical forcing which makes checking its claims onerous. For instance the much-debated 'authenticity' of John Shakespeare's Spiritual Testament is stated to be simply 'established' (50), while Cardinal Wolsey's actual hat is again transferred securely to a playhouse (155), despite Anne Barton's correction of that error in her 28 March 1991 *New York Review of Books* review of Greenblatt, 1976.

46 Greenblatt, 2001, 254.

47 Ibid., 248, puts it: Elizabethans 'look back with longing at the world they have lost', referring to a 'fifty year effect' post-Reformation.

48 See Hunt, 2004b, on the Eucharist in HAM. Hunt, 2004a presents similar readings of tolerance-implying theological mixtures in TGV, 1&2H4, H5, AWW, TN, and OTH.

49 The theory of young Shakespeare's employment by the Catholic Alexander Houghton, first proposed in O. Baker, 1937, 297–319, was severely dented by the investigations in Hamer, 1970. It was reprised in Honigmann, 1985, which presses, 59–76, for an 'early start' chronology for Shakespeare's play-writing career in support of this thesis. Honigmann, 1982, 53–90 also argues an early start, dating 1H6 to 1588 (88). My own small contribution to this discussion, Sokol, 2000, uncovers manuscript evidence indicating that 1H6 was unlikely to have been written before 1592, suggesting a 'late start' chronology.

50 Bearman, 2005, reviews and rejects 'financial' evidence of Shakespeare's father's recusancy, and Bearman, 2003, contests the authenticity of his 'spiritual testament'.

51 Malvolio, Angelo, and also Shylock are identified as power-seeking Puritans in Fisch, 1974; this holds that Shakespeare took 'Puritanism very seriously', analysing its beliefs and modes of thought, or 'dynamic'. On Angelo as a Puritan hypocrite see Ferreira-Ross, 1992. The evident notion that Falstaff's mock-godliness satirises Puritans has been reinterpreted: Poole, 1995, suggests a counter-parody of mocking Elizabethan portrayals of Puritans; Tiffany, 1998, argues Puritans may have liked the representation of anti-authoritarianism in the Henriad, and would not have thought that the portrayal of Falstaff parodied their values; M. Davies, 2005 holds that Falstaff/Oldcastle represents a Protestantism 'too bloated and too belated, too antique and inert, for the late Elizabethan war against Antichrist'. In an ambiguous counterpoise to any critique of extreme Protestantism, Shakespeare has atheistic Aaron complain that the religiously-inclined Lucius is given to 'twenty popish tricks and ceremonies' (TIT 5.1.76).

52 See Milward, 1973, 41–84, and Beauregard, 1999, on AWW.

53 See Daniell, 2001, on Shakespeare's language, and Hamilton, 1992, on his reflections of Church politics.

54 See Oxford DNB article by Patrick Collinson on the elder Edwin Sandys.

55 See Hunt, 2004a, Marotti, 2003, and many of the essays in Beauregard and Taylor, 2003. Of particular note in the latter is Hopkins, 2003, which offers an intriguing interpretation in which AWW presents 'images of reconciliation ... between apparently conflicting religious positions'. Topical readings of Shakespeare on religion need not only be about strife; indeed, the reading in Hopkins, 2003 considers not only Catholic/Protestant, but also Muslim/Christian reconciliation.

56 Hopkins, 2003, and Hunt, 2004a, 47–71, say much of interest about theological allusions in AWW, but miss the jokes in question. Noble, 1935, 196–7, cites remote biblical sources of Lavatch's remarks, but does not identify the passage from the Prayer Book; neither does Kirsch, 1981, 139–40, or Simonds, 1989, 47–9. Shaheen, 1993, 209, repeated in Shaheen, 1999, 270, remarks: 'the specific texts that lie behind [Lavatch's] words ... are not easily recognizable'. Milward, 1973, 110–20, discusses the reflections of the Prayer Book marriage ceremony in Shakespeare, but also misses these jokes.

57 See T. Smith, 1583, 98–101, for the arguments on both sides of this debate; see also Croft, 1983, and Sokol and Sokol, 2004, under WARD.

58 Hurstfield, 1958, 142.

59 See Sokol and Sokol, 2003, 30–4, 56–72.

60 As specified in the 1559 Act of Uniformity (1.Eliz.1 c.2), which applied until 1640.

61 Discussions of Shakespeare and companionate marriage include: Dash, 1981, 93; Dreher, 1986, 38; Boone, 1987, 54–6; and Hagstrum, 1992, 374–404. Boone, 1987, 49, is typical in claiming that companionate marriage was a product of Protestantism. This was denied by Professor Robert Miola (private communication), and his view is backed up by details in Sommerville, 1995, 129.

62 MacCulloch, 1996b, 421.

63 Ibid., 421. Ibid., 58–9 and 420–1, trace Cranmer slowly coming to accept a companionate theory of Christian marriage.

64 Anon., 1968, 239.

65 Lavatch's extended parody of the Prayer Book marriage ceremony has been overlooked in the considerable scholarship that has attempted to trace Shakespeare's uses of liturgical or scriptural texts, seemingly because Lavatch mirrors only the structures of meaning in the Prayer Book, not its wording. Noble, 1935, 83, is unique in noticing an allusion, but it misses the parody.

66 Hunter, 1959, 22n. This note identifies the same phrase used jocularly in ADO 2.1.298–300. Noble, 1935, 29, suggests two possible biblical sources.

67 A much milder skit on the same text, 'mutuall society, helpe and coumfort', possibly appears when Holofernes extends the invitation: 'I beseech your society' and Nathaniel accepts this with 'And thank you too, for society, saith the text, is the happiness of life' (LLL 4.2.157–9).

68 Sokol and Sokol, 2003, 119 and 127–9, describes how Shakespeare reflected on the limits of the 'one flesh' doctrine, and spoofed these.

69 Hunt, 2004a, 53, interprets the last of these utterances as 'strongly Calvinist'.

70 Shaheen, 1997, argues that in TRO 2.3.1–35 (in the Oxford lineation) Thersites presents a 'bitter prayer, a perversion of the Prayer Book'.

71 C. Davies, 1988, proposes a model in which 'stupidity' jokes can expose the false rationality of supposedly rational industrial societies and bureaucratic tyrannies.

72 See Benton, 1988, 51.

73 Booty, 1976, 48.

74 Ibid., 339; see also Collinson, 1967, 68–9, 71–83, 94–6, 123; and Collinson, 1994, 198, 240–1.

75 A mistake that seems to have taken hold widely of late is that a play-acted marriage ceremony could have made a valid Elizabethan marriage; because intent was all-important, no such possibility arose. See Swinburne, 1686, 105.

76 Thus, referring to the Stratford bawdy court in 1595, Brinkworth, 1972, 63, describes 'God's wounds' as 'an old Catholic oath still in currency – the Queen used it'.

77 Booty, 1976, 267; ibid., 402n., remarks that this is overlooked in a Royal Injunction of 1559 on the wafer.

78 An analysis of the music used in the royal chapel, in Bowers, 2000, shows that Elizabeth I used the most conservative version of the Prayer Book there, despite her own Act of Uniformity mandating the use of the more 'Reformed' version of 1559. Moreover, MacCulloch, 1996b, 35, tells of reported sightings of a crucifix there; see Collinson, 1994, 87–118, on Elizabeth's less than wholly Reformed personal inclinations.

79 Donne, 1960, 301.

80 See Erne, 2001, 211–12. This also resolves puzzles, finding in Geneva the 'one hill' (217–18), and all three Churches for Donne 'unbridelike'.

81 Collinson, 1994, 228.

82 See Coryate, 1611, 231–2, on synagogue behaviour, and ibid., 234, on the stripping 'euen naked' of converted Italian Jews.

5 'RACE', PART ONE

1 Michael Banton, quoted in Niro, 2003, 41.

2 For instance, Crewe, 1995, admits at its start, 'Even if the the term "race" is granted, recent studies have rightly emphasised the heterogeneity and historical specificity of "racial" construction.' Yet, as do many discussions, this then holds that Shakespeare's work is filled with colour-coded 'race-writing' and pursues a focus more relevant to our time than to Shakespeare's.

3 Sweet, 1997, proposes, in line with this distinction, that a 'racism without race' in Iberian culture gave rise to later American racist thought.

4 Shakespeare's age was, of course, aware of physical differences between geographically separated human groups. But then, as we shall see, geographical

influences, rather than biological lineage, were considered of prime importance in determining human variety. See Fiedler, 1974; Gillies, 1994; Feerick, 2003; and Floyd-Wilson, 2003 – these matters will be discussed at length in Chapter 6.

5 It is strange that some who seemingly would seek to historicise and relativise Racialist concepts still strive to find evidence that the Racialist sense of the term 'race' somehow transcended time and culture. So, in a reprise of her argument in Hendricks, 1996 (mentioned in the next note), Hendricks, 2000, 15–20, searches Elizabethan foreign language dictionaries for traces of Racialist words or concepts. Similarly, Iyengar, 2005, 1–2, seeks Racialist overtones in uses of 'race' by Shakespeare and William Towerson where this term bears entirely different meanings than the one indicating Race (this exercise seems to contradict the position taken in Iyengar, 2004, which is described in the next note).

6 The term 'race' does appear often in Elizabethan contexts, with meanings including: the passage of time; a natural or inherited disposition; any class of animals or things; one of the sexes; a cut, slit, mark or scratch; a ginger root. But, as Biswas, 1996 and Feerick, 2003 point out, only such non-Racial meanings attached to 'race' then. Iyengar, 2004, 95, confirms that only in the late seventeenth century did ' "race" also evoke . . . the belief that people with different skin-tones belong to different species'. Hendricks, 1996, 41–2, admits the same, yet claims, 43, that Shakespeare partly subscribed to a 'more modern idea [of race] based on physical appearance (i.e. skin color, physiognomy)', and so argues that 'the figurative evocation of India [in MND] . . . marks the play's complicity in the racialist ideologies being created by early modern England's participation in imperialism'. On how far Shakespeare's age was from viewing contemporary India in terms of racial superiority, see R. Barbour, 2003.

7 Is a concept of Race only the ill-begotten offspring of myths that supported beliefs in 'White' racial superiority from the eighteenth century onward, and which found pseudo-scientific support in the nineteenth and earlier twentieth centuries? Or is it properly associated with a long-held genteel distaste for non-paleskinned persons? (The pronouncements of Charles Lamb and his contemporary John Quincy Adams on Othello's skin colour, reprinted in Shakespeare, 1999, 279–81, indicate that this kind of bigotry may have reached a zenith in the early nineteenth century, but it is certainly not extinct.) Or is 'Race' actually useful as a rough and ready guide to minor genetic variations, as for example when recessive genes are concentrated in people of certain ancestries as a result of a 'founder effect'? The usefulness of Race in medical diagnostics may be an artefact of history; the Atlantic slave trade brought many West Africans to the Americas, and these, of course, had greater chances of sharing familial genetic traits than had Africans in general. Otherwise, there is more genetic variability within a purported African 'race' than between it and other 'races'.

8 In other ways discerning readings of OTH in Barthelemy, 1987, and in E. Berry, 1990, manifest these tendencies. Bassi, 2003, 64–5, argues that racial

interpretations which deny the stability of 'race' and yet assert its centrality contradict themselves, while 'cast[ing] a bridge between early modern England and the postmodern, multicultural United States, establishing a privileged axis which ignores important geo-historical variants'; this especially critiques Little, 2000.

9 See Baecker, 1999.

10 Hunter, 1964, 51, identifies a wide range of Elizabethan authors who 'describe Moors as existing in many parts of the globe'; these include Malabar, Malacca, Guinea, Ethiopia, Fukien, and America. Bartels, 1990, 434, finds 'Moor' used 'to designate a figure from different parts or the whole of Africa (or beyond) who was either black or Moslem, neither, or both.' D'Amico, 1991, 59, likewise describes Elizabethan confusion about 'Moors': 'how men of color – African, Moor, Ethiopian, Indian and Arab – would merge in the popular imagination'. Gillies, 1994, 32, comments that a 'blurring of racial outline is typical of the representation of exotics in Shakespeare and other Elizabethan dramatists', and Habib, 2000, 2, writes 'what notions of race the Elizabethans had were hopelessly confused, as they routinely combined Africans with Arabs, Indians and south Asians, and pre-Columbian Americans'. Referring to the many meanings of 'Moor' in Shakespeare's time, Neill, 1998, 364–6, alleges the Elizabethan 'language of difference' was 'shifting and uncertain . . . before the modern discourses of race and color'. A rare exception, W. D. Jordan, 1975, 5, claims that 'in Shakespeare's day . . . the terms *Moor* and *Negro* were used almost interchangeably'.

11 See Bartels, 1990, especially 434: 'the Moor was characterized alternately, and sometimes simultaneously, in contradictory extremes, as noble or monstrous, civil or savage'. See also Bartels, 2006a.

12 Sidney, 1962: 168 (sonnet 7); 169 (sonnet 9, obliquely); 175 (sonnet 20, eyebrows); 188 (sonnet 47). See ibid., 436, for commentary on the attractive black eyes of Penelope Devereux.

13 Hall, 1996, 62–122, contains a wide-ranging and politically purposeful survey of this field. For Crewe, 1995, 17–18, Lucrece's blood separating into two colours in LUC 1742–3 is exemplary.

14 TIT 4.2.71, MV 2.1.1, OTH 3.3.267–71.

15 Girard, 1991a, 49, and Girard, 1991b, speculate that MV was intended to communicate differently to different segments of its original audience, the groundlings being supposedly more receptive to racist outlooks.

16 See especially the rigorously historical Vaughan and Vaughan, 1997, which avoids all simple presumptions.

17 There is great uncertainty about the average literacy of Shakespeare's audiences (see Sokol, 1994a, 65 7), and about the availability to Elizabethans of printed texts (see Sokol, 2004). Word of mouth is still more elusive; none of the scant accounts we have of Shakespearian auditors' responses (e.g. Simon Forman's diaries, Henry Peacham's drawing, a few critical remarks) could contribute even one vote to a 'poll' intended to determine average racial outlooks.

18 Especially Bartels, 1997, re-interprets many of the early modern reports of Western African travel and exploration that have been often read as revealing inflexible racist stereotyping, arguing that on the contrary the advantage of European states lay in maintaining flexible and sympathetic rather than overweening attitudes toward Africans and 'Moors'.

19 A few examples are: Semple, 1987, 35, on Elizabeth's 1601 'intentions to deport her black subjects'; Baecker, 1999, 118, which makes parallel claims concerning 1599 [sic] and 1601; Andreas, 2002, 190, which refers to 'two edicts expelling the "Blackamoors" in 1596 and again in 1601'; Niro, 2003, 43, which claims 'Elizabeth twice entreated the wholesale removal of blacks and Moors from England'. Such an error is not seen in the treatments in Eldred Jones, 1965, 12–13, and Iyengar, 2004, 101.

20 Bartels, 2006b, 310, 311, 307.

21 Barthelemy, 1987, 3, 25, 84, 92, and Gillies, 1994, 25, seem to assume this. Vitkus, 2003, 102–3, holds that the racist myth recounted by Best was 'widely disseminated' and generally 'understood'. D'Amico, 1991, 64–5, connects the story of Ham's sin in Genesis with a supposed 'Christian tradition' that Africans were his descendants, and then with Best's claim that Ham was cursed on account of sexual incontinence. D'Amico, 1991 sees this in terms of religion: 227–8n. links Ham's curse with Islam; 179 claims that Ham's sinfulness typified 'the Christian tradition' in which 'deviations from the European norm, whether in appearance, custom or religion, signalled degeneration or sin'.

22 See W. D. Jordan, 1975, 17–19. Tokson, 1982, 13, describes Best's theory as one among others.

23 See Braude, 1997, and Sollors, 1997, 79–111.

24 Iyengar, 2004, 96.

25 Iyengar, 2005, 10; see ibid., 8–11.

26 See W. D. Jordan, 1975, 17–19, which, incorrectly, blames Jewish tradition for the theory of Hamitic Blackness.

27 Braude, 1997, reveals how belief in the post-medieval prevalence of the legend of Africans' Hamitic ancestry derived from Racialist pseudo-scholarly misrepresentations.

28 Eldred Jones, 1971, 21–31. The impact of Leo on England and English playwrights is also discussed in Eldred Jones, 1965, 21–6. Iyengar, 2004, 99, holds that Leo's career itself 'illustrates both European tolerance and intolerance'.

29 Morse, 1998, 72, proposes that in OTH criticism a 'predisposition to a-historical "racism" occludes further exploration', and, 74–5, finds a critic's collusive use of 'our' in a racially judgmental phrase frankly 'disgusting'. Baecker, 1999, 199, holds that Elizabethans 'found Africans to be no more or less exotic and barbaric than the Russians'. Bassi, 2003, objects to the racialisation of Shakespeare studies, concluding that although several of Shakespeare's plays 'feature non-European characters, yet "race" is not the category which can best guide us in interpreting them' (72).

30 For instance Suzman, 1988, in a reply to Semple, 1987, argues that '"blackness" is only one of several considerations' leading to the downfall of Othello.

31 Hodgen, 1964, 213–14.

32 W. D. Jordan, 1975, 3–45, cites John Hawkins, William Towerson, Thomas Stevens, George Best, Thomas Candish, Leo Africanus, and anonymous authors in Hakluyt and Purchas. Some studies such as Vaughan and Vaughan, 1997, and Sweet, 1997, but few, have explored more widely since.

33 W. D. Jordan, 1975, 43.

34 No new evidence has disrupted this conclusion in Folarin, 1977, 7.

35 Ibid., 6.

36 In a typical instance, Hall, 1996, 21, places side by side, without comment, accounts of English slaving in 1569 and 1637, suggesting a significant continuous English involvement with Atlantic slaving.

37 Zhou Xiaojing, 1998, 336, which in support misquotes Tokson, 1982, ix (where Tokson writes of this becoming true 'during the next two hundred years').

38 For example, Barker and Hulme, 1985, 204, asserts that TMP must be seen as 'a play imbricated within a discourse of colonialism' and accuses any contrary viewpoints of being 'complicit, whether consciously or not, with a colonialist mentality'.

39 Vaughan and Vaughan, 1997, holds that Elizabethan attitudes to Blacks were preponderantly negative, but also cites some positive ones, as does W. D. Jordan, 1975. Tokson, 1982, mentions that some European travellers found 'positive traits' among Black people (18), and devotes a final chapter, 120–35, to discussing 'Positive Aspects of the Image of the Black Man' in literature, albeit mainly to dismiss these as insignificant or tainted. More recently, and more forcefully, Bartels, 1997, 61, holds that in Shakespeare's England there was a 'significantly open' and wide 'range of meanings Africa could hold'. This argues that among these possible attitudes, racism was disadvatageous because an obstacle to imperial or mercantile success (62). Similarly, Dimmock, 2005, pictures English attitudes toward the Ottoman Turks as so positive (even with praises of Turkish religion) that, before James I's peace, strategic alliances against Spain were considered. See also Iyengar, 2004, and Hodgen, 1964, 367–73.

40 Zhou Xiaojing, 1998, 341.

41 See S. Kaplan, 1949, 277–333, from which the following historical details are taken.

42 The ruse also included sending copies of the tract to Lincoln, who never replied to a request that its sequel be dedicated to him, and to other anti-slavery leaders who replied, if at all, guardedly.

43 Gillies, 1994, 27. Similar propositions are presented in Andreas, 2002, 188, and luridly in Raley, 1997, and Little, 2000. Neill, 1989, 394, asks 'what it is in Othello that "poisons sight"' and proposes a possible Elizabethan 'racialist ideology'. Yet Neill, 1989, 399, comments, 'The audience can become deeply implicated in this network of interlocking prejudices and suspicions just because

it is Iago's habit to work by implication and association; feelings and attitudes that would hardly survive inspection in the light of reason are enabled to persist precisely because they work away in this subterranean fashion.'

44 Neill, 1989, uses this term to conflate adultery with racial adulteration; the beds actually called 'unproper' by Iago in OTH 4.1.67 are adulterous but not miscegenetic.

45 Sollors, 1997, 395.

46 A. Ward, 1996, 13. Gaikwad, 1967, 14–19, tells a more complicated story: from the fifteenth century the Portuguese authorities strongly encouraged their settlers to marry Indian women, and the Dutch did the same, while the British East India Company urged such marriages later on (this cites, 16, a 1684 letter).

47 A. Ward, 1996, 20–1, claims that the Anglo-Indians in India were very prosperous from 1600 to 1785, and details the new repressive orders of 1776–95.

48 Dalrymple, 2003, 1–54, chronicles the eighteenth-century decline from tolerance into bigotry of the British Indian administration, and, 50–1, details the new restrictions imposed on Anglo-Indians.

49 Ibid., 50.

50 David Worthington has kindly informed me that the John Henderson of the picture is 'almost certainly' the politician he and Steven Murdoch treated in the Oxford DNB. See the note on the cover illustration, at the end of the Introduction.

51 See for instance W. D. Jordan, 1975, 29–40; Tokson, 1982, 82–105; I. Smith, 1998, 179–80 (which also stresses Black jealousy); and multiple assertions in Barthelemy, 1987, and D'Amico, 1991. Even Bartels, 1997, which finds 'postcolonial' readings of OTH deficient, accepts that there was a stereotypic view of Africans as lustful, although it wittily wonders if the reports of nakedness often adduced as reasons for this might have been otherwise interesting 'to a people desperate to find new markets for their cloth' (58).

52 Loomba, 2000, 211, 222n., 206. Ibid. insists that these monstrous 'images . . . have not been imported from the nineteenth century', although it admits at the same time that some in the OTH playworld are 'sympathetic' to the 'Othello–Desdemona marriage'.

53 Morse, 1998, 74. This calls some aspects of Shakespearian racialising theories 'disgusting' (75), and equally attacks assumptions that Black women on Renaissance stages offer 'a female variant on the lusty moor', asserting 'their lust is no different from that of other [White] lusty women' (73).

54 Chedgzoy, 1998, 116.

55 Niro, 2003, 50.

56 Floyd-Wilson, 2003, 1–3, 35–47.

57 Indeed Floyd-Wilson, 2003, 23–47, proposes that alternative views of southern birth or Blackness, especially in relation to sexuality, were in the process of exchanging prominence at about Shakespeare's time. Spiller, 1998, 146, remarks on a change of the meanings of race from 'genealogy toward national ethnicity' during Shakespeare's time, although this is not the same as

from geographically determined humours to ethically significant skin colours. A similar change is alleged in Marcus, 2004, which claims that the Folio text of OTH was altered to become more 'racist' than the Quarto. But geohumoral thinking was still very much alive in John Milton's time, and later, as will be seen in Chapter 6.

58 See Tokson, 1982, 82–105, for texts indicating such stereotypes.

59 Ibid., claims that English drama represented the sexuality of Black men and women as evil, and miscegenation as evil, but, 95, allows that OTH was an exception because Shakespeare could 'imagine the possibility of a deep, devoted love evoked by a black man in the heart of a good white woman although the real nature of that man is still highly disputable'. Exceptionalism is also implied in Hunter, 1978b, an important essay on OTH and colour prejudice first published in 1967. Citing visual art, theology, and philosophy, this argues for longstanding negative associations of Blackness, yet finds, 47, that OTH has the power to 'manipulate . . . sympathies' in a contrary way (although that also had a historical basis in 'complicating factors' of Shakespeare's time).

60 I. Smith, 1998, 178–81, presents a theory of inverted stereotypes in which Iago takes on 'Black' characteristics and Othello 'White' ones, and cites other authors with similar views, 178.

61 Rymer, 1956, 132–64.

62 Alexander, 1968, 71.

63 Obtained by applying to Wells and Taylor, 1989, my custom programs WCSPEAK and LINES.

64 Yet even Aaron's literary sophistication may be seen as destructive, if we consider the view expounded in West, 1982, that TIT presents Romans and barbarians as equal in their contributions to the fatal decline of late Rome, because both are educated through Roman literature to embrace defunct ideals. Race is held accountable for this in Liebler, 1994, which examines classical sources and concludes, 278, that TIT suggests that the decline of late Rome was caused by the 'hybridization of its central leadership'.

65 Both Barabas and Muly Mohammet influenced Shakespeare's TIT, as seen in the verbal allusions at 5.1.135–6 (and its whole context) and 4.2.151 respectively. See Edelman, 2005, 31 and 55n., on the proposition that Aaron may have been a collaborative creation of Shakespeare and Peele.

66 Eldred Jones, 1965, 53, sees Aaron as ebullient, but I think here pushes this character's attractiveness too hard. I agree with the notion next expressed, ibid., 54, that in giving moral agency and choice to Aaron Shakespeare shows a non-Racialist 'preoccupation with men rather than types'.

67 I have in mind Edmund, Falconbridge, and Richard III. An exception is Don John, the bastard brother of the Prince in ADO, who says that his 'sadness is without limit' (1.3.3–37). It will be argued in Chapter 6 that, thanks to his inner vacuum, Iago can be neither sad nor glad.

68 Braxton, 2000, 225; see also 227ff. It has been argued that the deficiencies of Roman Law seen in TIT had bearing on the Elizabethan debate over a

reception of Roman-inspired Civilian Law: Bate, 1995, 28, suggests that the play opposes Roman law – exemplified, for instance, in Saturninus' 'chilling' insistence in TIT 4.4.54 that Martius and Quintus 'died by law' – with more humane English Common Law, governed by like precedent. Kerr, 1992, in a discussion connecting legal uses of evidence with classical rhetoric, likewise alleges that a 'darker side' of civil law informs arbitrary judgment in TIT.

69 Expounded in Hunt, 1988, 205, 214.

70 Bartels, 1990, 435, claims this, and links it to a vision of an evil Moor, but also insists on Aaron as 'unique' (445).

71 As in J. S. White, 1997.

72 Translated in Bullough, 1957–75, 7:241–52, reprinted with notes in Shakespeare, 2001, 370–86.

73 Her remarkable act of lying on her deathbed to defend her husband from blame is brilliantly treated in Frazier, 1985.

74 Rymer, 1956, 132.

75 On which see Shakespeare, 2001, 123n.

76 See Hurstfield, 1958, 139–41, and Bean, 1968, 13–14.

77 In MND Egeon does not die, but does disappear in a sinister way, on which see McGuire, 1989.

78 Claribel's marriage is treated with racist horror in the film *Prospero's Books*, and she is presented, according to Raley, 1997, 95, with 'tearful eyes and a bloody pudendum . . . enslaved', in a manner claimed, ibid., to be 'familiar to the imagination of Shakespeare's contemporaries'. It seems to me erroneous to attribute the racist sneers of Antonio and Sebastian (and much worse) to Shakespeare's culture, rather than a revulsion from these.

79 Yet this is denied in Cheadle, 1994, which holds that Brabantio's interest in Othello's marvellous adventures indicates prejudice against him, and similarly in Gillies, 1994, 139–40, which repeats an often-suggested denigration of early modern curiosity about outsiders in the remark that Brabantio 'and his daughter court their own seduction through an "errant" and voyeuristic wish-dreaming, a desire for the exotic as an embodiment of the repressed contents of mental domains . . . which they have previously refrained from "discovering"'. I have opposed such anti-epistemological views, which deny the possibilities of cross-cultural curiosity, understanding, or empathy, in Sokol, 1994b, and in Sokol, 2003, 48–76.

80 Gillies, 1994, 138, calls this tolerant remark 'strikingly implausible', and claims 'However "liberal" this [remark] may sound to the modern ear, the suggestion is clearly that the case has been rigged in Othello's favour.' Bartels, 2006a, 145, suggests more moderately that Othello's trial's outcome is driven by 'contingency'. We will consider its legal plausibility presently.

81 See Sokol and Sokol, 2003, 108–116, 212.

82 Andreas, 2002, 188.

83 Even after the revelation of Othello's terrible act he is called by Emilia a 'dull Moor' (5.2.232) and 'cruel Moor' (5.2.256) in a way that seems more descriptive

than racial. I think it is less than attentive to bracket, as does Bassi, 2003, 72, both Emilia and Brabantio with Iago, Gratiano, Bassanio, and Antonio, 'as the prototypical racists'. E. Berry, 1990, 319–21, also alleges racism in the speeches of Brabantio, Emilia, and even Desdemona.

84 This continued image of Othello's nobility, brilliantly treated in Gardner, 1963 (originally 1955), delivers an impression far more positive than the 'making more of the Moor' – the making of him as a better man than Aaron – argued for in Bartels, 1990, and suggested in Eldred Jones, 1965, 119.

85 Niro, 2003, 45; however, ibid., 48, sophisticates the matter finding, 'the simple reading of race in *Othello* remains troubled'.

86 Ibid., 46–7, citing Habib, 2000, 136. These are not alone in a tendency to detect racial bigotry in any language that might imply colour awareness.

87 Neill, 1998, 365–6. In a similar vein Loomba, 2000, 207–10, discusses the impact of the Spanish concept of *limpieza de sangre* and disagrees with the views of several writers claiming that Elizabethan England stood apart from this early Racialist ideology.

88 Dimmock, 2005, 203. This study, especially 9–10, agrees with Matar, 1999, that relying on Edward Said's *Orientalism* provides an inadequate basis for understanding English views of the 'East' in Shakespeare's time.

89 Bartels, 1997, 61, 62.

90 Ibid., 62.

91 Mallett and Hale, 1984, 313–66.

92 Ibid., 313–14; ibid., 333, adds that when some Venetian patricians did go to war in 1509 it was found that 'Many families had sold or lost their weapons and armour generations ago.'

93 Lewkenor, 1599, 15, 130–3 and passim.

94 See Muir, 1956. Certainly Shakespeare did include many specifics about Venice in MV and OTH, on which see McPherson, 1990, 51–81; for OTH, Lewkenor could have supplied most of these.

95 McPherson, 1988.

96 However, ibid., 464–5, argues it is taken from Francesco Sansovino.

97 See McPherson, 1990, 81–90.

98 Cited hereafter from Nashe, 1948.

99 See Sokol, 1994a, 99–109, 216–222.

100 Nashe, 1948, 60.

101 Sugden, 1925, 545, lists many reflections in English Renaissance drama of the stereotype of lascivious Venetian women, and Mahler, 1993, proposes that Italy at large, and in particular a misogynistic view of sexually rampant Italian women, came to represent vice for English Renaissance drama. But Hoenselaars, 1993, 44, claims that typical errors of distortion and projection concerning Italy are 'rooted in ethnocentric thought patterns', and points out that in Dekker's *All Fools* stereotyping associations of Italy with cuckoldry are superseded by an 'acknowledgement of vice not as specific but as a universal fault'.

102 Jack, however, soon makes her pregnant.

103 See McPherson, 1990, 86–7 on this cloistering, and 84–5 on Venetian husbands' famed jealousy.

104 Gardner, 1963, 352–5; see also 358.

105 Barthelemy, 1987, 152, 153. Ibid., 150–62, proposes that White men's anxieties are projected onto Black men, making 'sex . . . conventionally the black man's preoccupation' (151); this is very similar to the view of Winthrop Jordan commented on above.

106 See Lerner, 1979, 16, Bradshaw, 1992, and the debate between Nelson and Haines, 1983, and Nathan, 1988.

107 Cowhig, 1985, 9, for one, finds it 'clear' that Othello's marriage 'is fully consummated'.

108 Ibid., says of Desdemona: 'Beneath a quiet exterior lay the spirited independence which comes out in her defence of her marriage before the Senate.'

109 Yet E. Z. Cohen, 1976, 127, concludes that Iago's characteristics are 'sterility and coldness . . . asexuality', and in this contrasts him with Cassio, 'who survives'. Arguments to follow in Chapter 6 affirm this.

110 If, as Hadfield, 1998 suggests, Iago is intended to be seen as Spanish, then the proto-Racialist Iberian *limpieza de sangre* concept may have bearing on Iago, although (as discussed above) not on the whole play. Everett, 1987, made the same proposition as Hadfield, that Iago is Spanish – and argued that Roderigo and Othello are as well, so weaving a subtle account of how OTH portrays the Spanish enigmas of Shakespeare's time.

111 This asserts a counter-view to the notorious position taken in the essay 'Shakespeare and the Stoicism of Seneca', Eliot, 1934, 33–54. In this Eliot – aware that his opinion 'may appear subjective and fantastic in the extreme' – holds that in his final speech Othello is merely 'cheering himself up' (39). As many critics have said, such a position is tremendously reductive; in it, I believe, Eliot was attacking not Shakespeare or Othello, but the ideal of poetry put forward in G. Wilson Knight's 1930 essay 'The Othello Music' (reissued in Knight, 1960, 97–119). In it Knight acknowledged a mixture of baseness and nobility in Othello, but concluded that in the play's finale 'the *Othello* music itself sounds with a nobler cadence, a richer flood of harmonies, a more selfless and universalized flight of the imagination, than before' (119).

112 In this racist Iago avers 'or else I am a Turk', which is overlooked in Hoenselaars, 1995, a study of similar phrases.

113 Vitkus, 2003, 78–106, overlooks the impact of this and finds in OTH reflections only of an animosity and fear which it alleges underlay the demonizing attitudes of all Elizabethans to all Turks. Thus, ibid., 95, calls the astute Ottoman strategies disclosed in OTH 1.3 'morally questionable' (no reason is given). Such a position is overturned by Dimmock, 2005, which demonstrates very positive English attitudes to Turks before James came to the throne. But Dimmock proposes that *Othello* may signal a Jacobean withdrawal from an 'Anglo-Islamic link' with the Ottomans; I cannot see evidence for this in the playtext.

6 'RACE', PART TWO: SHAKESPEARE AND SLAVERY

1 Schorsch, 2004 rigorously investigates Jews who were involved with the Atlantic slave economy; it concludes that their behaviour was on average no better or worse than that of Christians of the same time and place. An important methodological position taken in this study is an avoidance of over-reliance on a few distorting, over-used anecdotes; a parallel problem with the over-use of selected 'race' materials has been discussed in the last chapter, while Goose, 2005, 113–15, critiques the over-use of certain materials that have been purported to prove Elizabethan xenophobia.

2 Schorsch, 2004, 167–9.

3 Iyengar, 2005, 203; see also ibid., 200–19, and Iyengar, 2004, 104.

4 J. H. Baker, 1990, 541. On paradoxes of *habeas corpus* in relation to imprisonment or slavery in Shakespeare's time see ibid., 168–9 and 537–44.

5 Hunt, 1997, 39, thinks it relevant that under the English Vagrancy Acts of 1547 and 1572 enslavement was briefly possible as a punishment for sturdy beggary, but admits that there is virtually no evidence that these punishments were ever applied. Slack, 1988, 122, explains why the 1547 Act was a 'spectacular failure' ('volunteer slaveowners did not materialize'); this failure is further discussed in MacCulloch, 1988, 98–9. Yet in discussing reflections of slavery on ERR and OTH, Hunt, 1997, and Slights, 1997, find characteristic of oppressive early modern society, respectively, 'virtual de facto enslavement' (40) and 'commodification of people as property' (383).

6 P. J. Cornish, 1996, discusses these writings in relation to theories of tolerance.

7 Terraciano, 1999, considers this 'Black Legend', and also a contrary 'White Legend' associated with the unusual freedom that Spanish kings allowed to debates over the justification of the Spanish actions in America. This argues that such freedom was granted when outrage against New World conquest, exploitation, expropriation, murder, and enslavement served royal interests, and when it did not such expressions were suppressed.

8 Hadfield, 1998, 338, comments that 'Finding anti-Spanish material would have presented no problem to any literate writer in the early 1600s.'

9 See Achinstein, 2001, 109.

10 Montaigne, 1942, 3:128–51.

11 Benzoni, 1579. On this see the notes to Benzoni, 1862 (a translation of the Italian original), and Sokol, 2003, 38. Sokol, 2004, 71, traces a copy to which Shakespeare may have had access.

12 See Anon., 1844, 6 (a reprint of 1610).

13 See Hoenselaars, 1992, 176–8, 227, 229–31, 235, 242, 287n., 266n., on the many, often satirical, theatrical references to English slaves.

14 Vitkus, 2000, 11–12, holds that historical enmity played a part in motivating Moorish pirates, and, 9–11, adds they also retaliated against Christian pirates. Davis, 2003, claims that as opposed to the purely economic motives of Atlantic planter–slavers, Muslim slavers seizing Europeans had additional motives of revenge (for the loss of Spain).

15 Vitkus, 2000, 3–4.
16 Ibid., 46n., quoting David D. Hebb.
17 Corsairs continued to seize English seamen and cargoes in the Mediterranean despite Elizabeth I's attempts to arrange trade-protecting treaties with Morocco; in support of an independent Portugal, she even made moves towards a military alliance with the Moroccans against Spain – for details see D'Amico, 1991, 7–40.
18 See the slave narratives collected in Vitkus, 2001, and the introduction to this collection, Matar, 2001.
19 Yet Davis, 2003, proposes that the methods of analysis that have been applied to Atlantic 'Black' slavery are equally illuminating with regard to Mediterranean 'White' slavery.
20 See Matar, 2001, 20–1, and Vitkus, 2001, passim.
21 Davis, 2003, 15. Ibid., 3–26, discusses the great difficulty of determining how many such slaves were taken, for many were ransomed.
22 Singh, 2004, 86, quoting Matar, 1999.
23 Iyengar, 2004, 101.
24 Slights, 1997, 383. But see Chapter 5, note 79.
25 See Heller, 1994, 56–8 on Bodin, 1606.
26 See under VILLEIN and COPY[hold] in Sokol and Sokol, 2004.
27 Yet Hunt, 1997, proposes ERR implies much Elizabethan servitude was slavish.
28 Gurr, 1996.
29 Sokol, 1994b.
30 See Seaver, 1995 on the actualities of apprentice indiscipline, and Burnett, 1997, Neill, 1998, and Anderson, 2005 on servants in Shakespeare.
31 See Bernthal, 1991 on this treason trial by combat.
32 So Baecker, 1999, 114, holds that generally for 'Shakespeare's Elizabethan audience . . . "slave" denoted a contemptible person and not necessarily a person owned by another'.
33 HAM 3.2.70, paralleling LUC 200 'fancy's slave!' Also: 'slave to [implicitly, erotic] slavery' (SON 133); 'false slave to false delight' (LUC, 927); 'a slave to' [implicitly, time and mortality] (SON 64); 'slave of nature' (R3 1.3.227); 'slave to patience' (ROM 5.3.220); 'slave to memory' (HAM 3.2.179); 'a slave to limit' (TRO 3.2.80); 'slaves of chance' (WT 4.4.540); and Mars is called an erotic 'slave' in VEN 101.
34 SON 57, SON 58, SON 141, SHR 1.1.217, ADO 3.2.151, TMP 3.1.66.
35 His mention of a 'pagan' may be a slur on Othello's religion, for although Othello is clearly a Christian, he is perhaps a *converso*. Vitkus, 2003, 77–106, argues at length for reading Othello's self-identification with a Turk as an image of a despised religious reconversion, a hated 'turn'.
36 Cummings, 1997, discusses the conception that 'thoughts are free' in the context of compulsions to confess used in association with English early modern heresy and treason trials, and trials for adultery, noting that the much-hated ex-officio oaths of the age would bind unwilling suspects to reveal their inner thoughts (despite Iago's claims for despised 'slaves').

37 Similar racism is rife in the play, with Lucius' brother-in-law Bassanius referring to Aaron's 'body's hue, / Spotted, detested, and abominable' (2.3.74), and (in the Folio text only) Titus himself responding to Marcus' description of a 'black ill-favoured fly, / Like to the Empress' Moor' (3.2.67) by describing a detestable 'coal black Moor' (3.2.77).

38 Braxton, 2000.

39 Eldred Jones, 1965, 53–4.

40 The heavy irony in this passage might possibly reflect Shylock's response to the Scholastic doctrine that 'all Jews collectively inherited servile status to Christians', discussed in Hsia, 1988, 114, or to the legal status of Jews as the king's property in England between the Conquest and their expulsion in 1290, on which see Holdsworth, 1903, 1:45–6, Pollock and Maitland, 1898, 1:468–75, and Routledge, 1982.

41 Thomas, 1983, 24–5 and 151.

42 Ibid., 137.

43 Spurgeon, 1935, 335; this finds the most animal imagery in OTH, but the bulk of animal images in MV vehemently negative.

44 Sokol, 1998, explicates some of these.

45 Epstein, 1977, 22a. The same passage is translated less fluently, but given closer scrutiny in the notes, in Fohrman, 1992, 22a.

46 Schorsch, 2004, 214.

47 On Bodin and his French contemporaries on slavery see Heller, 1994.

48 In Bodin, 1975, 225 and Bodin, 1606, 33–45.

49 Bodin, 1606, 43–5.

50 Anon., 1844, 6.

51 Similar confoundings of locations occur in the deliberate displacement in WT of the pastoral to Bohemia and away from the traditional Sicily, on which see Colie, 1974, 270–1, and the removal of Delphos in WT to an 'isle'; see Sokol, 1994a, 213n.

52 On the symbolic interplay of Africa and America in the play see the classic Fiedler, 1974, 167–200.

53 See Sokol and Sokol, 2004 under INDENTURE and PRENTICE.

54 Massed slave labour as in the Spanish New World was also used in parts of the ancient Roman world, while Elizabethan indentured servitude resembled to a degree the kinds of bond slavery implied by the biblical passages mentioned above in relation to MV, a status entered into for a fixed period of years, often to repay a debt.

55 Very few have doubted this. The very important revisionist article Skura, 1989, 44, finds 'E. E. Stoll and Northrop Frye are the only exceptions I have seen cited.' The same exceptions to the rule are also identified disapprovingly by Charles Frey in Frey, 1979. Yet Vaughan, 1988, holds that 'intentionalist' theories of Caliban's American identity '*should* be discarded . . . because . . . Shakespeare's contemporaries and their descendants for nearly three centuries did not associate *The Tempest*'s savage with American Indians'. Chapter 5 of Vaughan and Vaughan, 1991, attenuates this conclusion. The sophisticated Hantman, 1992, gives reasons against it.

56 Jamestown ties with Santa Fe New Mexico as the second-earliest European settlement within the United States, the earliest being St Augustine, Florida, which was founded by Spain in 1565.

57 These include Sokol, 1994c, 2003; Sokol and Sokol, 1996; here I will extend these in order to consider questions of tolerance.

58 Of course sea navigators were aware of the latitude of Virginia; English land explorers were too, as proved by the excavation of a complex portable instrument called a 'compass dial' by the Virginia rediscovery project. This may have been the very same ivory 'Dyall' that Captain John Smith twice wrote that he demonstrated to the 'king' of the Pamunkey Indians in December 1607, and by this means saved his own life. See Sokol, 2003, 26 and 133–5.

59 Aristotle, 1941, 1286, *Pol.* 7.7.19–38.

60 See Fink, 1941, 67–70.

61 Botero, 1611, 4–8, 13.

62 Ibid., 13.

63 Bodin, 1606, 550.

64 Botero, 1611, 12–13.

65 Bodin, 1606, 550.

66 See Floyd-Wilson, 2003, 5–11.

67 Ibid., 1; the popularity is described in detail ibid., 3ff.; see also Feerick, 2003, 34–40.

68 Ibid., 2.

69 See: ibid., 42; Bodin, 1606, 548, 550, 561; Botero, 1611, 8–10, 13.

70 William Harrison, quoted in Floyd-Wilson, 2003, 4.

71 Fink, 1941, 71–2 cites Thomas Wright and Nashe. Hoenselaars, 1992, 18–19, 105, 137, 180–1, 250n., 279–80n. treats dramatic reflections of climate theory in H5, JN, CYM, *The Alchemist, The White Devil*, and the anonymous play *Thomas Lord Cromwell* (1602). Hoenselaars, 1996, 14–16, adds TIT, ANT, and TN; Palmer, 2006 adds HAM.

72 Fink, 1941, 71–80, discusses eight allusions; Stroup, 1943 uncovers more.

73 Burton, 1972, 239.

74 Floyd-Wilson, 2003, 2.

75 Bodin, 1606, 550; see also Botero, 1611, 7, which adds that 'the land of the *Patagones*' has the same latitude as Germany, only south rather than north (this section is missing from earlier editions of Botero).

76 Anglerie, 1555, 219v and 220v contains the passages Shakespeare used for these and other details of *The Tempest*.

77 Hoenselaars, 1996, 14. Ibid., 14–16, refers to TIT, ANT, and TN in this regard, but claims Shakespeare was sceptical of climate theory. However, the examples given there from H5 and CYM seem to accord with Bodin's views.

78 Feerick, 2003, 66–70, describes attempts made to allay such fears. Similar fears, and some empirical (and some fanciful) bases for them, are discussed in Kupperman, 1984.

79 From a ms. *c.* 1607–12, in Strachey, 1953, 19.

80 These include Jourdan, 1610, Anon., 1844 (1610), and Purchas, 1625, 4:1734–58. See Kermode, 1962, xxvi–xxx, and Bullough, 1957–75, 8:295–9.

81 Although written accounts became available, earlier verbal ones were no doubt heard: Bullough, 1957–75, 8:240 warns that 'One must guard against ascribing to literary influences features [of *The Tempest*] which Shakespeare could well have got from talking with returned [Virginia] voyagers.' In their earlier years there the English were certainly not 'conquerors in Virginia' or 'Triumphant in America', as is suggested in Matar, 1999, 15. For an account of contemporary reactions to the often nearly catastrophic early history of Virginia see Knapp, 1992, especially 1–4, 204–19.

82 No earlier text survives from before the version published in Purchas, 1625, 4:1734–58, which was probably truncated and toned down. See ibid., 4:1751–2, 1756.

83 See Kermode, 1962, xxvii–xxx; Muir, 1972, 280; and Bullough, 1957–75, 8:239.

84 See especially J. Smith, 1986, 2:233–5, and Percy, 1922, 269–70.

85 P. L. Barbour, 1969, 1:68.

86 Anon., 1844, 15–16.

87 For instance Floyd, 1612, 322–3, gives a sarcastic account of dragooned and forcibly married English settlers; this is part of the Catholic side of a pamphlet war over Virginia discussed in Sokol and Sokol, 1996, 365–7, 378n. On the English response to this propaganda see Bond, 1997, 490–4.

88 Percy, 1922, 266–8 and 271–3. This manuscript, written in response to John Smith's version of events, is analysed in P. L. Barbour, 1971, 9–15.

89 This is discussed in Sokol, 2003, 173–81.

90 P. L. Barbour, 1969, 1:241–5.

91 This turmoil is described in Shirley, 1949, 227–8, P. L. Barbour, 1964, 109–20, and P. L. Barbour, 1969, 1:68, 125–9. Contemporary comments are found in Edward Maria Wingfield's manuscript 'Discourse of Virginia' in P. L. Barbour, 1969, 1:213–34, in Percy, 1946, 22, and in J. Smith, 1986, 2:188–90.

92 Strachey, 1953, 72–88, and much of Harriot, 1588, praise Algonkian material culture.

93 Purchas, 1625, 1753.

94 Strachey, 1953, 84.

95 Sanders, 1949, 129.

96 Harriot, 1588.

97 See Sokol, 1994c, and Sokol, 2003, Chapter 2.

98 The John White drawings, British Museum P&D 1906-5-9-1, and the Theodore de Bry engravings derived from them, are analysed and reproduced in Quinn and Hulton, 1964.

99 Thomas Harriot's captions to Plates XVI and XV in the unpaginated illustrative section of de Bry, 1590. The captions are discussed in Quinn, 1955, 1:430, 438.

100 de Bry, 1590 was an illustrated republication of Harriot, 1588; it was issued in four languages.

101 In fact Harriot mathematically investigated the social implications of food availability, calculating the agricultural potential of Virginia and the growth of human populations, respectively in his *Report* and in his unpublished mathematical papers, as described in Sokol, 2003, 48–76, and in greater mathematical detail in Sokol, 1974.

102 Harriot, 1955, 384–5. Harriot did not know that Virginia typically has colder winters than far more northerly England; according to Quinn, 1992, 4, the one winter he passed there (1585–6) was exceptionally warm. The effects of prevailing winds (and to a lesser extent the Gulf Stream) that render Europe's climate milder than eastern North America's, latitude for latitude, were not then understood, on which see Quinn, 1992, 14, and on the science see Seager, 2006. However, Botero, 1611, 3–4, does observe 'that those who lye to the West-wards in the same latitude, liue in a more colder temperature'.

103 Of course South American cannibals receive a favourable treatment in 'Of the Cannibals' in Montaigne, 1942, 1:215–29, which is virtually quoted (also critiqued) in TMP 2.1.149–74. But these cannibals are also cited as exemplifying the cruelty that derives from southern geohumoral influences (together with exceptional abilities in theology, mathematics, literature, astronomy) according to Botero, 1611, 9, 13.

104 Cornish and Clark, 1989, maintain, 291–2: 'There is considerable evidence that, in line with human relationships generally, in-servants and wage-labourers treated their employers argumentatively, aggressively, truculently.'

105 Thus Sokol, 2003 analyses a threat of Prospero becoming a black magician.

106 Brown, 1985, 68, reads Prospero's 'acknowledge mine' as a property claim 'when apportioning the plebeians to the masters'; this contradicts all of Shakespeare's other uses of 'acknowledge' which involve accepting kinship, responsibility, or guilt. See the epigraph to section 8 above, and Sokol, 2003, 188–94.

107 Straube and Mallios, 2000, 38.

108 Straube and Mallios, 2000, 30, describes features of the archaeological record eloquent of a deterioration of Algonkian–English economic relations at Jamestown from reciprocal, to unilateral, to non-existent.

109 It is possible Shakespeare heard of these from members of the London Virginia Company. He had many likely personal contacts within the Company, as indicated in Hotson, 1937, 219–26; Kermode, 1962, xxvii–xxviii; Hantman, 1992, 72–3; and the sources cited in Edwards, 1974, 250n.

110 Crashaw, 1610, 21–2 (the theme of conversion occupies 20–2). This prints a vehemently anti-Catholic 1609 sermon, which is ridiculed in Floyd, 1612, 319–25.

111 Virginia Council, 1906, 14.

112 Anon., 1610, 2–3, 6.

113 Sokol, 2003, 85–7, argues that Gonzalo distorts his borrowing into a sentimentalised parody.

114 Prosser, 1965, 261–4.

115 Montaigne, 1942, 2:108–24.
116 The 'Villaine' (TLN 2152) defender of Gloucester in LRF 3.7.71–8, Old Adam in AYL, even the despairing Steward in TIM, are cases in point.

7 AFTERWORD: TOLERANCE AS A SPECIES OF LOVE

1 Sokol, 2003, 163–98.
2 Aristotle, 1941, 994: *Nicomachean Ethics* 1125a 4–6. The Aristotelian Magnanimous Man, rendered in this translation as 'proud', is praised in all of Book 4 Chapter 3, 991–5.
3 See Shakespeare, 1995a, 67–9.
4 The following details come from Fraser, 1995, 130–4.

Bibliography

Achinstein, Sharon (2001). 'John Foxe and the Jews', *Renaissance Quarterly* 54: 86–120.

Alexander, Nigel (1968). 'Thomas Rymer and Othello', *Shakespeare Survey* 21: 67–77.

Anderson, Linda (2005). *A Place in the Story: Servants and Service in Shakespeare's Plays*. University of Delaware Press.

Andreas, James (2002). 'Shakespeare and the Invention of Humanism: Bloom on Race and Ethnicity', in *Harold Bloom's Shakespeare*. Ed. Christy Desmet and Robert Sawyer. 181–97. Palgrave.

Andrews, Michael Cameron (1983). 'The Stamp of One Defect', *Shakespeare Quarterly* 34: 217–18.

Anglerie, Peter Martyr (1555). *The Decades of the Newe World of East India*. Trans. Richard Eden.

Anon. (1594). *A Pleasant Conceited Historie, called The Taming of a Shrew.*

(1610). *A True and Sincere Declaration of the Purpose and Ends of the Plantation Begun in Virginia.*

(1632). *The Lawes Resolutions of Womens Rights: or, the Lawes Provision for Women.*

(1811). *The Statutes at Large of England.* 20 vols.

(1844). 'A True Declaration of the Estate of the Colony of Virginia', in *Tracts and Other Papers, 3*. Ed. Peter Force. Reprint of London, 1610. 1–27. Wm. Q. Force.

(1968). 'An Homilie of the State of Matrimonie', in *Certaine Sermons or Homilies*. Facsimile of 1623 edition. Ed. Mary Ellen Rickey and Thomas B. Stroup. 239–48. Scholars' Facsimiles and Reprints.

Aristotle (1941). *The Basic Works*. Ed. Richard McKeon. Random House.

Atkinson, David (1986). 'Marriage under Compulsion in English Renaissance Drama', *English Studies* 67: 483–504.

Babb, Lawrence (1944). 'Hamlet, Melancholy and the Devil', *Modern Language Notes* 59: 120–2.

(1951). *The Elizabethan Malady: A Study of Melancholia in English Literature from 1580 to 1642*. Michigan State College Press.

Bacon, Francis (1862–74). *Works*. Ed. James Spedding, Robert Leslie Ellis, and Douglas Denon Heath. 16 vols. Longmans.

Baecker, Diann L. (1999). 'Tracing the History of a Metaphor: All Is Not Black and White in Othello', *Comitatus* 30: 113–29.

Baker, J. H. (1986). 'The Law Merchant and the Common Law before 1700', in *The Legal Profession and the Common Law.* 341–69. Hambleton.

(1990). *An Introduction to English Legal History.* Third edition. Butterworths.

Baker, Oliver (1937). *In Shakespeare's Warwickshire and the Unknown Years.* Simpkin Marshall.

Barbour, Philip L. (1964). *The Three Worlds of Captain John Smith.* Houghton Mifflin and Company.

(ed.) (1969). *The Jamestown Voyages under the First Charter 1606–1609.* 2 vols. Cambridge University Press, for the Hakluyt Society.

(1971). 'The Honorable George Percy, Premier Chronicler of the First Virginia Voyage', *Early American Literature* 6: 7–17.

Barbour, Richmond (2003). *Before Orientalism: London's Theatre of the East, 1576–1626.* Cambridge University Press.

Barker, Francis, and Peter Hulme (1985). '"Nymphs and reapers heavily vanish": The Discursive Contexts of *The Tempest*', in *Alternative Shakespeares.* Ed. John Drakakis. 191–205. Methuen.

Bartels, Emily C. (1990). 'Making More of the Moor: Aaron, Othello, and Renaissance Refashionings of Race', *Shakespeare Quarterly* 41: 433–54.

(1997). 'Othello and Africa: Postcolonialism Reconsidered', *William and Mary Quarterly* 54: 45–64.

(2006a). 'Othello and the Moor', in *Early Modern English Drama: A Critical Companion.* Ed. Garrett A. Sullivan Jr, Andrew Hadfield, and Patrick Cheney. 140–51. Oxford University Press.

(2006b). 'Too Many Blackamoors: Deportation, Discrimination, and Elizabeth I', *SEL: Studies in English Literature, 1500–1900* 94: 305–22.

Barthelemy, Anthony G. (1987). *Black Face, Maligned Race: The Representation of Blacks in English Drama from Shakespeare to Southerne.* Louisiana State University Press.

Bartlett, John (1965). *Concordance to Shakespeare.* Macmillan.

Barton, Anne (1994). *Essays, Mainly Shakespearean.* Cambridge University Press.

Bassi, Shaul (2003). 'Country Dispositions: Ethnic Fallacies in Shakespeare Criticism', in *Shakespearean International Yearbook 3.* Ed. Graham Bradshaw. 59–76. Ashgate.

Basu, Sammy (1999a). 'Dialogic Ethics and the Virtue of Humour', *The Journal of Political Philosophy* 7: 378–403.

(1999b). '"Woe unto you that laugh now!": Humour and Toleration in Overton and Shaftsbury', in *Religious Toleration: 'The Variety of Rites' from Cyrus to Defoe.* Ed. John Christian Laursen. 147–72. Palgrave Macmillan.

Bate, Jonathan (ed.) (1995). *Titus Andronicus.* Third Arden Shakespeare edition. Routledge.

Bean, J. M. W. (1968). *The Decline of English Feudalism.* Manchester University Press.

Bearman, Robert (2003). 'John Shakespeare's "Spiritual Testament": A Reappraisal', *Shakespeare Survey* 56: 184–202.

(2005). 'John Shakespeare: A Papist or Just Penniless?', *Shakespeare Quarterly* 56: 409–33.

Beauregard, David N. (1999). ' "Inspired merit": Shakespeare's Theology of Grace in *All's Well That Ends Well*', *Renascence* 51: 219–39.

Beauregard, David N., and Dennis Taylor (eds.) (2003). *Shakespeare and the Culture of Christianity in Early Modern England*. Fordham University Press.

Bellamy, John (1979). *The Tudor Law of Treason*. Routledge & Kegan Paul.

Benedict, Philip (1996). '*Un Roi, Une Loi, Deux Fois*', in *Tolerance and Intolerance in the European Reformation*. Ed. Ole Peter Grell and Peter Scribner. 65–93. Cambridge University Press.

Benton, Gregor (1988). 'The Origins of the Political Joke', in *Humour in Society*. Ed. Chris Powell and George E. C. Paton. 33–55. St Martin's Press.

Benzoni, Girolamo (1579). *Histoire Nouvelle du Nouveau Monde: Extracted from the Italian and Enriched with Many Discourses by Urbain Chauveton*.

(1862). *History of the New World by Girolamo Benzoni of Milan, Shewing His Travels in America from A.D. 1541 to 1556*. Trans. from Italian by W. H. Smyth from the 1572 edition. Hakluyt Society.

Bergson, Henri (1911). *Laughter: An Essay on the Meaning of the Comic*. Trans. Cloudsley Brereton and Fred Rothwell. Macmillan & Co.

Berman, Harold J. (1994). 'The Origins of Historical Jurisprudence: Coke, Selden, Hale', *Yale Law Review* 103: 1651–738.

Bernthal, Craig A. (1991). 'Treason in the Family: The Trial of Thumpe v. Horner', *Shakespeare Quarterly* 42: 44–54.

Berry, Edward (1990). 'Othello's Alienation', *SEL: Studies in English Literature, 1500–1900* 30: 315–33.

Berry, Phillipa (2004). 'Hamlet's Ear', in *Shakespeare and Language*. Ed. Catherine M. S. Alexander. 201–12. Cambridge University Press.

Biberman, Matthew (2004). *Masculinity, Anti-Semitism, and Early Modern English Literature: From the Satanic to the Effeminate Jew*. Ashgate.

Biswas, D. C. (1996). 'Shakespeare and Racialism', in *Shakespeare: Varied Perspectives*. Ed. Vikram Chopra. 3–9. B. R. Publishing.

Black, Joseph (2001). ' "Pan is Hee": Commending *The Faerie Queene*', *Spenser Studies* 15: 121–34.

Blake, Norman Francis (1981). *Non-Standard Language in English Literature*. Deutsch.

Blank, Paula (1996). *Broken English: Dialects and the Politics of Language in Renaissance Writings*. Routledge.

Bluestein, Gene (1981). 'It Only Hurts When We Laugh: Ethnic Jokes and the International Theme', *Thalia: Studies in Literary Humor* 4: 10–13.

Boccaccio, Giovanni (1964). *Concerning Famous Women*. Trans. from the Berne 1539 edition by Guido A. Guarino. George Allen and Unwin.

Bodin, Jean (1606). *The Six Books of a Common-weale*. Trans. Richard Knolles.

(1970). *Colloquium Heptaplomeres de Rerum Sublimium Arcanis*. E-text of reissue of (ed.) Ludovicus Noack, Schwerin, 1857: www.gutenberg.org/etext/17859. Georg Olms Verlag.

(1975). *Colloquium of the Seven about Secrets of the Sublime*. Ed. Marion Leathers Daniels Kuntz. Princeton University Press.

(1984). *Colloque Entre Sept Scavans*. Commentary by Francois Berriot. Libraire Droz.

Boehrer, Bruce Thomas (1994). 'Bestial Buggery in *A Midsummer Night's Dream*', in *The Production of English Renaissance Culture*. Ed. David Lee Miller, Sharon O'Dair, and Harold Weber. 123–50. Cornell University Press.

Bond, Edward L. (1997). 'England's Soteriology of Empire and the Roots of Colonial Identity in Early Virginia', *Anglican and Episcopal History* 46: 471–99.

Boone, Joseph Allen (1987). *Tradition Counter Tradition: Love and the Form of Fiction*. University of Chicago Press.

Booty, John E. (ed.) (1976). *The Book of Common Prayer 1559*. Folger Shakespeare Library.

Boskin, Joseph, and Joseph Dorinson (1985). 'Ethnic Humor: Subversion and Survival', *American Quarterly* 37: 81–97.

Botero, Giovanni (1611). *Relations, of the Most Famous Kingdoms and Commonweales Thorough the World*.

Bowers, Roger (2000). 'The Chapel Royal, the First Edwardian Prayer Book, and Elizabeth's Settlement of Religion, 1559', *The Historical Journal* 43: 317–44.

Bradshaw, Graham (1992). 'Obeying the Time in *Othello*: A Myth and the Mess It Made', *English Studies* 73: 211–28.

Braude, Benjamin (1997). 'The Sons of Noah and the Construction of Ethnic and Geographical Identities in the Medieval and Early Modern Periods', *William and Mary Quarterly* 54: 103–42.

Braxton, Phyllis N. (2000). 'The Hue and Crime of Shakespeare's Aaron', *CLA Journal* 43: 207–28.

Bredvold, Louis I. (1924). 'Milton and Bodin's *Heptaplomeres*', *Studies in Philology* 21: 399–402.

Breight, Curtis C. (1996). *Surveillance, Militarism, and Drama in the Elizabethan Era*. Macmillan.

Brennan, Gillian E. (1994). 'The Cheese and the Welsh: Foreigners in Elizabethan Literature', *Renaissance Studies* 8: 40–64.

Briggs, E. R. (1978). 'Reflections upon the First Century of the Huguenot Churches in England', *Proceedings of the Huguenot Society* 23: 99–119.

Brinkworth, E. R. C. (1972). *Shakespeare and the Bawdy Court of Stratford*. Phillimore.

Brooks, Cleanth (1963). 'The Naked Babe and the Cloak of Manliness', in *Shakespeare Criticism, 1935–1960*. Ed. Anne Ridler. 228–54. Oxford University Press.

Brown, Paul R. (1985). ' "This thing of darkness I acknowledge mine": *The Tempest* and the Discourse of Colonialism', in *Political Shakespeare*. Ed. J. Dollimore and A. Sinfield. 48–71. Manchester University Press.

Bullough, Geoffrey (ed.) (1957–75). *Narrative and Dramatic Sources of Shakespeare*. 8 vols. Routledge & Kegan Paul.

Burn, John Southerden (1846). *The History of the French, Walloon, Dutch, and Other Foreign Protestant Refugees Settled in England.* Longman, Brown, Green, and Longmans.

Burnett, Mark Thornton (1997). *Masters and Servants in English Renaissance Drama and Culture.* Macmillan.

Burton, Robert (1972). *The Anatomy of Melancholy.* Ed. Holbrook Jackson. J. M Dent & Sons Ltd.

Busher, Leonard (1614). *Religions Peace or A Reconciliation, Between Princes & Peoples, and Nations.*

(1846). 'Religions Peace or A Plea for Liberty of Conscience', in *Tracts on Liberty of Conscience.* Ed. Edward Bean Underhill. Transcript of 1646 edition, which reprints 1614. 3–81. The Hanserd Knollys Society.

Castiglione, Baldasarre (1975). *The Book of the Courtier.* Trans. Sir Thomas Hoby, 1561. J. M. Dent.

Chapman, Antony J., and Hugh C. Foot (eds.) (1977). *It's a Funny Thing, Humour.* Permagon Press.

Cheadle, Brian (1994). 'The "Process" of Prejudice: *Othello* I.iii.128–45', *Notes and Queries* 41: 491–3.

Chedgzoy, Kate (1998). 'Blackness Yields to Beauty: Desirability and Difference in Early Modern Culture', in *Renaissance Configurations: Voices, Bodies, Spaces 1580–1690.* Ed. Gordon McMullan. 108–28. Palgrave Macmillan.

Christen, Oliver (2004). 'Making Peace', in *A Companion to the Reformation World.* Ed. R. Po-chia Hsia. 426–39. Blackwell Publishing.

Cioni, Maria L. (1982). 'The Elizabethan Chancery and Women', in *Tudor Rule and Revolution: Essays for G. R. Elton.* Ed. John W. McKenna and DeLloyd J. Guth. 159–82. Cambridge University Press.

(1985). *Women and Law in Elizabethan England with Particular Reference to the Court of Chancery.* Garland Publishing.

Clare, Janet (1999). *'Art made tongue-tied by authority': Elizabethan and Jacobean Dramatic Censorship.* Manchester University Press.

Clegg, Cyndia Susan (1999). 'Liberty, License, and Authority: Press Censorship and Shakespeare', in *A Companion to Shakespeare.* Ed. David Scott Kastan. 464–85. Blackwell Publishers.

Coffey, John (2000). *Persecution and Toleration in Protestant England 1558–1689.* Longman.

Cohen, Eileen Z. (1976). 'Mirror of Virtue: The Role of Cassio in Othello', *English Studies* 57: 115–27.

Cohen, Ted (2001). *Jokes: Philosophical Thoughts on Joking Matters.* University of Chicago Press.

Cohen, Walter (1982). *'The Merchant of Venice* and the Possibilities of Historical Criticism', *ELH* 49: 765–89.

Coke, Edward (1644). *Third Part of the Institutes of the Laws of England.*

Colie, Rosalie L. (1974). *Shakespeare's Living Art.* Princeton University Press.

Collinson, Patrick (1967). *The Elizabethan Puritan Movement.* Jonathan Cape.

(1994). *Elizabethan Essays.* Hambledon Press.

Cornish, Paul J. (1996). 'Spanish Thomism and the American Indians: Vitoria and las Casas on the Toleration of Cultural Difference', in *Difference and Dissent: Theories of Tolerance in Medieval and Early Modern Europe*. Ed. John Christian Laursen and Cary J. Nederman. 99–117. Rowman and Littlefield.

Cornish, W. R., and G. de N. Clark (1989). *Law and Society in England, 1750–1950*. Sweet and Maxwell.

Coryate, Thomas (1611). *Thomas Coryat's Crudities*.

Cowhig, Ruth (1985). 'Blacks in English Renaissance Drama and the Role of Shakespeare's Othello', in *The Black Presence in English Literature*. Ed. David Dabydeen. 1–25. Manchester University Press.

Craig, Martha (1969). 'The Secret Wit of Spenser's Language', in *Edmund Spenser: A Critical Anthology*. Ed. Paul J. Alper. 322–39. Penguin.

Crashaw, William (1610). *A Sermon Preached in London before the Lord Lewarre, Lord Gouernor and Captaine Generall of Virginia Febr 21 1609*.

Crewe, Jonathan (1995). 'Out of the Matrix: Shakespeare and Race-Writing', *Yale Journal of Criticism* 2: 13–29.

Croft, Pauline (1983). 'Wardship in the Parliament of 1604', *Parliamentary History* 2: 39–48.

Cummings, Brian (1997). 'Swearing in Public: More and Shakespeare', *English Literary Renaissance* 27: 197–232.

Dalrymple, William (2003). *White Mughals: Love and Betrayal in Eighteenth-Century India*. Flamingo.

D'Amico, Jack (1991). *The Moor in English Renaissance Drama*. University of South Florida Press.

Daniell, David (1984). 'The Good Marriage of Katherine and Petruchio', *Shakespeare Survey* 37: 23–31.

(2001). 'Shakespeare and the Protestant Mind', *Shakespeare Survey* 54: 1–12.

Dash, Irene G. (1981). *Wooing, Wedding, and Power: Women in Shakespeare's Plays*. Columbia University Press.

Davies, Christie (1988). 'Stupidity and Rationality: Jokes from the Iron Cage', in *Humour in Society*. Ed. Chris Powell and George E. C. Paton. 1–32. St Martin's Press.

(2002). *The Mirth of Nations*. Transaction.

Davies, Michael (2005). 'Falstaff's Lateness: Calvinism and the Protestant Hero in *Henry V*', *Review of English Studies* 56: 351–78.

Davis, Robert C. (2003). *Christian Slaves, Muslim Masters*. Palgrave Macmillan.

de Bry, Theodore (ed.) (1590). *America, Part I*. English version of multilingual edition of Thomas Harriot, *A Briefe and True Report*.

De Somogyi, Nick (1998). *Shakespeare's Theatre of War*. Ashgate.

D'Ewes, Sir Simon (1973). *The Journals of All the Parliaments during the Reign of Queen Elizabeth*. Facsimile of London, 1682. Irish University Press.

Dimmock, Matthew (2005). *New Turkes: Dramatizing Islam and the Ottomans in Early Modern England*. Ashgate.

Donne, John (1960). *Poems*. Ed. Sir Herbert Grierson. Oxford University Press.

Downs-Gamble, Margaret (1993). 'The Taming-School: The Taming of the Shrew as Lesson in Renaissance Humanism', in *Privileging Gender in Early Modern England.* Ed. Jean R. Brink. 65–78. Sixteenth Century Journal Publishers.

Dreher, Diane Elizabeth (1986). *Domination and Defiance: Fathers and Daughters in Shakespeare.* University Press of Kentucky.

Dummett, Ann, and Andrew Nicol (1990). *Subjects, Citizens, Aliens and Others: Nationality and Immigration Law.* Weidenfeld and Nicolson.

Dusinberre, Juliet (1975). *Shakespeare and the Nature of Women.* Macmillan.

Eastman, Max (1937). *Enjoyment of Laughter.* Hamish Hamilton.

Edelman, Charles (ed.) (2005). *The Stukeley Plays: The Battle of Alcazar by George Peele, The Famous History of the Life and Death of Captain Thomas Stukeley.* Manchester University Press.

Edwards, Philip (1974). *Threshold of a Nation: A Study in English and Irish Drama.* Cambridge University Press.

Eliot, T. S. (1934). *Elizabethan Essays.* Faber & Faber.

Ellis, David (2005). 'Falstaff and the Problems of Comedy', *Cambridge Quarterly* 34: 95–108.

Epstein, I. (ed.) (1977). *The Babylonian Talmud: Tractate Kiddusin.* Soncino Press.

Erne, Lukas (2001). 'Donne and Christ's Spouse', *Essays in Criticism* 51: 208–29.

Everett, Barbara (1987). ' "Spanish" Othello: The Making of Shakespeare's Moor', *Shakespeare Survey* 35: 101–12.

Feerick, Jean (2003). 'A "Nation ... now degenerate": Shakespeare's Cymbeline, Nova Britannia, and the Role of Diet and Climate in Reproducing Races', *Early American Studies* 1: 30–71.

Ferreira-Ross, Jeanette (1992). 'The Puritan Hypocrite in Shakespeare and Jonson', *Unisa English Studies* 30: 1–13.

Fiedler, Leslie A. (1974). *The Stranger in Shakespeare.* Paladin.

Fink, G. S. (1941). 'Milton and the Theory of Climatic Influence', *Modern Language Quarterly* 2: 67–80.

Finlay, Roger (1981). *Population and Metropolis: The Demography of London.* Cambridge University Press.

Fisch, Harold (1974). 'Shakespeare and the Puritan Dynamic', *Shakespeare Survey* 27: 81–92.

Fletcher, Angus (2002). 'Marvelous Progression: The Paradoxical Defense of Women in Spenser's Mutabilitie Cantos', *Modern Philology* 100: 5–23.

Floyd, John (1612). *The Overthrow of the Protestant Pulpit-Babels. Particularly Confuting W. Crashaws Sermon at the Crosse.*

Floyd-Wilson, Mary (2002). 'Delving to the Root: *Cymbeline,* Scotland, and the English Race', in *British Identities and English Renaissance Literature.* Ed. David J. Baker and Willy Maley. 101–15. Cambridge University Press.

(2003). *English Ethnicity and Race in Early Modern Drama.* Cambridge University Press.

Foakes, R. A. (1989). *Coleridge's Criticism of Shakespeare.* Athlone Press.

(2005). ' "Armed at point exactly": The Ghost in Hamlet', *Shakespeare Survey* 58: 34–47.

Fohrman, David (ed.) (1992). *Talmud Bavli: Tractate Kiddushin*. Mesorah Publications Ltd.

Folarin, Shyllon (19//). *Black People in Britain, 1555–1833*. Oxford University Press.

Fowler, Alastair (1960). 'Emblems of Temperance in *The Faerie Queene* Book II', *Review of English Studies* 11: 143–9.

Fraser, Agnus M. (1995). *The Gypsies*. Blackwell Publishing.

Fraunce, Abraham (1588). *The Arcadian Rhetorike*.

Frazier, Harriet C. (1985). ' "Like a Liar Gone to Burning Hell": Shakespeare and Dying Declarations', *Comparative Drama* 19: 166–80.

Freeman, Jane (2002). ' "Fair terms and a villain's mind": Rhetorical Patterns in *The Merchant of Venice*', *Rhetorica* 20: 149–72.

Frey, Charles (1979). '*The Tempest* and the New World', *Shakespeare Quarterly* 30: 29–41.

Furness, H. H. (ed.) (1899). *Much Ado About Nothing*. New Variorum Shakespeare. J. B. Lipincott Co.

Gaikwad, V. R. (1967). *The Anglo-Indians*. Asia Publishing House.

Galeotti, Anna Elisabetta (2002). *Toleration as Recognition*. Cambridge University Press.

Gardner, Helen (1963). 'The Noble Moor', in *Shakespeare Criticism 1935–1960*. Ed. Anne Ridler. 348–70. Oxford University Press.

Gascoigne, George (1907). *The Complete Works*. Ed. John W. Cunliffe. 2 vols. Cambridge University Press.

Gillies, John (1994). *Shakespeare and the Geography of Difference*. Cambridge University Press.

Girard, Rene (1991a). *A Theatre of Envy*. Oxford University Press.

(1991b). ' "To Entrap the Wisest" ', in *Shylock*. Ed. Harold Bloom. 291–304. Chelsea House.

Gleckman, Jason (2001). 'The Merchant of Venice: Laws Written and Unwritten in Venice', *Critical Review (Melbourne)* 41: 81–94.

Goose, Nigel (2005a). 'Immigrants in Tudor and Early Stuart England', in *Immigrants in Tudor and Early Stuart England*. Ed. Nigel Goose and Lien Luu. 1–38. Sussex Academic Press.

(2005b). ' "Xenophobia" in Elizabethan and Early Stuart England: An Epithet Too Far?', in *Immigrants in Tudor and Early Stuart England*. Ed. Nigel Goose and Lien Luu. 110–35. Sussex Academic Press.

Goose, Nigel, and Lien Luu (eds.) (2005). *Immigrants in Tudor and Early Stuart England*. Sussex Academic Press.

Greenblatt, Stephen (1976). 'Learning to Curse: Aspects of Linguistic Colonialism in the Sixteenth Century', in *First Images of America: The Impact of the Old World on the New*. Ed. Fred Chiappelli. 2 vols. 2:561–80. University of California Press.

(2001). *Hamlet in Purgatory*. Princeton University Press.

Grell, Ole Peter (1996a). *Calvinist Exiles in Tudor and Stuart London.* Scolar Press.

(1996b). 'Exile and Tolerance', in *Tolerance and Intolerance in the European Reformation.* Ed. Ole Peter Grell and Peter Scribner. 164–81. Cambridge University Press.

Grell, Ole Peter, and Peter Scribner (eds.) (1996). *Tolerance and Intolerance in the European Reformation.* Cambridge University Press.

Gross, C. (1908). *Select Cases Concerning the Law Merchant, 1270–1638.* Vol. 23. The Selden Society.

Gurr, Andrew (1996). 'Industrious Ariel and Idle Caliban', in *Travel and Drama in Shakespeare's Time.* Ed. Jean-Pierre Maquerlot and Michèle Willems. 193–208. Cambridge University Press.

Gwynn, Robin D. (1985). *Huguenot Heritage.* Routledge & Kegan Paul.

(1995). 'Marital Problems and the Position of Women in the French Church of London in the Later 17th Century', *Proceedings of the Huguenot Society* 26: 214–29.

Habib, Imtiaz (2000). *Shakespeare and Race: Postcolonial Praxis in the Early Modern Period.* University Press of America.

Hadfield, Andrew (1994). *Literature, Politics and National Identity: Reformation to Renaissance.* Cambridge University Press.

(1998). 'Race in *Othello*: The *History and Description of Africa* and the Black Legend', *Notes and Queries* 45: 336–8.

(2004). '*Hamlet's* Country Matters: The "Scottish Play" Within the Play', in *Shakespeare and Scotland.* Ed. Willy Maley and Andrew Murphy. 87–103. Manchester University Press.

Hagstrum, Jean H. (1992). *Esteem Enlivened by Desire.* University of Chicago Press.

Hall, Kim F. (1996). *Things of Darkness: Economies of Race and Gender in Early Modern England.* Cornell University Press.

Hamer, Douglas (1970). 'Was William Shakespeare William Shakeshafte?', *Review of English Studies* 21: 41–8.

Hamilton, Donna B. (1992). *Shakespeare and the Politics of Protestant England.* University of Kentucky Press.

Hantman, Jeffrey L. (1992). 'Caliban's Own Voice: American Indian Views of the Other in Colonial Virginia', *New Literary History* 23: 69–81.

Harding, D. W. (1969). 'Women's Fantasy of Manhood', *Shakespeare Quarterly* 20: 245–53.

Harries, Frederick J. (1991). *Shakespeare and the Welsh.* Facsimile of 1919 edition. Llanerch Publishers.

Harriot, Thomas (1588). *A Briefe and True Report of the New Found Land of Virginia.*

(1955). 'A Briefe and True Report of the New Found Land of Virginia, 1588', in *The Roanoke Voyages.* Ed. David Beers Quinn. 2 vols. 1:317–87. The Hakluyt Society.

Hartley, T. E. (ed.) (1981–95). *Proceedings in the Parliaments of Elizabeth I.* 3 vols. Leicester University Press.

Hassel, R. Chris (2003). 'The Accent and Gait of Christians: Hamlet's Puritan Style', in *Shakespeare and the Culture of Christianity in Early Modern England*. Ed. Dennis Taylor and David N. Beauregard. 287–310. Fordham University Press.

Hazlitt, W. Carew (ed.) (1887). *A Hundred Merry Tales: The Earliest English Jest-Book*. Facsimile of 1526. J. W. Jarvis & Son.

Heller, Henry (1994). 'Bodin on Slavery and Primitive Accumulation', *The Sixteenth Century Journal* 25: 53–65.

Hendricks, Margo (1996). ' "Obscured by dreams": Race, Empire, and Shakespeare's *A Midsummer Night's Dream*', *Shakespeare Quarterly* 47: 37–60.

(2000). 'Surveying "Race" in Shakespeare', in *Shakespeare and Race*. Ed. Catherine M. S. Alexander and Stanley Wells. 1–22. Cambridge University Press.

Highley, Christopher (2004). 'The Place of Scots in the Scottish Play: Macbeth and the Politics of Language', in *Shakespeare and Scotland*. Ed. Willy Maley and Andrew Murphy. 53–66. Manchester University Press.

Hinshelwood, R. D. (2007). 'Intolerance and the Intolerable: The Case of Racism', *Psychoanalysis, Culture & Society* 12: 1–20.

Hodgen, Margaret T. (1964). *Early Anthropology in the Sixteenth and Seventeenth Centuries*. University of Pennsylvania Press.

Hoenselaars, A. J. (1991). 'Broken Images of Englishmen and Foreigners in English Renaissance Drama', *Germanisch-Romanische Monatsschrift* 41: 157–73.

(1992). *Images of Englishmen and Foreigners in the Drama of Shakespeare and His Contemporaries*. Fairleigh Dickinson University Press.

(1993). 'Italy Staged in English Renaissance Drama', in *Shakespeare's Italy: Functions of Italian Locations in Renaissance Drama*. Ed. Michele Marrapodi, A. J. Hoenselaars, Marcello Cappuzzo, and Lino Falzon Santucci. 30–48. Manchester University Press.

(1994). 'World Citizens in *Henry V* and *The Merry Wives of Windsor*', in *Shakespeare: Cosmopolitisme et Insularité*. Ed. Marie-Thérèse Jones-Davies. 115–28. Belles Lettres.

(1995). 'The Elizabethans and the Turk at Constantinople', *Cahiers Élisabéthains* 47: 29–42.

(1996). 'Shakespeare, Foreigners, and National Ideologies', in *Shakespeare: Varied Perspectives*. Ed. Vikram Chopra. 11–33. B. R. Publishing.

(1998). 'The Other in the Mirror: Prejudice and Stereotypes on the English Renaissance Stage', *Cahiers Charles V* 24: 85–101.

Holderness, Graham, and Brian Loughrey (eds.) (1992). *The Taming of a Shrew*. Barnes & Noble Books.

Holdsworth, Sir William (1903–72). *A History of English Law*. 17 vols. Methuen.

Holt, Jim (2004). 'Punch Line: The History of Jokes and Those Who Collect Them', *The New Yorker* April 19 & 26: 184–90.

Honigmann, E. A. J. (1982). *Shakespeare's Impact on His Contemporaries*. Macmillan.

(1985a). 'Shakespeare and London's Immigrant Community circa 1600', in *Elizabethan and Modern Studies*. Ed. J. P. Vander Motten. 143–53. Seminarie voor Engelse en Amerikaanse Literatuur.

(1985b). *Shakespeare: The 'Lost Years'*. Manchester University Press.

Hope, Jonathan (2004). 'Introduction', in *Shakespeare and Language*. Ed. Catherine M. S. Alexander. 1–17. Cambridge University Press.

Hopkins, Lisa (2003). 'Is Paris Worth a Mass? *All's Well that Ends Well* and the Wars of Religion', in *Shakespeare and the Culture of Christianity in Early Modern England*. Ed. Dennis Taylor and David N. Beauregard. 369–81. Fordham University Press.

Hotson, Leslie (1937). *I, William Shakespeare*. Jonathan Cape.

Houghton, Walter E., Jr. (1942). 'The English Virtuoso in the Seventeenth Century', *The Journal of the History of Ideas* 3: 51–73 and 190–219.

Howell, W. S. (1956). *Logic and Rhetoric in England, 1500–1700*. Princeton University Press.

Hsia, R. Po-chia (1988). *The Myth of Ritual Murder*. Yale University Press.

Hunt, Maurice (1988). 'Compelling Art in Titus Andronicus', *SEL: Studies in English Literature, 1500–1900* 28: 197–218.

(1997). 'Slavery, English Servitude and *The Comedy of Errors*', *English Literary Renaissance* 27: 29–56.

(2004a). *Shakespeare's Religious Allusiveness: Its Play and Tolerance*. Ashgate.

(2004b). 'Taking the Eucharist Both Ways in *Hamlet*', *Cithara* 43: 35–47.

Hunter, G. K. (ed.) (1959). *All's Well that Ends Well*. Second Arden Shakespeare edition. Methuen and Co.

(1964). 'Elizabethans and Foreigners', *Shakespeare Survey* 17: 37–52.

(1978a). 'Elizabethans and Foreigners', in *Dramatic Identities and Cultural Tradition: Studies in Shakespeare and His Contemporaries*. 1–30. Liverpool University Press.

(1978b). 'Othello and Colour Prejudice', in *Dramatic Identities and Cultural Tradition: Studies in Shakespeare and His Contemporaries*. Ed. G. K. Hunter. 31–59. Liverpool University Press.

Hurstfield, Joel (1958). *The Queen's Wards: Wardship and Marriage under Elizabeth I*. Longmans Green and Co.

Iyengar, Sujata (2004). 'The Tolerance and Persecution of Africans in Early Modern England and Scotland', in *Voices for Tolerance in an Age of Persecution*. Ed. Vincent P. Carey. 95–106. Folger Shakespeare Library.

(2005). *Shades of Difference: Mythologies of Skin Color in Early Modern England*. University of Pennsylvania Press.

Japtok, Martin, and Winfried Schleiner (1999). 'Genetics and "Race" in *The Merchant of Venice*', *Literature and Medicine* 18: 155–72.

Jenkins, Harold (ed.) (1982). *Hamlet*. Second Arden Shakespeare edition. Methuen.

Jones, Eldred (1965). *Othello's Countrymen: The African in English Renaissance Drama*. Oxford University Press.

(1971). *The Elizabethan Image of Africa*. The University Press of Virginia.

Jones, Emrys (1981). 'The Welsh in London in the Seventeenth and Eighteenth Centuries', *Welsh History Review* 10: 461–79.

Jonson, Ben (1975). *Poems*. Ed. Ian Donaldson. Oxford University Press.

(1979). *Bartholomew Fair*. Ed. E. A. Horsman. Manchester University Press.

Jordan, Wilbur K. (1932–40). *The Development of Religious Toleration in England.* 4 vols. Harvard University Press.

Jordan, Winthrop D. (1975). *White over Black: American Attitudes toward the Negro, 1550–1812*. Reprint of 1968. W. W. Norton and Company.

Joubert, Laurent (1980). *Treatise on Laughter (Paris, 1579)*. Trans. Gregory David de Rocher. University of Alabama Press.

Jourdan, Silvester (1610). *A Discovery of the Barmudas.*

Kahn, Coppélia (1975). '*The Taming of the Shrew*: Shakespeare's Mirror of Marriage', *Modern Language Studies* 5: 88–102.

Kaplan, Benjamin J. (2004). 'Conscience, Conflict and the Practice of Toleration', in *A Companion to the Reformation World*. Ed. R. Po-chia Hsia. 486–505. Blackwell Publishing.

Kaplan, Sidney (1949). 'The Miscegenation Issue in the Election of 1864', *Journal of Negro History* 34: 274–343.

Kent, Joan (1973). 'Attitudes of Members of the House of Commons to Regulation of Personal Conduct', *Bulletin of the Institute of Historical Research* 46: 41–71.

Kermode, Frank (ed.) (1962). *The Tempest*. Second Arden Shakespeare edition. First published 1954. Methuen & Co.

Kerr, Heather (1992). 'Aaron's Letter and Acts of Reading: The Text as Evidence in *Titus Andronicus*', *AUMLA: Journal of the Australasian Universities Language and Literature Association* 77: 1–19.

Kirsch, Arthur (1981). *Shakespeare and the Experience of Love*. Cambridge University Press.

Klibansky, Raymond, Erwin Panofsky, and Fritz Saxl (1964). *Saturn and Melancholy*. Thomas Nelson.

Kliman, Bernice (ed.) (1996). *The Enfolded Hamlet*. www.leoyan.com/global-language.com/ENFOLDED.

Knapp, Jeffrey (1992). *An Empire Nowhere: England, America and Literature from Utopia to 'The Tempest'*. University of California Press.

Kniezsa, Veronika (1991). ' "Scotica Pronunciatione": Sixteenth- and Seventeenth-Century English Authors on Scots', *Scottish Language* 10: 1–8.

Knight, G. Wilson (1960). *The Wheel of Fire*. Methuen.

Kornstein, Daniel J. (1993). 'Fie Upon Your Law!', *Cardozo Studies in Law and Literature* 5: 35–56.

(1994). *Kill All the Lawyers: Shakespeare's Legal Appeal*. Princeton University Press.

Krishna-Menon, V. K. (1931). *A Theory of Laughter: With Special Relation to Comedy and Tragedy*. Allen & Unwin.

Kuntz, Marion Leathers (1998a). 'The Concept of Toleration in the *Colloquium Heptaplomeres* of Jean Bodin', in *Venice, Myth and Utopian Thought in the Sixteenth Century*. Ed. Marion Leathers Kuntz. 123–44. Ashgate.

(1998b). 'Harmony and the *Heptaplomeres* of Jean Bodin', in *Venice, Myth and Utopian Thought in the Sixteenth Century.* Ed. Marion Leathers Kuntz. 31–41. Ashgate.

(1998c). 'The Home of Coronaeus in Jean Bodin's *Colloquium Heptaplomeres*', in *Venice, Myth and Utopian Thought in the Sixteenth Century.* Ed. Marion Leathers Kuntz. 277–83. Ashgate.

(1998d). 'Structure, Form and Meaning in the *Colloquium Heptaplomeres* of Jean Bodin', in *Venice, Myth and Utopian Thought in the Sixteenth Century.* Ed. Marion Leathers Kuntz. Section III. n. p. Ashgate.

Kupperman, Karen Ordahl (1984). 'Fear of Hot Climates in the Anglo-American Colonial Experience', *William and Mary Quarterly* 41: 213–40.

Lambard, William (1576). *A Perambulation of Kent.*

Lane, Robert (1995). ' "The sequence of posterity": Shakespeare's *King John* and the Succession Controversy', *Studies in Philology* 92: 460–81.

LaRocca, John J. (1984). ' "Who Can't Pray with Me, Can't Love Me": Toleration and the Early Jacobean Recusancy Policy', *The Journal of British Studies* 23: 22–36.

Laursen, John Christian (1999a). 'Orientation: Clarifying the Conceptual Issues', in *Religious Toleration: 'The Variety of Rites' from Cyrus to Defoe.* Ed. John Christian Laursen. 10–11. Palgrave Macmillan.

(ed.) (1999b). *Religious Toleration: 'The Variety of Rites' from Cyrus to Defoe.* Palgrave Macmillan.

Laursen, John Christian, and Cyrus Masroori (1999). 'Annotated Bibliography of Religious Peace, Concord, and Toleration Literature: 1500–1700', in *Religious Toleration: 'The Variety of Rites' from Cyrus to Defoe.* Ed. John Christian Laursen. 229–45. Palgrave Macmillan.

Laursen, John Christian, and Cary J. Nederman (eds.) (1996). *Difference and Dissent: Theories of Tolerance in Medieval and Early Modern Europe.* Rowman and Littlefield.

Laursen, John Christian, and Cary Nederman (eds.) (1998). *Beyond the Persecuting Society: Religious Toleration before the Enlightenment.* University of Pennsylvania Press.

Lecler, Joseph (1960). *Toleration and the Reformation.* 2 vols. Association Press.

LeFave, Lawrence, and Roger Mannell (1976). 'Does Ethnic Humor Serve Prejudice?', *Journal of Communication* 26: 116–23.

Lerner, Lawrence (1979). *Love and Marriage: Literature in Its Social Context.* Edward Arnold.

Levin, Harry (1993). 'Shakespeare's Italians', in *Shakespeare's Italy: Functions of Italian Locations in Renaissance Drama.* Ed. Michele Marrapodi, A. J. Hoenselaars, Marcello Cappuzzo, and Lino Falzon Santucci. 17–29. Manchester University Press.

Lewkenor, Lewis (1599). *The Commonwealth and Gouernment of Venice: Written by the Cardinall Gasper Contareno.*

Liebler, Naomi Conn (1994). 'Getting It All Right: Titus Andronicus and Roman History', *Shakespeare Quarterly* 45: 263–78.

Lievsay, John Leon (1985). 'Shakespeare and Foreigners', in *William Shakespeare: His World, His Work, His Influence*. Ed. John F. Andrews. 3 vols. 1:233–40. Scribner's.

Little, Arthur L., Jr (2000). *Shakespeare's Jungle Fever: National-Imperial Re-Visions of Race, Rape, and Sacrifice*. Stanford University Press.

Littleton, Charles (1995). 'Social Interactions of Aliens in Late Elizabethan London: Evidence from the 1593 Return and the French Church Consistory "Actes"', *Proceedings of the Huguenot Society* 26: 147–59.

(2003). 'Acculturation and the French Church of London, 1600–circa 1640', in *Memory and Identity: The Huguenots in France and the Atlantic Diaspora*. Ed. Bertrand Van Ruymbeke and Randy J. Sparks. 90–109. University of South Carolina Press.

(2005). 'The Strangers, Their Churches, and the Continent', in *Immigrants in Tudor and Early Stuart England*. Ed. Nigel Goose and Lien Luu. 177–91. Sussex Academic Press.

Locatelli, Angela (1993). 'The Fictional World of *Romeo and Juliet*: Cultural Connotations of an Italian Setting', in *Shakespeare's Italy: Functions of Italian Locations in Renaissance Drama*. Ed. Michele Marrapodi, A. J. Hoenselaars, Marcello Cappuzzo, and Lino Falzon Santucci. 71–84. Manchester University Press.

Lockey, Brian C. (2006). *Law and Empire in English Renaissance Literature*. Cambridge University Press.

Londré, Felicia Hardison (1995). 'Elizabethan Views of the "Other": French, Spanish, and Russians in *Love's Labor's Lost*', *Elizabethan Review* 3: 3–20.

Loomba, Ania (2000). '"Delicious traffick": Alterity and Exchange on Early Modern Stages', in *Shakespeare and Race*. Ed. Stanley Wells and Catherine M. S. Alexander. 203–24. Cambridge University Press.

Luu, Lien (2005a). 'Alien Communities in Transition, 1570–1640', in *Immigrants in Tudor and Early Stuart England*. Ed. Nigel Goose and Lien Luu. 192–210. Sussex Academic Press.

(2005b). 'Natural-Born versus Stranger-Born Subjects: Aliens and their Status in Elizabethan London', in *Immigrants in Tudor and Early Stuart England*. Ed. Nigel Goose and Lien Luu. 57–75. Sussex Academic Press.

Maas, P. (1953). 'Henry Finch and Shakespeare', *Review of English Studies* n.s. 4: 142.

MacCulloch, Diarmaid (1988). 'Bondmen under the Tudors', in *Law and Government under the Tudors*. Ed. Claire Cross, David Loades, and J. J. Scarisbrick. 91–109. Cambridge University Press.

(1996a). 'Archbishop Cranmer: Concord and Tolerance in a Changing Church', in *Tolerance and Intolerance in the European Reformation*. Ed. Ole Peter Grell and Peter Scribner. 199–215. Cambridge University Press.

(1996b). *Thomas Cranmer: A Life*. Yale University Press.

Maclean, Hugh (ed.) (1968). *Edmund Spenser's Poetry*. W. W. Norton & Company, Inc.

Maclean, Ian (1980). *The Renaissance Notion of Woman: A Study in the Fortunes of Scholasticism and Medical Science in European Intellectual Life.* Cambridge University Press.

Maguire, Laurie E. (1995). 'Cultural Control in *The Taming of the Shrew*', *Renaissance Drama* 26: 83–104.

Mahler, Andreas (1993). 'Italian Vices: Cross-cultural Constructions of Temptation and Desire in English Renaissance Drama', in *Shakespeare's Italy: Functions of Italian Locations in Renaissance Drama.* Ed. Michele Marrapodi, A. J. Hoenselaars, Marcello Cappuzzo, and Lino Falzon Santucci. 49–68. Manchester University Press.

Maitland, F. W. (1911). 'The Deacon and the Jewess; or, Apostacy at Common Law', in *Collected Papers.* Ed. H. A. L. Fisher. 3 vols. 1:385–406. Cambridge University Press.

Malcolm, Noel (2006). 'Jean Bodin and the Authorship of the Colloquium Heptaplomeres', *Journal of the Warburg and Courtauld Institutes* 69: 95–150.

Maley, Willy, and Andrew Murphy (2004). 'Then with Scotland First Begin', in *Shakespeare and Scotland.* Ed. Willy Maley and Andrew Murphy. 1–19. Manchester University Press.

Mallett, M. E., and J. R. Hale (1984). *The Military Organization of a Renaissance State: Venice c. 1400 to 1617.* Cambridge University Press.

Marcus, Leah S. (1988). 'Cymbeline and the Unease of Topicality', in *The Historical Renaissance.* Ed. Heather Dubrow and Richard Strier. 134–68. University of Chicago Press.

(2004). 'The Two Texts of *Othello* and Early Modern Constructions of Race', in *Textual Performances: The Modern Reproduction of Shakespeare's Drama.* Ed. Margaret Jane Kidnie and Lukas Erne. 21–36. Cambridge University Press.

Marotti, Arthur F. (2003). 'Shakespeare and Catholicism', in *Theatre and Religion: Lancastrian Shakespeare.* Ed. Richard Dutton, Alison Findlay, and Richard Wilson. 218–41. Manchester University Press.

Martinich, A. P. (1995). *A Hobbes Dictionary.* Blackwell Reference.

Marx, Steven (1992). 'Shakespeare's Pacifism', *Renaissance Quarterly* 45: 49–95.

Maslen, R. W. (2003). 'The Afterlife of Andrew Borde', *Studies in Philology* 100: 463–92.

Matar, Nabil (1999). *Turks, Moors, and Englishmen in the Age of Discovery.* Columbia University Press.

(2001). 'England and Mediterranean Captivity, 1557–1704', in *Piracy, Slavery, and Redemption: Barbary Captivity Narratives from Early Modern England.* Ed. Daniel J. Vitkus. 1–52. Columbia University Press.

McAlindon, Thomas (2001). 'The Discourse of Prayer in *The Tempest*', *SEL: Studies in English Literature, 1500–1900* 41: 335–55.

McGuire, Philip C. (1989). 'Egeus and the Implications of Silence', in *Shakespeare and the Sense of Performance: Essays in the Tradition of Performance Criticism in Honor of Bernard Beckerman.* Ed. Ruth Thompson and Marvin Thompson. 103–15. University of Delaware Press.

McPherson, David (1988). 'Lewkenor's Venice and its Sources', *Renaissance Quarterly* 41: 459–66.

(1990). *Shakespeare, Jonson and the Myth of Venice.* University of Delaware Press.

Melchiori, Giorgio (1994). *Shakespeare's Garter Plays: Edward III to Merry Wives of Windsor.* Associated University Presses.

Milton, John (1825). *A Treatise on Christian Doctrine, Compiled from the Holy Scriptures Alone.* Trans. Charles R. Sumner. Cambridge University Press.

Milward, Peter (1973). *Shakespeare's Religious Background.* Indiana University Press.

Mintz, Lawrence E. (1977). 'Ethnic Humour: Discussion', in *It's a Funny Thing, Humour.* Ed. Antony J. Chapman and Hugh C. Foot. 287–9. Permagon Press.

Miola, Robert S. (2001). "An alien people clutching their gods'?: Shakespeare's Ancient Religions', *Shakespeare Survey* 54: 31–45.

Moens, W. J. C. (ed.) (1896–1916). *The Registers of the French Church, Threadneedle Street, 1600–1840.* 4 vols. Huguenot Society of London.

Monro, D. H. (1951). *Argument of Laughter.* Melbourne University Press.

Montaigne, Michel (1942). *Essays.* Trans. John Florio. 3 vols. J. M. Dent & Sons Ltd.

Morgann, Maurice (1972). *Shakespearian Criticism.* Ed. Daniel A. Fineman. Clarendon Press.

Morris, Brian (ed.) (1981). *The Taming of the Shrew.* Second Arden Shakespeare edition. Methuen & Co.

Morse, Ruth (1998). 'Othello: White Skin, Black Masks', *Cahiers Charles V* 24: 65–83.

Moschovakis, Nicholas (2002). ' "Irreligious piety" and Christian History: Persecution as Pagan Anachronism in *Titus Andronicus*', *Shakespeare Quarterly* 53: 460–86.

Muir, Kenneth (1956). 'Shakespeare and Lewkenor', *Review of English Studies* 7: 182–3.

(1972). *The Sources of Shakespeare's Plays.* Methuen & Co.

Mullini, Roberta (1993). 'Streets, Squares, and Courts: Venice as a Stage in Shakespeare and Ben Jonson', in *Shakespeare's Italy: Functions of Italian Locations in Renaissance Drama.* Ed. Michele Marrapodi, A. J. Hoenselaars, Marcello Cappuzzo, and Lino Falzon Santucci. 158–70. Manchester University Press.

Mulryne, J. R. (1996). 'Nationality and Language in Thomas Kid's "The Spanish Tragedy" ', in *Travel and Drama in Shakespeare's Time.* Ed. Jean-Pierre Maquerlot and Michèle Willems. 87–105. Cambridge University Press.

Murphy, Andrew R. (2002). *Conscience and Community: Revisiting Toleration and Religious Dissent in Early Modern England and America.* Penn State University Press.

Muss-Arnolt, William (1914). *The Book of Common Prayer among the Nations of the World.* SPCK.

Nashe, Thomas (1948). *The Vnfortvnate Traveller: or The Life of Jacke Wilton.* Ed. H. F. B. Brett-Smith from 1594 edition. Basil Blackwell.

Nathan, Norman (1988). 'Othello's Marriage Is Consummated', *Cahiers Élisabéthains* 34: 79–82.

Nederman, Cary J. (2000). *Worlds of Difference: European Discourses of Toleration, c. 1100–c. 1550.* Pennsylvania State University Press.

Neill, Michael (1989). 'Unproper Beds: Race, Adultery, and the Hideous in *Othello*', *Shakespeare Quarterly* 40: 383–412.

(1998a). '"Mulattos," "Blacks," and "Indian Moors": *Othello* and Early Modern Constructions of Human Difference', *Shakespeare Quarterly* 49: 361–74.

(1998b). 'Servant Obedience and Master Sins: Shakespeare and the Bonds of Service', *Proceedings of the British Academy* 101: 131–71.

Nelson, Alan H. (2000). Parish Register St Olave Silver Street, London (1561–1624). Typescript held at London Guildhall Library.

Nelson, T. G. A., and Charles Haines (1983). 'Othello's Unconsummated Marriage', *Essays in Criticism* 33: 1–18.

Nelson, William (1963). *The Poetry of Edmund Spenser.* Columbia University Press.

Nevo, Ruth (1980). *Comic Transformations in Shakespeare.* Methuen & Co.

Nicholl, Charles (2007). *The Lodger: Shakespeare on Silver Street.* Allen Lane.

Nicoll, Allardyce (1963). *The World of Harlequin: A Critical Study of the Commedia dell'Arte.* Cambridge University Press.

Nilsen, Don L. F. (1993). *Humor Scholarship: A Research Bibliography.* Greenwood.

Niro, Brian (2003). *Race.* Palgrave Macmillan.

Noble, Richmond Samuel Howe (1935). *Shakespeare's Biblical Knowledge and Use of the Book of Common Prayer, as Exemplified in the Plays of the First Folio.* SPCK.

Oberman, Heiko A. (1996). 'The Travail of Tolerance: Containing Chaos in Early Modern Europe', in *Tolerance and Intolerance in the European Reformation.* Ed. Ole Peter Grell and Peter Scribner. 13–31. Cambridge University Press.

Osgood, Charles Grosvenor (1915). *A Concordance to the Poems of Edmund Spenser.* Carnegie Institution.

Palmer, Daryl W. (2006). 'Hamlet's Northern Lineage: Masculinity, Climate, and the Mechanician in Early Modern Britain', *Renaissance Drama* 35: 3–25.

Percy, George (1922). 'A Trewe Relacyon: Virginia from 1609 to 1612', *Tyler's Quarterly Historical and Genealogical Magazine* 3: 259–82.

(1946). 'Observations by Master George Percy, 1607', in *Narratives of Early Virginia.* Ed. Lyon Gardiner Tyler. 5–23. Barnes & Noble.

Pérez-Ramos, Antonio (1988). *Francis Bacon's Idea of Science and the Maker's Knowledge Tradition.* Clarendon Press.

Petronella, Vincent F. (1984). 'Hamlet: The International Theme', *Hamlet Studies* 6: 18–22.

Pettegree, Andrew (1986). *Foreign Protestant Communities in Sixteenth-Century London.* Clarendon Press.

(1990). ' "Thirty years on": Progress towards Integration amongst the Immi-grant Population of Elizabethan London', in *English Rural Society, 1500–1800*. Ed. John Chartres and David Hey. 297–312. Cambridge University Press.

(1996). 'The Politics of Toleration in the Free Netherlands, 1572–1620', in *Tolerance and Intolerance in the European Reformation*. Ed. Ole Peter Grell and Peter Scribner. 182–98. Cambridge University Press.

Plato (1966). *Collected Dialogues*. Ed. Edith Hamilton and Huntington Cairns. Pantheon Books.

Plucknett, T. F. T. (1956). *A Concise History of the Common Law*. Fifth edition. Butterworth & Co.

Pollock, Sir Frederick, and F. W. Maitland (1898). *The History of English Law before the Reign of Edward I*. Second edition, reissued 1968. 2 vols. Cambridge University Press.

Poole, Kristen (1995). 'Saints Alive! Falstaff, Martin Marprelate, and the Staging of Puritanism', *Shakespeare Quarterly* 46: 47–75.

Popkin, Richard H. (1988). 'The Dispersion of Bodin's Dialogues in England, Holland and Germany', *The Journal of the History of Ideas* 49: 157–60.

(1998). 'Skepticism about Religion and Millenarian Dogmatism: Two Sources of Toleration in the Seventeenth Century', in *Beyond the Persecuting Society: Religious Toleration before the Enlightenment*. Ed. John Christian Laursen and Cary Nederman. 232–50. University of Pennsylvania Press.

Poulton, Diana (1983). 'Dowland's Darkness', *Early Music* 11: 517–19.

Powers, Alan (1994). ' "Gallia and Gaul, French and Welsh": Comic Ethnic Slander in the Gallia Wars', in *Acting Funny: Comic Theory and Practice in Shakespeare's Plays*. Ed. Frances Teague. 109–22. Associated University Presses.

Prest, Wilfred R. (1991). 'Law and Women's Rights in Early Modern England', *The Seventeenth Century* 6: 169–87.

Prosser, Eleanor (1965). 'Shakespeare, Montaigne, and the Rarer Action', *Shakespeare Studies* 1: 261–4.

Pugliatti, Paola (1996). *Shakespeare the Historian*. St Martin's Press.

Purchas, Samuel (1625). *Purchas His Pilgrimes*.

Quinn, David Beers (ed.) (1955). *The Roanoke Voyages 1584–1590*. 2 vols. Hakluyt Society.

(1992). *Thomas Harriot and the Problem of America*. Oriel College.

Quinn, David Beers, and Paul Hulton (1964). *The American Drawings of John White 1577–1590*. 2 vols. Trustees of the British Museum and University of North Carolina Press.

Rabb, Theodore K. (1963). 'The Editions of Sir Edwin Sandys's "Relation of the State of Religion" ', *Huntington Library Quarterly* 26: 323–36.

Raffield, Paul (2005). 'Contract, Classicism, and the Common-Weal', *Law and Literature* 17: 69–96.

Raley, Marjorie (1997). 'Claribel's Husband', in *Race, Ethnicity, and Power*. Ed. Joyce Green MacDonald. 95–119. Associated University Presses.

Ramsey, Jarold (1973). 'The Perversion of Manliness in Macbeth', *SEL: Studies in English Literature, 1500–1900* 13: 285–300.

Reeve, M. D. (1989). 'Conceptions', *Proceedings of the Cambridge Philological Society* 215 n. s. 35: 81–112.

Remer, Gary (1996a). 'Bodin's Pluralistic Theory of Toleration', in *Difference and Dissent: Theories of Tolerance in Medieval and Early Modern Europe*. Ed. John Christian Laursen and Cary J. Nederman. 119–37. Rowman and Littlefield.

(1996b). *Humanism and the Rhetoric of Toleration*. Penn State University Press.

Ricoeur, Paul (ed.) (1996). *Tolerance: Between Intolerance and the Intolerable*. Berghahn Books.

Righter (Barton), Anne (1967). *Shakespeare and the Idea of the Play*. Penguin Shakespeare Library edition; first edition, 1962. Penguin Books Ltd.

Riley, Denise (2000). *The Words of Selves: Identification, Solidarity, Irony*. Stanford University Press.

Rooley, Anthony (1983). 'New Light on John Dowland's Songs of Darkness', *Early Music* 11: 6–21.

Rosen, Alan (1997). 'The Rhetoric of Exclusion: Jew, Moor, and the Boundaries of Discourse in *The Merchant of Venice*', in *Race, Ethnicity, and Power*. Ed. Joyce Green MacDonald. 67–79. Associated University Presses.

Routledge, R. A. (1982). 'The Legal Status of the Jews in England, 1190–1790', *The Journal of Legal History* 3: 91–124.

Rymer, Thomas (1956). *The Critical Works*. Ed. Curt Zimansky. Yale University Press.

St German, Christopher (1975). *Doctor and Student*. 1523; first English editions c. 1532. Ed. T. F. T. Plucknett and J. L. Barton. Selden Society.

St John, Warren (2005). 'Seriously, the Joke is Dead', *The New York Times* May 22.

Sanders, Charles Richard (1949). 'William Strachey, the Virginia Colony, and Shakespeare', *The Virginia Magazine of History and Biography* 57: 115–32.

Sandys, Edwin (1605). *A Relation of the State of Religion*.

Schickler, F. de (1892). *Les Eglises du Refuge en Angleterre*. 3 vols. Libraire Fischbacher.

Schoenbaum, S. (1981). *William Shakespeare: Records and Images*. Scolar Press.

(1986). *William Shakespeare: A Compact Documentary Life*. Reprint of Oxford University Press edition, 1977. New American Library.

Schorsch, Jonathan (2004). *Jews and Blacks in the Early Modern World*. Cambridge University Press.

Schotz, Amiel (1991). 'The Law That Never Was: A Note on *The Merchant of Venice*', *Theatre Research International* 16: 249–52.

Schultz, Charles E. (1989). 'The Sociability of Ethnic Jokes', *International Journal of Humor Research* 2: 165–77.

Scouloudi, Irene (1987). 'The Stranger Community in the Metropolis 1558–1640', in *Huguenots in Britain and their French Background, 1550–1800*. Ed. Irene Scouloudi. 42–55. Macmillan Press.

Seager, Richard (2006). 'The Source of Europe's Mild Climate', *American Scientist* 94, July–August: 334–41.

Seaver, Paul S. (1995). 'Work, Discipline and the Apprentice in Early Modern London', in *Wellsprings of Achievement*. Ed. Penelope Gouk. 159–79. Variorum.

Semple, Hilary (1987). 'Shakespeare and Race', *Shakespeare in Southern Africa* 1: 30 8.

Seronsy, Cecil C. (1963). ' "Supposes" as the Unifying Theme in *The Taming of the Shrew*', *Shakespeare Quarterly* 14: 15–30.

Shaheen, Naseeb (1993). *Biblical References in Shakespeare's Comedies*. University of Delaware Press.

(1997). 'A Note on *Troilus and Cressida*, II.iii.1–37', *Notes and Queries* 44: 503–5.

(1999). *Biblical References in Shakespeare's Plays*. University of Delaware Press.

Shakespeare, William (1968). *The First Folio*. Facsimile of 1623 prepared by Charlton Hinman. W. W. Norton.

(1977). *The Merchant of Venice*. Ed. John Russell Brown. Second Arden Shakespeare edition. Methuen and Co.

(1987). *Hamlet*. Ed. G. R. Hibbard. Oxford University Press.

(1995a). *Antony and Cleopatra*. Ed. John Wilders. Third Arden Shakespeare edition. Routledge.

(1995b). *Editions and Adaptations of Shakespeare*. Chadwyck-Healey database, version 1.0.

(1995c). *King Henry V*. Ed. T. W. Craik. Third Arden Shakespeare edition. Routledge.

(1997). *The Riverside Shakespeare*. Second edition. Houghton Mifflin Company.

(1999). *Othello*. Everyman edition. Ed. John F. Andrews. J. M. Dent.

(2001). *Othello*. Third Arden Shakespeare edition. Ed. E. A. J. Honigmann. Thomson Learning.

Shapiro, James (1992). *Shakespeare and the Jews*. Columbia University Press.

Sharpe, Kevin, and Christopher Brooks (1976). 'History, English Law and the Renaissance', *Past & Present* 72: 133–42.

Shirley, John W. (1949). 'George Percy at Jamestown, 1607–1612', *The Virginia Magazine of History and Biography* 57: 227–43.

Sidney, Philip (1961). *Apology for Poetrie*. Ed. J. C. Collins. Clarendon.

(1962). *The Poems of Sir Philip Sidney*. Ed. William A. Ringler. Clarendon Press.

Simonds, Peggy Muñoz (1989). 'Sacred and Sexual Motifs in *All's Well That Ends Well*', *Renaissance Quarterly* 42: 33–59.

Singh, Jyotsna G. (2004). 'Islam in the European Imagination in the Early Modern Period', in *Voices for Tolerance in an Age of Persecution*. Ed. Vincent P. Carey. 85–92. Folger Shakespeare Library.

Skinner, Quentin (2000). 'Why Does Laughter Matter to Philosophy?' Passmore Lecture, December 2000, ANU: http://socpol.anu.edu.au/pdf-files/passmorelect2000.pdf.

(2002). 'Hobbes and the Classical Theory of Laughter', in *Visions of Politics*. 3 vols. 3:142–76. Cambridge University Press.

(2004). 'Hobbes and the Classical Theory of Laughter', in *Leviathan after 350 Years*. Ed. Tom Sorell and Luc Foisneau. 139–66. Oxford University Press.

Skura, Meredith Anne (1989). 'Discourse and the Individual: The Case of Colonialism in *The Tempest*', *Shakespeare Quarterly* 40: 42–69.

Slack, Paul (1988). *Poverty and Policy in Tudor and Stuart England*. Longman.

Slights, Camille Wells (1997). 'Slaves and Subjects in *Othello*', *Shakespeare Quarterly* 48: 377–90.

Smith, Bruce R. (2000). *Shakespeare and Masculinity*. Oxford University Press.

Smith, Ian (1998). 'Barbarian Errors: Performing Race in Early Modern England', *Shakespeare Quarterly* 49: 168–86.

Smith, John (1986). *Works*. Ed. Philip L. Barbour. 3 vols. University of North Carolina Press.

Smith, Raymond (1972). *The Archives of the French Protestant Church of London: A Handlist*. Huguenot Society of London.

Smith, Thomas (1583). *De Republica Anglorum*.

Sokol, B. J. (1974). 'Thomas Harriot – Sir Walter Ralegh's Tutor – on Population', *Annals of Science* 31: 205–12.

(1985). 'A Spenserian Idea in *The Taming of the Shrew*', *English Studies* 66: 310–16.

(1989). 'Painted Statues, Ben Jonson and Shakespeare', *Journal of the Warburg and Courtauld Institutes* 52: 250–3.

(1991). 'Figures of Repetition in Sidney's *Astrophil and Stella* and in the Scenic Form of *Measure for Measure*', *Rhetorica* 9: 131–46.

(1992). '*The Merchant of Venice* and the Law Merchant', *Renaissance Studies* 6: 60–7.

(1994a). *Art and Illusion in 'The Winter's Tale'*. Manchester University Press.

(1994b). 'Numerology in the Time Scheme of *The Tempest*', *Notes and Queries* 41: 53–5.

(1994c). 'The Problem of Assessing Thomas Harriot's A briefe and true report of his Discoveries in North America', *Annals of Science* 51: 1–15.

(1995a). 'Constitutive Signifiers or Fetishes in *The Merchant of Venice*?', *International Journal of Psycho-Analysis*. 76: 373–87.

(1995b). 'Macbeth and the Social History of Witchcraft', *Shakespeare Yearbook* 6: 245–74.

(1998). 'Prejudice and Law in *The Merchant of Venice*', in *Shakespeare Survey 51*. Ed. Stanley Wells. 159–73. Cambridge University Press.

(2000). 'Manuscript Evidence for an Earliest Date of *Henry VI Part One*', *Notes and Queries* 245: 58–63.

(2003). *A Brave New World of Knowledge: Shakespeare's The Tempest and Early Modern Epistemology*. Associated University Presses.

(2004). 'Shakespearian Sources in "Obscure" Continental European Publications', in *Not of an Age, But for All Time: Shakespeare across Lands and Ages*. Ed. S. Coelsch-Foisner and G. E. Szönyi. 65–75. Braunmüller.

Sokol, B. J., and Mary Sokol (1996). '*The Tempest* and Legal Justification of Plantation in Virginia', *Shakespeare Yearbook* 7: 353–80.

(1999). 'Shakespeare and the English Equity Jurisdiction: *The Merchant of Venice* and the Two Texts of *King Lear*', *Review of English Studies* 50: 417–39.

(2002). 'Where Are We in Legal-Historical Studies of Shakespeare?: The Case of Marriage and Property', in *Shakespearean International Yearbook 2*. Ed. John M. Mucciolo and W. R. Elton. 249–71. Ashgate.

(2003). *Shakespeare, Law and Marriage*. Cambridge University Press.

(2004). *Shakespeare's Legal Language*. Paperback reprint, corrected, of 2000 edition. Continuum.

Sollors, Werner (1997). *Neither Black nor White but Both*. Oxford University Press.

Sommerville, Margaret R. (1995). *Sex and Subjection: Attitudes to Women in Early Modern Society*. Arnold.

Spenser, Edmund (1961). *The Faerie Queene*. Ed. J. C. Smith, 1909–10. 2 vols. Oxford University Press.

Spicer, Andrew (2005). ' "A Place of Refuge and Sanctuary of a Holy Temple": Exile Communities and the Stranger Churches', in *Immigrants in Tudor and Early Stuart England*. Ed. Nigel Goose and Lien Luu. 91–109. Sussex Academic Press.

Spiller, Elizabeth (1998). 'From Imagination to Miscegenation: Race and Romance in Shakespeare's *The Merchant of Venice*', *Renaissance Drama* 29: 137–64.

Spurgeon, Caroline (1935). *Shakespeare's Imagery and What It Tells Us*. Cambridge University Press.

Stone, Lawrence (1979). *The Crisis of the Aristocracy, 1558–1641*. Revised edition; first published 1965. Clarendon Press.

Strachey, William (1953). *The History of Travell into Virginia Britania*. Ed. Louis B. Wright and Virginia Freund. Hakluyt Society.

Straube, Beverly A., and Seth Mallios (2000). *Jamestown Rediscovery Interim Report 1999*. APVA.

Stretton, Tim (1994). 'Women, Custom and Equity in the Court of Requests', in *Women, Crime and the Courts in Early Modern England*. Ed. Jenny Kermode and Garthine Walker. 170–89. UCL Press.

(1998). *Women Waging Law in Elizabethan England*. Cambridge University Press.

(1999). 'Widows at Law in Tudor and Stuart England', in *Widowhood in Medieval and Early Modern Europe*. Ed. Sandra Cavallo and Lydan Warner. 193–208. Longman.

(2002). 'Women, Property and Law', in *Early Modern Women's Writing*. Ed. Anita Pacheco. 40–57. Blackwell Publishing.

Stroup, Thomas B. (1943). 'Milton and the Theory of Climatic Influence', *Modern Language Quarterly* 4: 185–9.

Strype, John (1725–31). *Annals of the Reformation*. 4 vols.

Sugden, Edward H. (1925). *A Topographical Dictionary to the Works of Shakespeare and his Fellow Dramatists*. Manchester University Press.

Suzman, Janet (1988). '*Othello*, a Belated Reply', *Shakespeare in Southern Africa* 2: 90–6.

Sweet, James H. (1997). 'The Iberian Roots of American Racist Thought', *William and Mary Quarterly* 54: 143–66.

Swinburne, Henry (1686). *A Treatise of Spousals or Matrimonial Contracts.*

Taunton, Nina (2001). *1590s Drama and Militarism: Portrayals of War in Marlowe, Chapman, and Shakespeare's Henry V.* Ashgate.

Taylor, Gary (1985). *To Analyze Delight: A Hedonist Criticism of Shakespeare.* University of Delaware Press.

Teague, Frances (1994a). 'Introduction', in *Acting Funny: Comic Theory and Practice in Shakespeare's Plays.* Ed. Frances Teague. 9–26. Associated University Presses.

(1994b). '*Othello* and New Comedy', in *Acting Funny: Comic Theory and Practice in Shakespeare's Plays.* Ed. Frances Teague. 29–39. Associated University Presses.

Terraciano, Kevin (1999). 'The Spanish Struggle for Justification in the Conquest of America', in *Religious Toleration: 'The Variety of Rites' from Cyrus to Defoe.* Ed. John Christian Laursen. 93–126. Palgrave Macmillan.

Thomas, Keith (1983). *Man and the Natural World: Changing Attitudes in England 1500–1800.* Allen Lane.

Thompson, Ann (ed.) (1984). *The Taming of the Shrew.* The New Cambridge Shakespeare. Cambridge University Press.

(ed.) (2003). *The Taming of the Shrew.* The New Cambridge Shakespeare, updated edition. Cambridge University Press.

Thorne, S. E. (1985a). 'English Law and the Renaissance', in *Essays in English Legal History.* 187–95. Hambledon.

(1985b). 'Sir Edward Coke 1552–1952', in *Essays in English Legal History.* 223–38. Hambledon.

(1985c). 'Tudor Social Transformation and Legal Change', in *Essays in English Legal History.* 197–210. Hambledon.

Tiffany, Grace (1998). 'Puritanism in Comic History: Exposing Royalty in the Henry Plays', *Shakespeare Studies* 26: 256–87.

Todd, Barbara J. (1999). 'The Virtuous Widow in Protestant England', in *Widowhood in Medieval and Early Modern Europe.* Ed. Sandra Cavallo and Lydan Warner. 66–83. Longman.

Tokson, Elliot H. (1982). *The Popular Image of the Black Man in English Drama, 1550–1688.* G. K. Hall.

Trevor, Douglas (2004). *The Poetics of Melancholy in Early Modern England.* Cambridge University Press.

Vaughan, Alden T. (1988). 'Shakespeare's Indian: The Americanization of Caliban', *Shakespeare Quarterly* 39: 137–53.

Vaughan, Alden T., and Virginia Mason Vaughan (1991). *Shakespeare's Caliban: A Cultural History.* Cambridge University Press.

(1997). 'Before Othello: Elizabethan Representations of Sub-Saharan Africans', *William and Mary Quarterly* 54: 19–44.

Vickers, Brian (1968). *The Artistry of Shakespeare's Prose.* Methuen & Co. Ltd.

(1985). 'Shakespeare's Use of Prose', in *William Shakespeare: His World, His Work, His Influence.* Ed. John F. Andrews. 2 vols. 2:389–96. Scribner's.

Virginia Council (1906–35). 'Instructions Orders and Constitutions to Sir Thomas Gates knight Governor of Virginia' [Ashmolean Ms. 1147, fol. 175–90a, May 1609], in *The Records of the Virginia Company of London*. Ed. Susan Myra Kingsbury. 4 vols. III:12–24. Library of Congress.

Vitkus, Daniel J. (ed.) (2000). *Three Turk Plays from Early Modern England*. Columbia University Press.

(ed.) (2001). *England and Mediterranean Captivity 1557–1704*. Columbia University Press.

(2003). *Turning Turk: English Theater and the Multicultural Mediterranean, 1570–1630*. Palgrave Macmillan.

Walzer, Michael (1997). *On Toleration*. Yale University Press.

Ward, Andrew (1996). *Our Bones Are Scattered*. Henry Holt.

Ward, Joseph P. (2005). ' "[I]mployment for all handes that will worke": Immigrants, Guilds and the Labour Market in Early Seventeenth-Century London', in *Immigrants in Tudor and Early Stuart England*. Ed. Nigel Goose and Lien Luu. 76–87. Sussex Academic Press.

Wells, Robin Headlam (1985). 'John Dowland and Elizabethan Melancholy', *Early Music* 13: 514–28.

(2000a). ' "Manhood and chevalrie": Coriolanus, Prince Henry, and the Chivalric Revival', *Review of English Studies* 51: 395–422.

(2000b). *Shakespeare on Masculinity*. Cambridge University Press.

Wells, Stanley, and Gary Taylor (eds.) (1989). *William Shakespeare: The Complete Works*. Electronic edition. Oxford University Press.

West, Grace Starry (1982). 'Going by the Book: Classical Allusions in Shakespeare's *Titus Andronicus*', *Studies in Philology* 79: 62–77.

Whatley, William (1619). *A Bride-Bush: or a Direction for Married Persons*. A sermon delivered 1617.

White, Jeannette S. (1997). ' "Is black so base a hue?": Shakespeare's Aaron and the Politics of Race', *CLA Journal* 40: 336–66.

White, R. S. (1999). 'Pacifist Voices in Shakespeare', *Parergon* 17: 135–62.

Williams, Bernard (1996a). 'Toleration, a Political or Moral Question?', in *Tolerance: Between Intolerance and the Intolerable*. Ed. Paul Ricoeur. 35–48. Berghahn Books.

(1996b). 'Toleration: An Impossible Virtue?', in *Toleration: An Elusive Virtue*. Ed. David Heyd. 18–27. Princeton University Press.

Wilson, Christopher P. (1979). *Jokes: Form, Content, Use and Function*. Academic Press.

Wilson, John Dover (1953). *The Fortunes of Falstaff*. Cambridge University Press.

Wilson, Richard (2004). *Secret Shakespeare*. Manchester University Press.

(2005). 'Making Men of Monsters: Shakespeare in the Company of Strangers', *Shakespeare* 1: 8–28.

Wilson, Thomas (1553). *The Arte of Rhetorique*.

Woodbridge, Linda (2003). 'Jest Books, the Literature of Roguery, and the Vagrant Poor in Renaissance England', *English Literary Renaissance* 33: 201–10.

Wootton, David (2002). 'Pseudo-Bodin's *Colloquium Heptaplomeres* and Bodin's *Démonomanie*', in *Magie, Religion und Wissenschaften im Colloquium Heptaplomeres*. Ed. Karl Friedrich Faltenbacher. 175–225. Wissenschaftliche Buchgesellschaft.

Wrigley, E. A., and R. S. Schofield (1981). *The Population History of England, 1541–1871: A Reconstruction*. Edward Arnold.

Yaffe, Martin D. (1997). *Shylock and the Jewish Question*. Johns Hopkins University Press.

Yates, Frances (1947). 'Queen Elizabeth as Astraea', *Journal of the Warburg and Courtauld Institutes* 10: 27–82.

Young, Bruce W. (1988). 'Haste, Consent, and Age at Marriage: Some Implications of Social History for *Romeo and Juliet*', *Iowa State Journal of Research* 62: 459–74.

Zagorin, Perez (2003). *How the Idea of Religious Toleration Came to the West*. Princeton University Press.

Zhou Xiaojing (1998). 'Othello's Color in Shakespeare's Tragedy', *CLA Journal* 41: 335–48.

Zijlstra, Samme (2002). 'Anabaptism and Tolerance: Possibilities and Limitations', in *Calvinism and Religious Toleration in the Dutch Golden Age*. Ed. R. Po-chia Hsia and Henk van Nierop. 112–31. Cambridge University Press.

Zillmann, Dolf (1983). 'Disparagement Humor', in *Handbook of Humor Research*. Ed. Paul E. McGhee and Jeffrey H. Goldstein. 85–107. Springer-Verlag.

Zimmermann, Heiner (2006). 'Macbeth and Hercules', *Renaissance Studies* 20: 356–78.

Zito, George V. (1991). *The Sociology of Shakespeare*. Peter Lang.

Index

DATE DUE

OCT 2 2 2010	